STRANGERS

IN THE

ETHNIC HOMELAND

Strangers in the Ethnic Homeland

*Japanese Brazilian Return Migration
in Transnational Perspective*

TAKEYUKI TSUDA

Columbia University Press • New York

COLUMBIA UNIVERSITY PRESS
NEW YORK
PUBLISHERS SINCE 1893
NEW YORK   CHICHESTER, WEST SUSSEX

Copyright © 2003 Columbia University Press
All rights reserved
Library of Congress Cataloging-in-Publication Data
Tsuda, Takeyuki.
Strangers in the ethnic homeland : Japanese Brazilian return migration
in transnational perspective / Takeyuki Tsuda.
p.   cm.
Includes bibliographical references and index.
ISBN 0–231–12838–X (cloth) — ISBN 0–231–12839–8 (paper)
1. Brazilians—Japan.   2. Japan—Ethnic relations.   I. Title.
DS832.7. B73 T78 2003
305.895'6081'0952—dc21   2002067460

Columbia University Press books are printed on permanent and durable acid-free
paper.
Printed in the United States of America
c 10 9 8 7 6 5 4 3 2 1
p 10 9 8 7 6 5 4 3 2 1

To my late father, who made it all possible

CONTENTS

◦℧◦

ॐ

The Japenese Brazilians as Immigrant Celebrities

THE TRAIN SLOWS as it rolls into Shibuya station in Tokyo. It is past rush hour on the Yamanote line, but the car is still quite full with commuters. Outside on the station platform await hundreds of passengers, a blur through the windows as the train passes by them before coming to a precise stop. The doors open, allowing the passengers inside to shuffle out and a new group to file into the train in an orderly manner. Most of the men are dressed conservatively in suits, and the women are clad in the standard OL (office lady) style with knee-length skirts and stockings. Finally, just before the doors shut, a group of three men stroll in. Compared to those who preceded them, these Japanese appear quite different. Their demeanor is casual and leisurely. Two of them are dressed in shirts of bright, mixed colors and jeans with a stripe down the seam. The third wears a T-shirt that says **BRASIL**. They continue their conversation, speaking loudly in Portuguese.

"*Brincadera, cara. Ele 'ta falando, falando, mais o japonês não entende,*" one of them remarks, his hands in his pockets as he leans against the handrail.

"*Coitado. Viu, o japonês dele é antigo. É um dialeto de Okinawa também,*" another says. They laugh. A big, hearty laugh.

Instantly, the three men become the objects of peculiar glances from the surrounding Japanese. Some look up from their newspapers. Others pretend not to notice these strangers. Two Japanese women sitting beside me turn their eyes away from the men and look at each other. They exchange one word.

"*Gaijin* (foreigners)."

Ever since the first Japanese Brazilians began return migrating to Japan in the late 1980s in search of high-paying jobs in Japanese factories, they

x   Preface

have attracted a considerable amount of public attention. By now, most
Japanese have heard of the Brazilian *nikkeijin* (Japanese descendants born
and living outside Japan),[1] if not actually seen them on the streets, on
trains, or in other public areas. Despite their Japanese phenotype, they are
quite conspicuous in public not only because they speak Portuguese but
also because of their distinctly different dress and demeanor. When the
Japanese first encounter these strange descendants from Latin America,
most are quite confused and disoriented and cannot figure out exactly
who these people are. One young Japanese man described his initial reaction, widely shared among his compatriots:

> The first time the Japanese Brazilians came to town, I was really sur-
> prised. I thought, wow, look at these weirdos! What in the world are
> they, anyway? They looked Japanese, but they weren't real Japanese.
> They acted completely differently, spoke a foreign tongue, and dressed
> in strange ways. They were like fake Japanese, like a fake superhero you
> see on TV.

However, the Japanese Brazilians have become much more than peculiar ethnic curiosities. With an immigrant population currently estimated
at 280,000, they are the third largest group of foreigners in Japan, after the
Korean Japanese and Chinese,[2] and their numbers continue to grow
steadily despite Japan's prolonged economic recession. This means that
close to one fifth of the entire Brazilian nikkeijin population now currently resides in Japan. They have been accompanied by smaller numbers
of nikkeijin from other South American countries, namely Peru, Argenti-
na, Bolivia, and Paraguay.[3] The return migration of the nikkeijin has been

---

[1]There is some ambiguity and confusion over the general use of this Japanese ethnic term. Sometimes the original Japanese emigrants are not called nikkeijin and the term refers only to Japanese descendants born abroad.

[2]There are approximately 600,000 Korean Japanese who are still registered in Japan as "foreigners." Although 90 percent of them were born and raised in Japan (Ryang 1997:3), they are
not granted Japanese citizenship, and many have not naturalized. The population of Chinese
in Japan remains higher than that of Brazilian nikkeijin. In 2000, there were 335,575 Chinese
registered as foreigners in Japan. In addition, there are a good number of illegal visa overstay-
ers (32,896, according to 2000 figures).

[3]In 1995, there were 36,269 Peruvians, 2,910 Argentinians, 2,765 Bolivians, and 1,176 Paraguayans
registered as foreigners in Japan.

Ethnic diversity has finally come to Japan! Three foreign workers (a Peruvian and probably two Southeast Asians) sit on a train with Japanese schoolchildren. (All photographs are from the author's collection.)

part of a larger mass migration of foreign workers to Japan. The country currently has well over 800,000 unskilled foreign workers from various countries in Latin America, East and Southeast Asia, and the Middle East.

The Brazilian nikkeijin began return migrating to Japan in the late 1980s in response to a severe Brazilian economic crisis and a crippling shortage of unskilled labor in Japan. Most of them work in small and medium-sized firms in the manufacturing and construction sectors and perform unskilled "3K" jobs (the Japanese acronym for dirty, dangerous, and difficult) that are shunned by native Japanese. Although they are well educated and middle class in Brazil, they still earn five to ten times their Brazilian incomes as unskilled manual laborers in Japan and remit or take home well over $3 billion annually to Brazil, roughly equivalent to 6 percent of Brazil's entire export trade for 1996. They are by far the largest and most important source of legal migrant labor in Japan and have assumed a critical function in the Japanese economy as a flexible and relatively cheap labor force. Therefore, although the labor shortage has become less acute during Japan's decade-long recession, many Japanese manufacturing firms have become dependent on Japanese Brazilian workers and would not be able to stay in business without them. The Brazilian nikkeijin have also become prominent consumers in Japanese society (especially of electronic and household goods) in the towns and communities where they are concentrated and spend an amazing $50 million per month on international phone calls.

Because almost all of the Japanese Brazilians initially go to Japan with intentions to work only for a couple of years and then quickly return home with their savings, they have been called *dekasegi*, the Japanese word for temporary migrant worker.[4] However, about half of them have already become long-term or permanent immigrant settlers in Japan. As a result, although many of the earlier migrants were single male sojourners, a majority have now migrated with their families or have called over family members to Japan in anticipation of a prolonged or indefinite stay. Others have become circle migrants who shuttle back and forth between Brazil and Japan.

Most of the Japanese Brazilian migrants are of the second and third generations (*nisei* and *sansei*), who were born and raised in Brazil, do not speak Japanese very well, and have become culturally Brazilianized to various degrees. Therefore, their migration to Japan is a "return migration" only in the sense that they are returning to their ancestral ethnic homeland.[5] Despite their Japanese descent, however, they are ethnically rejected and treated as foreigners in Japan because of narrow definitions of what constitutes being Japanese and have become the country's newest ethnic minority, joining the ranks of the Korean Japanese, Burakumin, Ainu, and Okinawans.[6]

There has been a disproportionate amount of interest among Japanese academics and students in the Brazilian nikkeijin, and a staggering number

---

[4]"Dekasegi" literally means one who "goes out" to earn money. The word originally referred to Japanese workers from rural agricultural areas who migrate within Japan in search of work.

[5]The use of the term "homeland" becomes quite complicated for ethnic return migrants like the Japanese Brazilians who have both a natal and an ethnic or ancestral homeland. See Tsuda (forthcoming 1, 2) for an analysis of how return migration influences the Japanese Brazilians' conception of homeland.

[6]The Burakumin are a former outcaste group, and the Ainu are aboriginals who are mainly found in Hokkaido. The Okinawans inhabit the Ryukyu islands south of the main Japanese archipelago and not only are seen as an ethnic minority by mainland Japanese but also maintain a separate ethnic identity and historical consciousness.

of research papers, questionnaire surveys, reports, and master's theses have already been produced. At least seven books in Japanese have been published on the subject so far, although most are journalistic accounts and factual presentations (Fujisaki 1991, Ninomiya 1992, Ninomiya and Rodosho 1994, H. Takahashi 1995, Y. Takahashi 1992, Watanabe, ed. 1995, Watkins 1994). A comprehensive bibliography on foreign workers in Japan compiled by the Japan Institute of Labor in 1995 included 102 citations just on nikkeijin return migrants. There have also been a number of Japanese Brazilian graduate students in Japan as well as non-nikkeijin Brazilian researchers studying nikkeijin return migration.

American researchers have not been slow to jump onto the bandwagon either. Despite the considerable linguistic abilities that the topic demands (fluency in both Japanese and Portuguese), a good number of academics and students based in the United States are studying (or have studied) the Brazilian nikkeijin in Japan, and many more are undoubtedly on their way. Researchers based in Europe and even Australia are also taking an interest in the topic. In fact, the field of nikkeijin studies in Japan has become so crowded recently that some Japanese Brazilians have been interviewed more than once by different researchers. In fact, the author was told by two separate Japanese researchers that they contacted specific nikkeijin only to be told that a certain Japanese American graduate student from the University of California had already done an interview with them a few months ago. Two books in English on the subject have already been published. *Circle K Cycles* by novelist Karen Yamashita (2001) is a compilation of personal experiences, observations, and fiction, and *No One Home: Brazilian Selves Remade in Japan* by anthropologist Daniel Linger contains a number of interview transcripts with Japanese Brazilians in Japan.

The Japanese Brazilians have also become instant celebrities in the mass media. Enough articles have been written about them in Japanese national and local newspapers as well as in magazines to fill several thick volumes. There are also a good number of Japanese television documentaries about the nikkeijin return migrants, and even television dramas about them. They are also featured on news programs, talk shows, and quiz and game shows. Although interest in the Japanese Brazilians has waned recently with Japan's recession and the general loss of concern at all levels in the country's foreign worker problem, the media coverage continues. In Brazil, the nikkeijin dekasegi have received prominent coverage not only in Japanese Brazilian community newspapers but also in leading national Brazilian papers and magazines. There have also been nationwide television news programs and radio broadcasts devoted to them. In the United States, prominent articles (including front-page coverage) about the Japanese Brazilians in Japan have appeared in major newspapers and news magazines, including *The New York Times*, the *Wall Street Journal*, the *Los Angeles Times*, the *San Francisco Chronicle*, the *Christian Science Monitor*, and *Time* magazine. They have even made the ABC evening news.

Some Japanese Brazilians are quite amazed when they are told of the incredible international media attention they have received. One informant remarked, "Strange, I never knew we were so famous." Indeed, some cannot quite figure out why they generate so much interest in Japan and elsewhere. After all, they simply came to Japan to earn some money and then to quickly head home.

The amount of academic and media attention that the Brazilian nikkeijin have received is especially remarkable for two reasons. Compared to immigration levels to which Americans are normally accustomed, the number of nikkeijin in Japan is rather small and may be reaching an upper limit, even if Japan enters another period of robust economic growth. In addition, Japanese Brazilian immigrants are relatively unproblematic from an economic, political, and social standpoint. They are legally accepted by the Japanese government and do not suffer from serious economic exploitation or human rights abuses in Japan, although they are sometimes exploited by transnational labor broker agencies. In general, they enjoy favorable working and housing conditions compared to other foreign workers and do not live in segregated ghettos, nor are they becoming an impoverished underclass. Most of the Japanese Brazilians have good access to medical care, health insurance, and other public services. They have not brought with them any health or social problems (like disease, crime, or drugs), nor have they been the target of any concerted negative public reaction or backlash. Since most still consider themselves to be temporary sojourners, they are not yet experiencing the problems associated with long-term immigrant settlement, such as employment and housing discrimination, job competition with native workers, and lack of social and political rights. On an ethnic level, they have not been really controversial either. As Japanese descendants, most are not phenotypically different from the Japanese, and they are not targets of notable ethnic discrimination (see chapter 3). In general, it can be safely said that they have not yet caused any profound changes in Japanese ethnic beliefs, national identity, or racial composition. They are adapting to Japan rather smoothly without the significant social or family disruption and psychological problems that some immigrant minorities experience (see chapters 5 and 6). The most serious current social issues among Japanese Brazilian immigrants are the educational problems some of their children face in Japan and the adaptational difficulties such children have when they return to Brazil (see the epilogue).

So why are the Japanese Brazilians in Japan so inherently fascinating? I hope that this book will make some of the reasons clear. Of course, there are many other examples of "ethnic return migrants" like the nikkeijin who return to their ancestral homelands after living abroad for generations. The most famous example is the ethnic Germans from Eastern Europe and the former Soviet Union, who have "returned" to Germany after the collapse of communism. Other examples include foreign-born ethnic Chinese and Koreans who have migrated back to China and Korea, Spanish expatriates in Europe who have recently returned to Spain, and the "return" of Jews residing in various countries to Israel, although the circumstances here are quite different from the other cases. In Latin America, the Japanese-descent nikkeijin are not the only ones returning to their ethnic homelands. Approximately 45,000 Latin Americans of Italian descent have returned to Italy, and smaller populations of ethnic Germans, Portuguese, and Spanish are also migrating "back" to Europe.

Ethnic return migrants are interesting because many have become immigrant minorities in their countries of ethnic origin despite their ancestral ties and presumed ethnic similarities with the host populace. Because of the ethnic affinity that the Japanese Brazilians feel with the Japanese, their ethnic and socioeconomic marginalization in Japan is quite disorienting and introduces complications in their identity and adaptation that other immigrants in Japan do not face.

Acknowledgments

As always, a research project of this scope could not have been successfully completed without the continuous support and assistance of numerous individuals. This includes people from three different countries. First and foremost, I would like to express my deepest gratitude to George De Vos, professor emeritus of anthropology at the University of California at Berkeley, who has been my intellectual mentor and friend for many years. Since that day in September 1990 when I first walked into his office, a young and wide-eyed graduate student of twenty-one years, I have learned much from our close association and our many long conversations, and he has been a continuous source of intellectual inspiration. I owe a great deal to him for my intellectual growth over the years. I will also never forget his emotional support during the difficult year after my father's premature death as well as the constant encouragement, enthusiasm, and assistance he has so generously provided throughout my academic career.

I am also deeply indebted to Wayne Cornelius, director of the Center for Comparative Immigration Studies and the Center for U.S.–Mexican Studies at the University of California at San Diego, who has provided continuous and critical support for my research (intellectually, institutionally, financially, and otherwise) as well as for my academic career. Starting with our field research trip to Japan in November 1992, we have worked closely on Japanese immigration issues, and I have also benefited greatly from my participation in his research and from the various other opportunities he has opened up for me. Under his generous sponsorship, I was able to spend two years as a visiting research fellow at the Center for U.S.–Mexican Studies in order to write up my dissertation and then to prepare the manuscript for this book. The experience and resources available to me during this period proved to be invaluable.

I would also like to gratefully acknowledge the assistance and support of Nelson Graburn, professor of anthropology at the University of California at Berkeley, who served as my advisor and the chair of my dissertation committee and from whom I took a number of courses while I was a graduate student. I have known him since my arrival at Berkeley and have always deeply appreciated his thoughtful advice, insightful comments, and skill as a teacher and discussant. I thank him for his constant intellectual support and his firm encouragement and guidance throughout my years as a graduate student. His serious dedication to students is quite remarkable.

My stay in Porto Alegre, Brazil was made possible by Cicero Vaz, professor of psychology at the Instituto de Psicologia at the Pontifícia Universidade Católica do Rio Grande do Sul (PUCRS), who generously provided me with housing, office space, and personal research support, as well as much-needed doses of assurance and encouragement. The four and a half months under his tutelage were critical for getting my project and fieldwork off to a solid start and proved to be a very memorable period. I would also like to thank Elisa Ludwig, my Portuguese tutor in Porto Alegre, whose patience and teaching skill was critical for my mastery of the language. Finally, I am very grateful to André Jacquemin, professor of psychology at the Universidade de São Paulo in Ribeirão Preto, who was my sponsor during the last half of my stay in Brazil. With his generous assistance and support both within and outside the university, I was able to take advantage of a new research environment, which broadened my fieldwork in Brazil both empirically and analytically.

In Japan, my institutional research affiliation was arranged at the University of Tokyo by Kenichiro Hirano, professor in the Department of Social and International Relations. I sincerely appreciate his many efforts on my behalf. In addition, I was kindly assisted by Takamichi Kajita, professor of sociology at Hitotsubashi University, and Toshio Iyotani, professor of economics at the Tokyo University of Foreign Studies, both of whom provided the necessary personal advice, guidance, introductions, and research support to ensure that my fieldwork would be successful. Takashi Miyajima, professor of sociology at Rikkyo University, was also very helpful during my stay in Japan. Along with the many other university professors whom I had the pleasure to meet, I cannot even begin to thank the countless employers, labor brokers, local residents, factory workers, school teachers, journalists, local officials, and government bureaucrats who were kind enough to find time in their busy schedules to answer my many questions. One individual I would like to personally mention is Mr. Junichi Kitazawa of the International Exchange Office in Ota city, Gunma Prefecture, who assisted me in finding a factory job and arranged numerous interviews for me with local officials and employers. Much of my work during the first phase of my stay in Japan would not have been possible without his experience, contacts, resources, and persistence.

The entire project has been generously funded by numerous grants and fellowships. My research in Brazil was supported by a Foreign Languages and Area Studies Fellowship from the U.S. Department of Education and by a Regents Fellowship from the University of California at Berkeley. During my fieldwork in Japan, I was funded by a Fulbright-Hays Doctoral Dissertation Research Abroad Fellowship and a grant from the Wenner-Gren Foundation for Anthropological Research (Grant no. 5757). My dissertation write up was made possible by generous support from the Center for U.S.–Mexican Studies at the University of California at San Diego, as well as a fellowship from the Social Science Research Council and the American Council of Learned Societies and a grant from the Center for Japanese Studies at the University of California at Berkeley.

Various ideas and analyses that were eventually incorporated into this book were presented at numerous conferences, workshops, and departmental colloquiums. I thank the various individuals who invited me to these occasions and the audiences for their helpful comments and questions. This manuscript (in whole or in part) has also benefited considerably from comments and suggestions at various stages by (among others) Arjun Appadurai, Roy D'Andrade, Robert Cole, Wayne Cornelius, George De Vos, Suzanne De Vos, Nelson Graburn, Germaine Hoston, William Kelly, Jeff Lesser, Tanya Luhrmann, Roshni Rustomji-Kerns, Saskia Sassen, Marcelo Suárez-Orozco, and Ayumi Takenaka, as well as two anonymous but very thoughtful reviewers of the completed book manuscript. As always, errors in fact and interpretation are the sole responsibility of the author.

Last, and most important, my heartfelt gratitude and deepest thanks go out to the hundreds of Japanese Brazilians and Brazilians in both Brazil and Japan who so willingly and openly allowed me to share their lives and experiences for close to two years and to participate in their jobs, social activities, and families to an extent that far surpassed my initial expectations.

I appreciate their sincere and enthusiastic response to me and my research as well as their many thoughtful comments and insightful observations about their lives in both countries. I can still vividly remember each encounter and conversation and all the wonderful moments and enjoyable times I spent with those many individuals whose paths briefly crossed with mine. The remarkable kindness, hospitality, and emotional warmth extended to me so unselfishly by so many different Brazilians on so many different occasions will never be forgotten. *Muito obrigado e boa sorte!*

STRANGERS
IN THE
ETHNIC HOMELAND

INTRODUCTION

๛

Ethnicity and the Anthropologist
Negotiating Identities in the Field

INTRODUCTION: A HOT SUMMER DAY

It was an autumn day in September when I stepped off the train into the scorching heat after a three-hour trip from central Tokyo to Ota city in Gunma Prefecture. I had arrived in Japan just four days earlier to start phase 2 of my fieldwork after close to nine months in Brazil. As I walked out onto the station platform, I looked up at the imposing structure of the shopping center that towered over the station, which brought back fleeting memories of those grand, indoor shopping centers in Brazil (*os shoppings*). In fact, "the shopping" in Brazil had become such a symbol of progress that every sizable Brazilian city seemed to need a glamorous shopping or two to demonstrate that it had fully emerged from the rural backwaters to become a modern, proud city. However, I had no time to reminisce about my experience in Brazil. I was in Japan and had changed my mentality accordingly. Unlike Brazil, which had been a completely foreign country for me, Japan was familiar, and as a Japanese descendant from the United States, I always felt I belonged here, although I had never stayed in the country for longer than a month and a half. Compared to the uncertainty I felt when stepping off the plane in Brazil, I felt confident in Japan: I was a partial insider and knew how to behave, how to adapt and mix in with the Japanese, and what to expect. Usually, I could be ethnically "Japanese" enough to get by without any problems and avoid some of the difficulties that complete foreigners would conceivably have. Therefore, I did not expect the disorienting confusion that would confront me in the coming weeks of fieldwork—not because of my status as a foreigner, but precisely because I was *not* completely foreign in Japan.

Ota city and the adjacent Oizumi town are part of an industrial area in Gunma Prefecture that has the highest concentration of Brazilian nikkeijin (Japanese descendants born and raised outside of Japan) in Japan. In 1996, 10 percent of the town's population of 42,229 consisted of registered foreigners (this excludes unauthorized immigrants), 76 percent of whom were nikkeijin. The nikkeijin are employed both in the factories of large multinational companies and in hundreds of smaller, subcontracting firms. The Japanese Brazilian immigrant community is quite cohesive and supported by an expanding array of ethnic businesses. The local government has welcomed the Japanese Brazilians and provides many services. The schools in the area have created special classes and instruction for nikkeijin children. Even local Japanese businesses post signs and instructions in Portuguese and sometimes even hire Portuguese-speaking salesmen. A number of nikkeijin labor broker companies operate in the area, providing extensive employment and housing services.

Being a nikkeijin myself (a second-generation Japanese American), I had decided to work in a factory with the Brazilian nikkeijin as a dekasegi (temporary migrant worker) in order to conduct participant observation in the true anthropological spirit. From what I had heard so far, however, my prospects of getting a factory job were not very good. Despite the contacts my Japanese professors in Tokyo had with employers hiring foreign workers, none of them had been able to secure a job for me. After arriving in Japan, I had come once to Ota city in order to speak with Mr. Honkawa, a local government official responsible for its international residents. He had kindly agreed to contact employers on my behalf but had not yet succeeded in placing me in a factory. Armed with a bunch of *shokaijo* (letters of introduction), which are a basic necessity in Japan if one wishes to get anything done, I had returned to Ota city again in order to discuss any possibilities with him. It had been quite an effort to collect the shokaijo from my Japanese professors on such short notice, and I was hoping that they would do the trick, in standard Japanese fashion.

The building where Mr. Honkawa's office was located was not far from the station. As I stepped up to the entrance, the automatic glass doors slid open, beckoning me inside. I proceeded up to the International Exchange Office and entered with a polite and formal bow and the standard Japanese greeting. The office workers looked up and welcomed me, smiles of familiarity on some of their faces. Mr. Honkawa was on the telephone but gestured for me to wait in one of the comfortable armchairs on the other side of the room where guests were received. As I sat down, an impeccably dressed and made-up OL (office lady) emerged from an adjacent room with a wooden tray bearing a cup of tea. The young woman gracefully placed the teacup on the low table before me with a "*dozo*" (please help yourself) and a slight bow. I thanked her politely and took a sip. I had gone through the ritual many times before, and it was all so very routine. The Japanese demeanor and subtle body comportment expected in such situations were so conditioned that they had already become automatic reflexes for me—part of my Japanese "habitus."

Mr. Honkawa was off the phone in a few minutes and quickly came over. I stood up to greet him with a formal bow, and he began a short, pleasant chat. How was my trip from Tokyo? How was I adapting to Japan? What did I think of the heat?

After a few minutes, I presented him with my letters of introduction from my three Japanese professors and from the Tokyo Fulbright office. Mr. Honkawa seemed surprised that I had so quickly and diligently obtained the shokaijo and took a few minutes to read them, expressing his approval. He neatly put them back into their envelopes and placed them on the table before him.

"Well, as I told you on the phone, we tried talking to the presidents of five local companies that employ lots of Japanese Brazilians, but unfortunately, they were all unwilling to allow you to work," Mr. Honkawa reported. "Also, our *kyokucho* (bureau director) spoke with one of the managers at Watanabe Industries, but unfortunately, they aren't hiring any foreign workers right now."

Mr. Honkawa then began going through a list of reasons why employers were hesitant to hire me. They did not want researchers observing their operations and treatment of foreign workers, they thought a period of four months was too short to train and employ me, they were worried about my personal safety, they were not as willing as before to hire new workers because of the recession, etc.

There was a slight pause. "However, there is one remaining possibility. I spoke with someone named Matsushita Guilherme—he's a Japanese Brazilian who is the manager of a local Brazilian food store. Speaks good Japanese. He's agreed to show up at two o'clock and may be able to do something for you. By the way, if the factory job doesn't work out, how would a job at a Brazilian food store be?"

"No, that wouldn't work," I was quick to reply. "It has to be a factory where I can observe Japanese and Japanese Brazilian workers together."

Mr. Honkawa looked a bit troubled, betraying the expression of some-one who has run out of options. By that time, I had basically given up on the prospect of being able to work in a factory in Ota or Oizumi.

"Please, don't be too concerned, Mr. Honkawa," I tried to reassure him. "Even if I can't work in a factory, I could live in this community, contact various Japanese Brazilians, interview them, and maybe socialize with them on the weekends. This was basically what I was doing in Brazil." It was a very disappointing alternative for me, but I had no choice, and I did not want Mr. Honkawa to feel bad about letting me down after his many sincere efforts.

"Well, let's see what Guilherme has to say," Mr. Honkawa concluded.

I tried to keep my hopes up but was rather pessimistic about the last remaining option. If important Japanese professors and high-ranking local government officials could not find me a job, what could a local Brazilian food store owner do for me?

It was a while before Guilherme appeared, arriving close to 20 minutes late in standard Brazilian fashion. He carried nothing besides a cellular phone and was casually dressed, his attire marking him as a Japanese Brazilian. Despite his Japanese physical appearance, his comportment was distinctly *un*-Japanese. He did not bother to bow, nor did he go through any of the formal Japanese greetings.

Guilherme and I exchanged *meishi* (business cards), and Mr. Honkawa handed him my letters of introduction, carefully mentioning the names of the prestigious Japanese institutions from which they came. Guilherme did not seem too interested in the letters of introduction. After all, he was Brazilian, not Japanese.

I began with an extensive self-introduction and expressed my desire to work in a factory with Japanese Brazilians. Again, I laid down all the condi-tions: I would work strictly as a volunteer without pay, I would never use the name of the company in my research, I would wear a uniform and would do the same work as the Japanese Brazilians, and I would do overtime.

There was a long pause after my words. Guilherme looked at my meishi again, his face hesitant. "Well, working in a factory is a complicat-ed issue since you are on a cultural activities visa, even if it's strictly as a volunteer for research purposes," he remarked with a troubled expression. He paused for a few moments, still thinking the matter over, then asked, "How long did you say you would work?"

"Four, maybe five months," I said, my final hopes sinking. I knew my intention to work only for a relatively brief period was also a serious disadvantage. At most, I expected an "I'll try my best, but I can't promise anything." Such a response would have been equivalent to a refusal in my mind.

Finally, Guilherme spoke. "Well, I can get a job for you at the air conditioning unit of Toyama Electric right away. There are lots of Japanese Brazilians in that factory. Can you start working tomorrow?"

I was dumbfounded and speechless at the unexpected offer. I had not expected him to be able to find me a job, least of all right on the spot. Start working in a factory tomorrow? Suddenly, the prospect seemed daunting. I had expected at least one week to psychologically prepare myself for a grueling and fast-paced assembly line job.

"Tomorrow?" It was my turn to sound hesitant.

"Yes." The response was matter of fact. He seemed a bit puzzled at the sudden tone of reluctance in my voice after my eager plea. I wanted a factory job, didn't I?

"Uh, well . . . I can't really start working so soon," I was finally able to gather together a coherent response. "My baggage is still at a Tokyo hotel and it would take at least two days for it to get here."

"Monday then?"

There was another pause on my part. "Yes, I think I can start working on Monday."

Guilherme was already standing up. "O.K. I will meet you in front of the Ota station Sunday around noon and will drive you to the company apartment where you will be living."

I stood up, bowed, and thanked him profusely with every polite Japanese expression I could think of. Guilherme smiled briefly, shook my hand, and quickly departed, leaving Mr. Honkawa and me to marvel at what had just happened. Very un-Japanese, I thought, watching Guilherme leave the room.

The letters of introduction remained on the table.

IDENTITY AND THE FIELDWORKER:
THE SUBJECTIVE BASIS FOR "OBJECTIVITY"

And so began my fieldwork experience in Japan. On Sunday, Guilherme picked me up at the Ota train station as promised (he was only 15 minutes late this time). As I soon found out, Guilherme was one of those middlemen who introduce Brazilian nikkeijin to Japanese-run labor broker firms, which technically hire the nikkeijin and then place them in various Japanese factories. The next day, I found myself working side by side with Japanese and Japanese Brazilian workers in the inspection section of one of the air conditioner assembly lines at Toyama Electric in Oizumi town. The factory was huge, with roughly 10 percent of the work force nikkeijin (including a good number of Japanese Peruvians). I was also housed in a nearby apartment with Japanese Brazilians. I conducted participant observation in this environment for four and a half months before I moved to Kawasaki city in Kanagawa Prefecture, another region with a sizeable Japanese Brazilian populace.

I had attempted to find a factory field site by dutifully following an ethnic adaptational pattern that had been so successful for me in the past—acting as "Japanese" as possible. Yet, for the first time, this strategy had shown severe limitations. Instead, it had been a Brazilian sense of informality and a willingness to bend the rules—the *jeitinho brasileiro* (the Brazilian way of doing things)—that had finally landed me a factory job. However, I did not fully anticipate that the manner in which I gained ac-

The inspection section of the air conditioner assembly line at Toyama factory, where the author worked for four and a half months.

The cramped quarters in which most Japanese Brazilians live in Japan. Usually, two Japanese Brazilians would be assigned to a room of this size, called a *hachijyoma* (a room with eight tatami mats).

cess to the field would determine the way I was ethnically perceived by the "natives" (both Japanese and Japanese Brazilians) and therefore significantly influence my effectiveness as a fieldworker.

In this chapter, I wish to provide a candid account of my personal experiences in the Toyama factory and how my ethnically ambiguous status influenced my fieldwork and collection of ethnographic material. This type of self-reflexivity in the field is becoming increasingly prevalent in anthropology in recent years and is best summarized by what Tedlock (1991) calls a shift from participant observation toward the observation of participation.[1] As is true with all anthropologists, I had quite idiosyncratic field experiences, a product of my peculiar personal qualities and the particular

---

[1] An increase in self-reflexivity in ethnographic writing was noted as early as 1972 by Nash and Wintrob and has now become standard practice, especially after the publication of *Writing Culture: The Poetics and Politics of Ethnography* (Clifford and Marcus 1986).

dynamics of the social milieu I confronted. However, I hope my personal reflections will shed light on some enduring issues and problems related to fieldwork.

Since anthropological data is obtained through interaction with informants, it is undeniable that the personal characteristics of anthropologists directly affect the process of field research. Therefore, a consideration of anthropologists' self-experiences in the field helps clarify their relationships with informants, how the ethnographic data was obtained, and the personal biases and cultural factors that structure their selective perceptions. This is necessary for understanding the inherent limitations, incompleteness, and general reliability of the ethnographic analysis.

In this manner, a self-reflexive discussion of the fieldworker's subjectivity is not fundamentally incompatible with the understanding of the scientific process of fieldwork, but is essential to it. As Hortense Powdermaker (1967:9) once observed, "A scientific discussion of field work method should include considerable detail about the observer: the role he plays, his personality, and other relevant facts concerning his position and functioning in the society studied." Indeed, an ethnography that completely ignores the anthropologist's own experiences in the field in favor of a sanitized and depersonalized account can be considered problematic on methodological grounds despite the resulting aura of scientific objectivity (cf. Whitehead and Conaway 1986:3).[2] Ultimately, this distorts the nature of the anthropological endeavor, in which the subjective experiences of the observer in the field are intricately involved with what is observed and the reactions of the observed. Given the multitude of methodological and epistemological difficulties inherent in fieldwork, a frank assessment of the personal subjectivities involved is a means to salvage what objectivity is possible. As George Marcus notes, "objectivity (rather than the often presumed subjectivism) . . . arises from . . . a scrupulous, methodological practice of reflexivity" (1995:112).

However, as Myerhoff and Ruby (1982:7, 24) point out, there is a fine line between self-reflexiveness and self-centered narcissism. According to

---

[2]A number of writers have discussed how accounts of the anthropologist's personal experiences were suppressed in early ethnographic writing because of concerns about scientific objectivity (see also Abu-Lughod 1986:10, Myerhoff and Ruby 1982, Nash and Wintrob 1972, Scheper-Hughes 1992:23, Tedlock 1991:71–72). When personal experiences in the field have been discussed, they generally have appeared in separate publications (Bowen 1964, Levi-Strauss 1969, Maybury-Lewis 1965, Powdermaker 1966, Rabinow 1977).

Rosaldo (1989:7), the problem with current, self-reflexive ethnographies is "the tendency of the self-absorbed Self to lose sight altogether of the culturally different Other" (see also Scheper-Hughes 1992:28). The purpose of anthropological self-reflexivity should not be self-exploration but methodological clarification and a better understanding of how the informants' lives were observed and interpreted.[3] Some knowledge of the self is a prerequisite for knowledge about others encountered in the field, which is why Clyde Kluckhohn (and to a lesser extent, Margaret Mead) instructed their graduate students in anthropology to undergo psychoanalysis (see Mead 1952:345; Nader 1986:98, 113).

Anthropologists in the past have relied on the theoretical frameworks they use to analyze ethnographic materials to self-reflexively understand the fieldwork process itself. Some classical examples include Berreman's (1972:xvii–lvii) analysis of his field experiences in a Himalayan village from a social interactionalist perspective and Devereux's (1967) use of clinical psychology to reflect on fieldwork and methodology in social science. In a similar vein, I will examine how fieldwork involves a constant negotiation of identity between anthropologists and their informants. A number of researchers have discussed the relationship between the anthropologist's evolving sense of identity and the fieldwork process (Kondo 1986, 1990; Myerhoff and Ruby 1982; Whitehead and Conaway 1986).[4]

Identity refers to a conscious awareness of who one is in the world based on association with certain sociocultural characteristics or membership in social groups. The individual's identity consists of two components: the self and social identity. The self (or self-identity) is the aspect of identity that is experienced and developed *internally* through the individual's own subjective perceptions and experiences of the social environment. However, an identity is also *externally* defined by others in accordance with stan-

---

[3]Mel Spiro makes a similar point:

> In this regard, the psychoanalysts' stress on self-reflexivity, like that of the psychological anthropologists discussed below, is very different from that of many postmodernists who also stress its importance. . . . For while the former two deploy their counter-transferential experience in the service of understanding the object (patients and non-Western peoples, respectively), the latter . . . deploy it instead in the service of their own "self-growth." (1996:762)

[4]Interactions in the field could be analyzed as encounters between different cultural systems instead of focusing on the individual characteristics of the anthropologist (Lutz 1988:14–15). However, since personal characteristics are also culturally constituted to a certain degree, they involve contrastive cultural systems as well.

dardized cultural norms and social roles, which can be called the individual's social identity.

Self-identity and social identity are not conceptually exclusive as some have suggested (e.g., Castells 1997:6–7), since both influence the individual's composite perception of identity. Others have questioned this distinction altogether because both are ultimately mediated and constituted by cultural meanings and constructs (Kondo 1990:34). However, collapsing the distinction may be equally problematic because identity is not only a matter of cultural constructs but one of *competing* cultural constructs. In other words, it is undeniable that discrepancies and conflicts frequently occur between the cultural categories that individuals use to define their inner selves (self-identity) and the cultural categories imposed on them by others (as their social identity).[5] This can lead to a fragmented experience of identity, the domination of one of these aspects of identity over the other, or some type of synthesis between these incongruous elements. Since identities are internally experienced and externally defined in various ways as individuals engage in relationships with different people in constantly shifting social contexts, they develop multiple and sometimes conflicting selves (cf. Ewing 1990).

Undoubtedly, the identities that anthropologists bring to the field have a profound impact on the fieldwork process. When anthropologists enter the field, they are perceived by the natives in a certain manner in accordance with pre-existing social categories and roles (cf. Berreman 1972; Kondo 1986; Lutz 1988). In other words, the observer is also being observed by the natives, and what they observe has a significant influence on the observer's research possibilities and access to ethnographic knowledge (cf. Escobar 1993:383). As Gerald Berreman remarks (1972:lvi), "The nature of [the anthropologist's] data is largely determined by his [social] identity as seen by his subjects" (cf. Cicourel 1964:42). The social identities that informants ascribe to anthropologists structure not only how they will be perceived but also what will be freely divulged to them and what they will be allowed to observe.[6] As a result, fieldworkers must engage in a constant "presentation of self" and "impression management" in an at-

---

[5]Kondo also recognizes that despite attempts to transcend the self/society binary, the distinction insidiously persists (1990:37).

[6]Horowitz's (1989) and Whitehead's (1986) discussions of their personal field experiences are good illustrations of this point.

tempt to negotiate their identities in a manner that will allow them to be accepted by the natives and provide access to the type of ethnographic data desired.

Anthropologists in the past have frequently been seen by the natives as religious missionaries, or suspected of being spies or various types of government officials (see Berreman 1972; Du Bois 1986:224; Nader 1986:100; Weidman 1986:255). Others have been seen as journalists, reporters, artists, prostitutes, and even ancestor spirits or deities (Horowitz 1989; Landes 1986; Williams 1967:43–44). In such cases of mistaken social identity, anthropologists have struggled to convince their informants that they are actually researchers and do not have other motives or agendas. However, it is not only their professional identities that are at stake—fieldworkers must also deal with informants' perceptions of their ethnic, national, gender, and class identities. In other words, the *whole* self must be continuously negotiated with the natives throughout the fieldwork process in a manner that will be favorable for research purposes. In the following sections, I explore my own experiences in this regard with a strong emphasis on the ethnic aspects of identity.

WHO IS THE ANTHROPOLOGIST?: THE RESEARCHER'S AMBIGUOUS ETHNICITY IN A "MULTIETHNIC" FIELD SITE

One of my primary objectives in the field was not only to understand the Japanese Brazilians' experience in Japan and their ethnic perceptions of the Japanese but also to study *Japanese* ethnic attitudes toward the Japanese Brazilians. I wished to avoid a one-sided study that focuses exclusively on the Brazilian nikkeijin immigrant minority without any understanding of the ethnic reactions of the Japanese majority. Of course, I realized that this type of "multiethnic" fieldwork would be quite complicated since I would have to be accepted by two separate groups constituted through mutual social exclusion and quite distinct in identity and self-consciousness. However, I felt well positioned to study both sides of this ethnic encounter given my own ethnicity and past experiences.

Before going to Japan, I had spent eight and a half months in Brazil in the cities of Porto Alegre and Ribeirão Preto in the states of Rio Grande do Sul and São Paulo, where I conducted almost 70 interviews with various Japanese Brazilians and participated extensively in community activities. I was openly accepted by both Japanese Brazilian communities because of my ethnic status as a fellow nikkeijin from America who spoke Japanese and was becoming proficient in Portuguese. Therefore, I expected ready access and acceptance by the Japanese Brazilians in Japan as well. At the same time, I felt that because of my Japanese descent and my unusually strong Japanese cultural background, I would also be readily accepted among the Japanese, as had always been the case in the past. However, the maintenance of such dual social identities in the field was a much more complicated and delicate process than I had initially imagined.

ACCEPTANCE AND UNDERSTANDING: JAPANESE BRAZILIAN PERCEPTIONS OF THE ANTHROPOLOGIST

As expected, the Japanese Brazilians responded to me with friendliness and active interest, and I was quite successful in establishing rapport and gaining acceptance. I had no problems negotiating either my ethnic identity among them as an American nikkeijin or my professional identity as an anthropologist because they were quite familiar with these social identities and quite sympathetic toward such people. My informants were very conscious of their nikkeijin counterparts in the United States—the Japanese Americans (*nipo-americanos*)—and were generally quite interested in me. There was a strong feeling of commonality between us as Japanese descendants born and raised abroad who shared some similar ethnic experiences, and this facilitated interaction from the very beginning. My proficiency in Portuguese and extended stay in Brazil undoubtedly strengthened this ethnic bond and the feeling of common background. Of course, before I introduced myself to individual Japanese Brazilians, there was some initial confusion about my ethnicity. For instance, one nisei woman remarked, "I wasn't quite sure whether you were a [Japanese] Brazilian or a Japanese at first. I saw you together with the Brazilians and you wore the same uniform, but you also spoke Japanese to the Japanese workers." Others had similar initial impressions. "I found your accent [in Portuguese] to be strange when I first saw you," another remarked after I finally had a chance to formally introduce myself. "But now I understand. It's an American accent."

In addition, I was directly sharing the experiences of the Japanese Brazilians in Japan by assuming the social class identity of a dekasegi and working alongside them on the assembly line. Since I had found my job through the same labor broker firm that supplied Toyama with Japanese Brazilian workers, I wore the same blue uniform (which was different from the gray uniforms of the Japanese Toyama workers), which immediately symbolized our ethnic and social class solidarity.

My reasons and motives for being in the factory—that is, my professional identity as an anthropologist researcher—were also readily understood and accepted, if not openly welcomed by the Japanese Brazilians. Since many of them are relatively well educated, they could easily relate to the concept of a graduate student doing research in a foreign country and conducting participant observation in a factory with his informants. Most knew what an *antropólogo* was, and others were familiar with *pesquisa de campo* (fieldwork). A few even told me they had taken anthropology or sociology courses while they were university students. I was sometimes asked what conclusions I would draw from my research about them, how the Japanese Brazilians were different from the Japanese Americans, or whether my thesis would be published as a book. Others openly wondered when I would be conducting an interview with them. Of course, my social identity as a graduate student researcher in the factory indicated that I was not an ordinary dekasegi in Japan like the Japanese Brazilians. However, this apparent difference in social class identity did not create any distance between us since the Brazilian nikkeijin were middle-class in Brazil. Like them, I had experienced a decline in social class status in Japan by assuming the identity of a dekasegi. The only difference was that I maintained some semblance of my former middle-class identity in the factory, whereas they did not.

This ethnic and professional acceptance among the Japanese Brazilians was further reinforced by the general tendency of Brazilians to be friendly, receptive, and hospitable even toward outsiders and strangers. Call it national character or Latino warmth, but the contrast with ordinary Japanese was quite stark. In fact, I did not find my acceptance among the *non-nikkeijin* Brazilians in the factory to be any less than among the Japanese Brazilians despite our supposedly greater ethnic distance. Both Japanese Brazilians and Brazilians were equally interested in the Japanese American in their midst. In fact, word of my presence spread among them in the factory so that after a while, some of the individuals I met for the first time had already heard about me from their companions. "Yeah, you're that Japanese American researcher guy, right?" a few confirmed when I introduced myself.

Because of my ethnic and social class affinity with the Japanese Brazilians and their complete understanding of my professional identity as an anthropologist, I was considered an insider among them as much as someone born and raised in the United States could be. As far as some of them were concerned, I was like one of them—another nikkeijin dekasegi trying to earn money in Japan—except that I happened to have research motives as well. Of course, a strong consciousness of difference between them and me always remained, even in the factory. I was sometimes told: "Your life in Japan must be easier than ours because you are an American [i.e., more respected than Brazilians in Japan]" or "because you are a researcher."

Undoubtedly, my status as a partial insider among the Japanese Brazilians made them more willing to talk for long hours about personal feelings and experiences that they might have been reluctant to divulge to outsiders, especially to Japanese researchers from Japan.[7] In fact, virtually all of them were receptive to my requests for interviews and almost no one expressed any reluctance.[8] I conducted a total of 47 interviews with the Japanese Brazilians in both Oizumi/Ota and Kawasaki, an industrial city adjacent to Tokyo that has a lower concentration of foreign workers. Most were two to three hours long, with a few lasting up to five or six hours. A good portion of my informants in Oizumi and Ota worked directly with me in the factory, providing me with an ideal opportunity to build rap-

---

[7]Most of the time, the benefits in the field that I enjoyed as a "nikkeijin" were taken for granted by both me and my Japanese Brazilian informants. However, there were a few occasions when they would make me acutely aware of my ethnic advantage. The most vivid illustration was when I participated in a project about foreign workers with Japanese professors and graduate students. One Japanese Brazilian I interviewed for this project told me that he was initially reluctant to become an informant because he thought he would have to talk to a Japanese and was quite relieved when he found that an American nikkeijin would interview him. I first began with the questions assigned to me by the Japanese project coordinators, to which he gave short, mechanical, and noncontroversial answers. "I don't want to say anything bad about the Japanese," he told me. When that task was finished and I began with my own personal questions, he relaxed visibly and said, "Ah, now we can *really* talk." The tone of the interview changed quite dramatically, allowing him finally to open up and speak frankly about his critical impressions of the Japanese.

[8]Only one Japanese Brazilian was uncertain of my identity as an anthropologist and initially expressed some reluctance to be interviewed when I first called him because he suspected that I might have been a missionary. Despite his initial hesitation, however, he ended up being one of my best informants, eventually talking to me well past midnight and driving me the long distance to his apartment and back.

port and even friendship before the interview. However, I also branched out broadly (by using the snowball approach) and contacted individuals outside the factory, who were just as open and receptive to my research and included some of my best informants. I also conducted interviews with Japanese Brazilians who were not factory workers, such as ethnic business owners, graduate students, and those working as liaisons and assistants for local governments and labor broker firms, and finally, with leaders of nikkeijin assistance organizations.

The only problem I encountered with the Japanese Brazilian dekasegi was simply one of time. Interviews were often very difficult to arrange because of their hectic work schedule, which frequently included overtime until late at night as well as work on Saturdays. Most of them (myself included) would be very tired after a long day of work, and many would have other commitments on Sundays, virtually the only day off for some. Appointments were sometimes canceled (or no one would be home when I arrived) and a good number of interviews required two or three separate visits to complete. However, once I was able to schedule an interview, even those who were the most busy were very willing to talk for a long time, and I never felt like a nuisance or unwanted intrusion.[9]

AMBIGUITY AND SOCIAL DISTANCE: JAPANESE PERCEPTIONS OF THE ANTHROPOLOGIST

Compared to the receptive and accessible Japanese Brazilians, the Japanese workers at the Toyama factory were a completely different story. The contrast was virtually night and day. This was personally quite dismaying since I had never had any doubts about my ability to be openly accepted as an ethnic "Japanese." I had been socially comfortable with various Japanese my entire life, beginning with my many years in Japanese Saturday school, then during my short trips to Japan to visit relatives, and later in encounters with Japanese professors, graduate students, and other youth. My different background as a Japanese descendant born and raised

---

[9]Since many Japanese Brazilians experience frustrations and difficulties in Japan as an ethnic minority, speaking to someone else who was sympathetic, interested, and could understand their experiences was also partly therapeutic for some; I felt this "cathartic" function of my interviews on some occasions.

in America had been less an ethnic hindrance than a cultural asset and a focus of active interest and appreciation. In addition, I spoke Japanese almost like a native and could even pass as one for most purposes if I wanted, since I became completely synchronized with the Japanese social environment after a few months in Japan. However, during my fieldwork, the Japanese I encountered and the dynamics of the social situation were completely different. I was dealing with Japanese factory workers, not students or professors, and I was in an assembly plant, not a school or university.

Negotiating an Ethnic Identity: From Nonperson to Ethnic Anomaly

Although most of the Japanese Brazilians are not phenotypically distinct from the Japanese, because those in the factory wore a different, blue-colored uniform as temporary migrant workers contracted from outside broker firms, this became an ethnic marker that clearly distinguished them from the Japanese workers at Toyama. Since I wore the same uniform, the ethnic and social class identity of "*nikkei burajirujin dekasegi rodosha*" (Brazilian nikkeijin migrant worker) was automatically imposed upon me by the Japanese. This external perception of my social identity was apparently confirmed by my behavior—not only did I work on the assembly line, I spoke in Portuguese to the Japanese Brazilians all the time, ate lunch with them in a separate room reserved for nikkeijin workers, and clustered with them during break. As far as the Japanese were concerned, I was as Brazilian as samba and carnaval, and there was no reason to think otherwise. It was a disorienting experience—a true case of mistaken identity.

Therefore, I was treated by the Japanese in the same way that the Japanese Brazilians are treated on the factory floor—with ethnic isolation and utter indifference. Close to a thousand Japanese Brazilians had been working in Toyama for several years now and they had long since lost their ethnic novelty. Because of the linguistic and cultural barriers, most of the Japanese workers were unwilling to interact with these ethnic strangers or had decided that it was simply not worth the effort. On their part, the Japanese Brazilians had grown accustomed to this neglect and socialized only among themselves. As a result, the Japanese had learned to react to the Brazilian nikkeijin with detached indifference, limiting interaction mainly to work instructions and an occasional stray remark. All that really mattered was that the Brazilian nikkeijin continued working diligently, and so far they had without causing any real problems.

The anthropologist in the field.

The reaction to me was no different. None of the Japanese workers talked to me (except to give me work orders) and no one showed any type of personal interest in me or bothered to ask who I was. There were no greetings, no smiles of recognition in the morning, no small talk. It was as if I was not there as a person and the only thing they cared about was my physical presence as an automaton installing utility cables and pressure gauges onto the machines. In fact, no one even bothered to ask or remember my name and instead simply called me "*gaijin-san*" (Mr. Foreigner).

In fact, I was reminded of Clifford Geertz's famous description of how indifferently the natives initially reacted to him and his wife when they first arrived in a Balinese village. His words fit my experience very aptly:

> Everyone ignored us . . . people seemed to look right through us with a gaze focused several yards behind us. . . . Almost nobody greeted us; but nobody scowled or said anything unpleasant to us either, which would have been almost as satisfactory. . . . If we ventured to approach someone . . . he moved, negligently but definitely, away . . . they acted as if we simply did not exist. (1973:412–13)

However, whatever the initial reaction of the natives, many anthropologists stick out in the field like a sore thumb. As Geertz quickly adds:

> The indifference, of course, was studied; the villagers were watching every move we made, and they had an enormous amount of quite accurate information about who we were and what we were going to be doing. (1973:413)

This obviously was not the case for me since I was not ethnically "visible" in the field. I knew that at Toyama, the Japanese workers were *not* watching me, studying me, or wondering who I was. In fact, they *knew* who I was—another faceless Japanese Brazilian migrant worker out of hundreds who worked temporarily in the factory and constantly circulated in and out. There was nothing special about me, and therefore, no reason to bother to interact with me. The persistent social neglect and lack of attention from the Japanese workers quickly became unbearable. It was such a stark contrast to the previously positive receptions of me in Japan.

For a while, I tried to convince myself that my status as a virtual nonperson on the factory floor would be a significant advantage. After all, was this not the ideal fieldwork situation—to be able to observe without being observed, without distorting the "natural" behavior of the natives by the presence and watchful gaze of the anthropologist? However, it was patently obvious that if I remained personally undistinguishable in the field— the same as the other Japanese Brazilians who worked diligently around me—I would never have access to the Japanese workers, nor would I ever be able to conduct interviews with them about their attitudes toward the Brazilian nikkeijin. More important, a good fieldworker is socially engaged, not passive, withdrawn, and observing from an "objective" distance in an effort not to disturb the social environment. The most interesting observations and insights in anthropology come from active *inter*action with informants, not inaction.[10] Therefore, the social identity that the Japanese had imposed on me as a "Japanese Brazilian migrant worker" was clearly detrimental.

---

[10]In fact, informants' perceptions and reactions to the disruptive presence of the anthropologist reveal much about their culture and society (cf. Devereux 1967). As Luhrmann notes, "the anthropologist learns to use his or her own responses and adaptation to the new culture, and the new culture's responses to the anthropologist, as a significant source of data about the culture" (1994b:73).

At times, I almost expected something to happen—some collective event or incident that would reveal to the Japanese who I really was and cause them to open up to me, something analogous to the police vice raid on the Balinese cockfight that apparently allowed Geertz to show his solidarity with the villagers and made him the center of attention and affection.[11] I waited, but that "magic moment" obviously never came.

I knew that passivity in the field would lead nowhere. Thus, my attempt to negotiate my identity with my Japanese informants began in earnest. Despite my persistent efforts, however, considerable confusion and ambiguity remained about who I was and what my motives were.

At first, the task of clarifying my ethnic and professional identity to the Japanese workers and gaining their understanding and acceptance seemed simple enough. I would begin talking to them in Japanese, then quickly find a chance to personally introduce myself. Yet, given the difficult situation I was in, my presentation of self was fraught with difficulties from the very beginning and did not lead to the smooth social acceptance I had hoped. The fundamental problem was that I had to disrupt their previous ethnic and social class perceptions of me as a "Brazilian nikkeijin" and "dekasegi" a number of times before I could convey to them who I *really* was (i.e., my self-identity). Whenever I began speaking to a nearby Japanese worker, the reaction would frequently be subdued surprise since the Japanese Brazilians are not expected to speak fluent Japanese. After a short chat, I would then explain that actually, I am not Japanese Brazilian but from the United States. This would elicit another expression of surprise. What was an American doing in an electrical appliance factory in Japan? "Actually," I would continue, "I'm a graduate student from the University of California conducting research on Brazilian nikkeijin dekasegi." Another surprise. Sometimes there would be an expression of acknowledgment; at other times, the response would simply be, "Really?"

Not only did my presentation of self cause a number of expected surprises for my informants, the self-identities that I claimed did not easily fit into their familiar social categories, both ethnically and professionally. I would avoid introducing myself ethnically as a "nikkeijin," but as someone

---

[11]There are other examples of unexpected incidents that have helped anthropologists establish rapport and a sense of social solidarity with their informants. For example, Kornblum (1989:1–2) describes how his willingness to defend a family of gypsies he was studying from attack in a dispute with Serbian immigrants near Paris allowed him to be accepted as one of them.

who was "born in America" (*amerika umare*) or "from America" (*amerika shusshin*). Since I could not be accepted by the Japanese as long as I was perceived as another nikkeijin foreigner, this was a conscious attempt on my part to distance myself from the Brazilian nikkeijin in the factory by negotiating an identity as an ethnic "Japanese," that is, as a Japanese descendant who could speak and behave "Japanese" and was therefore completely different from most nikkeijin. However, there were too many incongruities between the way I presented myself ethnically and the way I behaved. In Erving Goffman's words, I had serious problems with "impression management." Despite my attempts to demonstrate my "Japaneseness" in front of the Japanese workers, I wore the blue nikkeijin uniform and spent most of my time with the Japanese Brazilians speaking Portuguese, seemingly indicating that I belonged more with them than with the Japanese.

Fundamentally, my ethnic status remained ambiguous for the Japanese workers. Although I was seen more as a nikkeijin than as a Japanese, I did not conform to their stereotype of a foreign-born nikkeijin either—the way I spoke Japanese simply sounded too native. In fact, I was asked more than a few times whether I was Japanese by Toyama workers who did not know me personally, although my uniform clearly indicated that I was not. Of course, since I was not a *hakujin* (a white person), I did not fit their standard conception of an "American" either. And if I was really American, why in the world did I speak Portuguese?[12]

Negotiating a Professional Identity: Dekasegi or Researcher?

The Japanese workers also had trouble making sense of my professional self-identity as an anthropologist and researcher since they had no ready-made social category through which they could comprehend what I claimed to be doing. Coming from a working-class background without higher education, few had any idea what social science research was about, to say nothing of an anthropologist conducting participant observation in a factory. I certainly did not conform to their limited notion of a graduate student researcher, which was probably dominated by images of working in science laboratories or studying in large libraries with lots of obscure

---

[12]In fact, there was considerable confusion among the Japanese workers about what language I was using with the Japanese Brazilians. Some of the Japanese even asked me whether Brazilians speak English.

books. The concept of participant observation or fieldwork simply did not exist for them. Therefore, my declared professional self-identity seemed inconsistent with my actual working-class social identity in the factory as a dekasegi. Why would an American researcher from the well-known University of California work as a lowly, unskilled migrant worker in Japan, even if it were for research purposes? It was simply too hard to believe for some. Perhaps, the only indication that I might indeed be some sort of researcher was my peculiar and persistent habit of scribbling down notes on a small pad during short breaks in production.

Thus, I was very difficult to socially categorize and to culturally understand, which is generally a prerequisite for sustained social interaction in any society. Not only was my ethnic and professional status quite ambiguous, there was considerable discrepancy between my self-asserted identities and my actual behavior. This resulted in a conflict between my inner sense of self (as a "Japanese" and as an anthropologist) and the manner in which I was perceived by the Japanese workers through the standard social identities of nikkeijin and dekasegi. Although a number of the Japanese workers seemed to completely accept what I told them about myself at face value, most remained uncertain.

No one openly challenged my personally asserted identities, but I received many hints that they were doubtful, confused, or simply did not believe me. Sometimes, I was asked, "You are really a dekasegi, aren't you?" Even some of those Japanese informants I came to know quite well as personal friends were quite skeptical at first. One Toyama worker, who ended up being one of my closest friends and best informants in Oizumi, admitted during our final dinner together that despite our numerous conversations, he had initially refused to believe that I was actually a researcher. "Only when you asked me for an interview did I begin to realize that maybe you were a researcher," he told me. This revelation was quite surprising to me since he had given me no indication of his doubts. It was also disorienting since it showed how little the other Toyama workers probably trusted my identity claims.

This was true even among my supervisors. For instance, during my final days in the factory, my *hancho* (group leader) came up to me and observed: "You must not have been able to save lots of money during your stay in Japan because you didn't do a lot of overtime." I reminded him that I was a student and had not earned a salary for my work because I had a fellowship. The most extreme reaction came from a *kumicho* (foreman) at one of the sections where I worked for a few days. On the first day, I had introduced myself extensively to him, and we even had a friendly chat during break. However, one of my co-workers later told me that when I had left for the restroom, the kumicho told the other workers that he thought I was crazy and had simply lost my mind. "He can't deal with the fact that he's a dekasegi in Japan, so he's creating some kind of fantasy that he's American and doing research," the kumicho supposedly concluded.

Other Barriers to Social Acceptance

There were other barriers that prevented me from being socially accepted by the Japanese at the Toyama factory. My employment through an out-side nikkeijin labor broker firm indicated that I was not only a nikkeijin foreign worker but a *hi-seishain* (a nonregular, temporary worker) who did not belong to the Toyama company as a direct employee. In fact, *Japan-ese* hi-seishain employed in a similar manner experienced the same social isolation at Toyama that the nikkeijin did. Therefore, my blue uniform constantly felt like a stigma that branded me not only as a nikkeijin for-eigner but also as an outside employee who could not be socially accept-ed as part of the firm. My lack of acceptance was probably exacerbated by the fact that the Toyama workers in my section were considered *heisateki* (closed, exclusionary) even by Japanese workers from other sections.

Even among the Japanese workers who accepted my self-identity as a university researcher, the consciousness of my higher social class status sometimes became a barrier. One worker even told me directly, "Generally, I don't like college-educated types—they think they are so smart." One of my closest Japanese informants spoke to me about how he was nervous and hesitant when I first began interviewing him because of an "inferiority com-plex" (*rettokan*)—as a less-educated factory worker, he felt he could not say anything that was intelligent enough for a graduate student's research. I was conscious of this potential problem and therefore made a special effort not to emphasize my social class identity as a university researcher to my Japan-ese informants after the initial introduction. In this sense, my willingness to do manual factory work actually helped reduce this sense of difference.

One other social barrier should be mentioned—gender. Christena Turner, who also conducted participant observation among Japanese workers, discusses this issue at length:

> There is very clear gender segregation in most situations in Japan and a high consciousness of gendered differences in language and cultural

practice. One of the consequences of this situation is that women are less threatening because they are less powerful. Another consequence is that a female researcher has the freedom to speak to women and to men alone or in groups, whereas it is more difficult for men to speak either to a woman alone or even to small groups. (1995:27)

As a male anthropologist, I encountered especially serious problems of access to female informants because of the considerable segregation that existed between male and female Japanese workers at Toyama. Men and women generally sat separately during break at different tables and stood in separate groups during the morning assembly, talking only among themselves. At a group level, conversations across gender lines were quite rare, and any notable interaction occurred only between certain individuals (motivated partly by romantic interest among the younger workers). Sometimes, I felt that the gender segregation was almost as notable as the ethnic segregation in the factory.

Therefore, my gender identity was another obstacle to fieldwork. Most of the female workers were quite shy and simply did not talk to the foreign workers in the factory, *especially* if they were men. After a while, however, I became quite skilled at cornering hapless female workers on the factory floor and forcing them to talk to me, at which point they discovered that I spoke Japanese and was rather easy to converse with. Fortunately, I was able to engage a number of female workers in friendly and extensive conversation, and even the shyest among them eventually opened up to me, telling me at length about her personal frustrations and the discrimination she felt as a female employee. However, *all* of them were very reluctant to be interviewed outside the factory, and I did not wish to force the issue. I obviously realized that it would be highly inappropriate for me to meet them at home, especially if they lived alone in company dormitories. Even my offers to meet them at *kissaten* (cafés and coffee houses) were received with strong reluctance. The contrast was again quite vivid with Japanese Brazilian women, who were just as sociable, accessible, and willing to talk and associate with me as the men. My requests for personal interviews were never considered threatening, and even when I visited them alone in their apartments, it was never an issue. As a result, my nikkeijin interview sample is quite balanced, according to the sex ratio of Japanese Brazilian migrants in Japan.

Therefore, because of these numerous ethnic, social, and gender barriers, I was never accepted by the Japanese workers at Toyama at the group level despite my persistent attempts to negotiate my identity in a favorable manner and constantly engage them in conversation on the assembly line. Collectively, there was always uncertainty, hesitation, and distance. In fact, a few times, I would attempt to forcibly break out of the social segregation and isolation I experienced in the factory by sitting at a table during break with only Japanese workers. However, this felt strange and a bit awkward (a nikkeijin worker would *never* sit at a table with all Japanese and vice versa), and I had trouble integrating myself into the conversation. Few of the Japanese workers paid any personal attention to me, and I was not given opportunities to talk about myself or my background. The topics of conversation would be other Toyama workers, an upcoming company social event, an issue related to the Ota/Oizumi area, or agriculture (the dominant activity in the region before the industrial factories were relocated from the metropolis). Therefore, the occupational, regional, and social class barriers between us became quite evident. It was very different from the conversations I would have with Japanese students or middle-class professionals, where we had plenty of common topics to discuss. Although I kept telling myself at Toyama that I am much more "Japanese" than I ever was "Brazilian," after unsuccessfully attempting to socialize with Japanese workers, I would always return to my Japanese Brazilian companions, realizing how much more comfortable I was with them, how they knew me personally and could relate to me, and how I felt I belonged with them. I appreciated their complete acceptance, openness, and warmth. "I guess I am a Brazilian after all," I would mutter to myself.

As a result, social acceptance among the Japanese workers was possible only at an individual level. Fortunately, a limited number of individuals were able to overcome their uncertainties and the numerous barriers between us to understand who I was and establish the basic trust and friendship necessary for frank conversations and an informative interview. Even at a group level, however, I certainly had much closer relationships with the Japanese than the other nikkeijin workers, and many Toyama workers were willing to speak to me individually on the assembly line and answer questions, sometimes quite frankly. I remember a number of interesting conversations during brief breaks in production, especially with workers from other sections who had been temporarily transferred to my section (called *oen*). This became one vital source of ethnographic information.

However, the Toyama workers (and not just the women) were very reluctant to be extensively interviewed about the Japanese Brazilians. The topic of nikkeijin workers was controversial, and even if they completely believed who I was, they were not comfortable enough with me to reveal their true feelings. In addition, although I spoke Japanese, claimed to be an American, and consciously disassociated myself from the Brazilian nikkeijin in front of my Japanese informants, my close affiliation with the Japanese Brazilians made the prospect of an interview about them more difficult. There was also considerable management pressure to treat the Brazilian nikkeijin well and avoid any potential conflicts. For some, this meant not talking about the nikkeijin to outsiders in general, especially in regard to their negative opinions and resentments. In fact, one Japanese worker confided to me during our interview that he had been told specifically by his supervisor not to talk with me.[13] Even those Japanese workers with whom I was quite friendly politely declined my requests for interviews. I received a quite diverse range of creative excuses, such as: I am busy with the baseball league after work, I have to take care of my mother at home, it's better to talk to older people with more opinions, I don't have much contact with the nikkeijin, I have to prepare for my wedding, I will not be coming to work the next two weeks and my home phone is disconnected for repairs. After a while, the persistent refusals became quite routine, but they undoubtedly remained the most disappointing aspect of my fieldwork in Japan.

Outside the Factory: Greater Control Over the Presentation of Identity

Many of the problems I experienced at Toyama were the product of the peculiar social environment that prevailed in the factory, which made it difficult to establish and maintain an ethnic and professional self-identity that would be conducive to fieldwork. The obstacles were considerably less with Japanese informants outside the factory since they had not seen me in a factory uniform working with the Japanese Brazilians and did not closely associate me with the nikkeijin. Therefore, I had much more control over the presentation of my self as a person with a strong "Japanese" background. Not only was I able to speak more extensively about my ethnic background

---

[13]In fact, on the day of the interview, this supervisor had come over to my section specifically to tell me that she thought it was not a good idea for me to talk to this individual. "He tends to get drunk and say inaccurate things," she told me. "I don't want you to get a bad impression of the Japanese."

and experiences, I had many more opportunities outside the factory to demonstrate my "Japanese" manners and demeanor, including bowing, bringing *omiyage* (gifts) to house visits, and properly using greetings, expressions of gratitude, and honorific Japanese. As a result, I was perceived as a Japanese descendant from the United States who was culturally "Japanese" enough to be ethnically accepted, a self-identity that I had failed to establish within the factory. In fact, I was told by my Japanese informants a number of times that they did not feel any "*iwakan*" (sense of incongruity) with me, nor did I appear to be a foreigner to them despite my origins overseas. Given my comportment, language ability, and knowledge of Japan, there was no reason for them to doubt the "Japanese" ethnic self-identity that I asserted.

Outside the factory, there was less difference in social class as well, which enabled me to more effectively negotiate a favorable professional self-identity as a "student researcher." Most of my informants tended to be well-educated individuals of middle-class status for whom the concept of a graduate student from a foreign country working on a thesis was more familiar. Also, since they had not seen me as a factory worker, my professional self-identity did not conflict with the working-class social identity I assumed at Toyama, which was the main reason my claim to be a researcher had little credibility there. In fact, I would not immediately tell my informants that I worked in a factory with the Japanese Brazilians as a participant observer so that I would be seen exclusively as a student researcher. This undoubtedly facilitated my social acceptance and increased the willingness of my informants to assist my research by agreeing to interviews. As I was told by a number of them, "We are very sympathetic to students studying in Japan"—especially ones who had come all the way from the United States. At the same time, my professional status was not so high (like that of a "professor"), which would have inhibited spontaneity and intimacy.[14]

Therefore, my assertion of a respected ethnic and professional self-identity outside the factory did not conflict with my Japanese informants' external social perceptions of my identity, leading to considerably better rapport and social acceptance. In fact, my relationships with them resem-

---

[14]This problem was directly mentioned by one of my professors, who felt his informants were not willing to frankly divulge their opinions in front of him. Since professor is a very respected status in Japan, some Japanese informants undoubtedly become status-conscious, which restricts the conversation.

bled my previous experience with Japanese students, professors, and relatives. As a result, most of the 46 interviews I conducted with Japanese were with those I met outside the factory.

In addition to Japanese workers and city residents, I interviewed company employers, labor brokers, local government officials, journalists, police officials, school teachers (responsible for classes with Japanese Brazilian children), and immigration policy makers at federal government ministries. Japanese employers as well as labor brokers were generally quite accessible for interviews and willing to talk for long hours. Most of the managers at smaller subcontracting companies (which are the primary employers of the Japanese Brazilians) were quite frank and honest during interviews, in contrast to managers at larger firms, who were generally less forthcoming. Local and federal government officials directly involved with the foreign worker problem were also relatively accessible. As expected, local government officials, especially in the rural cities of Oizumi and Ota and even at the prefectural level, were very friendly, frankly voiced their opinions, and answered questions to the best of their abilities. In contrast, federal bureaucrats and immigration policy makers were experts at being vague, dodging difficult questions, professing ignorance, and mechanically uttering government ideology. A common experience among those studying institutions of power in a society is that the further one "studies up" (Nader 1972), the less willing to talk are the informants. An increase in institutional power seems to correspond to a decrease in the amount of information freely divulged.

TATEMAE VS. *HONNE:* ACCESS TO THE PRIVATE

Of course, successful fieldwork does not merely consist of securing the basic rapport and social acceptance necessary to conduct interviews with informants. One of the key tasks for the field researcher is to obtain access to private information that is normally concealed from outsiders. This includes personal opinions, private attitudes, and inner feelings hidden from public view (called the *honne* in Japan)[15] that contradict and subvert official ideologies and socially approved attitudes (the *tatemae*). This is an important distinction that my Japanese informants themselves

---

[15]Using the social interactionist metaphor of the theater, Gerald Berreman calls this the "back region" (or "backstage") of the natives' lives (1972:xxxiii–v).

frequently made, referring to their ethnic prejudices toward the Japanese Brazilians as the honne that they usually kept hidden (see chapter 2 for further discussion and illustrations).

Needless to say, most of my Japanese informants were initially reluctant to reveal their honne feelings and tended to utter politically correct, tatemae attitudes about the Brazilian nikkeijin. This reluctance was undoubtedly increased by my own status as a nikkeijin. However, because I had negotiated an ethnic self-identity as a culturally Japanese descendant from the United States, this naturally put a certain amount of distance between me and the Brazilian nikkeijin, making it easier for my Japanese informants to divulge their negative opinions and prejudices about the culturally foreign Japanese Brazilians.

Nonetheless, in order to encourage my informants to freely discuss other prejudices they harbored about the Japanese Brazilians, I had to disassociate myself from the nikkeijin dekasegi in terms of social class status as well. As I will discuss in chapter 2, because of postwar Japanese economic prosperity, middle-class status has become a defining attribute of Japanese ethno-national identity.[16] In contrast, the nikkeijin are generally viewed as descendants of indigent rural Japanese of low social class who were supposedly forced to leave their homeland and emigrate abroad many decades ago (when Japan was poor). Such Japanese social class prejudices persist even toward current generations of Brazilian nikkeijin, who continue to be seen as poor. Therefore, my attempts to successfully negotiate a "Japanese" ethnic self-identity and fully distance myself from the nikkeijin involved demonstrating that I was not only racially and culturally Japanese, but of a middle-class (Japaneselike) social background as well. In addition to my professional status as a university student, I had to frequently tell my Japanese informants that my parents had come to the United States for graduate study instead of as poverty-stricken emigrants (even if I did not mention this fact, I was always asked about it). Once I mentioned my parents' social class background, some of my Japanese informants even said, "Oh, so you aren't a *real* nikkeijin." This was usually the most critical factor that changed the initially hesitant tone of the interview and enabled my informants to open up to me and speak more freely about their ethnic and social class prejudices about the Brazilian nikkeijin.

---

[16]Because of relatively low income disparities between blue- and white-collar workers in Japan, even my Japanese informants who were factory workers did not identify themselves as "working class" but felt they lived well-off, middle-class lives.

I also had to establish a certain amount of friendship, trust, and intimacy with my Japanese informants before they would openly reveal their honne feelings and private attitudes about the Brazilian nikkeijin to me. Therefore, my first outing with my informants (or visit to their home) would generally consist of a relaxed, informal conversation in which I would completely and honesty divulge not only the motives for my research but also details about my personal background. The substantive interview would be conducted on the second meeting or visit. Only then would the honne about the Japanese Brazilians emerge.

The *location* of the interview was just as critical as the level of intimacy I had established with my informants. I frequently had to find an appropriate private space in which honne feelings and prejudices could be freely expressed without the concern of being overheard by others. I quickly found that public areas such as cafés and restaurants were the worst places for such interviews. One Japanese worker even apologized to me after we left an interview session at a café for not being able to say what he "truly felt" about the nikkeijin. "I was worried that the others around me would hear what I was saying and look strangely at me," he said. Fortunately, the café had closed and we were able to move to a more private location, where I ended up asking him similar questions to which I got more honest and frank answers. The best places for interviews were undoubtedly in the privacy of homes or apartments or in a secluded corner at an empty (or noisy) restaurant out of earshot of other people. In fact, when we were looking for places to interview, one Toyama worker even suggested that I interview him in his car.

Thus, my effort to obtain access to my Japanese informants' private ethnic attitudes and prejudices was a time-consuming and painstaking process that involved negotiating an appropriate ethnic and professional identity, cultivating trust and friendship, and skillfully managing the use of space. This undoubtedly limited the size of my interview sample. However, as one of my informants said, "one honne is better than a hundred tatemaes."

EXISTENTIAL ANXIETIES IN THE FIELD

Multiple Loyalties, "Identity Prostitution," and Ethnic Marginality

As shown by the discussion thus far, the presentation of self and the management of a workable identity in the field is a dynamic process that requires the anthropologist to negotiate a number of different identifications with various types of informants. Especially in multiethnic field sites, the success of participant observation depends greatly on the "versatility" of anthropologists—their ability to assume and enact various social identities and therefore obtain access to different ethnic groups. In this sense, anthropological fieldwork has even been compared to theatrical acting (for example, see Turnbull 1986).[17]

The situation is undoubtedly exacerbated when the two groups that are being studied are ethnically segregated and mutually exclusive, if not antagonistic. As will be discussed in chapter 3, most of the Brazilian nikkeijin are treated as "foreigners" in Japan because they cannot speak or act Japanese and are therefore ethnically rejected and excluded from Japanese social groups. Partly because of this marginalization, the Japanese Brazilians come to view the Japanese in an unfavorable manner and define a "Brazilian" counteridentity in opposition to the cultural differences of the Japanese.

Therefore, I could not be accepted into both groups by negotiating one coherent ethnic identity but had to assume a social identity as a "nikkeijin" with the Japanese Brazilians and as a "Japanese" with my Japanese informants, maintaining dual and conflicted ethnic loyalties. The situation was especially disorienting in the factory, where the two ethnic groups were in close proximity. I found myself constantly moving back and forth between the Japanese Brazilians and the Japanese, which involved switching not just languages but attitude and mentality as well. At one moment, I would be displaying my identity as a "nikkeijin" while conversing with a group of Japanese Brazilians during break, and the next moment, I would switch back to my "Japanese" identity when I returned to the assembly line and began speaking to a Japanese Toyama worker. In an effort to demonstrate my ethnic allegiance to the Japanese Brazilians, I would distance myself from the Japanese in their presence by agreeing with the critical and negative remarks they made about the Japanese (although I did not believe what I was saying) and then do the same in the company of the Japanese by adopting a detached and critical perspective toward the Brazilian nikkeijin. At times, I felt considerable discomfort at this manipulation of my ambiguous ethnicity through the display of dif-

---

[17]Gold (1958:217) describes participant observation as "role pretense"—a process of pretending to occupy certain roles through proper external behavior, regardless of the anthropologist's own background or identity.

ferent identities in different situations and the constant switching of ethnic allegiances, depending on what was most advantageous for my research at a certain moment. This type of behavior can be called "identity prostitution"—the selling of one's identity for instrumental advantage. Uneasy feelings of inauthenticity and expediency frequently result.

Identity prostitution can also create a certain amount of existential unease by fragmenting the self. Individuals are able to maintain a sense of inner coherence despite the existence of multiple and conflicting self-identities by remaining within one frame of reference at any particular moment and compartmentalizing previous, incompatible experiences into a different level of consciousness (cf. Ewing 1990). The individual's various self-identities usually exist in a *preconscious* state outside immediate awareness (cf. Erikson 1980 [1959]:127) until they are brought to consciousness by external social pressures and enacted in behavior. Because previously enacted identities that conflict with the identity currently being presented have been temporarily suppressed and "forgotten," the internal inconsistencies within the self are not reflexively examined.[18] This enables individuals to engage contradictory selves in different social contexts without experiencing overt self-conflict and dissonance.

However, the constant switching of identities that is sometimes involved in fieldwork can threaten the individual's ability to maintain a sense of cohesion and continuity in the self. My attempt to gain acceptance from both the Japanese Brazilians and the Japanese forced me to enact mutually incompatible "nikkeijin" and "Japanese" ethnic identities in rapid succession or even simultaneously, bringing them into direct conflict. Because of the simultaneous presence of both identities in my consciousness, I could not keep them separate, which threatened my internal sense of ethnic consistency and fragmented my experience of self. I felt ethnically unanchored and decentered because of my inability to commit myself exclusively to either ethnic group and resolve my identity crisis.

Despite my efforts to fully immerse myself in the lives of both my Japanese Brazilian and Japanese informants through the manipulation of my conflicted identity, I remained an ethnically marginal person in the field who did not completely belong to either group. I was a partial

---

[18]Ewing calls this the "contextual unconscious" (1990:268). The use of this term is problematic because in most cases, identities not currently being displayed in a certain context are not repressed into the individual's unconscious to become inaccessible to the person.

insider but also a partial outsider to both the Brazilian nikkeijin and the Japanese. At the same time, I became conscious of the benefits of such ethnic marginality for fieldworkers, despite its inherent limitations. *Partial* insiders enjoy better access to informants and a greater ability to empathize with the "native's point of view" than do total outsiders, and their presence in the field is less disruptive. However, they cannot expect complete acceptance and access to their informants' personal and private experiences, as can *total* insiders (i.e., native anthropologists). However, unlike total insiders, marginal fieldworkers, as partial outsiders, can maintain a certain amount of psychological detachment from the group under study, making them less susceptible to the group's cultural assumptions, ideological justifications, and biases. Like a complete outsider, a partial outsider discovers cultural differences in the encounter with informants, thus helping to illuminate their cultural system of behavior and consciousness, which a total insider may take for granted. When the research deals with the interaction of two different ethnic groups (especially if they are mutually antagonistic), marginality allows the anthropologist to take a critical step back and objectively evaluate the experiences, attitudes, and identities of *both* groups as someone who does not completely identify with or is not fully invested in either. Hopefully, the result is a balanced analysis in which both groups are judiciously represented and their motives and reactions sufficiently explained, rather than a biased perspective in which the anthropologist "takes sides."

Ethnically marginal anthropologists may enjoy other unexpected advantages over complete insiders in certain cases. Although marginality usually prevents full access to the private lives of informants, it may ironically be a privileged status when internal group conflict is involved. This was especially relevant with the Japanese Brazilians. Because they experience a severe decline in social status from their middle-class occupations in Brazil to blue-collar jobs in Japan, there is considerable resentment and jealousy directed toward those Brazilian nikkeijin who have been promoted to a higher status in the factory, as translators and cultural liaisons, by the Japanese. Such individuals are frequently seen as self-serving "asskissers" and ethnic betrayers who obsequiously "act Japanese" to improve their social standing in the eyes of the Japanese at the expense of their hapless ethnic fellows (see chapter 6). Likewise, there is also considerable envy directed toward Japanese Brazilians who have come to Japan as privileged graduate students on fellowships, instead of as dekasegi.

At certain times, I felt that my Japanese Brazilian informants were more comfortable talking about these internal ethnic conflicts and problems to me as a marginal, partial outsider than they would be to an insider Japanese Brazilian anthropologist. Native anthropologists are likely to become involved in these internal status conflicts as well, which ironically restricts open access to informants and information. One Japanese Brazilian graduate student who was also studying the nikkeijin dekasegi in Japan told me that when he first started to do research, he figured he had an unique advantage as an ethnic insider to the community. However, he quickly realized that he was mistaken, as he experienced considerable trouble relating and talking with his dekasegi compatriots because of jealousies and conflicts caused by his higher status in Japan as a graduate student. "I discovered that I am just as much an 'outsider' to the Japanese Brazilian dekasegi community as any other researcher," he concluded.

Although I was of the same "high" social status in Japan, such resentment was never directed toward me since I was a Japanese American, a partial outsider to whom the same standards that the Japanese Brazilians used to assess each other did not apply. Therefore, I was not involved in their internal tensions and status rivalries. Undoubtedly, my willingness to work in a factory as a dekasegi also helped prevent any conflicts and resentments over my higher status as a student researcher in Japan. Although I was frequently used by the Japanese as a translator on the factory floor and "acted Japanese" in front of them, I was obviously not considered an ethnic betrayer by the Japanese Brazilians, and my privileged treatment by the Japanese was never a source of envy or a barrier to fieldwork.

Social Identities Versus the Inner Self

The psychological strain of fieldwork was not limited to my attempts to manipulate my identity as both "nikkeijin" and "Japanese" and the resulting ethnic marginality I experienced in the field. Because anthropologists must conform to certain socially acceptable identities in order to fit in with the natives, they are frequently obliged to subordinate and even hide their own subjective consciousness of who they really are in a self-induced act of "symbolic violence." There can be considerable conflict and dissonance between the multiple social identities that anthropologists must deploy in the field in order to further their research agendas and their true, inner sense of self.[19]

---

[19]Gold (1958) also mentions this conflict between the anthropologist's social identity and the self. Conaway (1986), Kondo (1986), and Whitehead (1986) have discussed this issue with respect to their gender and ethnic identities.

Among the Japanese Brazilians, my external compliance with my social identity as a "nikkeijin" was actually quite different from my inner self-consciousness since I had always identified quite strongly with the Japanese and had never considered myself an American nikkeijin in the past. I had always been very conscious of my "Japaneseness," especially within my family because we spoke only Japanese at home and maintained Japanese customs. In addition, my parents never identified themselves as nikkeijin and insisted that my brother and I were "pure Japanese" and that it would be shameful if we could not speak and behave Japanese. Since I grew up in an exclusively white neighborhood in the northern suburbs of Chicago and never had any Japanese American friends (or even Asian ones) in my youth, I had no opportunity to explore the meaning and history of the Japanese American ethnic heritage or experience. Instead, from fourth grade to the end of high school, my parents sent me to a Japanese Saturday school, where I studied with students from Japan. This intense and frequently grueling experience not only forced me to maintain my Japanese in a native environment but also further strengthened my identification with the Japanese as I eventually adapted smoothly at the school and developed close friendships with many Japanese students.

My lack of identification with American nikkeijin during my youth was reinforced by my parents' tendency to actively distance themselves from the nikkeijin and regard them with considerable contempt. Having come to the United States for graduate study, they looked down on Japanese Americans, whom they saw as descendants of originally poor Japanese who had abandoned Japan to escape poverty in rural areas. Because of this snobby elitism and "ethnic" prejudice, they socialized exclusively within the Japanese expatriate business community and actively avoided the Japanese Americans. For these various reasons, I saw the American nikkeijin as people with a different ethnic and historical background who had lost much of the Japanese language and their Japanese consciousness by the second and third generation. Despite my increased contact with Japanese Americans since graduate school, I continued to feel quite ethnically different from most of them because of my much closer affiliation to Japan and stronger Japanese self-identity.

Therefore, I felt quite hypocritical at times identifying as a bona-fide American nikkeijin in Japan to further my research. The identity dissonance was most acute when the Japanese Brazilians seemed to assume in certain comments and remarks that I shared their nikkeijin immigration legacy—that my parents had left difficult rural conditions in Japan, had emigrated as agricultural contract laborers to the United States, and after much suffering and discrimination, had urbanized, educated their children, and attained middle-class status. This was undoubtedly part of the ethnic commonality we shared as fellow "nikkeijin," and I simply acknowledged such remarks.[20]

More important, however, my attempts to adequately negotiate a social identity as an American nikkeijin among the Japanese Brazilians obliged me to partly conceal the "Japanese" aspect of my self-identity by acting more like a nikkeijin foreigner in Japan than I actually was. Since the Japanese Brazilians develop strong anti-Japanese counteridentities in response to their negative experiences in Japan, I was afraid that I could alienate them if I asserted my "Japaneseness" too strongly in their presence. Therefore, I attempted to downplay and even conceal my Japanese language ability and my close associations with the Japanese in an attempt not to differentiate myself from them as someone who was more "Japanese." In order to ensure their complete trust and acceptance, I was playing the role of the "nikkeijin foreigner" at the expense of my true ethnic self.

I had analogous experiences with the social class identity of "dekasegi" that I had assumed among the Brazilian nikkeijin. Although I initially introduced myself as a graduate student researcher, since I worked as a migrant laborer and lived in company housing with the Japanese Brazilians, I acted as a "dekasegi" literally all of the time, except when I was conducting interviews or organizing notes in my room. For their part, the Japanese Brazilians treated me as a bona-fide dekasegi and generally did not mention my graduate student status or my research in the factory. Since I was asked by the broker firm not to mention that I was working as a "volunteer" without pay, the Japanese Brazilians in the factory did not know I had a research fellowship and simply assumed that I was living off the money I earned in the factory. Sometimes I even wondered if they had forgotten that I was actually a student researcher. Again, I felt a considerable amount of dissonance and discrepancy between who I was socially expected to be and my inner feelings about who I actually was.

---

[20]In Brazil, I had been asked about my family migration history several times by the *issei* (first-generation nikkeijin), and when I told them that my parents had emigrated as students, they became quite conscious of the status difference between themselves and my parents, although their attitude toward me did not change. As a result, I decided not to reveal this information to my informants in Japan and simply "pass" as someone with a "nikkeijin" past.

Of course, the psychic tension between social identity and inner self is not peculiar to fieldwork but is part of everyday life. However, the dissonance can become stressful at times, especially for anthropologists who have decided to totally immerse themselves in the field and must assume a discrepant social identity on a constant basis. Since I was working, living, talking, socializing, eating, sleeping, and drinking with Japanese Brazilians literally twenty-four hours a day, there were moments when I would become tired of being a "nikkeijin dekasegi." In fact, I was reminded of what Evans-Pritchard, after weeks of living only with the Nuer, had once called "Nuerosis" (1977 [1940]:13). At times, I truly needed an escape from the unrelenting demands of the field. For some anthropologists, this involves the creation of a private space, isolated from the field, in order to reaffirm and maintain one's true self-identity. For instance, Kondo (1986; 1990), a Japanese American anthropologist who conducted fieldwork in Japan, talks about how she finally distanced herself from the restrictive "Japanese daughter" role that had been imposed on her by her Japanese host family by moving into a private apartment, thus saving her inner self from collapse and fragmentation. In a similar vein, Laura Bohannan's remarks about her experiences studying the Tiv of west Africa are illustrative:

> It was only in the privacy of my hut that I could be my real self. Publicly, I lived in the midst of a noisy and alien life. If I wanted conversation in my own language, I had to hold it with myself. . . . If I wanted counsel from my own people, I had to turn to my books. . . . It was the one means of hanging on to myself, of regaining my balance . . . of retaining my own values. (Bowen 1954:153–54)

My escape from the field involved not only moments of social isolation but also frequent trips to Tokyo. I would eagerly rush off to the city to meet Japanese professors or relatives or to participate in a research meeting or project, in order to salvage and reassert certain aspects of my inner self-identity as a "Japanese" and a "student" that I had to suppress when doing fieldwork in Oizumi. In other words, I would switch to a different social environment that I felt was more congenial to the true expression of my inner self.

My attempts in the field to maintain a social identity as an ethnic "Japanese" among my *Japanese* informants were characterized by some personal ambivalence as well. I have always felt that the Japanese cultural standards to which I willingly conform in Japan are somewhat incompatible with my Americanized attitudes and "natural" behavior in the United States, especially in terms of hierarchical deference and the suppression of personal opinions for social consensus. Yet the identity dissonance was not as acute with my Japanese informants because I felt that the role of a "Japanese" was closer to my true ethnic self and background than that of a "Brazilian nikkeijin."[21]

In this manner, I felt that I could not completely reveal my true self-identity to either my Japanese Brazilian or my Japanese informants if I were to be ethnically accepted by both groups. Among the Japanese Brazilians, I downplayed and sometimes concealed my "Japaneseness," and among my Japanese informants, I deemphasized, if not suppressed, inappropriate aspects of my American "nikkeijin" self. At best, only different fragments of my true self that happened to be compatible with my external social identity could be properly expressed. In fact, a certain amount of violence to the inner self may be an unavoidable component of fieldwork (cf. Crapanzano 1977).[22]

FIELDWORK BETWEEN SELF AND OTHER

The active involvement of the self in fieldwork has become increasingly prominent in contemporary anthropology. Although anthropologists have always conducted "participant observation," they used to be detached

---

[21]Anthropologists also conform to the social identity assigned to them in the field because of certain conscious or subconscious psychological gratifications. As Devereux notes:

> [The anthropologist's] subjects force him into the procrustean bed of an ascribed status, chosen in accordance with their own needs. If the participant observer then feels that he must accept this status, he has a plausible reality-excuse for not scrutinizing the unconscious gratifications he may derive from it. (1967:234)

Although I attempted to break out of the social identity of "Brazilian nikkeijin" that was attributed to me at Toyama, it is undeniable that I also had a strong wish to play along with this identity because it was personally fulfilling and gratifying. The fact that the Japanese (as well as Japanese Peruvians and a few first-generation Japanese Brazilians) mistook me for a Japanese Brazilian was confirmation of how advanced my command of Portuguese and Brazilian mores had become and filled me with a sense of personal competence and accomplishment. The same can be said of my attempts and wish to play the role of a "Japanese" on the factory floor.

[22]In this manner, the process of fieldwork and ethnography inflicts mutual "violence." Just as anthropologists supposedly do violence to native experience through their power over ethnographic writing and representation (see Clifford 1988 for an analysis of ethnographic authority), natives do violence to the anthropologist's self in the field through the imposition of preconceived social identities.

observers more than engaged participants.[23] In Malinowski's time, the idea of complete participation in the natives' lives was still a novel one, and something that the anthropologist did only occasionally. In his reflections on fieldwork, Malinowski suggests:

> In this type of work, it is good for the Ethnographer sometimes to put aside camera, note book and pencil, and to join in himself in what is going on. He can take part in the natives' games, he can follow them on their visits and walks, sit down and listen and share in their conversations. I am not certain if this is equally easy for everyone . . . but though the degree of success varies, the attempt is possible for everyone. (1961 [1922]:21)

However, in a number of contemporary ethnographies, the anthropologist has become a total participant and actual member of the society or group under study.[24] According to Tanya Luhrmann, "Anthropology has encouraged, in recent years, increasing immersion in the native culture. . . . Rather than watching what is being done, there is more emphasis on doing what is done" (1994b:75). Some recent examples of such "total immersion" fieldwork include Abu-Lughod's (1986) work among a Bedouin community in Egypt where she was adopted as a family daughter, Kondo's (1990) and Turner's (1995) studies of the Japanese workplace as actual company employees, and Luhrmann's (1989) ethnography of witchcraft based on her actual membership in a cult. The participation aspect of fieldwork through the direct assumption of native social identities has been emphasized as the dominant methodology and the means of observation. This frequently requires the anthropologist to identify closely with the natives, reducing the distance between the observer and the observed. Undoubtedly, the advantages of this type of fieldwork include not only better rapport but also greater in-depth access to native experiences. As Bourdieu observes, the traditional status of the anthropologist as a "detached observer" had produced excessively mechanistic, objectivist, and structural descriptions of native behavior (1977:1). Total immersion field-

---

[23]As Schwartz and Schwartz (1955:344) note, participant observation can range from "passive" to "active"—from socially detached observer to complete participant (cf. Gold 1958:217).

[24]According to Nash and Wintrob (1972), an increase in the personal involvement of ethnographers with their subjects in anthropological fieldwork has been continuing for decades.

work enables us to move beyond analyses based exclusively on symbolic structures and cultural norms and directly consider the subjective experience of identity, self, and emotion.

Undoubtedly, when we are directly involved in the lives of our informants, the need for self-reflexive awareness of how our identities are deeply embedded in the fieldwork process becomes even more critical. Just as we analyze the other, we must also analyze our self throughout the fieldwork encounter. In other words, when taking on the social identity of a "native," the anthropologist must maintain an independent and distinct inner self through a conscious monitoring of self-experience. A total collapse and dissolution of an autonomous inner self in the field through the complete internalization of a native social identity (that is, "going native") would destroy the critical distance and detachment between anthropologist and informant that makes external observation and meaningful analysis possible.[25] So the constant dissonance and psychic tension I experienced in the field between my external social identity and my internal sense of self seems to be a necessary component of fieldwork. In our uncertain discipline, existential unease may actually be the key to "objectivity."[26]

Multiple Identities at Stake

Self-reflexiveness in the field is also critical because knowledge is never found in the abstract but is always situated in a certain context, that is, obtained from a particular perspective. This is especially the case in anthropology, where knowledge is not simply extracted by detached observation but produced in human interaction (Scheper-Hughes 1992:25) and therefore depends heavily on the anthropologist's social position in the field.

---

[25]Kondo makes a similar observation in regard to her field experience:

> I found that a lessening of distance through intense participation in [my informants' lives] . . . was productive in many ways. Yet the complete elimination of distance through identification proved to be too extreme and led to distressing conceptual ambiguity. Some degree of remove from the Other was necessary in order to recover meaning from the experience.

In her study of witchcraft through membership in various magical groups, Luhrmann (1989:320) also notes that had she identified completely as a witch and had come to believe in the truth of magical ideas (instead of maintaining an identity as an anthropologist), she would not have been able to write an observer's text.

[26]Devereux (1967) seemed to have this fundamental insight in mind when he entitled his book about fieldwork *From Anxiety to Method in the Behavioral Sciences*.

Therefore, the negotiation of identity in the field directly constitutes the acquisition of anthropological knowledge. As the social status of the anthropologist among the natives constantly shifts, this leads to multiple sources of knowledge (cf. Kondo 1986; Rosaldo 1989:169, 181). Therefore, we must constantly remain reflexively self-conscious of how our presentation of various identities in the field results in different relationships with informants and different perspectives on the society being studied. As we move through various social relationships, our identities must be renegotiated as we constantly reposition ourselves vis-à-vis new informants in changing contexts. Depending on the identity that the anthropologist engages, the distance between self and other constantly shifts in productive ways. My inner self was always in dynamic flux in the field as I engaged in a continuous process of affiliation with and distancing from both my Japanese and nikkeijin informants, resulting in multiple perspectives and differential knowledge commensurate with the ethnic diversity of my field site. Without a certain amount of personal flexibility and willingness to engage numerous selves in the field, the anthropologist will miss the opportunity to view the society from different vantage points, which is the basis for analytical objectivity. The result will be a rather limited and one-sided ethnography that fails to capture the rich diversity inherent in any field site. Evidently, this type of identity manipulation for research purposes has its negative psychological consequences, including the unease caused by "identity prostitution," marginality, and the fragmentation of the self, but it may be necessary for good fieldwork.

However, as this chapter has made clear, anthropologists have only partial control over their efforts to define and manage appropriate identities for themselves in the field since these identities are also socially defined for them by the natives, who perceive the fieldworker's presentation of self and subsequent conduct in a certain way through preconceived social categories. Therefore, the negotiation of identity in the field is never complete but continues to be actively contested. The success of this constant effort varies depending on situational circumstances, thus facilitating or restricting the research possibilities for the anthropologist. With the Japanese Brazilians, the management of an appropriate self-identity as an "American nikkeijin researcher" was a smooth process since the ethnic and professional categories I used to define myself were quite familiar to them and favorably regarded. With the Japanese workers at Toyama, the negotiation of my personal ethnic and professional status was fraught with difficulties because inherent inconsistencies and contradictions in my presentation of self and my actual behavior led to a conflict between internally asserted and externally imposed identities. As a result, my efforts were met with a variety of responses ranging from skepticism to doubts about my sanity.

As a result, one of the great ironies of my field research in Japan was that those who were the most inaccessible and reluctant to be interviewed were not the powerful bureaucrats in the federal government but simple, unskilled Japanese factory workers. Although anthropologists generally have been reluctant to "study up" because of the inherent problems of conducting fieldwork among society's institutional power holders (Nader 1972), my greatest difficulties were with "studying down." Fortunately, I had considerably more control over the definition of my identity with Japanese informants outside the factory since there were fewer social situational factors that contradicted the proper impressions I wanted to convey, allowing me to conceal my life as a nikkeijin dekasegi and behave only in ways consistent with someone who was ethnically "Japanese" and a "student."

Fieldwork as a Process of Self-Discovery

Not only does the social identity that the anthropologist assumes among the natives influence fieldwork, fieldwork in turn influences the anthropologist's identity. In other words, as anthropologists attempt to understand others by negotiating their identities in the field, they attain a new understanding of themselves (Crapanzano 1977; Myerhoff and Ruby 1982; Rabinow 1977:5). The impact of field experiences on the anthropologist's self is undoubtedly much greater in total immersion fieldwork.[27]

Openly embracing and directly involving ourselves in a culture becomes an occasion for self-discovery and subjective identity formation through the recognition of cultural differences and similarities between ourselves and our immediate social environment. The contrast (if not conflict) between the social identity we adopt in the field and our inner sense of self is highlighted, making clear who we are and who we are *not*. Adopting the ethnic identity of a nikkeijin among the Japanese Brazilians threw

---

[27]Likewise, the implications of fieldwork for the self are also greater when the anthropologist is ethnically related or similar to the informants. Had I been an American of non-Japanese descent, the difficulties of acceptance I experienced among the Japanese workers or my experiences of ethnic commonality with the Brazilian nikkeijin would not have had such a powerful personal meaning.

into relief those incongruous aspects of my inner self that made me much more "Japanese" than they, thus strengthening my sense of ethnic affinity with the Japanese. In addition, by assuming the ethnic role of a Japanese among my Japanese informants, I experienced Japanese cultural attitudes and behaviors that were quite discrepant with my own dispositions and discovered serious limits to my "Japanese" ethnic identity in the factory environment. This made me aware of my cultural differences that were the product of my American upbringing as a nikkeijin, and this consciousness was reinforced by feelings of ethnic affinity and commonality with the openly receptive Brazilian nikkeijin. In this manner, both my "Japanese" and "American nikkeijin" identities were simultaneously strengthened in the field and seemed to pull me in different directions. Despite my initial identity crisis, what eventually emerged was a compartmentalized but coherent multiple ethnic identity in which my two different selves would be engaged separately depending on the immediate social situation.[28]

Undoubtedly, this continuing process of identity development and self-discovery during fieldwork in turn brings new insight into the lives of our informants. As Whitehead and Conaway note, "The processes of field adjustment, data collection, and interpretation are influenced by both the self the fieldworker brings to the field and the self the fieldworker *becomes*" (1986:2–3, emphasis mine). The French historian, Tzvetan Todorov, describes this intricate relationship between self knowledge and knowledge of others as follows:

> The process can be described in these terms: knowledge of others depends on my own identity. But this knowledge of the other in turn determines my knowledge of myself. Since knowledge of oneself transforms the identity of this self, the entire process begins again: new knowledge of the other, new knowledge of the self, and so on to infinity. (1995:15)

My own struggles to negotiate and develop an appropriate identity in response to a complex field situation (my new knowledge of my self) undoubtedly influenced and structured my perception and analysis of my in-

---

[28]This compartmentalization of my total ethnic self has continued after completing fieldwork. I am now much more conscious of expressing the "American nikkeijin" component of my self in the United States and reserving the "Japanese" component for when I am in Japan, or with Japanese in the United States.

formants' ethnic experiences as well (my knowledge of the other).[29] In other words, my own identity experiences as an American "nikkeijin" in Japanese society served as a partial basis of comparison and contrast from which I could better analyze and reflect upon the ethnic experiences of the Japanese Brazilians as fellow nikkeijin confronted with analogous identity issues in their ethnic encounter with the Japanese. In the process, various analytical constructs and a theoretical framework gradually emerged through which I could capture the essence of their lives. Therefore, not only does the anthropologist's self-development in the field result in a distinctive understanding of the other, it is inextricably involved in the development of theory as well. While self-reflexively discussing her own field experiences, Kondo makes a similar point:

> The *specificity* of my experience [as an anthropologist in the field]—a particular human being who encounters particular others at a particular historical moment and has particular stakes in that interaction—is not opposed to theory: it *enacts* and *embodies* theory. That is to say, the so-called personal details of the encounters, and of the concrete processes through which research problems emerged, are constitutive of theory; one cannot be separated from the other. (1990:24, italics in original)

Although the anthropologist's self-knowledge acquired in the field can result in an enhanced understanding of and insight into the lives of his or her informants, it can also obviously have a pernicious, distorting effect. I was constantly aware of the danger of simply projecting my ethnic experiences onto the Japanese Brazilians and the Japanese, thus allowing my own ethnic preoccupations and concerns to masquerade as "native experience." This problem is analogous to the countertransference that occurs in psychoanalysis between the analyst and the patient and can be a serious impediment to objective understanding (see Devereux 1967). This danger is greater in total immersion fieldwork, where the psychological distance between anthropologist and native has been greatly reduced or in some cases, completely dissolved. While we must resist exoticizing the different

---

[29]Of course, the anthropologist's personal experiences and self-development *outside* the field can also lead to new insights about the experiences of informants. For instance, Renato Rosaldo claims that his bereavement after his wife's death helped him to better understand the Ilongot headhunter's grief, rage, and emotional motivation (1989:1–21).

experiences of the "Other" as incommensurable and ultimately inscrutable, we must also avoid glimpsing others only to see a pale reflection of ourselves (cf. Lutz 1988:216).

ETHNOGRAPHIC REPRESENTATION
OF THE EXPERIENCE OF COLLECTIVITY

Conducting in-depth research through close contact with various types of informants from different perspectives in multiethnic field sites reveals regularities and consistent trends in the interview and ethnographic materials. However, one also becomes acutely aware of the intricacies and richness of individual difference. The deeper one delves into the research, the harder it becomes to make facile generalizations about an entire ethnic group. Yet, at the same time, an exclusive focus on the particularities of individual experiences at the expense of generalization can blind the researcher to broader patterns that make analytical and theoretical explanation of group experience and behavior possible. When considering the narrative strategies for ethnographic writing, the anthropologist strives to represent the diversity inherent in the natives' lives while remaining aware of regularities and commonalities in experience.

In order to do this, one can simply break up the members of the ethnic group under consideration into finer groups and categories broad enough to represent general types of experiences but specific enough to recognize individual variation. These designated categories of people can then be analyzed in relation to each other. This is done on occasion in this book, for instance when I make distinctions between "Japanized nikkeijin" and "Brazilianized nikkeijin." Although this approach is obviously much more sensitive than generalizing about an entire ethnic group as one homogeneous entity, the main problem is that these different categories are not mutually exclusive, with some individuals belonging to more than one category and others not belonging to any at all. Eventually, these artificial categories take on a personality of their own, although they do not represent anyone in particular, and ultimately come to replace the specificity of actual individuals. The description, although perhaps elegant, becomes contrived and forced, with real people eventually dropping out of the analysis. Therefore, ethnographers who adopt this type of representation end up doing exactly what they initially intended to avoid—confining an entire range of individuals into a pre-made and rigid ideal type, thereby reducing their complexity to disembodied generalities.

The approach I have adopted is an attempt to smoothly integrate the presentation of individual diversity within a generalized ethnographic description. The frequency or generalizability of certain collectively held ethnic experiences is indicated by quantitative words such as "most," "few," "many," "all," "none," "some," "lots of," and "a good number of."[30] At the same time, specific individual examples are constantly brought up, to either serve as illustrations of the general experience being discussed or demonstrate the range of individual variation. Specific individuals whose experiences do not conform to these generalized representations are also mentioned (sometimes to be analyzed separately as a different type of collective experience). The aim is to focus on collective experiences while showing how individuals share them differently.

Nonetheless, generalized statements about entire ethnic groups are sometimes difficult to avoid because our informants' consciousness of their racial and cultural differences is frequently based on stereotypical and simplistic representations of other groups. My Japanese Brazilian informants made sense of their ethnic experiences and constructed a distinct ethnic identity in a transnational context by contrasting themselves with homogeneous images they had of both the Brazilians in Brazil and the Japanese in Japan. A similar process of collective ethnic differentiation occurred among my Japanese informants in response to their ethnic encounter with the Brazilian nikkeijin in order to better understand what it meant to be Japanese. Reducing the ethnic other to stereotypes brings one's ethnic distinctiveness into sharp relief. Yet a distinction must be made between our informants' stereotyped ethnic representations and *our* representation of their experiences of ethnic stereotypes. While giving sufficient voice to the collective images natives use to constitute their ethnicity, anthropologists must not describe an ethnic group's experiences in the same manner in which the natives ethnically describe themselves.

---

[30]Although some ethnographers claim that such words give the "illusion of quantitative specificity" (Ohnuki-Tierney 1993:7), I find them indispensable. The reader can be assured that the use of such quantitative words in the ethnographic description is not haphazard, but was chosen with care based on numerous extensive interviews and many hundreds of hours of close participant observation.

ABOUT THE BOOK

I hope I have captured this diversity inherent within generalities when exploring the ethnic consequences of Japanese Brazilian return migration and their encounter with the Japanese. This book analyzes the impact of migration on the minority status, ethnic identity, and adaptation of the Japanese Brazilians within the context of migrant nationalism, transnational communities, and globalization. I consider what happens when the experience of ethnicity is no longer confined to one locality but negotiated in multiple transnational contexts. In contrast to the relatively greater stability and predictability of ethnic experiences among those who remain territorially confined to a bounded social context, individuals who are physically displaced through transmigration and subject to the forces of globalization are more likely to reconfigure and reconceptualize their ethnic status and identity, as exposure to new ethnic groups problematizes their previous ethnic experiences and assumptions. I consider my research to be part of a fundamental shift in current anthropology and sociology toward the examination of transnational and global processes and their impact at the local level.

Of course, transnational migration does not simply affect the migrants themselves—it has an equally important impact on the majority host society that must deal with immigrants in its midst. However, ethnographies about ethnicity and immigration focus almost exclusively on the experiences of the immigrant minority without any in-depth consideration of the ethnic experiences of majority individuals in the host society, who are either reduced to an oversimplified, monolithic entity or a social constant to which immigrants react and inevitably assimilate. In order to overcome such shortcomings, I will also situate Japanese Brazilian immigrants in Japan within a broader understanding of Japanese ethnic and national identity by analyzing how majority Japanese react to the sudden presence of Japanese-descent, Latino immigrants in their country in terms of their ethnic assumptions and identities.

The first part of this book analyzes the impact of the return migration of the Japanese Brazilians on their ethnic minority status. Although they are a socially prominent and culturally respected positive "Japanese" minority in Brazil, when they migrate to Japan, they suddenly become an ethnically disparaged and marginalized negative "Brazilian" minority of low social class status. In chapter 1, I discuss the construction of a strong transnational "Japanese" ethnic identity among the Japanese Brazilians in

Brazil through essentialized perceptions of their Japanese racial and cultural differences and their identification with positive global images and information about Japan, which have become the basis for their social status and prestige as a "positive minority" in Brazil. In chapter 2, I then examine how they become a "negative minority" when they migrate to Japan by analyzing the sociocultural, psychosocial, and situational aspects of Japanese prejudice and discrimination toward them, which are based on negative perceptions of their migration legacy, their presumed low social class status, and their "Brazilian" cultural behavior.

The second part of the book analyzes the impact of migration to Japan on the ethnic identity of the Japanese Brazilians in the context of an emerging transnational migrant community. Chapter 3 describes how the Japanese Brazilians are rejected as culturally Brazilian foreigners by the Japanese despite their Japanese descent and socially marginalized as casual migrant laborers on the periphery of the Japanese working class. In addition, they experience ethnic discrimination, confront derogatory Japanese images of Brazil, and develop negative attitudes about Japanese society and culture. In contrast to their previous transnational ethnic identification with the Japanese, their unfavorable experiences in Japan as a negative immigrant minority cause them to strengthen their Brazilian national sentiments as a "counteridentity" asserted in opposition to the Japanese. This type of migrant nationalism indicates that transnational migration, instead of being counterhegemonic, can in some cases unintentionally contribute to the nation-state's hegemonic agendas because it exposes migrants to experiences abroad that reaffirm and increase their national loyalties.

However, this resurgence of Brazilian nationalism among Japanese Brazilian return migrants in Japan occurs within the larger setting of a transnational community. In chapter 4, I examine the nature of transnational migrant communities by analyzing the economic, personal, and institutional networks that have developed between Japanese Brazilians in Japan and Brazil in the technologically constituted space of media and communication networks. Such transnational connections enable the constant flow of information, commodities, and people across national borders and allow the Japanese Brazilians to maintain social relationships that transcend the constraints of spatial distance and transgress the boundaries of the nation-state. However, this transnational community does not produce a corresponding transnational consciousness that overrides national loyalties because it lacks the ideological institutions, cultural coherence, and spatial integrity necessary to challenge and subvert

the hegemonic influence of the nation-state over individual consciousness. As a result, a disjuncture between consciousness and community
has developed in which migrants strengthen their national identities despite their membership in a transnational community.

The last part of the book deals with the behavioral and adaptational
consequences of migrant identities. Chapter 5 argues that the development of migrant nationalism among most Japanese Brazilians in Japan
leads to a form of ethnic resistance that facilitates their adjustment to their
negative minority status. Through the behavioral assertion and performative enactment of their nationalist Brazilian "counteridentities," they are
able to resist assimilative Japanese cultural pressures and protect their self-
image from the psychologically degrading effects of their negative minority status and low social class status. However, such ethnic resistance
among the Japanese Brazilians does not change their subordinate social
class position in Japan nor seriously challenge dominant Japanese ethnic
ideologies. In addition to reproducing their socioeconomic marginalization by precluding social mobility, their ethnic resistance also reinforces
the hegemony of the Japanese nation-state by causing a reaffirmation of
ethno-national identity among the Japanese, who experience a renewed
awareness of their Japanese cultural distinctiveness when confronted by
the culturally different Japanese Brazilians. The resurgence of national
sentiment among both migrants and hosts indicates that the unrelenting
forces of global migration do not always weaken the nation-state as a primary source of identity in the modern world.

In contrast to those who resist Japanese ethnic hegemony by asserting
their cultural differences, chapter 6 discusses the psychological difficulties
and problems experienced by a minority of Japanese Brazilians who attempt some form of cultural assimilation (and even try to "pass" as Japanese). Although this type of adaptation leads to better Japanese social acceptance and occupational mobility, it has negative psychological
consequences and can cause identity diffusion, psychological stress and
unease, alienation from ethnic peers, and ultimately, the internalization of
a negative ethnic self-image.

The conclusion contextualizes the ethnic experiences of the Japanese
Brazilians by examining two types of globalization (contiguous and noncontiguous) and their divergent impact on ethnic identity. Instead of simply expanding identity toward transnational possibilities, globalization
can cause a paradoxical intensification of local differences, producing a
number of disjunctures between globalization, identity, community, and

the nation-state. In the second part of the conclusion, I argue that the ethnic encounter between the Japanese Brazilians and the Japanese has produced exclusionary ethnic identities through a decreased emphasis on racial commonalities and an increased emphasis on cultural differences.

Although the Japanese Brazilians initially come to Japan as temporary sojourners, current trends indicate that they will be a permanent presence in Japanese society. The epilogue is therefore devoted to their future minority status and ethnic adaptation in Japan. Although the current generation of Japanese Brazilian immigrants will remain a culturally distinct minority, if ethnic resistance continues among their descendants, they could suffer from continued cultural disparagement and discriminatory social subordination. However, the experiences of Japanese Brazilian children currently in Japanese schools indicate that, unlike their parents, they will eventually escape a degraded minority status by assimilating and disappearing into the majority Japanese populace.

I wish to stress that this book is not simply a narrow ethnographic or empirical description of Japanese Brazilian immigrant experiences but is also intended to address fundamental theoretical issues related to minority status, ethnic prejudice and discrimination, identity, nationalism, transnationalism, and globalization. In other words, the study aims to be rich in ethnographic description while remaining theoretically engaged. I have attempted to smoothly intertwine ethnographic description with theoretical explanation. My study can be characterized as an "analytical ethnography" in contrast to a "narrative ethnography" because it is organized according to a certain line of theoretical argument.

In this sense, this book is a contribution to the growing number of theoretically informed ethnographies that examine local migrant and ethnic communities from a transnational and global perspective. However, although I appropriate and further develop many of the concepts and theories currently associated with transnationalism and globalization studies (as I find them useful), my work is also a sustained critique of the assumptions of this literature.

A NOTE ABOUT ETHNIC TERMINOLOGY

Japanese Brazilian ethnic terminology is quite complex, diverse, and confusing, indicating the ambiguous nature of their ethnicity and their constantly shifting identities. In addition to "Japanese Brazilian" (*nipo-brasileiro* in Portuguese, or less commonly *japonês-brasileiro*), a multitude of other terms are used, including "*japonês,*" "*brasileiro,*" "*nikkei,*" "*descendente*" (or "*descendente japonês*"), as well as the Japanese generational terms "issei," "nisei," "sansei," depending on the location, the social situation, and the context of speech. There is also a distinct difference between the ethnic terms used in Brazil and those used in Japan.

Although I have been employing the term "Japanese Brazilians" in line with "Japanese Americans," these types of hyphenated minority categories are a very American way of labeling ethnic groups and are not generally used in Brazil.[31] The Japanese term "nikkeijin" is also rarely used and is salient mainly among the Japanese of Japan. Instead, the Japanese Brazilians refer to themselves exclusively as "japonês" in Brazil.

After migration to Japan, the ethnic terminology that the Japanese Brazilians use to refer to themselves changes dramatically. Instead of "japonês," they call themselves "brasileiros" in Japan, indicating both the alienation they suddenly feel from the strong "Japanese" ethnic identity they developed in Brazil and a concomitant increase in their ethnic consciousness of being Brazilian. As a result, "japonês" is implicitly redefined to refer exclusively to the Japanese of Japan.[32] This also entails a redefinition of the meaning of "brasileiro" since in Brazil, it was used exclusively to refer to Brazilians of non-Japanese descent and almost never to the Japanese Brazilians themselves. Therefore, "brasileiro" suddenly takes on a double connotation in Japan that can be a source of confusion when it is not clear to which of the two types of Brazilians (Japanese descendants or non-Japanese descendants) the speaker is actually referring, especially since there are some of the latter in Japan as well. To avoid such confusion, many Japanese Brazilians would refer to a non-nikkeijin Brazilian by saying: "*Ele/ela é brasileiro mesmo*" (literally meaning "He/she is a 'true' or 'real' Brazilian"). In addition, the word "nikkeijin" (*os nikkeis* in Portuguese) becomes much more prevalent among the Japanese Brazilians in

---

[31]Likewise, the general ethnic category of *asiatico* (Asian), which figures so prominently in the United States (as in Asian American), hardly appears at all in Brazil. Brazilians do not lump together all people of Asian descent and collectively refer to them as Asian or Asian Brazilian (cf. Maeyama 1984:455–56). Instead, only finer ethnic categories are used such as *japonês, coreano* (Korean), and *chinês* (Chinese).

[32]Interestingly enough, however, I have noticed that sometimes when the Japanese Brazilians refer to their lives in Brazil, they again call themselves japonês. This shows the power of speech context (that is, the social context speech *refers* to, as opposed to the immediate social context the speaker is in) in determining the use of ethnic terminology.

Japan. However, although it is frequently used in their print media (Portuguese newspapers, brochures, books, advertisements, etc.), it is less common in everyday speech. Likewise, the use of the term "descendentes" or "descendentes japoneses" becomes more common in Japan. Finally, the Japanese Brazilians also frequently use the word "dekasegi" (*os dekasseguis* in Portuguese) to speak about themselves collectively.

I have tried to avoid causing confusion when using these different ethnic categories. Although it is not common practice among the Japanese Brazilians themselves, I use the term "Japanese Brazilian," which is the most general and least ambiguous because its meaning is fixed and always refers to the same ethnic group regardless of the immediate social context. To add variety, I also call the Japanese Brazilians "Brazilian nikkeijin" or simply "nikkeijin," since this Japanese ethnic term is also not context dependent.

Part 1

∾

MINORITY STATUS

CHAPTER 1

ᴄ𝕽ᴜ

When Minorities Migrate

The Japanese Brazilians as Positive Minorities in Brazil and
Their Return Migration to Japan

A COMPLETE and comprehensive ethnography of transnational processes
requires multisited fieldwork (Marcus 1995; cf. Clifford 1992) in the various
countries involved. In the case of transnational migrants, fieldwork
must ideally be conducted in both the sending and the receiving country
in order to understand the influence of migration on their ethnicity and
identity and analyze the transnational linkages between the two countries
that frame their experiences. Moreover, it is impossible to fully understand the ethnic status and identity of migrants in the host society without first understanding their prior status and identity in their home country, since their sociocultural experiences back home inevitably condition
how they interpret and react to their ethnic experiences abroad (cf. Basch,
Glick Schiller, and Blanc 1994:109; De Vos 1982a; Herskovits 1941).
Therefore, without sufficient knowledge of the premigratory ethnic experiences of the Japanese Brazilians in Brazil, any analysis of their postmi-
gratory experiences in Japan would be ethnically decontextualized at best.

THE BENEFITS OF BEING MINORITY:
THE ETHNIC STATUS OF THE JAPANESE BRAZILIANS
IN BRAZIL

Japanese emigration to Brazil began in 1908 and continued in significant
numbers until the early 1960s. Like the Japanese who came to the United
States, the emigrants to Brazil originated from all parts of Japan, ranging
from Hokkaido to Okinawa. During the prewar period, 1908 to 1941, approximately 190,000 Japanese entered Brazil. Many were farmers suffering from difficult conditions in Japan's rural areas, which were plagued by

overpopulation, declining agricultural prices, increasing debt, and unemployment, as well as harsh climatic conditions in the northern regions. Others were second and third sons who did not inherit land from their parents under the old Japanese *ie* (household) system and had limited economic opportunities. In addition to such factors that "pushed" the Japanese out of Japan, the expanding, labor-deficient Brazilian coffee plantation economy served as the necessary "pull" factor that drew them to Brazil. New immigrant workers were needed because of the abolition of slavery in 1888 and the decline of immigration from Europe (especially Italy). Japanese emigration was also encouraged by active recruitment and propaganda efforts by the Japanese government, which was concerned with overpopulation and poverty in rural areas, and by the establishment of "emigration companies" to recruit and transport emigrants to Brazil.[1] In addition, the discriminatory closing of the United States to further Japanese immigration starting with the "Gentlemen's Agreement" in 1908 and culminating in the Immigration Act of 1924 diverted the migrant flow southward.

Although most Japanese emigrants went to Brazil as dekasegi, with dreams of returning to Japan in several years with considerable wealth, reality proved much more difficult. They earned much less than expected as contract laborers, suffered harsh conditions on the coffee plantations, and initially found it difficult to acquire their own land to cultivate. Eventually, many became small proprietors in Japanese *colônias*, rural agricultural enclave communities established on land set aside with the assistance of the Japanese government. As the years wore on, returning to Japan with significant personal wealth became increasingly unlikely, and a vast majority of the Japanese settled permanently in Brazil with their families.[2] However, many of them remained unassimilated and relatively isolated in their ethnic enclaves and continued to dream of eventual repatriation.

The outbreak of World War II led to some repressive measures against the Japanese in Brazil, although nowhere as severe as those against the Japanese Americans. Most important, however, the war eliminated any re-

---

[1]Staniford (1973b:9) also notes that Japanese immigrants in Brazil encouraged relatives who remained behind to join them in Brazil. However, others claim that such chain migration was not a major factor (see Fukunaga 1983).

[2]Fukunaga (1983:111–13) and Maeyama (1982:46) estimate that over 90 percent of the Japanese who emigrated to Brazil before World War II eventually settled. Only about 15,000 of the Japanese emigrants returned to Japan during this period (Fukunaga 1983:71–72).

maining hope of an eventual return to Japan. In contrast to their unassimilated parents, many of the Brazilian-born, second-generation nisei began serious and active efforts to integrate themselves into Brazilian society in the postwar years. Another wave of Japanese immigrants arrived after the war (this time, mainly because of economic difficulties in war-torn Japan), some of whom were better educated and of higher social status than previous immigrants. From 1953 to 1962, 50,000 Japanese emigrated to Brazil. Generally, these postwar emigrants went with the intention of settling permanently, and many became small landholders in agricultural enclaves right away.[3]

Currently, there are about 1,228,000 Japanese Brazilians in Brazil, the largest community of Japanese descendants outside of Japan. Almost all of the population (91 percent) is concentrated in the southwestern and southern regions of Brazil.[4] The state of São Paulo has by far the highest number of Brazilian nikkeijin with a population of 887,000 (the city of São Paulo itself has 326,000). The second largest population is in the state of Paraná, which has 138,000 Japanese Brazilians, most of whom live in the large cities of Curitiba and Londrina. The states of Rio de Janeiro, Espírito Santo, and Minas Gerais have a combined total of 87,000 Japanese Brazilians. Much smaller populations are scattered in the southernmost states of Santa Catarina and Rio Grande do Sul (1,682 and 3,811 respectively), as well as the northeastern (28,000), northern (33,000), and central-western regions (49,000) of Brazil. Most of the Japanese Brazilians are now second-generation nisei (30.9 percent) or third-generation sansei (41 percent), with a small but increasing population of *yonsei* (fourth generation).[5] The first-generation *issei* now comprise only 12.5 percent of the entire nikkeijin population and are mostly postwar Japanese emigrants.

As Brazil's oldest and by far largest Asian minority, the Japanese Brazilians are now generally well integrated into Brazilian society. Most of them are urbanized and live in large cities in the most developed regions, with only a small minority residing in the rural colônias.[6] Even in the colônias

---

[3]See Tsuda (2001) for an analysis of the history of the Japanese in Brazil.
[4]The population statistics presented here are mainly derived from the São Paulo Humanities Research Center (1987–1988) survey on nikkeijin, which includes both pure Japanese descendants and those of mixed descent.
[5]Most of the yonsei are still children and close to 62 percent are of mixed descent.
[6]Ninety percent of the Japanese Brazilians live in cities, with only 10 percent left in rural areas. The rural colônias established before World War II have effectively disappeared, and those that currently exist are composed of more recent postwar immigrants (frequently on land directly inherited from the prewar colônias).

that remain, virtually all of the youth have moved to the cities in order to pursue advanced education and professional careers.[7] Most of the Brazilian nikkeijin are middle class, well educated, and socially integrated in Brazilian society. The intermarriage rate is reported to be around 45.9 percent (Yamanaka 1997:20), and as a result, 6 percent of the nisei and 42 percent of the sansei are of mixed descent. A considerable degree of cultural assimilation has occurred among the nisei and sansei.[8]

Despite their socioeconomic and cultural integration in mainstream Brazilian society, however, the Japanese Brazilians continue to assert a rather prominent "Japanese" ethnic minority identity, which remains considerably stronger than their identification with majority Brazilians or the Brazilian nation (cf. Maeyama 1996:398). Because of a strong consciousness of the racial, cultural, and social differences from other Brazilians that distinguish and define them as "Japanese," the Japanese Brazilians continue to emphasize their minority ethnic identity despite a growing realization that they have become considerably Brazilianized. Many of my informants privileged the Japanese side of their dual ethnic identity, claiming that they feel more "Japanese" than "Brazilian." Only a relatively small proportion of them had fully adopted a majority Brazilian identity. According to one survey of nikkeijin in the cities of Bastos (São Paulo) and Assai (Paraná), 74 and 79 percent of the respondents respectively claim that they have a "Japanese consciousness" and only about 7 percent say that they do not feel Japanese (Kitagawa 1996:185–87).[9] The following sections examine the various components of this experience of Japanese ethnic distinctiveness among the nikkeijin in Brazil.

PRIMORDIAL ETHNICITY:
RACIAL VISIBILITY AND THE ESSENTIALIZATION
OF A JAPANESE ETHNIC IDENTITY

Race is the most prominent marker that differentiates the Japanese Brazilians as ethnically "Japanese" in Brazil. In fact, the experience of being

---

[7]Despite the nostalgia and legacy of the colônias, they have mainly become residences for the elderly issei and rural retreats for youth returning from the cities to visit their parents and perhaps to help out on the farm during weekends or holidays.

[8]Many of the first-generation issei remain culturally unassimilated (cf. Saito 1976, 1978).

[9]Since these are two of the most cohesive Japanese Brazilian communities in Japan, the numbers may be higher than in other communities.

racially identified as "*japonês*" is undoubtedly familiar to anyone of Japanese descent who has lived in Brazil. It happened to me for the first time a few days after I had arrived in Brazil. I was walking innocently down the street in downtown Porto Alegre, when suddenly:

"*Oi, japonês!* (Hey, Japanese!)"

Startled, I turned around to find a Brazilian street vendor beckoning to me, trying to interest me in his goods.

"*Só três mil cruzeiros, japonês.*" He was holding up a bag of apples. "*Mais barato do que nas lojas.*" Realizing that he had caught my attention, he continued his upbeat sales pitch, telling me how fresh and delicious his apples were. I hesitated before the proper words in Portuguese came out.

"*Não obrigado* (No thank you)."

My hesitation was due less to my still inadequate Portuguese than to the way I had been addressed directly by my ethnicity. It was the first time in my life that I had been greeted by a stranger in such a manner.

I reached the downtown bus station where a row of buses waited. I checked the signs designating the various routes. My bus had not yet arrived. However, because I was still unfamiliar with the bus system, I approached the attendant to confirm that I was waiting at the right spot (and also to practice my Portuguese). After indicating that I had the correct bus stop, he gestured toward the bench.

"*Espera aqui, japonês* (Wait here, Japanese)."

There it was again. I was beginning to realize that this would be a common occurrence in Brazil. In the following days, I would experience it numerous times—strangers calling me "*japonês*" in public (sometimes for no apparent reason), store clerks referring to me as "*japonês*," a pedestrian muttering "*japonês*" as I walked past, questions ending with the ethnic designation, "*japonês*."

"You might as well get used to it," one of my nisei friends told me. "There are so few Japanese living in Rio Grande do Sul that you have Brazilians who have hardly ever seen a Japanese person."

Of course, children are merciless in this regard since they react with an unrefined spontaneity that adults have learned to politely hide in public. I will never forget the little Brazilian boy who grabbed his mother's skirt, pointed to me as I walked past, and said, "Mommy, Mommy. Look! A japonês!" Nor will I ever forget the group of smiling Brazilian children who surrounded me on the street and greeted me with every Japanese word they knew. *Sayonara, arigato. . . .* The other experience that remains vividly in my mind was a particular bus ride I took from downtown Porto Alegre. A little girl who sat next to her mother, across from me, spent most of the bus ride staring at me, her large, cute eyes studying my features intently. I shifted uncomfortably in my seat, averted my eyes for a while, then glanced back at her. The stare continued. After a few minutes, I realized that it was hopeless—there was no way I could shake off her probing eyes. My Japanese ethnicity was being located and essentialized by the silent gaze of a mere child! The gaze was more powerful and meaningful for me than any utterance. I could easily fill the absence of words with my own imagination: "So, this is what a Japanese looks like. The slanted eyes, the flat face, the small nose. How intriguing." Even after I got off the bus, the gaze seemed to follow me relentlessly. In contrast to children, ethnic curiosity is expressed in a more muted form among adults as concerns for decorum intervene and the novelty wears off after numerous encounters. Yet the gaze was always there, making me acutely aware of my peculiar Japanese appearance that clearly differentiated me from the surrounding blend of Brazilian faces.

In fact, this racial designation as japonês is not simply confined to places like Porto Alegre where the sight of a Japanese descendant is quite rare. It prevails throughout Brazil, including the city of São Paulo, which has the highest concentration of Japanese Brazilians in the country. Of course, in such areas, it is less frequent and more of a confirmation of ethnic difference than a reaction to ethnic novelty. Nonetheless, when ethnic appellations are based on physiognomy, it inscribes a racially constituted ethnic awareness (cf. Fanon 1967:109–12). Although my distinctive Asian appearance had never been a real focus of attention in the United States, it was suddenly thrust into my self-consciousness in Brazil, becoming a prominent component of my "Japanese" ethnic identity.

Was it ethnic prejudice? For a moment, I was reminded of Frantz Fanon's experience in France as a black man from Martinique:

"Look, a Negro!" It was an external stimulus that flicked over me as I passed by. I made a tight smile.

"Look, a Negro!" It was true. It amused me.

"Look, a Negro!" The circle was drawing a bit tighter. I made no secret of my amusement.

"Mama, see the Negro! I'm frightened!" . . . Now they were beginning to be afraid of me. I made up my mind to laugh myself to tears, but laughter had become impossible. . . .

I subjected myself to an objective examination, I discovered my blackness, my ethnic characteristics; and I was battered down by tom-

toms, cannibalism, intellectual deficiency, fetishism, racial defects, slave-ships. . . .

What was it? Color prejudice. (1967:111–12, 118)

Of course, the issue is one of subjective interpretation. The external ethnic stimulus I received in Brazil was somewhat similar, but unlike Fanon, I was not ethnically burdened by a historical legacy of colonialism, exploitation, and slavery at the hands of the Brazilians. Even during my first week in Brazil, I fully realized that Japaneseness did not have the negative connotations there that blackness had in France for Fanon. For me, the Brazilian insistence on racially inscribing me as japonês was simply a recognition of *diferença* and not a prejudicial reaction in which difference is negatively perceived (cf. Park 1999:682). At worst, there may have been a tint of ridicule or banter at times, but never overt denigration or dislike. In general, I was much more amused than offended. After a while, it became routine, expected.

However, the emphasis placed on racial difference in Brazil is not always this subtle. I soon realized that certain Brazilians pull their eyes upward with their fingers to indicate the *olhos puxados* (slanted eyes, or literally "pulled eyes") of the Japanese Brazilians. However, this gesture is not necessarily intended as an affront to the nikkeijin, but is simply an amusing commentary on their different physiognomy. In contrast to the United States, where the gesture is considered to be an ethnic insult, when it was used in Brazil to refer to people or things Japanese, the context was basically neutral or playful. One of the most typical examples I observed was when my landlady in Riberão Preto (state of São Paulo) described the children of her Japanese Brazilian friend to an acquaintance. "Their father is Brazilian, but they still look very Japanese," she remarked, pulling her eyes up with her fingers for emphasis. I have also seen the gesture used when referring to products made by the Japanese. The worst case that I encountered was actually personally solicited—one of my attempts to gather derogatory ethnic humor about the Japanese Brazilians. "Why do the japonês have eyes like this?" my Brazilian friend asked, repeating the now familiar gesture. "Because they spend all their time frying pot stickers."

The peculiar Japanese physiognomy has even been conveniently appropriated by Brazilian commercials. A television ad for Toshiba products ends with a magnifying glass passing over the eyes of a Japanese face. "*Abre os olhos* (Open the eyes)," the ad exhorts. The commercial undoubtedly pokes fun at the Japanese, but seemingly has a double connotation that asks consumers to open their eyes to the quality of Japanese products. Again, local context is everything, making an unmitigated ethnic insult in one society a good-humored advertising gimmick in another.

My Japanese Brazilian informants seemed generally to share my interpretation of such ethnic experiences in Brazil. In fact, most were very accustomed to their constant racial designation as japonês, whether by ethnic appellation or gesture, and very few were bothered by it.[10] "It's simply how people behave here in Brazil," one nisei man explained. "And it happens to other ethnic groups as well. Brazilians frequently say, 'Hey, black!' 'Hey, German!' or 'Hey, Jew!'" A few mentioned that they would be offended if they were called "Jap," but most claimed it did not happen.

Others even read positive meanings into the experience. "My kids came home from school one day somewhat bothered that they are always called japonês by the other kids," one Japanese Brazilian mother remarked. "I told them that the Brazilians are not making fun of them. I told them that being Japanese is a source of pride. The Japanese are respected and admired in Brazil."

Even the slanted eyes gesture was taken in stride as simply ethnic humor. "It's just a joke. No one takes it seriously," one man expressed a common opinion. It was quite remarkable that only one informant was personally offended by the gesture, claiming that behind the jovial exterior was a serious attempt to ridicule the funny appearance of the Japanese. Yet even she admitted that the tendency to express ethnic prejudice in a jocular manner takes much of the bite out of Brazilian ethnic discrimination.

Despite the apparent lack of pejorative connotations, the attention given to the racial phenotype of the nikkeijin in Brazilian society has a significant impact on their ethnicity. Although some researchers consider racial identity separately from ethnic identity (see Glick Schiller and Fouron 1990), an individual's self-consciousness of ethnic membership is based not only on the experience of cultural differences but also on an awareness of racial distinctiveness based on shared descent (cf. Alonso 1994:391). The relative importance of race in defining an ethnic identity depends on its perceived visibility as a means to differentiate a certain group from the rest of society.

Because physical appearance is the primary means of ethnic differentiation in Brazil, racial phenotype has become the most fundamental factor

---

[10]Maeyama claims that many Japanese Brazilians become angry when they are called "japonês" and say "I am not japonês. I am brasileiro" (1996:322). However, his impressions seem to be based on earlier postwar experiences and are no longer true today.

that ethnically identifies the Japanese Brazilians as a "Japanese" minority and clearly distinguishes them from other Brazilians (cf. Saito 1976:196–97). In Brazilian society, the nikkeijin are immediately recognizable because of their distinctive "oriental" appearance (*traços orientais*), which is seen as markedly different from whites (*brancos*), blacks (*pretos*), and mixed-descent *mestiços* of all types (including *mulatos, morenos,* and *pardos*) (cf. Maeyama 1984:455). Brazilians give much attention to these phenotypic differences because of the high Brazilian sensitivity to racial characteristics, including slight differences in skin color.[11] Therefore, the Japanese Brazilians are always referred to as "japonês" by other Brazilians simply because of their facial features, not only in unfamiliar contexts when names are not known (such as in the streets, stores, and public areas) (cf. Maeyama 1984:448) but also when they are talked about among familiar acquaintances. Their distinctive racial appearance is much more prominent as an ethnic marker of Japaneseness in Brazil than it is for the Japanese Americans in the United States, where there are many Asian Americans of non-Japanese descent; an Asian phenotype does not denote Japanese ancestry as it usually does in Brazil, where most Asians are of Japanese descent.[12]

The tendency among mainstream Brazilians to single out the Brazilian nikkeijin as "japonês" constantly reminds them of their Japanese descent and ancestral roots. In fact, few Japanese Brazilians can escape the externally imposed awareness of their distinct racial features. As some of them mention, they have no choice but to be seen as "japonês" by other Brazilians because of their physical appearance. "Because of our faces, we can't deny that we are japonês, even if we wanted to," a middle-aged nisei woman remarked. "We are reminded of this whenever we walk down the street." Others spoke about how their racial visibility is a clearly evident and immutable feature that forever marks them as a distinctive "Japanese" ethnic minority, regardless of how culturally Brazilian they have become (see also Reichl 1995:47). "Even if we become completely Brazilian and act as Brazilian as possible, we will always be seen by Brazilians as Japanese because of our faces. There's no way to avoid this," a young Japanese Brazilian student said, a hint of resignation in his voice. "We can go to a soccer

---

[11]Because of the considerable racial intermixture in Brazil, Brazilians (unlike Americans) have a wide array of racial categories. Harris and Kottak (1963), in their study of racial categories among Brazilians in a fishing village in coastal Bahia, uncovered 40 categories used to describe phenotypic differences.

[12]It is interesting to note that those of Korean and Chinese descent in Brazil are also called "japonês" and frequently have to correct this misnomer (cf. Maeyama 1984:455).

game and cheer on our favorite São Paulo team, or even dance samba in the streets, and in the midst of it, someone will say, 'Hey, japonês.'"

Therefore, this racially inscribed "Japaneseness" is experienced by the Brazilian nikkeijin as a primordial ethnic identity based on innate characteristics acquired by birth that cannot be denied or changed. In a society where minority identities are essentialized by racial phenotype, they seemingly cannot be actively contested, resisted, and modified (cf. Mason 1986:6), in contrast to culturally constructed ethnic identities, which are more subject to negotiation. Among Japanese Brazilians of mixed descent (*mestiços*), racial difference is considerably more open to negotiation and manipulation. Yet, despite their greater racial ambiguity, it seems that even they are frequently unable to escape the essentialized, primordial nature of their ethnicity in Brazilian society and are designated as "japonês" because of their lingering "Japanese" physiognomy (see also Capuano de Oliveira n.d.:17). A sansei mestiço named João even mentioned that his nickname was "João japonês." Even some mestiços who felt that they do not "look very Japanese" claimed they were sometimes categorized as "japonês."

Since minority identities always imply a certain amount of ethnic marginalization, by racially essentializing the Japanese Brazilians as "Japanese," many Brazilians partake in a discourse of ethnic exclusion (whether inadvertently or not). Despite the cultural assimilation of the Japanese Brazilians in Brazil, mainstream Brazilians continue to find it difficult to conceptualize them as part of majority society because they do not belong to one of the three "founding" races of the Brazilian nation (white, black, Indian), a notion popularized by the famous Brazilian scholar, Gilberto Freyre (Capuano de Oliveira n.d.:18). As a result, those Brazilian nikkeijin who wish to be fully accepted as majority Brazilians rather than treated as an ethnic minority sometimes say, "*a cara não ajuda* (the face does not help)" (cf. Smith 1979:59). However, I saw indications that some Brazilians who develop close relationships with culturally assimilated second- and third-generation Japanese Brazilians are eventually able to see beyond the racial surface and do not continue to designate them as "Japanese." For instance, consider these remarks by a Brazilian woman:

> When I first met Fábio [a Japanese Brazilian sansei], I thought he would act very Japanese. But he didn't fit the stereotype. I eventually realized that he is very Brazilian—the way he talks, the way he greets you, his open hospitality. If it weren't for his appearance, I would think he was a true Brazilian. In fact, I don't see him as Japanese that much anymore.

In a heterogeneous and inclusive society where the definition of a dominant "majority group" remains perpetually indefinite and racially diffuse, it seems that sociocultural assimilation will enable the Japanese Brazilians to participate in a majority Brazilian ethnicity, despite perceptions of racial difference. However, as we will see in the next section, most of them have no problem with being classified as "japonês," by their race, since they do not wish to discard their minority Japanese ethnicity in favor of a Brazilian national identity in the first place. In fact, their "Japaneseness" is less of an ethnic stigma to be avoided than a positive asset to be maintained.

THE JAPANESE BRAZILIANS AS A POSITIVE MINORITY AND THE DEVELOPMENT OF A TRANSNATIONAL "JAPANESE" CONSCIOUSNESS

The ethnic differences among the Brazilian nikkeijin that constitute their prominent "Japanese" ethnic identity are not limited to their perceived racial characteristics but also extend to their experience of sociocultural distinctiveness, which is regarded as a product of their Japanese heritage and upbringing. However, their "Japaneseness" becomes the locus of identification because they are a "positive minority" whose ethnic qualities are favorably regarded in Brazilian society. In contrast to most minority groups, which are usually assumed to suffer from low socioeconomic status, prejudice, and discrimination (e.g., see Giddens 1989:245; Ogbu 1978:21–25; Joppke 1998:287; Simpson and Yinger 1972:11) and can therefore be called "negative minorities," the Japanese Brazilians occupy a higher socioeconomic status than the majority Brazilian populace and are respected, if not admired for their "Japanese" cultural attributes.[13] As a result, many of

---

[13] Although positive minorities are quite rare, one example is the Swedish-speaking minority in Finland. Although they no longer dominate the social elite and enjoy only moderately higher occupational status than the majority Finnish population, they continue to be seen as upper class and receive a certain amount of prestige for speaking Swedish (Liebkind 1982). Likewise, certain Asian minorities in the United States now occupy a relatively high socioeconomic and educational status and may be respected for the ethnic qualities that produce such social achievement. However, since many are subject to negative ethnic stereotypes, their positive minority status is quite ambiguous. Historical examples of positive minorities include westerners living in various colonized societies. Not only were they the dominant power holders in these societies, but they were frequently seen by certain sectors of the native populace as culturally superior (see Luhrmann 1994a).

them take pride in their ethnic heritage and have developed a transnational Japanese ethnic identity while generally distancing themselves from what they perceive negatively as "Brazilian."

Social Class Status

The postwar socioeconomic success of the Japanese Brazilians is one reason for the social prestige they enjoy as a "Japanese" minority in Brazil. Despite their humble origins as contract workers on Brazilian plantations, they went on to distinguish themselves in agriculture, creating very successful agricultural cooperatives and introducing various fruits and vegetables into the standard Brazilian diet (see Andô 1973; Saito 1973, 1976, 1978:21–27; Utsumi 1986). Since urbanizing, they have experienced considerable social mobility (see Maeyama 1989; Miyao 1980; Saito 1961:131–57, 1976:189–92) and are predominantly middle class in occupational status. According to a census of Brazilian nikkeijin, 43.3 percent are professionals, managers, or office workers, and another 20.9 percent are in private business (São Paulo Humanities Research Center 1987–1988). As a result, most earn salaries that are considerably above the Brazilian average. Thirty-one percent of them earn less than $400 per month, 48.2 percent earn between $400 and $1,600, and 21.4 percent earn more than $1,600. In contrast, wage levels for the general Brazilian populace are as follows: 61.9 percent earn less than $400, 30 percent earn between $400 and $800, and only 5.7 percent earn more than $1,600 (São Paulo Humanities Research Center 1987–1988). In fact, some of my informants even mentioned a general ethnic perception among Brazilians that the Japanese Brazilians are rich. A marriage with a nikkeijin man is understood in Brazilian society to be *garantido* (guaranteed), that is, economically secure.

The higher educational status of the Japanese Brazilians is also frequently a focus of attention. About 20 percent are university educated (Centro de Estudos 1992), which is over three times the Brazilian average.[14] As a result, like Asians in the United States, they are overrepresented at top universities such as the most prestigious, Universidade de São Paulo (see Maeyama 1983:69; Miyao 1980; Saito 1978:206–207; Smith 1979:64). The most popular ethnic joke in Brazil about the Japanese

---

[14]According to statistics published by IBGE (1992), only 6 percent of the entire Brazilian population over 10 years old is university educated.

Brazilians is undoubtedly the following: "If you want to enter the University of São Paulo, kill a Japanese."

Because of their social success, urban middle-class status has now become a distinctive ethnic attribute that defines the Brazilian nikkeijin as "Japanese" and distinguishes them from the rest of Brazilian society as a socioeconomically privileged positive minority. Because of strong class consciousness in Brazil, socioeconomic status is a quite effective means to differentiate ethnic groups. The Japanese Brazilians sometimes express considerable pride in their past social accomplishments and identify ethnically with their relatively high social class status, claiming that most of them are well-off and very few are of low social class. According to Robert Smith (1979:67), some feel that their socioeconomic success is the result of applying traditional Japanese values in Brazil, thus directly associating their respected middle-class status with their Japanese ethnic identity.

Positive Images of Japan

The positive minority status of the Brazilian nikkeijin is also based on favorable cultural perceptions of Japaneseness in Brazilian society, which are undoubtedly a product of Japan's prominent and respected position in the global order as an economic superpower. Although Japanese direct foreign investment and trade with Brazil has been relatively low, plenty of positive images about Japan's industrial development, prosperity, and advanced technology have been transmitted to Brazil through global mass media and telecommunications networks (see Tajima 1998:191). Reports and stories about Japan in Brazilian newspapers, magazines, and television programs have saturated Brazilian society with favorable impressions and information.[15] In addition to current news, there are plenty of stories about Japan's economic accomplishments and prosperity[16] as well as new Japanese products and technological innovations. The effectiveness of these images is further enhanced by the limited but increasing availability of high-quality Japanese products in Brazil (video/electronic equipment as well as automobiles), which are admired for their reliability and technological superiority. Even such mundane products as Panasonic batteries

---

[15]Some have even claimed that favorable images of Japan, fostered by the mass media, prevail throughout Latin America (see Nakagawa 1983:63).

[16]When the author was in Brazil, Japan's serious and prolonged recession did not receive prominent media coverage.

are prominently labeled "*technologia japonesa*" to make them more appealing and marketable. In fact, because Brazilian tariff restrictions have raised the price of Japanese imports in Brazil, they have become high-priced luxury items, increasing their commodified value and desirability as embodiments of Japanese economic and technological prowess. This is especially true for Japanese automobiles, which have been generally sold for twice their U.S. price as true luxury cars in Brazil, in contrast to the connotations of middle-class affordability and practicality they have in the United States.[17] I was quite surprised when I first observed the reaction of one of my Brazilian friends to a Japanese car. "The Honda is a *beautiful* automobile," she said admiringly as a black Accord passed by. It was as if she had just seen a Mercedes. Japanese products generally have more positive cultural connotations than American and European brands, which are frequently manufactured in Brazil and tailored for the lower-end Brazilian market.

This favorable Brazilian perception of Japan is based not only on specific knowledge and commodified images about the country but also on general impressions of the First World (*primeiro mundo*) that come mainly from the United States, which dominates the global flow of mass media and popular culture. In fact, when specific knowledge about Japan is lacking, generalized and rather idealistic images about the First World are quickly substituted as if it were synonymous with Japan. Although very few of the Brazilians I spoke with had a clear idea of the actual living conditions in Japan, since images of relatively privileged and luxurious Euro-American standards of living are readily available through American movies and TV shows, they were automatically applied to Japan by virtue of the country's First World status.

This global dissemination of positive impressions about Japan as a techno-economic power and First World nation has greatly enhanced the degree of ethnic respect the Japanese Brazilians receive in Brazil. In fact, the ethnic status of the Japanese in Brazil has fluctuated historically depending on the changing position of Japan in the global order (see Tsuda 2001). The nikkeijin were not held in high ethnic regard in the past when Japan's international status was unfavorable and negative images of the Japanese prevailed. In the early twentieth century, when Japan was still a backward Asian nation attempting to catch up with the West, Japanese

---

[17]The situation is gradually changing as Japanese auto makers begin to open plants in Brazil. Brazilian tariffs on imported goods have tended to fluctuate but will be gradually reduced over the long term, increasing the amount and affordability of imports.

immigrants were perceived by the Brazilian political elite as an "inferior race" who would have negative effects on Brazilian racial composition (see Lesser 1999:chapter 4). Although the ethic of hard work among the Japanese was always admired by some Brazilian officials, they were generally regarded as a problematic immigrant group with inscrutable customs and habits who simply refused to be assimilated. During the period of Japanese imperialist expansion and World War II, the Japanese in Brazil were seen as a serious threat to Brazilian national security (the "yellow peril") and were subject to considerable ethnic repression, leading to Japanese ultranationalist fervor within the immigrant community (see Lesser 1999:chapter 5). As a result, after the war, many of the nisei attempted to escape their negative minority status by distancing themselves from their Japanese ethnic identity and better integrating themselves into mainstream society by negotiating an identity as Brazilians (see Cardoso 1973; Sakurai 1993:86–87).[18]

However, because of Japan's global emergence as a preeminent First World nation in the postwar period, the Japanese Brazilians have experienced a dramatic change in their ethnic status from a previously negative to a currently positive minority. Although this rise in status is partly a result of their notable success as a socially mobile immigrant group, virtually all of my older informants agreed that the amount of respect they receive in Brazil has increased considerably with Japan's sudden rise in the world order. The observations of an issei woman were representative of her contemporaries:

> Although we were not involved in Japan's postwar growth, we have certainly benefited from it. Japan's great success has always reflected well on us and as a result, our standing in Brazil has improved dramatically. Indeed, some act as if we actually participated in Japan's economic miracle.

"Some Brazilians don't clearly differentiate the Japanese in Brazil from the Japanese in Japan," one informant observed. "For them, a Japanese is a Japanese, regardless of whether he lives in Brazil or Japan. Therefore, what the Japanese [in Japan] do instantly becomes a reflection of who we [Japanese Brazilians] are."

---

[18]Even before the end of the war, some of the acculturated urban nisei had begun negotiating synthetic ethnic identities and expressing loyalty to the Brazilian nation in an attempt to overcome Brazilian discrimination (see Lesser 1999:123–24, 130–31; Maeyama 1982, 1996).

Indeed, the Japanese Brazilians have capitalized on the currently pro-Japanese climate by asserting and embracing their "Japaneseness," in contrast to their attempts to assimilate to Brazilian society in the early postwar period (see Moreira da Rocha 1999:289–90, 295).[19] In fact, because Japan is now part of the First World, there is a certain prestige in being associated with that country instead of Third World Brazil. In fact, Brazilians tend to denigrate their country in general, and such criticisms have become part of the national discourse (the government is corrupt and does not function properly, the country is not very serious, it has major economic and social problems, etc.). By developing a strong transnational ethnic identification with Japan, the Japanese Brazilians are able to distance themselves from such negative images (cf. Linger 2001:25; Reichl 1995; J. Saito 1986:246). Undoubtedly, with the development of modern communications and mass media that reach out to people across national borders, it has become easier for second- and third-generation immigrant minorities to identify transnationally with distant ethnic homelands by appropriating positive images that circulate in the global ecumene. Ethnic identities in the modern world are becoming less dependent on actual interaction and experiences with other people because ethnic "encounters" can now be imagined over large geographical distances through the global production and dissemination of mass media (cf. Gupta and Ferguson 1992:10–11; Harvey 1989:289). As Arjun Appadurai observes (1996:53–54), globalization has increased the power and possibilities of the social imagination among ordinary people.

Ethnic Stereotypes and Positive Perceptions of Cultural Difference

The favorable understandings of Japan in Brazilian society have also enhanced the perception of the *cultural* differences of the Japanese Brazilians. This is another important component of their positive minority status that conditions their ethnic consciousness, causing them to emphasize their "Japaneseness" instead of their Brazilian identities. The dissemination of positive images about Japan in Brazil has included favorable portrayals of Japanese culture. For instance, when I was in Brazil, the main Brazilian tel-

---

[19]Some researchers have noted a desire among second- and third-generation immigrant minorities to explore and assert their past ethnic heritage (Hansen 1952). This type of "ethnic revival" occurs not only because they feel that they are losing their ethnic distinctiveness due to assimilation. Since they are now well established and secure in majority society, they are able to assert a minority ethnic identity without compromising or threatening their social position.

evision network, Globo, ran a documentary series, *O Milagre Japonês* (The Japanese Miracle), which also highlighted traditional Japanese cultural values as a necessary context for understanding the country's economic competitiveness, efficiency, and technological success.

In fact, there is considerable interest among some non-nikkeijin Brazilians in Japanese culture, which has lately come to be seen as refined, fashionable, chic, and exotic (Maeyama 1996:491; Moreira da Rocha 1999:289, 295; Reichl 1995:45). Although many of these Brazilians are introduced to Japanese culture by their Japanese Brazilian friends, much of their interest is also generated by their exposure to Japanese cultural images through television, films, and print media. When I lived in Porto Alegre (which has only a small Japanese Brazilian population), the local Catholic university held a series of demonstration classes on Japanese culture, including tea ceremonies and flower arranging. I was surprised to find that these classes were not only well attended but consisted overwhelmingly of non-nikkeijin Brazilians (cf. Moreira da Rocha 1999:290–91). Indeed, Japanese language classes offered both at the university and in more informal contexts consist not only of nikkeijin but also of a good contingent of Brazilian students as well. "It's amazing how many Brazilians want to learn Japanese," one Japanese Brazilian university student remarked. "It has no practical value for them—they just do it out of personal interest in Japanese culture. I am frequently asked by my [Brazilian] friends how long it will take them to learn the language." One issei woman who taught Japanese was initially surprised at the number of Brazilian students who eagerly attended her classes. "These classes were intended for nikkeijin students," she explained. "So we didn't know what to do with the Brazilians who showed up. But we couldn't tell them they had no right to learn Japanese because they are Brazilian."

Japanese cuisine has also become somewhat popular in Brazil (see Moreira da Rocha 1999:289). I have known a number of Brazilians who profess a personal love for sushi (eaten properly with chopsticks, of course). I have also been amused to find Brazilians who have learned to sing traditional Japanese songs (*enka*) and participate in karaoke contests held by the local Japanese Brazilian community. Japanese new religions have also been quite successful in Brazil. As Moreira da Rocha remarks, "Lately, it has become fashionable in Brazil to know about Japanese things, to learn cookery, to be able to read some *kanji*, and to sit *zazen* [and to] learn . . . *chanoyu* [Japanese tea ceremony]" (1999:295).

Likewise, the cultural differences of the Japanese Brazilians—which are associated with their Japanese ancestry—are regarded in an overwhelmingly positive manner. There is notable consensus among Brazilians that the japonês are hardworking, honest, intelligent, trustworthy, and responsible (cf. J. Saito 1986; Smith 1979:58–59).[20] In the past, the work ethic and ability of the japonês became so legendary in some rural areas of southern Brazil (especially Paraná) that it was said they could grow crops on infertile soil, which was referred to as *terra para japonês* (land for the Japanese). The Japanese Brazilians are also sometimes seen as more timid, reserved, and calm than Brazilians, characteristics that can have positive connotations. Such positive stereotypes and attitudes were quite evident in my interactions with mainstream Brazilians, which resulted in numerous unsolicited ethnic comments about the Japanese Brazilians such as the following:

"The japonês are very respected. They do the work of ten Brazilians," a Brazilian waiter told me, when he found out that I had interviewed a Japanese Brazilian woman in his restaurant.

"Japonês, eh?" an agent at a Brazilian bus terminal confirmed when I gave him my name, mistaking me for a Japanese Brazilian. "They are good people. Very intelligent, hardworking."

"We trust the japonês very much, much more than Brazilians," an old Brazilian lady told me. "I have many Japanese friends and they are always honest, responsible."

"You see, he is japonês," my professor in Porto Alegre observed when one of his students showed up unexpectedly to fulfill an obligation he did not need to honor. "He has a sense of responsibility lacking among Brazilian students."

My Brazilian housemate in Riberão Preto had this to say:

> The Japanese [Brazilians] are seen much better than the Koreans. We trust the Japanese very much—they are good people. The Koreans— sometimes you can't tell what they're up to or what they're like. They are new immigrants and haven't been around in Brazil too long, whereas the Japanese have been here for many decades.

Because the Japanese Brazilians are perceived in such favorable cultural terms in Brazilian society, it can be argued that they sometimes experi-

---

[20]For instance, in one survey, non-Japanese descent Brazilians were asked to choose various adjectives to describe the Japanese Brazilians. The most frequently chosen were: hard-working, diligent, responsible, dedicated, intelligent, competent, educated, and intellectual (T. Saito 1986). As Jenkins (1994) notes, although characterizations of other ethnic groups are often pejorative, this is not always the case.

ence "positive discrimination." In contrast to "negative discrimination," which excludes certain minority groups from full participation in majority society, not only are nikkeijin socially accepted, they are actually favored over members of the majority group in some cases. I have heard many times that some employers prefer them over non-Japanese descent Brazilians because they are seen as hardworking, well educated, and trustworthy (Smith 1979:58–59).

In fact, the only notable negative image of the Japanese Brazilians that I encountered in Brazil was a sense that the japonês are somewhat unreceptive toward ethnic outsiders (see below). I have also heard Brazilians mention that the japonês are too timid and restrained and that the women are too submissive to men, although the reference was more to Japanese in Japan. Although much of Brazilian ethnic prejudice is expressed through joking behavior, the jokes about the japonês that I actively collected from Brazilians tended to emphasize the positive aspects of the Japanese Brazilians, such as their academic achievements (although my own "Japanese" ethnic status undoubtedly made complete access to any nasty jokes difficult). In addition to the above-mentioned joke about killing a Japanese to enter the University of São Paulo, I heard another joke of this type that involves plugging a Japanese into an intelligence measuring machine. The reading goes off the scale, causing the machine (made in Brazil) to break and making the Japanese stupid like a Portuguese (in contrast to American attitudes toward the British, the Portuguese are frequently portrayed in Brazilian jokes as bumbling idiots). Other jokes poked fun at either the facial features or the strange and complicated last names of the Japanese Brazilians. Also, the stereotype of Asians in the United States as "geeks" or "nerds" seems to be much less prominent in Brazil.

In addition to such general understandings of the nikkeijin as a positive minority, many Brazilians further emphasize the "Japanese" cultural qualities of the nikkeijin by explaining their behavior ethnically (cf. Maeyama 1984:448, 1996:312). There is a strong tendency among a good number of Brazilians to automatically interpret many of the distinctive aspects and behaviors of the Japanese Brazilians (such as their high academic achievement, politeness, greater social reserve, cleanliness, etc.) in favorable terms as positive "Japanese" cultural qualities. A Japanese Brazilian mother gave a typical example of this Brazilian ethnic reasoning in regard to her son:

> When my son gets good grades in school, they say, "Of course, it's because he's Japanese. He is intelligent." When he does a really careful and

neat job on a class assignment, they say, "Of course, it's because he's Japanese." When he keeps his desk clean in the classroom, they say, "Of course, he is Japanese."

The process at work can be called "ethnic attribution"—the propensity to simplistically explain and interpret the behavior of those from a different ethnic group that corresponds to standard stereotypes as a collective ethnic trait while ignoring other possible explanations (cf. Hagendoorn 1993:35; Verkuyten 1997). Because the members of other ethnic groups are not directly familiar, it becomes easier to attribute their behavior to ethnic causes without considering possible individual or situational determinants.[21] In fact, as a Japanese descendant in Brazil, I experienced this type of positive ethnic attribution. My "Japanese" intelligence was credited for my relatively quick mastery of Portuguese more than a few times. On the day I left Porto Alegre, I told my Brazilian friends who drove me to the bus terminal that I had spent much of the previous night cleaning my apartment before I moved out. Again, the inevitable ethnic conclusion: "*Ele é japonês* (He is Japanese)."

Because of the Brazilian tendency to impose positive cultural stereotypes on the Japanese Brazilians through the ethnic attribution of their behavior, most of my informants continued to retain a strong consciousness that they are culturally "Japanese" to a certain extent and are significantly different from other Brazilians. As was the case with their experience of race, an identity emerges in a hegemonic context through external ethnic definitions. In fact, because Brazilians expect Japanese Brazilians to behave in a respectable "Japanese" manner, some of my informants felt that they could not act in inappropriate (i.e., "un-Japanese") ways as members of the Japanese community or do anything that would embarrass or tarnish their favorable reputation. It is possible that even those individuals who do not initially feel their "Japaneseness" very strongly eventually develop a consciousness of ethnic difference because they are constantly designated as culturally "Japanese" by other Brazilians (cf. J. Saito 1986:241). This is one reason even the sansei, whose Japanese cultural affiliation tends to be weaker than that of the nisei, continue to have stronger Japanese than Brazilian ethnic sentiments.

---

[21]This concept of ethnic attribution is derived from attribution theory in social psychology (see Brown 1986:chapters 4 and 5), which describes how individuals attribute behavior to either internal or external causes.

However, these cultural definitions of "Japanese" ethnicity are not only hegemonic constructs simply imposed on the self-consciousness of the Japanese Brazilians. Because of their positive connotations, they are actively asserted by the Japanese Brazilians themselves. When talking about their cultural differences, my nikkeijin informants agreed with the way they were ethnically characterized in Brazilian society and claimed that they *are* indeed more hardworking, diligent, honest, educated, intelligent, and responsible than most Brazilians, whom they stereotypically portrayed as lazy, easygoing, irresponsible, immature, and dishonest (see also Flores 1975:95; Reichl 1995:49, 51, 55; T. Saito 1986; Smith 1979:58).[22] In fact, it was remarkable how their comments about their positive cultural qualities were frequently accompanied by negative images of majority Brazilians. Consider the reflections of one young nisei man:

> We feel lots of cultural differences in relation to other Brazilians. Lots. Our cultural level is higher. We work harder, are more diligent, and intelligent. Brazilians like the beach too much and spend too much time partying and enjoying themselves. If you ask a Japanese [Brazilian] to do something, you can be assured it will be done. If you ask a Brazilian . . . who knows what will happen? They aren't serious about work and are unreliable.

The comments of an older Japanese Brazilian store owner emphasized some of the same themes from a different perspective:

> Living in Brazil, we see lots of things we don't like. Brazilians are laid back and never show up on time and sometimes don't even keep their appointments. I always have problems with this when I hire Brazilians at my store. Lots of them are lazy and irresponsible and are out to deceive others. In contrast, Japanese [Brazilian] employees can be trusted—you can always expect them to be honest and efficient.

It should also be noted that some of the ethnic comparisons the Japanese Brazilians made between themselves and mainstream Brazilians were

---

[22]Many Japanese Brazilian respondents in T. Saito's survey (1986) characterized Brazilians in this unfavorable manner. Few saw Brazilians as educated, hard-working, intelligent, or responsible. However, negative portrayals were less frequent in regard to Brazilian women, where female stereotypes were more prevalent.

more neutral in tone. For instance, they also characterize the Brazilians as friendly, talkative, sociable, and happy (cf. T. Saito 1986; Smith 1979:58), in contrast to which they saw themselves as more restrained, shy, and formal and less emotional and outgoing in demeanor. In general, however, the discourse of ethnic difference among the Japanese Brazilians invoked negative characterizations and stereotypes of majority Brazilians. In fact, according to a 1995 Datafolha poll of Japanese Brazilians living in São Paulo, 59 percent admitted that they are prejudiced against Brazilians, whereas only 35 percent felt that Brazilians were prejudiced against them (cited in Linger 2001:25).

Of course, the Brazilian nikkeijin do not always use such negative stereotypes when interacting with individual Brazilians and obviously acknowledge that there are well educated Brazilians who have positive qualities. However, ethnic identity is frequently experienced through ethnic stereotypes (see Bun and Kiong 1993:157–58; Hagendoorn 1993:31; Verkuyten 1997), since it is based on perceptions about collective group differences. By representing the ethnic other in a simplistic and demeaning manner, the Japanese Brazilians are able to define themselves more favorably through the use of positive ethnic stereotypes about "Japaneseness."[23] This increases their awareness and appreciation of the cultural qualities that differentiate them from other Brazilians and identify them as ethnically "Japanese."

In fact, even my informants of mixed descent tended to identify more strongly with the Japanese side of their ethnic identities and deemphasized their Brazilianness. Although most mestiços are racially classified as japonês in Brazilian society, they do not challenge or contest this hegemonic imposition of ethnic categories because of the predominantly favorable connotations of Japaneseness. Instead of regarding these essentialist assumptions about their ethnicity as symbolic violence to be resisted, they willingly complied, if not actively encouraged such external ethnic definitions. This was vividly shown in the manner in which my mestiço nikkeijin informants responded to my research. When I told them that I was studying the japonês in Brazil, they sometimes indicated to me (either on the phone or at the start of the interview) that they were of mixed de-

---

[23]As the social psychologists Jaspars and Warnaen (1982) have shown in a study of Indonesian ethnic identity, ethnic groups use self-attributed, positive stereotypes to differentiate themselves from other groups.

scent. However, if there had been no such indications and if my informants looked racially "Japanese" to me, I assumed that they were japonês and not mestiço, thus inadvertently partaking in the essentialist imposition of primordial Japanese ethnicities prevalent in Brazil. Most of them either did not correct my ethnic assumption or simply "passed" as a pure Japanese descendant throughout the interview, all too willing participants in the promotion of their "Japaneseness." Their mixed descent would be revealed to me only in response to a probing question or through my contact with them after the interview. The most memorable case occurred when I was interviewing a married couple in Ribeirão Preto. The wife, who was of mixed descent, proceeded to answer all my questions as if she were of pure Japanese descent; only toward the end of the interview did her husband reveal to me that her father is Italian. I was a bit surprised and asked her why she did not consider herself Italian instead of Japanese. "I don't want to be seen as Italian," she muttered, looking down.

Symbolic Ethnicity: The Construction of Cultural Distinctiveness

For most of my informants, therefore, the cultural benefits of being a Japanese minority were quite clear (cf. Ferreira and Asari 1986). Supposedly, there are few negatives to being "Japanese" in Brazil. In fact, to my initial surprise, virtually everyone from the younger generations claimed (sometimes emphatically) that they had *never* experienced any ethnic discrimination or exclusion in Brazil.[24] Although the Japanese Brazilians are undoubtedly influenced by Brazil's ideology of "racial democracy" that denies that there is ethnic discrimination in the country,[25] the fact that they generally reported only positive experiences as an ethnic minority is very significant.

However, the cultural differences that make such distinct Japanese ethnic identities possible cannot simply be asserted by ethnic decree—they

---

[24]Even in the 1970s, Saito (1976:197) observed that the Japanese Brazilians no longer encountered any resistance or barriers to social mobility in the cities. His informants (even older issei) felt they were not subject to ethnic prejudice (1976:192). However, Smith (1979:58) suspects that latent ethnic prejudice still existed during this period but was not overtly expressed in the form of discrimination.

[25]Of course, reality is quite different. For instance, there is considerable discrimination toward blacks who migrate from the Nordeste (the poorer and less developed northeast region of Brazil) to the industrialized cities of the south to work in factories and live in shantytowns.

must be actively developed and maintained through family socialization processes and the internal dynamics of the ethnic community. The family environment within which the Japanese Brazilians are raised is quite different from that of other Brazilian families, which creates certain enduring differences in cultural and behavioral orientation (cf. Handa 1987:720–21; J. Saito 1986:241). This is especially true for those raised in rural Japanese colônias, a majority of whom grow up speaking Japanese at home and become quite proficient in the language (Kitagawa 1997:181–85). Despite strong influences from Brazilian society later in life (especially through education in Brazilian schools), the effects of such early family socialization remain and continue to exert a substantial influence on thinking and behavior throughout the life course (cf. Saito 1978:129–31). Although this is especially true for the nisei, whose parents are immigrants from Japan, these differential socialization patterns continue to influence the sansei. In addition to subconsciously internalizing certain cultural and behavioral orientations within the family, many nikkeijin children feel considerable pressure from their parents to learn Japanese and to behave in certain ways worthy of the Japanese (see also Maeyama 1984:448; 1996:312, 397).

Despite the continued influence of primary socialization, however, the Japanese Brazilians are considerably assimilated and have lost many of their "Japanese" cultural differences through their substantially greater exposure to Brazilian society. Unlike earlier generations who lived predominantly in isolated Japanese colônias, a majority of them are well integrated in mainstream Brazilian society; they are raised, educated, and work in close contact with other Brazilians and socialize with Brazilian friends. As a result, many nisei feel a significant generation gap with their first-generation Japanese parents in terms of attitudes, demeanor, and orientation toward Brazil (cf. Maeyama 1982:37–49; Saito 1978:125–26). Although the issei initially view the cultural assimilation of their children in Brazil as undesirable (cf. Saito 1976:195), they eventually come to accept it as inevitable. One issei mother in Porto Alegre spoke about her experiences in this regard:

> At first, we see our children becoming more and more Brazilianized and try to prevent it. We try to make them speak Japanese at home and insist that they not lose their Japanese ways. Then we find that it is useless and begin to see the loss of Japanese culture as inevitable. Eventually, we realize that it's probably better this way.

Therefore, except for a minority who are still from the rural colônias, most younger Japanese Brazilians no longer maintain Japanese traditions or customs and do not speak proficient Japanese, communicating in Portuguese even at home (see also Saito 1976:196–97). As a result, they have become much more culturally Brazilian than Japanese.

This weakening of their Japanese cultural distinctiveness has made it harder for the Japanese Brazilians to maintain a separate "Japanese" ethnic identity. However, for positive minorities, a complete loss of their ethnic differences and identities is equivalent to a loss of cultural virtue and status. The Brazilian nikkeijin therefore attempt to preserve their cherished "Japanese" cultural differences through the symbolic re-creation of ethnic traditions such as festivals, rituals, food, music, and dress. In this manner, tradition (including ethnic tradition) becomes an object of nostalgic longing to be regained in a reconstituted form precisely when it is in danger of vanishing (Ivy 1995).[26]

The Japanese Brazilians practice such "symbolic ethnicity" (see Gans 1979, 1994) within their ethnic communities, which remain socially cohesive despite their dispersal in the cities and consist of very active associations and clubs, which run a multitude of ethnic activities and events ranging from festivals, large dinners, and performances featuring Japanese karaoke, theater, traditional music, and dance to various sporting events and Miss Nikkei beauty pageants (see also Cardoso 1973).[27] A good number of the Brazilian nikkeijin still actively participate in these ethnic associations,[28] which provide them with constant opportunities to engage in symbolic activities that are understood to represent a distinctive "Japanese" culture (see also Ferreira and Asari 1986:217–18; Linger 2001:25 Saito 1976:195). When such ethnic activities and performances are directed toward people outside the ethnic community, they become

---

[26]This point is illustrated in various contexts by Marilyn Ivy, who examines the reappropriation of vanishing phantasms in modern Japan. According to her analysis:

> Only from the position of loss can one assert that nothing has been lost; only when the seamless, unquestioned transmission of custom has been interrupted, does "tradition" emerge. The realization of loss is forestalled, denied, by an insistence that nothing is lost. It is denied by an idealization, a memorialization of place, a bracketing of practices, an assertion of continuity. (1995)

[27]The Japanese Brazilians show much more interest in Japanese music and other aspects of Japanese culture than Japanese Americans in Hawaii (Centro de Estudos 1992).

[28]Survey research shows that 35 percent to more than half of the Japanese Brazilians are active participants (Centro de Estudos 1992; Ferreira and Asari 1986:217–18; Reichl 1995:45).

opportunities to publicly demonstrate and affirm Japanese cultural differences in front of majority Brazilians, who express an active interest in such displays of "Japanese culture." In larger and better established nikkeijin communities (especially in the city of São Paulo and certain cities in Paraná state), there are half-day Japanese schools, many Japanese restaurants and food stores, and large ethnic festivals. Instruction in the Japanese language or culture (such as the tea ceremony or flower arranging) is also available through either Japanese schools or more informal classes (see Moreira da Rocha 1999). There are also many informal social gatherings among nikkeijin families and friends for dinners and parties that provide opportunities to cook Japanese food, speak Japanese (when possible), and sing Japanese songs (Japanese karaoke is the favorite activity at these gatherings).

In this manner, despite the absence of sufficient cultural differences in their everyday behavior or language necessary to maintain a "Japanese" minority identity, the Japanese Brazilians find special occasions in which to symbolically reenact and reconstruct their distinctive cultural heritage and traditions. Although these traditional Japanese cultural forms have been significantly altered in Brazil as they have been appropriated and re-created by Japanese descendants (see Moreira da Rocha 1999 in the case of Japanese tea ceremonies), their distinctiveness in Brazil is enough for them to be experienced as "Japanese" and therefore function as ethnic "emblems of contrast" and "boundary markers" (Barth 1969) that differentiate the Japanese Brazilians from mainstream Brazilians.

Ethnicity becomes "symbolic" precisely when a well-integrated and culturally assimilated positive minority finds it beneficial to continue asserting their ethnic differences instead of becoming subsumed in the majority. Even as the cultural characteristics that initially defined an ethnic group continue to weaken through assimilation, a strong ethnic identity can persist among its members on a subjective level through the symbolic invention of ethnic traditions (see Yinger 1981:258–59). Some scholars claim that this persistence of a residual symbolic ethnicity is the last stage before the full assimilation of the minority group (DeSantis and Benkin 1980) while others believe that such symbolic ethnic identifications will persist (Thompson 1974; Yinger 1981).

The symbolic maintenance of a separate identity by an ethnic community frequently involves the exclusion of other ethnic groups that threaten to "dilute" its cultural distinctiveness. In the case of the Japanese

Brazilians, this involves the social marginalization of the majority. In contrast to their social acceptance in Brazilian society, the Japanese Brazilians did not admit non-Japanese descent Brazilians into their ethnic associations until recent decades (cf. Smith 1979:67). In addition, a certain amount of ethnic self-segregation among the nikkeijin in their personal relationships continues. Some of them (including sansei) associate and socialize predominantly, if not exclusively with their ethnic fellows in closed social groups and do not have very active social relationships with mainstream Brazilians (Saito 1978:151–52).[29] Even those who relate more openly with Brazilians outside the Japanese community claim that they are more comfortable and get along better with their fellow japonês because of cultural similarities. Certain businesses run by Japanese Brazilians reportedly discriminate against Brazilians when hiring. Marriage with a Brazilian was considered taboo or strongly discouraged in the past. Although attitudes toward intermarriage have become considerably more tolerant in recent decades (see Butsugan 1980; Saito 1978:182–84; Smith 1979:65–66; Willems and Baldus 1942:532–33) and close to half of the nikkeijin are now marrying outside their ethnic group, the intermarriage rate is still notably lower than among Japanese Americans.[30] A number of nikkeijin families (including those in which the parents are nisei) still strongly encourage their children to marry another japonês instead of a Brazilian (cf. Reichl 1995:45). Indeed, it is usually the Japanese Brazilian parents who object to an intermarriage; the Brazilian parents are generally tolerant and accepting. As a result of such ethnic exclusiveness, nikkeijin communities and groups have a reputation among Brazilians for being *fechado* (closed and unreceptive). In fact, most Japanese Brazilians feel that they practice much more discrimination toward mainstream Brazilians than vice versa. This situation in which there is more exclusionary discrimination from the minority than the majority may be a characteristic of positive minority groups in general.

The negotiation of a distinctive Japanese identity among the Japanese Brazilians through the maintenance of exclusionary ethnic boundaries is

---

[29]This strong tendency to socially cluster with ethnic peers is also documented in research surveys (J. Saito 1986:245), although the Centro de Estudos study (1992:278) indicates greater interaction between the Japanese Brazilians and mainstream Brazilians.

[30]The intermarriage rate among Japanese Americans reached an all-time high of 75 percent in 2000 (*Pacific Citizen*, January 12–February 1, 2001).

symbolized by their ethnic terminology. The Brazilian nikkeijin refer to themselves exclusively as "japonês" and almost never use the more ethnically inclusive terms of "nipo-brasileiro" or "japonês-brasileiro" (see also Maeyama 1996:398). In contrast, non-nikkeijin Brazilians are usually called "gaijin" ("foreigners"), a custom passed down through the generations from the issei that has now become completely habitual among most Japanese Brazilians, including the sansei (see also Maeyama 1984:448, 1996:313–14; Saito 1978:179). Although "gaijin" has lost much of its original meaning among recent generations (in fact, a few sansei did not even know that it means "foreigner" in Japanese), its use still designates majority Brazilians as ethnic outsiders, thus clearly indicating who is "japonês" and who is not (cf. Sakurai 1993:57).

In this manner, a strong ethnic consciousness of "Japaneseness" is maintained within the nikkeijin community through differential family socialization, the communal performance of symbolic ethnicity, and the partial exclusion of ethnic "gaijin." Since many of the Japanese Brazilians believe that the positive "Japanese" cultural qualities they have acquired from their parents and grandparents have been maintained within their ethnic communities, this sense of generational continuity creates feelings of transnational ethnic affinity with the Japanese of Japan. Indeed, a number of Japanese Brazilians feel they are culturally similar to the Japanese (cf. Ferreira and Asari 1986:218).

POSITIVE MINORITIES BUT UNCERTAIN FUTURES

Despite the potential inclusiveness of majority Brazilian society, few Japanese Brazilians have taken full advantage of this ethnically tolerant social environment. Instead of adopting a Brazilian national consciousness, they have asserted, if not insisted on their Japanese ethnic distinctiveness, based on an awareness of racial, social, and cultural contrasts that identify them as a positive minority group.

Being "Japanese" in Brazil has many advantages since it not only is associated with high socioeconomic status but also involves a positive contrast between First World (Japan) and Third World (Brazil) and between Japanese and Brazilian culture. For the nikkeijin, the maintenance of a "Japanese" ethnic identity becomes a way of differentiating themselves from the negative aspects of Brazilianness while affiliating themselves with the contrasting positive aspects of Japaneseness. Their ethnic minority status is often a source of much pride and self-esteem[31] and for some, it even leads to a sense of superiority over what is considered Brazilian. In fact, Kitagawa's study of two Japanese Brazilian communities found that 86 percent of those surveyed have a lot of pride in their Japanese descent and 11 percent have some pride, rates that are *higher* than for the Japanese in Japan (Kitagawa 1996:188, 1997:133). The result is a relatively strong transnational identification as ethnic "Japanese" that continues to take precedence over their identities as Brazilian nationals. Indeed, many nikkeijin are reluctant to fully adopt a majority Brazilian identity. Even as some unwittingly become assimilated, they continue to emphasize their remaining cultural differences (even if they are only symbolic) in an attempt to hold on to the last vestiges of a respected minority status. In this sense, the persisting minority status of the Japanese Brazilians is not so much imposed by ethnic exclusion from mainstream Brazilians, as Vieira (1973) argues, but is voluntarily maintained through ethnic self-assertion and segregation to a considerable extent (cf. Capuano de Oliveira n.d.; Reichl 1995). In other words, it is based more on their ethnic exclusion of majority Brazilians than on their own marginalization in Brazilian society.

Nonetheless, the development of identity is always embedded within dominant contexts of power and inequality (cf. Comaroff 1987; Kondo 1990). Ethnic and migrant identities are constructed as individuals actively contest, appropriate, and subvert the hegemonic cultural meanings and categories imposed on them (Basch, Glick Schiller, and Blanc 1994; Charles 1992; Hall 1990; Ong 1996). However, as the Japanese Brazilian case demonstrates, the negotiation of identity does not always involve such struggles since the externally imposed identity may be consonant with the individual's subjective experiences. Instead of resistance and subversion, the assertion of an ethnic minority identity among the Japanese Brazilians in Brazil involves acquiescence, if not active promotion of their ethnicity as hegemonically constituted. Perhaps most of them have been so successfully co-opted by the hegemonic system that an assertion of an independent self-consciousness is no longer possible. Yet, as a positive minority, they may have no need to challenge dominant ethnic perceptions of their "Japaneseness" when it is so favorably construed. Instead, discrepant inner

---

[31]Studies have shown very high levels of self-confidence and self-esteem among the Japanese Brazilians (J. Saito 1986:249–50).

voices emphasizing their Brazilianness may be actively suppressed in favor of hegemonic understandings of their Japanese ethnicity.

However, even the ethnic status of positive minorities is subject to unpredictable shifts in dominant attitudes and perceptions, leaving them vulnerable to historical vicissitudes. Although the Japanese Brazilians are socioeconomically secure and well regarded in Brazil, their positive minority status has been dependent on the relatively recent change in Japan's global image and therefore remains fundamentally insecure. A few older issei still remember the past experiences of prejudice and discrimination against the Japanese Brazilians partly caused by Japan's wartime status as an imperialist menace and are less enthusiastic than the younger generations about their dramatic postwar rise to positive minority status. Perhaps they are aware that a negative turn of historical events in the future could just as quickly erode the ethnic gains they have recently made, possibly returning them to their former, *negative* minority status. Such lingering ethnic unease is occasionally shared by younger Japanese Brazilians as well. Mario, a prominent nisei businessman in São Paulo, spoke about such feelings:

> The status of the Japanese Brazilians is closely linked to Japan, although most of us have had nothing to do with the country. How Japan is perceived directly influences how we are perceived here in Brazil. I am bothered by this. If Japan does something bad, or its status in the world declines, it will have a negative effect on us in Brazil as well. I think the Japanese Brazilians should be judged independently on their own merits and not simply in reference to Japan.

Mario had not realized that the next change in the ethnic minority status of the Japanese Brazilians would come not from a decline in Japan's global status, but from return migration to Japan itself.

FROM EMIGRATION TO IMMIGRATION

Approximately eighty years after the first Japanese emigrants set foot in Brazil, the tables were turned on the Japanese Brazilians in a cruel twist of fate. Beginning in the early 1980s, the Brazilian economy crumbled and entered a prolonged and severe period of crisis, overburdened by foreign debt, hyperinflation, and high underemployment. Meanwhile, in one of the greatest economic miracles of modern history, the Japanese economy grew beyond all expectations to become the second largest in the world. Confronted by shrinking economic fortunes in Brazil and lured to Japan by an abundance of high-paying factory jobs, the descendants of the original Japanese emigrants to Brazil are again migrating across the Pacific Ocean, this time to take advantage of the economic opportunities in Japan and improve their financially stagnant lives at home. An interesting migration legacy that started with emigration *from* Japan at the beginning of the century ended with immigration *to* Japan at the end of the century.

The Causes of Japanese Brazilian Return Migration[32]

It is widely acknowledged as current wisdom in migration studies that immigration flows cannot be sufficiently explained by economic factors that simply push migrants out of the sending country and pull them to the receiving country (Castles and Miller 1993:21–22; Cornelius, Martin, and Hollifield 1994; Portes and Böröcz 1989). However, economic pressures remain the dominant force that initially instigates most labor migration. Research surveys conducted among Japanese Brazilian migrants show that 61 to 84 percent of the respondents cite purely economic reasons as the principal motive for migrating (JICA 1992; Kitagawa 1993).

The causes of Japanese Brazilian return migration can be partly understood through a microeconomic, rational choice model. According to this rather simple perspective, migration is motivated by rational, economic decisions that individuals make in response to income disparities between specific countries (Borjas 1989:457–85; Rothenberg 1977; Todaro 1969). Because of a severe wage differential between Brazil and Japan, the nikkeijin are able to earn 5 to 10 times their middle-class Brazilian incomes in Japan, even as unskilled factory workers. In Brazil, close to 60 percent of them earn less than $800 per month (São Paulo Humanities Research Center, 1987–1988) and according to the Brazilian census, the average salary for all Asians in Brazil (most of whom are Japanese Brazilians) is a mere $377 (cited in Japan Institute of Labor 1995). In contrast, 40 to 46 percent of them earn between $2,000 and $3,000 per month in Japan, with 25 to 40 percent earning more than $3,000 per month (Kitagawa 1992, 1993). Because they are legal immigrants and the most ethnically

---

[32]For a detailed analysis, see Tsuda (1999a).

preferred among Japanese employers, the Brazilian nikkeijin are in high demand in Japan (even during the current recession), and Japanese companies generally have to pay good wages in order to attract them. As a result, the Japanese Brazilians save an average of about $20,000 per year in Japan (Japan Institute of Labor 1995:135), which is approximately four or five times their average yearly income in Brazil.

The Japanese Brazilians are very aware that the money they can earn in Japan in just a few years may take decades to earn in Brazil. Such economic incentives are the fundamental cause of their return migration. One of my informants summarized this rational decision-making process as follows:

> We hear about the incredible wages in Japan and start doing these calculations—comparing our Brazilian salaries with how much you can earn in Japan. Then we say, wow, our monthly salaries in Brazil can be earned in Japan in a few days. Despite the sacrifices and difficulties, we end up migrating to Japan because the economic opportunity is just too good to pass up.

Like many other contemporary migrants, most Japanese Brazilians intend to save as much money as possible in Japan in a relatively short period of time (two to three years) and then return to Brazil to buy a house, purchase consumer goods, or open a business. A good number also send remittances back home to support their families.[33]

Many Japanese Brazilians who consider return migration face opposition from family members (especially wives and even parents). Although the family can become a barrier to migration in this respect, many of my informants simply felt that the tremendous economic opportunities awaiting them in Japan were too good to pass up. One of my close friends in Oizumi, Roberto, recounted his experience to me:

> When I was thinking about whether I should go to Japan as a dekasegi, my wife did not want me to leave. She felt that it would be bad for our

---

[33]According to research surveys, the most important financial objectives of the Japanese Brazilians are purchasing a house in Brazil and opening a business, followed by remitting money to family back home and saving money for educational purposes (Japan Institute of Labor 1995; Kitagawa 1993).

children if I was absent from the family for a number of years. I knew it was not good for them to be without a father and that they would miss me, but it was hard to make ends meet during the Brazilian crisis. I told my wife that I would be missing a once-in-a-lifetime opportunity if I didn't go to Japan. And I could support the family from Japan, at least economically, by sending remittances. By improving our economic footing, the family would ultimately be stronger.

Many other Brazilian nikkeijin have resolved this conflict between family and migration by relocating to Japan with their families.

Even on a purely economic level, however, such cost-benefit calculations by migrants are insufficient to initiate mass migration without the presence of other economic push-pull pressures caused by macrostructural economic conditions in both the migrant sending and the receiving country (see Massey 1988; Portes 1978; Sassen 1988). These include the hierarchical international division of labor between core and peripheral countries, the development and expansion of the capitalist mode of production, the dislocations of economic development, cyclical fluctuations in economic conditions, and the impact of structural economic changes on labor supply and demand.

Undoubtedly, the primary structural economic push factor that caused the Japanese Brazilians to emigrate was the Brazilian economic crisis of the 1980s. This long-term deterioration of the Brazilian economy was characterized by massive hyperinflation, stagnant or declining economic growth, and increasing unemployment and underemployment. Economic statistics for Brazil during the 1980s and early 1990s paint a grim picture. While Brazil's external debt continued to mount, reaching $123.9 billion by 1987, the annual economic growth rate remained very sluggish or declined for most of the period despite a brief growth spurt in the mid-1980s. During this period, unbelievable rates of hyperinflation hit Brazil in three successive waves, which crested to higher and higher levels each time, reaching a 2,000 percent annual rate by 1993. Meanwhile, the combined rate of unemployment and underemployment had climbed to 15 percent by 1991. Although the government attempted to resuscitate the economy and control hyperinflation by implementing a series of eight different economic plans, they were ineffective and sometimes counterproductive. The Brazilian finance minister was changed more than 10 times in the 1980s.

Many of the Brazilian nikkeijin bore the brunt of the economic crisis. Since most did not suffer from severe unemployment,[34] it was not an inability to find jobs but a decline in income and purchasing power that pushed them out of Brazil. The real value of wages was constantly eroded by the corrosive effect of hyperinflation despite the indexing of salaries.[35] This was further exacerbated as the market for professional and highly skilled jobs dried up, making it increasingly difficult for the well-educated, middle-class Japanese Brazilians to find satisfying jobs commensurate with their higher qualifications and income expectations.[36] Therefore, on the economic level, the return migration of the Brazilian nikkeijin has been driven by a serious labor market mismatch in the Brazilian domestic economy.

Although the Japanese Brazilians suffered much less from the Brazilian economic crisis than those at lower socioeconomic levels, their relatively high socioeconomic status ironically made them *more* willing to migrate than their lower-class compatriots. It is not always the level of *absolute* economic deprivation that motivates people to migrate, but *relative* deprivation caused by a discrepancy between expectations and economic reality. Because the Brazilian nikkeijin had enjoyed a comparatively privileged and high standard of living and had developed higher expectations about their quality of life, they were less willing than others to let their deteriorating wages lower their living standards during the economic crisis. As a result, they opted to emigrate in order to maintain their privileged lifestyle in contrast to many poorer Brazilians, who accepted worsening economic conditions and remained behind. When reflecting on the reasons for migrating to Japan, remarks such as the following from a nikkeijin woman were very typical:

We never suffered from a lack of money or had serious economic problems back home. There was always enough to live on, to put food on the table, to buy basic necessities. The problem was that because of the economic cri-

---

[34]Only 3.5 percent of those Japanese Brazilians surveyed by one study had been unemployed before going to Japan (Japan Institute of Labor 1995).

[35]In the greater São Paulo area (where most Japanese Brazilians live), the real value of wages fell 8 percent in 1987 and 21.6 percent in 1990, despite some brief increases in real wages in the 1980s.

[36]This was also true among other middle-class Brazilians who decided to emigrate during this period (see Margolis 1994:79; Martes 2000:52, 72). Such conditions seem to prevail throughout Latin American countries (see Piore 1979).

sis and Brazilian inflation, we couldn't do anything more than this with our salaries—couldn't buy a house, buy a car, or plan for our futures.

In this manner, labor migration is sometimes the result of the unmet expectations of the relatively well-to-do instead of simply the desperation of the economically dispossessed. Frequently, the latter also do not have the resources or the international social connections to migrate abroad. This is one important reason why migrant flows often consist of better-educated individuals of higher socioeconomic status (see Grasmuck and Pessar 1991; Margolis 1994; Massey 1988).

In fact, the Brazilian nikkeijin were not the only ones who emigrated from Brazil during the country's economic crisis. Numerous other Brazilians also left for North America and Europe during this period because of declining economic fortunes. As a result, by 1996, there were 1.56 million Brazilian migrants living abroad, including 600,000 in the United States, 40,000 in Italy, 36,000 in Germany, 32,000 in Portugal, 20,000 in England, 13,000 in Australia, and 10,000 in Spain (Sasaki 1999:245). Many of these emigrants are middle class and relatively well educated, but perform low-status, unskilled jobs in their host countries that are shunned by native workers (see Goza 1999:771; Margolis 1994:chapters 4, 5; Martes 2000:chapter 2, 3; Sales 1996:100).

In addition to economic push factors in the migrant sending country, there must also be sufficient structural economic demand for migrant labor in the receiving country for migration to be initiated. In the Japanese Brazilian case, the severe and extended economic crisis in Brazil coincided with a growing economic "crisis" of a different sort in Japan—an acute shortage of unskilled labor in the late 1980s. According to statistics compiled by the Japanese Ministry of Labor, an average of 48 percent of the companies in the manufacturing sector were suffering from labor shortages in 1989, and the proportion increased to 60 percent in 1990 (Minister of Labor Secretariat Policy Planning and Research Department 1993). The labor shortage was a product of decades of unprecedented and unbridled economic expansion, unfavorable demographic changes (a declining birth rate and an aging population),[37] and

---

[37]The birth rate had declined by almost 32 percent from 2.14 children per family in 1965 to 1.46 in 1993—the world's lowest fertility rate. Japan has the fastest growing elderly population among industrialized countries. The proportion of the population over the age of 65 grew from 7.1 percent in 1970 to 10.3 percent in 1985 and then jumped to 14.5 percent in 1995.

the increasing unwillingness of better-educated and socially mobile Japanese youth to do unskilled jobs. In addition, rural labor supplies were depleted, further large increases in the employment of women and the elderly became unfeasible, and labor-saving mechanisms such as automation and further rationalization of production had begun to show serious limitations. As a result, labor-deficient firms became dependent on foreign workers as the only realistic and cost-efficient source of labor power. This rising demand for migrant labor was a powerful economic incentive that "pulled" the Japanese Brazilians to Japan.

Although strong macroeconomic pressures in *both* sending and receiving countries are the fundamental forces that initiate migration, the simultaneous conjunction of economic push forces in one country and pull forces in another does not, by itself, specify the *destination* of the migrant flow. Therefore, any attempt to comprehensively explain migration flows requires a "migration systems" approach, a dynamic and multicausal perspective that examines various transnational economic and sociopolitical connections between various sending and receiving countries that serve as bridges and links that channel and direct migrants to specific countries (see Kritz and Zlotnik 1992; Castles and Miller 1993:2–4; Fawcett 1989; Fawcett and Arnold 1987). In order to understand why the Brazilian nikkeijin migrated specifically to Japan in the late 1980s instead of to other advanced industrialized countries in need of migrant labor at the time, we must consider historical and contemporary sociopolitical linkages between Brazil and Japan.

What is notable about Japanese Brazilian return migration is that it occurred in the relative *absence* of close economic or political relationships between the two countries. Despite Japan's global economic expansion, it was not actively involved in the Brazilian economy in the 1980s,[38] and political ties and relations have also been weak.[39] Instead, it was transnational *ethnic* connections between the Brazilian nikkeijin and the Japanese

---

[38]Although Japanese foreign investment in Brazil rose briefly from the end of the 1960s to the early 1970s, it fell to miniscule levels in the 1980s. Likewise, Japanese trade with Brazil remains quite low. Since 1985, the total value of Japanese exports to Brazil has ranged from $1.44 billion to $1.8 billion, a mere 0.3 to 0.4 percent of the entire Japanese export trade.

[39]Except for a brief period of contact between the two governments at the beginning of the century to negotiate the acceptance of Japanese emigrants, there have not been any sustained political interactions, military conflicts, or relations of colonialism between the two countries that could have influenced migration from Brazil to Japan.

that directed the migrant flow specifically to Japan. As described in the first part of the chapter, the Japanese Brazilians in Brazil have developed strong transnational sentiments of affiliation with Japan, which has not only resulted in a relatively strong "Japanese" ethnic consciousness but also produced feelings of nostalgic longing for the ancestral homeland (see Tsuda forthcoming 2). In one survey of Japanese Brazilians, 86 percent of the respondents expressed a desire to visit the country of their parents and grandparents (Centro de Estudos 1992).

Therefore, when the Brazilian economic crisis of the late 1980s created considerable pressure to emigrate, the Japanese Brazilians naturally turned to Japan, not only because of the abundance of high-paying jobs there but also because of the strong consciousness of their ethnic connections to their ancestral homeland. Without this transnational ethnic link, the migrant flow would not have been initially directed toward Japan, given the country's highly restrictionist policies toward unskilled migrant workers, which made it very difficult for even the nikkeijin to obtain work visas before the revised Japanese immigration law was implemented in 1990. However, despite such difficulties, Japan seemed familiar and culturally accessible for the Japanese Brazilians. The very first migrants were also able to obtain sponsorship for visas and find jobs through their relatives in Japan. Given the importance of such ethnic ties in enabling the Japanese Brazilians to establish an immigrant "beachhead," it is significant and not coincidental that the first Japanese Brazilians who began emigrating in the mid-'80s were generally first-generation issei (most of whom have retained Japanese nationality) and second-generation nisei (with dual nationality), who had the closest ethnic attachments to Japan.

However, nikkeijin return migration was also caused by a strong awareness among the *Japanese* of their transnational ethnic ties with the Japanese Brazilians. With the revised Immigration Control and Refugee Recognition Act of 1990, the Japanese government decided to legally admit the nikkeijin without restriction up to the third generation because they were Japanese descendants with presumed cultural commonalities with the Japanese (see also Miyajima 1993:59; Sellek 1996:263; Yamanaka and Miyajima 1992).

Because Japanese immigration policy forbids the acceptance of any type of unskilled foreign worker, in the 1980s, Japan was suddenly confronted with a rapidly expanding stock of illegal immigrants from various Asian countries, who had come in response to the country's growing demand for foreign labor. There was considerable pressure on the Japanese government to lift the ban on unskilled migrant workers from certain sectors of the business community that were suffering the most from the labor shortage. Government ministries representing business interests also began taking a more liberal stance toward immigration. In addition, there was pressure from various nikkeijin associations and politicians in Brazil to eliminate the restrictive immigration barriers (Fujisaki 1991; Yamanaka 1996).

Faced with such economic and political pressures, the Japanese government decided to openly accept nikkeijin immigrants as a convenient means to alleviate a crippling labor shortage and reduce the influx of illegal foreign workers (cf. Kajita 1994:172; Sellek 1996:263). However, immigration policy makers from various ministries insist that this was not their true intent and do not officially recognize the nikkeijin as unskilled migrant workers. Instead, they ideologically justify the policy as an opportunity provided by the benevolence of the Japanese government to those of Japanese descent born abroad to explore their ethnic heritage and visit their ancestral homeland (Kajita 1994:170). Of course, Japanese ministry bureaucrats admit that the nikkeijin are in fact working in Japan, but it is repeatedly stressed that this will enable them to experience their ethnic homeland by visiting relatives, traveling, and learning the Japanese language and culture. By thus appealing to an ideology of transnational ethnic affiliation with the Brazilian nikkeijin based on common ancestry, the Japanese government was able to acquire a much-needed and docile migrant labor force without contradicting, at least at the level of official appearances, the fundamental principle of Japanese immigration policy that no unskilled foreign workers will be accepted.

In addition, because Japanese ethnic ideology privileges common descent as the basis for cultural affinity, government officials assumed that the nikkeijin would be culturally similar to the Japanese and would assimilate smoothly to Japanese society, in contrast to other foreigners (Roth 1999:47; Sasaki 1999:258; Yamanaka and Miyajima 1992:20). As a result, immigration policy makers viewed nikkeijin migrants as an effective way to deal with the labor shortage without disrupting Japan's cherished ethnic homogeneity (Miyajima 1993:59), thus avoiding the social disruption and ethnic conflict associated with culturally and racially different foreigners.

This effective use of an ideology of transnational ethnic affinity by the Japanese government made the open admission of the nikkeijin politically acceptable. In fact, the proposed change in immigration policy was generally supported by policy makers and did not cause any serious controversies or objections among the involved government ministries, in contrast to the conflicts that were occurring over other proposed revisions to the immigration law. Nor did the nikkeijin policy raise any concerns among the Japanese public or mass media, despite the intense public debates at the time about whether Japan should open its doors to migrants from Asia and the Middle East.

As a result, while the government strengthened the ban on the importation of unskilled foreign workers in 1990,[40] it implemented a virtual open-door policy toward the nikkeijin. Under the new immigration provisions, the nikkeijin are allowed to enter Japan on two types of visas, both of which are modifications of previous visa categories, more tailored to their needs. For the second-generation nisei, the previously restrictive requirements and procedures for obtaining the *Nihonjin no Haigusha* (Spouse of Japanese) visa were simplified, making it much easier for them to enter Japan, as long as they can prove their Japanese descent. The Ministry of Justice also set aside a new *Teijyusha* (Long-Term Resident) visa category for the sansei. These special visas have no activity restrictions, and although they are of limited duration (six months to three years), they can be renewed an indefinite number of times, as long as the individual's documents are in good order.[41] However, the legal status of the Japanese Brazilians in Japan is not as favorable as that of European-descent Brazilian immigrants in Germany, Portugal, and Italy, many of whom are granted citizenship upon "return" to their ethnic homelands. Nonetheless, because of the ethnic bias inherent in most immigration policies, the Japanese Brazilians, with their renewable work visas, are much better off than Brazilian immigrants in other countries who are not ethnic return migrants. For instance, many Brazilians in the United States are undocumented and must constantly worry about possible apprehension and deportation by the Immigration and Naturalization Service (Margolis 1994:175–78).

---

[40]The revised immigration law includes tough employer sanctions that impose fines of up to 2 million yen (about $20,000) or prison terms of up to 3 years on those employers and labor brokers who knowingly recruit and hire illegal aliens. This law was again revised in May 1997, further increasing penalties on organizations or individuals smuggling or assisting the illegal entry of foreign workers into Japan.

[41]The Spouse of Japanese visa for the nisei is generally for three years, whereas the Long-Term Resident visa for the sansei is generally for one year (despite its name).

The change in Japanese immigration policy opened the floodgates, enabling the mass immigration of the Japanese Brazilians. By the early 1990s, the first group of nikkeijin who had migrated to Japan began returning to Brazil with substantial earnings, and stories about their economic success were widely noticed and disseminated within the community. Although dekasegi migration to Japan initially was seen as a shame and embarrassment in the nikkeijin community and an indication of economic failure, such cultural attitudes weakened and quickly dissipated as the migrant returnees made the dream of quick riches in Japan seem readily attainable. As a result, not only did migration to Japan become socially accepted, it became an incredible economic opportunity too good to be passed up. By the early 1990s, a migrant rush to Japan (called the dekasegi "boom") was on, as the Japanese consulate in São Paulo was suddenly flooded with visa applications and flights headed for Japan were booked with eager Japanese Brazilians ready to take advantage of the economic opportunities awaiting them in their ancestral homeland.

In this manner, a "culture of migration" was firmly established among the Japanese Brazilians in Brazil. A community with a culture of migration is one in which positive attitudes and a high regard for the economic benefits of out-migration has developed and become firmly entrenched, creating a cultural propensity to move abroad for economic reasons (Cornelius 1991:112). As a result, migration becomes prevalent and routine to the point where the community's members are dependent on it as a critical means for economic survival, sustenance, and advancement. Although the return migration of the Japanese Brazilians is only a little over a decade old, about 18 percent of the entire Brazilian nikkeijin population of 1.2 million currently resides in Japan, and the number of immigrants continues to grow despite Japan's deep recession. This percentage is even more remarkable when we consider that it does not include a large group of individuals who have already migrated to Japan and returned to Brazil and that close to 45 percent of the Japanese Brazilian populace consists of very young and older individuals who generally do not migrate because of their age.

In addition to increasing the sheer volume of Japanese Brazilian dekasegi, the culture of migration also greatly diversified the migrant flow. As the economic advantages of return migration became culturally acknowledged and valued in the Brazilian nikkeijin community, an increasing number of individuals of higher socioeconomic status began to migrate.[42] Such individuals can be classified as "opportunity migrants" who migrate not because they are economically impoverished, but because they find themselves unable to support their middle-class standard of living and aspirations and wish to improve their deteriorating economic situation. Similarly, many of the Brazilians who emigrate to the United States are opportunity migrants whose middle-class status was being threatened by the Brazilian crisis (Goza 1999:771; Margolis 1994:29, 86; Martes 2000:72–73; Sales 1998:33). The development of a culture of migration in the Brazilian nikkeijin community also diversified the migrant flow in terms of generation and age. Although the first group of migrants were mainly issei along with a contingent of nisei, most dekasegi are now nisei and sansei, and the issei have become only a small minority (see table 3). At the same time, the migrant flow now consists of more younger people.[43]

Transnational social networks that link the sending community to the host country are another variable that considerably increases migrant flows. Their impact on nikkeijin migration will be analyzed in greater detail in chapter 4. Effective transnational labor broker and employment networks have been established between Brazil and Japan, which recruit Japanese Brazilians in Brazil and channel them into specific jobs in Japan. By automatically providing potential Japanese Brazilian migrants with jobs and housing in Japan as well as other services, this transnational labor broker network has encouraged further migration by greatly simplifying the process and reducing its risks and uncertainties.

Transnational personal networks between Japanese Brazilians living in Brazil and Japan have also expanded and diversified the migrant flow by increasing the number of chain migrants called over by their families or friends in Japan. A good number of nikkeijin have been encouraged to migrate by acquaintances living in Japan who speak positively about the

---

[42]A research survey conducted by the Japan Institute of Labor (1995) shows that before June 1990, only 21.2 percent of the migrant flow consisted of Japanese Brazilians who were "office workers" in Brazil (government bureaucrats, teachers, white-collar company workers, professionals, private business owners, and bankers). The proportion of such individuals almost doubled to 38.5 percent among those who entered Japan between June 1990 to April 1991. In contrast, the proportion of "technical workers/vocational workers" (including farmers) declined from 32.6 to 27.9 percent during the same two periods.

[43]Among those surveyed by the 1995 Japan Institute of Labor study, the proportion of migrants over 40 declined from 33.8 percent before June 1990 to 24.3 percent between June 1990 and April 1991, while those in their 20s increased in the same two periods from 10.1 to 42 percent.

economic opportunities there. Others migrate to join their spouses, who have decided to remain in Japan longer than expected and therefore wish to reunite with their families. However, there remains a notable economic component to such family chain migration since much more money can be earned and saved in Japan if both spouses are working as migrant laborers and it becomes no longer necessary to send remittances back home (cf. Yamanaka 2000:142). In fact, the number of Japanese Brazilians who cite relatives and friends in Japan as the *primary* reason they decided to migrate remains quite small.[44]

In this manner, various sets of causal variables—economic, ethnic, and sociocultural—have contributed to the return migration of the Japanese Brazilians in different ways. Once economic forces *instigated* migration, transnational ethnic connections *channeled* migration to Japan, while the creation of a culture of migration and transnational social networks further *expanded and diversified* the migrant flow. When the relative importance of these various influences on migration is considered, it becomes evident that a full understanding of any migration system requires an analysis of both economic and noneconomic factors. Although economic push-pull factors may be the initial and underlying force that fundamentally drives labor migration, they account for the movements of migrants only in a very general sense and do not explain the specificity of the migrant flow, in terms of either precise destination or exact composition. In other words, economic forces do not completely explain why the Japanese Brazilians migrated to Japan instead of to other First World countries with labor shortages, nor why so many opportunity and chain migrants eventually emigrated as well. Therefore, we cannot ignore the important ethnic and sociocultural forces that direct, shape, and expand the migrant flow.

In fact, once migration is initiated by economic factors, the sociocultural structures that are subsequently developed continue to sustain the migrant flow even if the original economic causes of migration somewhat weaken. Indeed, a severe and prolonged recession in Japan since 1992 has significantly reduced the economic incentives among the nikkeijin to migrate. On the Brazilian side, economic uncertainty has definitely continued in Brazil with the persistence of low wages and limited employment opportunities, an increase in the cost of living for the middle class (Martes 2000:64), and two major currency crises in recent

---

[44]According to one research survey, only 15.5 percent of all nikkeijin migrants were of this category (Japan Statistics Research Institute 1993).

years.[45] Nonetheless, since the implementation of the *Plano Real* in 1994, inflation has been brought under control and the economy has become more stable, compared to the crisis years of the 1980s. Although the economic reasons to migrate have therefore weakened to a certain extent, the number of Japanese Brazilians in Japan has continued to steadily increase (see table 1 below). Since migration is now culturally encouraged and highly effective transnational migrant labor and social networks have made the process so simple and easy, the stigma and personal cost of migration have been greatly reduced. Therefore, it takes less economic pressure nowadays to convince the nikkeijin to leave Brazil.[46] As a result, the migrant flow has become self-sustaining and somewhat independent of its original economic causes, making it relatively insensitive to cyclical economic fluctuations in either the host or the home country that can potentially reduce the level of migration.[47]

Basic Characteristics of the Japanese Brazilian Immigrant Population in Japan

By any measure, the continued expansion of the Japanese Brazilian immigrant population in Japan is remarkable. Table 1 shows the number of Brazilian nationals registered as foreigners in Japan since 1988.

---

[45]In early 1999, the global economic crisis that began in Asia finally hit Brazil, resulting in a sudden flight of foreign capital from the country despite an enormous $41.5 billion rescue loan package from the International Monetary Fund. Partly under international pressure, the government was forced to end its policy of supporting its currency's value at artificially high levels, causing a 40 percent decline in the currency's exchange rate against the dollar that resulted in a sharp projected increase in annual inflation (from under 2 percent to 17 percent) and an expected decline in economic growth. A similar devaluation of the currency occurred in 2001, this time caused by economic problems in Argentina and a worldwide economic slowdown, which reduced foreign investment in Brazil. The value of the currency declined to a record low as it lost 20 percent against the dollar, making it difficult for Brazil to repay its large foreign debt and forcing the central bank to raise interest rates. As a result, the IMF offered another emergency loan of $15 billion to Brazil in order to restore investor confidence in the country by preventing it from defaulting on its foreign debt.

[46]This does not mean that more nikkeijin are now migrating for noneconomic purposes. The latest surveys show that economic reasons for migration continue to predominate among the Japanese Brazilians (Kitagawa 1997:103).

[47]Likewise, Massey (1988) notes

the tendency for emigration to become progressively independent of the economic conditions that originally caused it. Once a critical takeoff stage is reached, the movement of population alters social and economic structures within sending communities in ways that increase the likelihood of subsequent migration.

Portes (1989:612–13) makes similar observations.

TABLE 1 Numbers of Foreigners from Brazil
Registered in Japan 1988–2000

1988	4,159
1989	14,528
1990	56,429
1991	119,333
1992	147,803
1993	154,650
1994	159,619
1995	176,440
1996	201,795
1997	233,254
1998	222,217
1999	224,299
2000	254,394

Source: Japanese Ministry of Justice, Immigration Bureau Statistics

These numbers include a few Brazilians of non-Japanese descent who are legally admitted to Japan on Teijyusha visas as spouses of the nikkeijin and make up a relatively small portion of the total immigrant population. In the absence of official statistics, it is very difficult to estimate what percentage of the Brazilian population in Japan consists of individuals who are not nikkeijin. Although I have seen estimates of about 4 percent, this figure seems too low based on my personal experiences. About 8 percent of my sample of informants and their spouses were non-nikkeijin Brazilians. In addition, the above statistics do not include issei who have retained Japanese nationality as well as nisei who are dual nationals and do not have to register as foreigners in Japan.[48] Although there are no official statistics, surveys indicate that about 10 percent of the nikkeijin dekasegi have Japanese nationality,[49] which would put the total current Brazilian

[48]Under the current Japanese *jus sanguinis* (blood-based) nationality laws, if either parent is a Japanese national, the offspring are automatically granted Japanese nationality as long as they are registered with the Japanese government within a certain period after birth.

[49]Two survey research projects conducted among nikkeijin immigrants in Japan (see Cornelius 1998; Japanese Institute of Labor 1995) place the figure at 9 percent and 13 percent respectively.

immigrant population at about 280,000. Despite the increasing number of mixed-descent mestiços among the Japanese Brazilians, they probably make up less than 10 percent of the entire immigrant population in Japan, although statistics vary widely.[50]

As is true with most immigrants, the Japanese Brazilians are not evenly distributed in Japan but are concentrated in certain industrial areas. The regions with the highest concentrations are the Tomo area of Gunma Prefecture (consisting primarily of Oizumi, Ota, and Tatebayashi cities) and the cities of Hamamatsu, Toyota, and Toyohashi in Aichi Prefecture. Large populations are also found in the Nagoya city area, as well as in Kanagawa Prefecture adjacent to Tokyo city, especially in and near Kawasaki, Tsurumi, and Fujisawa cities. The coastal areas of Shizuoka Prefecture also have notable numbers of Japanese Brazilians. The prefectures with the largest numbers of Brazilian nikkeijin are: Aichi (29,787), Shizuoka (25,012), Kanagawa (13,958), Saitama (10,804), Gunma (10,305), Chiba (6,727), and Tokyo city (6,238). The cities with the highest nikkeijin concentrations are Ota/Oizumi (4,222) and Hamamatsu (6,714). Other cities with notable populations are Nagoya (3,831), Tokyo (3,556), Kawasaki (1,698), Fujisawa (1,375), and Osaka (1.364).[51]

When compared with the overall age distribution of the Japanese Brazilians in Brazil, more of the nikkeijin migrants in Japan are in the middle age brackets and fewer are from the youngest and oldest age groups (see table 2). In terms of generational distribution, the migrant population in Japan consists of fewer issei and yonsei (fourth generation) and many more nisei than the general Japanese Brazilian population in Brazil (see table 3). Issei tend not to migrate as much; many are simply too old, and others feel embarrassed about returning to their homeland to take low-status jobs (see chapter 2; Yamanaka 1997:21). Also, there are few yonsei in the immigrant population because most are still children and the only ones in Japan are those who have accompanied their sansei parents. Nisei are overrepresented in Japan partly because many are still young, and it is easier for them to obtain a visa than for the sansei.

---

[50]Since the Japanese government does not officially count the number of mestiço nikkeijin entering or living in Japan, this percentage is only a very rough estimate based on my own research sample and two surveys of nikkeijin conducted by the Japan Statistics Research Institute (1993) and JICA (1992) in which 17.3 percent and 5.6 percent of the respondents were of mixed blood. In my sample, about 6 percent were of mixed descent.

[51]These population figures are from 1995 except for Ota/Oizumi and Fujisawa.

TABLE 2 Age Distribution of the Japanese Brazilians

Japan		Brazil	
Age	*%*	*Age*	*%*
0–14	9	0–15	31.5
15–24	26.8	16–30	22.7
25–44	50.1	31–45	19.4
45–64	13.9	46–60	15.1
over 65	0.2	over 61	9.7

Source: Japanese Ministry of Justice, Immigration Bureau (1994 statistics) and São Paulo Humanities Research Center (1987–88)

Contrary to rumors in the nikkeijin community, the Japanese Brazilians who migrate to Japan are not necessarily of lower socioeconomic background than those who remain behind in Brazil. Survey data indicate that over 20 percent of them are university educated[52] and that 65 percent had middle-class occupations in Brazil,[53] figures that are roughly equivalent with those for nikkeijin living in Brazil (São Paulo Humanities Research Center 1987–1988; Centro de Estudos 1992).[54] In stark contrast to their social status in Brazil, a vast majority of the Japanese Brazilians in Japan work as unskilled or low-skilled manual laborers in the factories of small and medium-sized companies.[55] Only 3.5 to 10 percent of the nikkeijin immigrants are office workers (JICA 1992; Kitagawa 1992). They

---

[52]The questionnaire surveys by Kitagawa (1997) and the Japan Statistics Research Institute (1993) both report that over 20 percent of the Japanese Brazilians in Japan are university educated. The Centro de Estudos Nipo-Brasileiros survey (1992) shows a lower rate, with only 14.3 percent of the respondents being university educated.

[53]The occupational breakdown was as follows: white-collar office worker (25 percent), public official (4 percent), entrepreneur (14.5 percent), professional (7.7 percent), student (27.9 percent), farmer (5.7 percent), housewife (2.5 percent) (Kitagawa 1997:97). Only 0.8 percent were unskilled workers. Other survey reports show similar results (see JICA 1992; Kitagawa 1992, 1993).

[54]Frequently, middle-class migrants with better social and educational resources are the first to leave, paving the way for poorer, lower-class migrants later (Margolis 1994:92; Piore 1979). In the Japanese Brazilian case, however, we do not observe such sequential migration because only nikkeijin (and their Brazilian spouses), who are predominantly middle class, are allowed to legally enter Japan.

[55]According to surveys, up to 90 percent of the Japanese Brazilians are in unskilled or semi-skilled jobs (JICA 1992; Kitagawa 1992).

TABLE 3 Generational Distribution of the Japanese Brazilians

Japan		Brazil	
Generation	*%*	*Generation*	*%*
issei	7.5	issei	12.5
nisei	46.4	nisei	30.8
sansei	36.9	sansei	41.3
yonsei	0.0	yonsei	12.9

Source: Kitagawa (1997) and São Paulo Humanities Research Center (1987–88)

are usually translators and liaisons in Japanese labor broker firms and companies, local government offices, or assistance organizations. A very small but growing number of them have also opened ethnic businesses that cater to the Japanese Brazilian immigrant community. Close to 75 percent of the nikkeijin dekasegi are employed in the manufacturing industry, but there are also sizable numbers working in the construction (7.4 percent) and food service industries (7.9 percent). A few also work as elderly caretakers or nurses in hospitals and nursing homes (4 percent).[56] I have also heard of Japanese Brazilians employed as golf caddies, building security officers, hotel maids, janitors, newspaper deliverers, and gas station attendants, and even in funeral homes. The companies in which they work vary greatly in size from small subcontractors employing a few dozen workers to larger subcontractors employing hundreds.

Much of the daily lives of the Japanese Brazilians is dominated by long days in the factories. Since many of them work overtime in order to increase their migrant earnings, this leaves them with relatively little time for recreation and social life. During the height of the Japanese bubble economy in the late 1980s and early 1990s, they were working an average of more than 10 hours a day, and a vast majority worked overtime all day on Saturday as well (Kitagawa 1992). Although the Japanese Brazilians lead economically centered lives in Japan, it is the ethnic aspects of their migrant experiences that are the most interesting and will be the focus of the remainder of this book.

---

[56]These figures are from the Japan Institute of Labor study in 1995. The Japanese government's immigration statistics (for 1994) show that 80 percent of the Brazilians registered as foreigners in Japan work in manufacturing, 5.2 percent work in the service sector, and 9.5 percent work in offices.

CHAPTER 2

From Positive to Negative Minority

Ethnic Prejudice and "Discrimination" Toward
the Japanese Brazilians in Japan

INTRODUCTION:
THE IMPACT OF MIGRATION ON MINORITY STATUS

WHEN MIGRANTS relocate to a new society, they usually acquire a completely different ethnic status. Those who were part of the majority society back home find that they have become an immigrant minority in the host country. However, even for those who were already ethnic minorities in their countries of origin, migration entails a significant change in ethnic status from one type of minority to another.

This is true even for ethnic return migrants. Although they are considered ethnic minorities in the countries where they reside because of their foreign origins, when they migrate "back" to their ancestral homelands, they are usually not socially incorporated as part of the majority host society either. Despite the absence of racial differences with the host populace, they become a new type of ethnic minority because of the cultural differences they have acquired while living abroad for generations. Their social segregation in their ethnic homeland as culturally foreign minorities is further exacerbated if they become unskilled migrant workers who are a marginalized part of the working class.

The racial phenotype that marks the nikkeijin as a minority in Brazil ceases to be a source of ethnic differentiation in Japan, making them strictly a cultural minority. However, the cultural basis for their new minority status in Japan is quite different from the cultural aspects of their former minority status in Brazil. Whereas in Brazil they were perceived as culturally "Japanese," in Japan they become an ethnic minority because they are seen as so culturally "Brazilian." This is analogous to what has happened to ethnic Germans who have return migrated from Eastern Europe and the former Soviet Union to Germany. Although they were seen as "German" ethnic minorities in their countries of birth, when they "return" to their German ancestral homeland, they are seen as "Russians," "Poles," and "Romanians" by majority Germans and therefore become new ethnic minorities (see Münz and Ohliger 1998).

In the case of Japanese Brazilian return migration, the change from a "Japanese" to a "Brazilian" ethnic minority status is also accompanied by a dramatic shift from a "positive" to a "negative" minority status. This "decline" involves a sudden drop in both social class position and cultural status in Japan. Although the Japanese Brazilians are a socially successful middle-class minority in Brazil that is culturally respected for its "Japanese" qualities, they become low-status factory workers in Japan who are culturally disparaged to a certain extent for their "Brazilian" behavior. As a result, they are subject to both social class prejudice and ethnic prejudice in Japan, which has the potential to lead to ethnically discriminatory behavior.

This chapter examines the negative minority status of Brazilian nikkeijin immigrants in Japan by exploring the nature of Japanese prejudice and discrimination toward them. Since I interviewed only a limited number of Japanese and conducted participant observation in only one factory and two cities in Japan, my sample is by no means representative. However, because my Japanese informants were in daily contact with the Japanese Brazilians, my analysis does give some sense of how the Japanese have reacted to nikkeijin immigrants and how this has affected Japanese ethnic attitudes and assumptions. In addition, given the regularity of many of the responses of my informants, they undoubtedly represent some widely held attitudes in Japanese society about the Brazilian nikkeijin.

ETHNIC PREFERENCE BASED ON COMMON DESCENT

In general, ethnic prejudice toward the Japanese Brazilians was not very pronounced among the Japanese I interviewed. Although the nikkeijin are perceived to be culturally Brazilian and therefore not ethnically Japanese, because they are of Japanese descent, most Japanese feel a certain amount of affinity with them and prefer them to foreigners of non-Japanese descent, who are completely alien. Even those Japanese informants who actively disliked foreign workers in general and wished they would promptly leave Japan said that they could at least tolerate the presence of nikkeijin immigrants and learn to live with them if necessary.

Many of my informants mentioned how they felt *shitashimi* (familiarity and affinity) toward the Brazilian nikkeijin because of their shared descent, and sometimes even referred to them as *doho* (brethren) or *miuchi* (companions of the inner circle). Therefore, there was a strong sense that the nikkeijin could somehow be comprehended despite their different behavioral patterns and language. For example, this type of general sentiment was expressed by a Japanese factory worker in Oizumi:

> Discrimination and disparagement is less toward the Brazilian nikkeijin because they have a Japanese face. This creates a feeling of commonality with them as our brethren. Since we see them as people who were originally Japanese, we feel closer to them than other foreigners. There is much more discrimination toward the Korean Japanese.

Therefore, some of my informants felt safer and more at ease with the Japanese Brazilians than with other foreign workers. According to one local Japanese business owner:

> At least with the nikkeijin, we feel their blood ties as part of the Japanese group and a sense of commonality and security, in contrast to other foreign workers whom we approach with caution because some of them look scary and are a source of fear. I tend to relax more and feel safer with nikkeijin because of this sense of affinity.

Because my informants' ethnic preferences were based on perceived degrees of racial closeness in this manner, a few of them mentioned that discrimination and prejudice were higher toward mixed-descent nikkeijin (*konketsu*), who are seen as more foreign in contrast to nikkeijin of pure Japanese descent.

SOCIAL CLASS PREJUDICES TOWARD THE NIKKEIJIN DEKASEGI

Although the Japanese Brazilians are ethnically preferred by the Japanese over other immigrants, they have still become a negative minority in Japan as unskilled factory workers performing low-status jobs that are actively shunned and denigrated by most Japanese. In fact, many of my Japanese informants had negative stereotypes of the nikkeijin as people of low socioeconomic origins in general who had suffered a long history of poverty and migration. Therefore, the Brazilian nikkeijin are subject to a certain amount of social class prejudice from majority Japanese, based on both their current low occupational status in Japan and their stigmatized migration legacy.

The negative Japanese perception of the migration history of the Japanese Brazilians begins with the emigration of their parents and grandparents from Japan. Depending on the attitudes that a society has toward emigration in general, considerable social stigma can be attached to those who leave the homeland permanently because of economic difficulties. Emigration as a response to economic hardship was never culturally approved in Japan, nor did it ever become widespread, despite efforts by the Japanese government to promote it as a means to deal with serious rural overpopulation and poverty. Since the beginning of the Meiji Period in 1868, when Japan was finally opened to the rest of the world after centuries of isolation, only 1.04 million Japanese have emigrated permanently, a very small number compared with the current Japanese population of over 127 million.[1] Although it has become quite common nowadays for Japanese to leave the country for a temporary sojourn abroad for business or educational reasons, permanent emigration is still seen as somewhat improper. Such attitudes were evident in my conversations with various Japanese, but a young female freelance journalist expressed them most clearly:

> For a Japanese, to leave Japan permanently is abnormal—it is not a proper thing to do. So we always wonder why an individual left Japan and divide emigrants into two categories: those who left because they had no intellectual or personal ability and thus couldn't live in Japan and those who had too much ability and for whom Japan was too narrow to realize their potential. Therefore, they needed to be accepted in a different world.

Because most Japanese emigrants to Brazil originated from poor rural areas and left the country because of serious economic difficulties, they were seen by many of the Japanese I spoke with as uneducated people of low social class who did not have the ability to survive economically in Japan and thus had no choice but to abandon their homeland and emi-

---

[1]Emigration statistics calculated from *Kokusai Jinryu*, July 1990.

grate abroad to escape their hopeless poverty (cf. Maeyama 1982:32, 1996:9–10).[2] Such social class prejudices toward the issei were expressed by my Japanese informants in various ways, but a statement by an older, middle-class Tokyo resident was somewhat representative:

> The Japanese do not perceive the nikkeijin well. They are seen as people who were from rural villages and were poor. They were the type of low-level people who couldn't survive in Japan, so they had to discard Japan and go abroad. They are seen as *nihonjin shikkaku* (not worthy of being Japanese)—people who didn't have much ability.

A middle-aged housewife in Oizumi was even more explicit in her portrayal of Japanese emigrants as poverty-stricken, social failures:

> The nikkeijin are low-class people (*teikyu na hito*). They were Japanese *ochikobore* (social dropouts) who were poor and uneducated. These were people who had nothing in Japan, so said to themselves, "Regardless of how horrible things are overseas, they can't be worse than my life in Japan." Therefore, they abandoned their own country and fled abroad.

Such pejorative attitudes toward emigrants are especially strong in countries like Japan where the standard cultural attitude and expectation is that one should struggle and endure at home whatever the circumstances, instead of giving up and emigrating (cf. Staniford 1973b:13). Although not always prevalent among my informants, such attitudes were expressed by some, including an official who worked for the Oizumi municipal government:

> We Japanese say *ganbare* (keep trying and put in the effort) and we don't give up easily. The Japanese are originally village people. They stay where

---

[2]Japanese attitudes toward those who emigrated as colonists to occupied Asian territories such as Manchuria during the prewar period of imperialist expansion are quite different (see Staniford 1973a). Although many of the colonists emigrated because of economic difficulties at home as well, they were promoting Japan's national interests and imperialist aspirations abroad, while others were members of the Japanese elite. As a result, they were not socially stigmatized but somewhat glorified. In addition, unlike the Japanese emigrants to the Americas, they returned to Japan after World War II.

they are born and don't move around. So if you abandon and leave your country because of problems, this is disapproved of and not liked. One should stay and try one's best, as a matter of necessity.

Therefore, when speaking about the emigration legacy of the nikkeijin, my informants used phrases such as "*akiramepokkata*" (they gave up too easily), "*nihon o suteta*" (they abandoned or discarded Japan) or "*nihon o nigeta*" (they fled Japan). Many of them were not aware that most of the emigrants left Japan as dekasegi only for a temporary sojourn abroad and planned to return in several years with a fortune. Except for a minority, they did not intend to permanently "abandon" Japan, despite the economic desperation some of them faced.

A minority of my Japanese informants held less prejudiced opinions of the issei and described them as hapless victims of bad fate and circumstances beyond their control instead of attributing their low social class status and subsequent emigration to personal failure and inadequacy. For instance, one Japanese factory worker said:

> I read a book about nikkeijin emigrants once. Even if they had intelligence, if they lived in rural areas and were the fifth child, they couldn't get educated or inherit property like the eldest son. Therefore, even if they had ability, they didn't have the opportunity. If they had the chance in Japan, they might have succeeded and realized their potential. So it wasn't something that was within their own power. I consider it more a product of their birth and upbringing. Japan was a poor country back then and there were lots of poor people who had no choice but to go abroad.

Some of my informants also regarded the Japanese emigrants as more resourceful and courageous than other poor Japanese who stayed behind in Japan. In contrast to the majority, who felt that the nikkeijin issei were "quitters" who fled abroad instead of struggling at home, these informants felt that the emigrants were the ones who were willing to continue struggling in an active attempt to improve their lives abroad instead of passively accepting their poverty in Japan.

Social class prejudices toward Japanese emigrants were more prevalent among older Japanese than among the younger generation, who are not as familiar with the history or the circumstances under which the Japanese emigrated abroad. Born and raised in an age of prosperity, they do not have a historical memory of an earlier period when Japan was still a country with acute economic disparities and stronger social prejudice toward the poor. In general, my younger informants felt that they have less ethnic prejudice toward the nikkeijin when compared with their elders.

Although the derogatory attitudes that many of my Japanese informants had about the emigration of the nikkeijin apply mainly to the issei and are not directly relevant to their nisei and sansei descendants, they color the Japanese view of the nikkeijin in general. A number of my informants associated the Brazilian nikkeijin with poor rural farmers and low social class status, whether they were talking about issei, nisei, or sansei. Even some who were conscious that many nikkeijin descendants have attained a higher socioeconomic position in Brazil continued to see them in a negative light because they were supposedly raised by poor, uneducated parents. In this sense, the stigma of low social class attached to the original Japanese emigrants tends to persist even into the younger generations of nikkeijin. For instance, one middle-class Japanese housewife in Oizumi frankly observed: "Even if lots of the nisei are now middle class and well educated, I think if you get to know them better, their low social origins will eventually come out. When the parents are poor and uneducated, it undoubtedly shows up in their children." One Japanese Brazilian graduate student in Japan discussed this lingering ethnic stigma he continues to feel from the Japanese:

> I don't know if I sometimes imagine this, but even as a sansei, I feel we are looked down upon because we are the descendants of poor and unfortunate emigrant people who had to leave Japan. As an immigrant descendent, I feel they will look down on us forever from a position of superiority and a sense that they were fortunate for not having had to leave Japan. Older Japanese always seem to bring this up. They ask about your parents and grandparents and about your parents' occupation in Brazil in order to figure out your family's background. They try to reconstruct the history of your *ie* (household).

The social class prejudices that many Japanese have toward Brazilian nikkeijin are not only based on images of their stigmatized and impoverished emigration legacy but also a product of negative perceptions of their currently low social class status in Japan as dekasegi. Since migration in

general tends to have strong negative social class connotations of poverty
and economic misery in Japan and has never been valued, glorified, or
seen as integral to the formation of the nation-state, the category of
"dekasegi" has quite negative social class connotations. It originally referred to poor Japanese farmers from rural areas in the colder northern regions of Japan (such as the Tohoku area and Hokkaido) who migrate to
the warmer southwestern cities in search of temporary work as seasonal laborers during the winter. Therefore, the dekasegi is seen as a person of low
social class who has to constantly migrate to avoid poverty. Since the
Japanese Brazilians are also classified as dekasegi, they are subject to the
same type of class prejudice from majority Japanese as poor people who
could not survive economically in Brazil and were thus forced to come to
Japan to earn the needed money. Consider this typical comment by a
middle-aged doctor:

> Our attitude toward the nikkeijin is the same as the image of poverty we
> have of Japanese dekasegi—they are people who suffered in Brazil and
> couldn't eat and survive so have come to Japan. It is sad. So our preju-
> dice toward them is not because they are nikkeijin, but because they are
> of a low class level. It the same prejudice we have toward Japanese who
> are poor.

Some of my Japanese informants seemed to simply assume that the
Japanese Brazilians are poor in Brazil by virtue of their status as dekasegi
in Japan. This image is reinforced by the dominant perception of Brazil
(and other Third World countries) as impoverished and underdeveloped
in general (cf. Lie 2001:33), especially among Japanese factory workers,
who generally had no idea how advanced and modernized parts of Brazil
are. Few were aware that the Japanese Brazilians enjoy a relatively high
standard of living there as part of its urban middle class and are migrating
to Japan not as economically dispossessed people but to take advantage of
the tremendous wage differential between the two countries in order to
better their lives in Brazil.

A few of the Japanese I interviewed were better informed about the socioeconomic background of the Japanese Brazilians through their exposure
to the Japanese media, which seems to self-consciously avoid commonly
held social class prejudices about the nikkeijin as poverty-stricken migrants
by emphasizing their middle-class status in Brazil. Other informants rea-
soned that the nikkeijin, as Japanese descendants, would at least have

higher standards than ordinary Brazilians and must be better off and more socially successful. For such individuals, the Japanese Brazilians have return migrated as lowly dekasegi not necessarily because of their destitution, but because Brazil itself is a poor and economically troubled Third World country in contrast to rich, First World Japan. In this manner, blame is shifted from individual poverty to general national poverty.

When the unfavorable image of the current economic desperation of the nikkeijin dekasegi is combined with the perception of them as descendants of low-class Japanese emigrants, it seems to create a double stigma that worsens their socioeconomic evaluation. In other words, the nikkeijin, as descendants of those who initially fled to Brazil because they could not survive in Japan, have now returned to Japan because they could not survive economically in Brazil either. Therefore, their migration legacy is seen as involving a double economic failure—first in Japan, then in Brazil. "I think the nikkeijin are no good, poor people," said one resident of Oizumi, who was the most explicit about his feelings. "They went to Brazil as poor immigrants, but couldn't succeed in Brazil, so they come back to Japan now. If they tried hard, they would not be so poor." Others see the difficult migration history of the Japanese Brazilians with pity, as is evident in this statement by an older, retired man:

> The Brazilian nikkeijin are people who are really *kawaiso* (unfortunate, deserving pity) because they suffered in both Japan and Brazil. They had to leave Japan because they couldn't live here, but since the economic and political situation is so bad in Brazil, they have to come back to Japan because they couldn't survive there either. There is nothing so *nasakenai* (miserable, lamentable).

A few of my more outspoken informants even viewed the dekasegi motives of the Japanese Brazilians as downright shameful and despicable, as shown by the comments of a middle-aged housewife:

> I just can't respect these dekasegi nikkeijin. They come to Japan from Brazil just for the money after their parents left Japan decades ago. If they abandoned Japan and fled to Brazil because they were poor and couldn't survive here, that's where they should stay instead of coming back again because Japan is now rich and they are still poor in Brazil. I just don't like this type of dirty consciousness (*kitanai konjyo*).

As is apparent in the above comments and those from other informants, the emigration and return migration of the nikkeijin has strong negative connotations because of an expectation that those who leave Japan should come back only when they have achieved superior status and wealth, not as lowly dekasegi in search of money again. This type of social class stigma is, of course, especially strong toward the original issei emigrants who have now return migrated to Japan, especially since a number of them left decades ago with considerable fanfare and hopes of making a fortune in Brazil.[3] In addition to their advanced age, the embarrassment of returning to Japan as lowly dekasegi (equivalent to an admission of migrant failure in Brazil) is another reason there are few issei in Japan. One issei dekasegi I interviewed told me he would never visit his relatives in Japan because of this shame, even though he was a *jun-nisei* who had emigrated to Brazil with his parents when he was very young.

Because of the dominant association of the Japanese Brazilians with low social class origins and current migrant poverty, it was no surprise that most of my Japanese informants assumed that they are not only impoverished in Brazil but also live very poorly as immigrants in Japan. The Japanese Brazilians in Japan receive good salaries (sometimes earning higher hourly wages than Japanese full-time workers) and are provided with quality housing by their companies or labor broker firms. However, because most Japanese do not have much contact with them, their negative images about Japanese Brazilian impoverishment in Japan are based not on actual empirical fact or observation but simplistic preconceptions about the low-class poverty of migrant foreigners in general in comparison to the Japanese.

Partly because of decades of increasing prosperity and declining income inequality in Japan after World War II, an egalitarian social class ideology has developed in the country where most Japanese perceive

---

[3]As Roosens (1994:99) notes, migrants who return home after an extended period abroad are frequently seen unfavorably in this manner by their former countrymen:

> Particularly when the natives who stayed behind had to endure difficult times in order to improve their socio-economic situation, returnees are resented as disloyal people who fled their community and nation when their presence and efforts were badly needed. They are seen as people who return home when the battle is over.

themselves to be economically well-off and therefore middle class.[4] In this manner, Japanese ethno-national identity is defined not only by race and culture but also by a sense of First World prosperity so that being Japanese has become synonymous with being middle class. As is the case with perceived racial and cultural differences, the social class basis for Japanese national identity is given distinctive meaning through contrasts with external others, in this case, immigrant workers from Third World countries, who are seen as uniformly poor and therefore of low social class (cf. Lie 2001:28–33). In other words, the rich First World versus poor Third World dichotomy has simply been mapped onto social class differences at the domestic level so that the Japanese are perceived as middle class while immigrant workers are seen as low class.

Middle-class Japanese I met or interviewed (students and white-collar workers) generally believed that the nikkeijin immigrants in Japan were earning low wages and living in crowded and dilapidated housing. Therefore, when they actually met the nikkeijin dekasegi or were told of their living conditions in Japan, they were quite surprised that they were not living in poverty. For instance, when I went on a research trip to Toyohashi (in Aichi Prefecture) to study the foreign worker problem with a group of Japanese graduate students, they were amazed that the Japanese Brazilians they met did not seem *mijime* (miserable, wretched) and were "properly dressed with nice shirts and socks." Another group of undergraduate students on a class assignment to interview nikkeijin workers expected them to be living in squalor and were thus impressed and amazed to find that they lived in clean apartments built to the same standards as those for the Japanese, earned good wages, and had decent lives in Japan.

---

[4]The relatively low consciousness of social class differences among Japanese has been noted by researchers such as De Vos (see 1992:chapter 1 for a summary), Turner (1995), and Dore (1986:105). Although 36 percent of Americans identify with the middle class and a larger 61 percent see themselves as either working or low class (*The New York Times*, March 5, 1996, A8), there is no such cleavage in class consciousness among the Japanese, with about 90 percent considering themselves middle class (see Turner 1995:10; van Wolferen 1990:268). Kelly (1993:195–96) also discusses the discourse on a "classless class-consciousness" that has emerged in Japan. Since World War II, economic inequalities between rich and poor in Japan have decreased, and the country now has one of the lowest income disparities in the world, with the richest 20 percent earning only 4.3 times the income of the poorest 20 percent (World Bank 1992) (although Douglass [2000:100] claims that economic disparities in Japan are much wider than they appear in public data).

In addition to being associated with low-class immigrant poverty in Japan, the Brazilian nikkeijin are also subject to notable social status prejudice from middle-class Japanese because of their working-class jobs in Japanese factories. The social stigma attached to unskilled "3K" factory jobs characterized as *kiken* (dangerous), *kitanai* (dirty), and *kitsui* (difficult)[5] has grown in recent years as an increasingly better-educated populace has actively shunned such degrading and demeaning occupations. As a result, factory work is now seen as reserved only for the least educated sector of the Japanese populace at the lowest rungs of the social hierarchy (and for a growing number of foreigners). Those who are still stuck in working-class jobs are subject to a certain amount of disdain and disrespect as people without much personal ability. Such negative attitudes were expressed by a number of my white-collar informants, including a female journalist:

> Manual workers who are Japanese are now disappearing and most Japanese do work that requires them to use their heads. So we don't respect those who are still assembly-line workers. If they have the will and put in the effort, they should be able to rise in social status to become at least a factory manager. But those who are still unskilled workers have abandoned the challenge, so we don't respect them. In this day and age, when Japan is rich and there are plenty of chances to get a university education, there is something wrong with these people. They either had no ability, didn't try, or didn't have a chance to get a proper education.

In fact, one Japanese factory worker I came to know well talked about the social inferiority he feels as a blue-collar worker in Japanese society:

> I am always conscious about my low status as a worker without a university education. I feel this even among my relatives. When we get together, those who are university educated keep to themselves and don't bother to associate with us, because they look down on us. Japan is a really close-minded society.

Since even many middle-class Japanese do not know that the nikkeijin are also of middle-class background, they tend to equate the Japanese

---

[5]These jobs can also be called "5K" because they are also disliked (*kirai*) and despised (*keibetsu sareru*). Of course, in English, they would be "5D" jobs (dirty, dangerous, difficult, disliked, and despised).

Brazilians with unskilled working-class Japanese and regard them with the same type of social disdain (cf. Lie 2001:33). A resident of Oizumi expressed a commonly held sentiment among some middle-class Japanese when he said: "I see the nikkeijin as low status because of their educational level, just like Japanese factory workers. Both are at about the same level. So when compared with the average Japanese level, the nikkeijin are much lower."

However, social class prejudices toward Japanese Brazilian immigrants were prevalent even among Japanese blue-collar workers. Although they perform the same factory jobs as their nikkeijin counterparts on the assembly line, they also assumed that the nikkeijin are much poorer, and thus of lower social class. In fact, most of the workers at Toyama (including some supervisors) believed that the Japanese Brazilians were hired at very low salaries in order to cut production costs and few were aware that they were being paid high hourly wages. This ignorance was reinforced by the Toyama management (as well as nikkeijin labor broker firms), who instructed their workers not to talk about their wages in order to avoid conflict.[6] In fact, a group of Japanese women workers even told me that there was a general rumor that the nikkeijin earn under $1,000 a month, which they figured was not enough to survive in Japan. A retired Toyama worker summarized the general impression that many of them have of the economic plight of the nikkeijin:

> I hear conditions are terrible in Brazil and they can't live over there, so they come to Japan for the money and are stuffed six to a room in pig-pens by labor broker companies who don't treat them as humans. Since the cost of living here is much higher, they find they can't survive in Japan and can't buy anything because it's too expensive. I doubt they are able to save any money.

ETHNIC PREJUDICE BASED ON NEGATIVE PERCEPTIONS OF JAPANESE BRAZILIAN CULTURAL BEHAVIOR

Disappointed Ethnic Expectations

As we have seen, the nikkeijin tend to be economically stigmatized as a negative minority in Japan because of unfavorable images about their past

---

[6]I have heard of other factories in which the nikkeijin and Japanese workers are told not to discuss their wages.

migration legacy, prejudiced assumptions about their current migrant poverty, and their degraded social class status as unskilled factory workers in Japan. However, negative minority status has a cultural component as well. The Japanese Brazilians are also subject to a certain amount of ethnic prejudice because their *cultural* differences are regarded negatively by many Japanese.

Many of my Japanese informants expected the nikkeijin to be culturally Japanese because of racialized conceptions of ethnicity and were disappointed when they realized how Brazilian they have become. Racial descent is of primary importance in the definition of Japanese ethnic identity (see Kajita 1994:169–70; Kondo 1986:76; Yoshino 1992) and takes precedence over "culture" as the first and foremost criterion that determines who can be considered "Japanese,"[7] because those who are "racially" Japanese (i.e., of Japanese descent) are assumed to be "culturally" Japanese as well (see also Kondo 1986). This assumed correspondence between race and culture is the result of Japan's ideology of ethnic homogeneity in which all Japanese are seen as the same race and as culturally similar in thinking and behavior (cf. Yoshino 1992:120).[8] This attitude was exemplified by the comments of one neighborhood doctor to whom I spoke:

> When you live in Japan, you come to take this for granted. Everyone looks Japanese and we all think and act in more or less the same way. So when we see someone who has a Japanese face, we end up thinking that they are like the Japanese—that they will speak and behave like the Japanese [i.e., be culturally Japanese].

This essentialist ethnic assumption applies not only to the Japanese in Japan but also, to a lesser extent, to those of Japanese descent born abroad, because it is assumed that Japanese culture will be transmitted

---

[7]This is shown in the case of the Korean Japanese and other foreigners of non-Japanese descent, who can never be considered ethnically Japanese even if they are born and raised in Japan and have become *culturally* indistinguishable from the Japanese (Wagatsuma 1982:313). Yoshino provides a close analysis of such ethnic attitudes among his Japanese informants and among scholars of the *nihonjinron* tradition (1992:24, 115–19; see also Befu 1993:115–16). Harootunian (1988:438) makes a similar point in his historical analysis of Japanese national identity (cf. Weiner 1997a).

[8]In this manner, when race and culture are seen as correlated, they tend to be conflated (Medina 1997).

through family socialization to those of Japanese descent regardless of national boundaries. Therefore, there was a strong expectation among most of my Japanese informants that the Brazilian nikkeijin should have literally "inherited" a considerable amount of Japanese culture, even if they were born in a foreign country, because they were raised by Japanese parents. The Japanese undoubtedly realize that the Japanese Brazilians have become culturally foreign to a certain extent, and some are not sure how much of the Japanese language and behavior they have retained abroad. Despite this, however, many Japanese anticipate that there will be strong cultural commonalities and continuities. Such essentialist ethnic attitudes toward the nikkeijin are clearly expressed in the following statement by a local store owner, which echoes the sentiments of many of my Japanese informants:

> We think the Brazilian nikkeijin, as descendants of Japanese, must have retained good Japanese traditions because even if born abroad, they grew up in Japanese families. So they must be like the Japanese, at least a little . . . if their face is pure Japanese, we have the idea that their customs and attitudes will be at an above average Japanese level.

In this manner, despite geographical separation and different national backgrounds, a consciousness of transnational ethnic commonality with the nikkeijin has been created among the Japanese because of essentialist ethnic feelings of cultural similarity based on the primacy of racial and blood ties (cf. Roth 1999:28). Therefore, the cultural foreignness of the nikkeijin and the inability of most of them to speak the language properly are disillusioning and disappointing for most Japanese (cf. Ono and Wakisaka 1973:537–38).[9] Although some of those I interviewed felt that this loss of Japanese culture was more or less natural, many of them expressed their reactions with such words as *gakkari* (disappointed), *kitai hazure* (did not meet expectations), *shitsubo* (disappointing, disillusioning). In this manner, the loss of Japanese culture among the Japanese Brazilians becomes a *stigma*—an attribute that is discrediting because it is incongruous with social expectations (see Goffman 1963:3). Some Japanese I spoke with mentioned that the nikkeijin who cannot speak Japanese

---

[9]Surveys show that only 20 to 30 percent of the Japanese Brazilians in Japan can communicate in Japanese (Kitagawa 1992, 1993). About 10 to 13 percent have no speaking ability.

are seen as "second-rate Japanese" or "inadequate Japanese" (see also Taji-ma 1995:190, 1998:191–92).

Since the ethnic stigma that most nikkeijin carry is seen to be the result of personal deficiencies and failings, they are frequently held responsible for their cultural inadequacy (cf. Goffman 1963:4). Many of my Japanese informants who spoke about this issue generally faulted the issei parents for not raising their children according to Japanese cultural standards by properly teaching them the Japanese language in Brazil. Others, such as the local store owner cited above, pointed to what they perceived to be a lack of personal effort and intellectual ability among the Japanese Brazilians:

> It all depends on how much the nikkeijin know the Japanese language and cultural customs. Despite the high expectations we initially have of them, we become very disappointed when we meet them because they can't speak Japanese. It is all a personal attitude problem of the nikkeijin. If they are trying hard to learn the Japanese language here, I respect them for it and see it as admirable. Unfortunately, such nikkeijin are very few. With those who make no effort to learn Japanese, we say, *nanda* ("What the hell?"). Although they are nikkeijin, they are *darashiganai* (lazy and not disciplined), and I start to wonder if they really want to work hard and begin to doubt their way of living. We feel they are lazy people (*namakemono*) and look down on them.

A "Low" Brazilian Culture

The Japanese Brazilians are stigmatized because of their alien Brazilian cultural characteristics as well. It should be noted here that not all of my Japanese informants viewed the cultural attributes of the Japanese Brazilians in a generally negative manner. A few Japanese I spoke with had positive impressions of the Japanese Brazilians and liked their friendly openness, lightheartedness, and casualness, in contrast to which they portrayed the Japanese as cold, formal, too socially self-conscious, and sensitive. Most of these rare individuals had very close relationships with the nikkeijin, and they sometimes even claimed that they preferred to spend time with the Japanese Brazilians because they felt more comfortable and less socially inhibited than with the Japanese. In general, however, most of my Japanese informants had ethnic prejudices about the "Brazilian" cultural characteristics of the nikkeijin.

Immigrant minorities can be ethnically stigmatized when their country of origin is viewed negatively in the host society (cf. Goffman 1963:4). A number of Japanese I spoke with had negative images of Brazil not only as backward and underdeveloped (*okureteiru kuni*) but also as a country with a "low culture" (*hikui bunka*) and directly associated the nikkeijin with such images by virtue of their Brazilian origins. For instance, one female worker from Toyama had this to say:

> The Japanese see all of the Third World as poor. Since their level of economic production is low, we then associate them with low living and educational standards, high crime, and lack of developed cities. So the negative image is not about Brazil in particular, but about all Third World countries in general. The Japanese look down on the nikkeijin because they are from a country with low standards, culturally and educationally.

The nikkeijin also automatically become the target of some common, negative stereotypes of the "Brazilian" or "Latino" character, as shown by this typical comment by an older Japanese woman:

> The Brazilians [implicitly including Japanese Brazilians] are typical Latino types (*laten-kei*)—even if they don't have money to live tomorrow, they decide to enjoy life today and worry about tomorrow when it comes. They are open and jovial people, but also careless, irresponsible, and lazy (*darashiganai, iikagen*). Warm countries are like this.

A Japanese worker further elaborated on this sentiment:

> Brazil is a really laid-back country, and I think it was good for the nikkeijin. I don't think they worked very diligently out there. I hear Brazilians take two hours off for lunch and they work one day, then don't work the next, even if they are employed at a company. . . . The Brazilian nikkeijin are very loose about time too. They live day by day, and don't bother to plan ahead.

However, some Japanese give the nikkeijin higher marks in contrast to supposedly low Brazilian standards by virtue of their Japanese descent. "Even if the nikkeijin are at a low cultural level," one informant remarked, "I figure they must be better than Brazilians because of their Japanese heritage."

A Deficient Culture of Work

Derogatory opinions about the cultural differences of the nikkeijin as a negative minority are not only derived from preconceived notions of Brazil or Brazilian culture but also based on evaluations of the actual behavior of the nikkeijin. Despite the connotation of the term, ethnic "prejudice" consists not only of rigid *pre*conceptions and *pre*judgments, as Simpson and Yinger suggest (1972:24), but also of pejorative attitudes based on direct observations and experiences with members of the ethnic group.

Most important here are the opinions that the Japanese have of the work habits of the nikkeijin. In general, the Japanese workers on the assembly line at Toyama gave the Brazilian nikkeijin rather low marks for their work ethic and saw them as lazy, slow, irresponsible, and careless on the job. In fact, among all the Japanese workers with whom I spoke about this issue, only two had good opinions of the nikkeijin, and one had a lukewarm evaluation. Most had rather negative comments such as the following:

> The nikkeijin don't work very well, so the Japanese workers are forced to pick up the slack. They don't do all the required procedures and sometimes skip machines if the assembly line starts moving faster. Even a stupid Japanese would not do these things. They don't share the Japanese perception of work and are *iikagen* (irresponsible, careless) and *zatsu* (crass and not meticulous). It is because of their different culture, customs, and upbringing. Sometimes we even wonder if they have the ability to do even such simple work.

> The nikkeijin don't work hard, and can't do the work properly. Lots of people are disgruntled about them because they can't work well and trouble the Japanese workers who have to work extra to make up for them. The nikkeijin are different from the Japanese because of their lower educational level and the way they are raised, and that's why they are so cheap. The number of defects has gone up much more since the foreign workers came, and they have lowered Toyama's image. They come from a country of low culture and are suddenly asked to work with technology they have never seen before in Brazil. It's obvious that they will fail.

Again, we see the process of ethnic attribution here: the negatively perceived work habits of the Japanese Brazilians are attributed solely to their ethnic characteristics (i.e., "Brazilian culture"), while other situational and individual determinants that hinder their performance are conveniently overlooked. For instance, most Japanese workers do not seem to fully recognize the fact that the nikkeijin generally tend to be new workers with less experience in the factory because of their high turnover rate as a marginal and disposable migrant labor force. Nor was anyone aware that the Japanese Brazilians were generally office workers in Brazil and are not accustomed to strenuous physical labor. Indeed, this type of overgeneralization, where the unfavorable behavior of certain individuals from unfamiliar social groups is ethnically attributed as a collective *cultural* trait, is one of the primary causes of ethnic prejudice and negative stereotypes.

In contrast to the Japanese workers, the Japanese *employers* I interviewed had favorable impressions of their Brazilian nikkeijin employees. Although considerable variation in individual ability is noted, most employers acknowledge that the Japanese Brazilians work hard, always do overtime, and are more dedicated and diligent on the job than Japanese seasonal workers or part-timers (cf. Roth 1999:58). However, a good number look unfavorably at other aspects of nikkeijin behavior and work habits within the factory. The Japanese Brazilians are sometimes seen as excessively individualistic, uncooperative, and lacking in harmonious group coordination and spirit as well as personal initiative. A number of employers mentioned that the nikkeijin do not assist each other and create internal conflicts and even harass each other on occasion (see chapter 6). Other minor complaints included improper wearing of uniforms, inappropriate displays of affection between couples on the factory floor, and even jaywalking in front of the factory. Such perceived negative behavior is again ethnically attributed by these employers to "Brazilian" cultural differences. The observations of the following manager are quite typical:

> The cultural differences of the nikkeijin cause problems. They are too individualistic, selfish, and think only about their own personal needs and not of others. They have no group consideration and don't help each other but instead, harass those among them who try to do more to raise group efficiency. Also, even the better nikkeijin do only what they are told and don't try to do more, unless they are asked. In nikkeijin society in Brazil, it is said that they listen only to superiors and don't do the work voluntarily by themselves. So we have to give them strict orders.

The Japanese Brazilians are also seen as irresponsible and completely lacking in company loyalty because they frequently quit their jobs and move to firms offering higher wages and more overtime. Often, they leave the company without properly informing the management, break their contracts, or simply disappear from the job without notice. This tendency among the nikkeijin to frequently change companies for personal profit is a flagrant violation of what is usually considered to be culturally proper Japanese employee behavior: the company's benevolent paternalism is expected to result in hard work and loyalty from the workers.[10] Because of such behavior, some of these employers claim that the Japanese Brazilians care only about themselves and show absolutely no gratitude toward the company despite its efforts to provide them with housing, other services, and job security during production downturns. The refusal of the nikkeijin to properly conform to such Japanese ideologies of employee loyalty was noted by a number of company managers and labor brokers and again interpreted as a product of "Brazilian" culture (cf. Roth 1999:97–100). For instance, one employer explained:

> It is mainly a matter of cultural differences. They do not share our sense of work or obligation. In the Japanese system, the worker becomes a member of the company and dedicates himself to the company. In return, the company gives him security through lifetime employment and looks after him personally. So even Japanese with ability want to stay at the company, even if they can move to a better one. But the Brazilian nikkeijin and Peruvians quit without a second thought because they don't feel this loyalty to the company and say the salary is better in another company. Sometimes, ten nikkeijin leave all at once, and we can't produce. The nikkeijin do such disruptive things without a second thought because all they care about is themselves. They work today and disappear tomorrow.

A manager of a labor broker firm had similar impressions:

> It is a difference in customs between Japan and Brazil. Even Japanese part-time workers don't do this [switch jobs frequently], because they

---

[10]See Cole (1971), De Vos (1975a), Dore (1973), and Rohlen (1974) for discussions about traditional paternalistic relationships in Japanese corporations, which are also sometimes couched in an ideology of family in small firms (see Kondo 1990). Although paternalistic cultural norms mainly apply to full-time employees (*seishain*) at large firms and are less operative in the more marginal sectors of the economy where migrant workers are employed, a certain amount of company loyalty is still expected among temporary workers in small and medium-sized firms.

feel a sense of obligation and gratitude toward the company. Most nikkeijin don't have these feelings at all because they have a different national character (*kokuminsei*). There are some who are not like this and are proper, but only about 5 percent. The rest are irresponsible.

Of course, these behavioral patterns that Japanese employers dislike are not simply the result of "cultural differences" but are due to the nikkeijin's status as temporary migrant workers whose behavior is based on completely different motivations than that of native workers. As dekasegi, the predominant goal of the nikkeijin is economic, and since they wish to earn as much money as possible in a short period of time, they quickly leave the company if they find a job that pays better or offers more overtime. In addition, because of their intention to remain in Japan only temporarily, they feel no personal attachment to the firms where they work. A highly developed and extensive labor broker system that gives them ready access to a wide range of job possibilities also makes it easy for them to quickly change jobs. However, the employers I spoke with did not mention such noncultural reasons for the behavior of the nikkeijin. Again, we see the origins of prejudice in the process of "ethnic attribution," in which the disliked behavior of another group is simplistically explained as an ethnic/cultural characteristic and other motivations for such behavior are not considered. This demarcates the Japanese Brazilians as a negative minority group whose perceived cultural differences are held in low regard.

The Japanese Brazilians in Public

The behavior of the Japanese Brazilians outside the factory also creates negative cultural impressions among a number of Japanese. The most frequent complaints from local Japanese residents about the Japanese Brazilians is that they are a disturbance (*meiwaku*) because they make excessive noise in apartments, turn up their stereos too loud, and party until late at night on weekends (see also Japan Institute of Labor 1995; Roth 1999:167; Tsuzuki 2000:331; Watanabe et al. 1992; Yamashita 2001:110). A Japanese factory worker who had lived in an apartment building with nikkeijin described the disturbance they caused:

> In my last apartment, I had nikkei neighbors on both sides and had plenty of experiences with the "cheerfulness" (*akarusa*) of South America. The neighbors on the right were quiet, but those on the left were the

happy type. They would party, talk loud, sing in the bathtub, and play the guitar until late at night without any consciousness that they were in Japan and disturbing others. It wasn't that they were always noisy, but sometimes they seemed to have ten or twenty people in a room. We wanted them to be quiet but didn't complain directly to them.

A few Japanese residents also mention that the nikkeijin do not take off their shoes when entering apartments.[11] Another public problem cited ad nauseam is the supposed inability of the Japanese Brazilians to properly separate their garbage into burnable and nonburnable trash when putting it out. However, this problem has subsided with better distribution of information in Portuguese, including instructions at garbage dumping sites and numerous practical living guidebooks.

The behavior of the nikkeijin in the streets is also viewed unfavorably. It is sometimes mentioned that they do not obey traffic signals or jaywalk. Even in the town of Oizumi, which has the highest concentration of Japanese Brazilians in Japan and where the residents have become used to constantly encountering foreigners in the streets, some Japanese still do not like to see nikkeijin walking around in groups, dressed in a strange manner, speaking loudly in Portuguese, and otherwise behaving in ways that seem alien. Of course, only a minority of the nikkeijin behave in ways that call attention to themselves in the streets, but when they do, they are extremely conspicuous. Some of my Japanese informants also regarded the dress styles of the nikkeijin as "*hade*" (gaudy, loud), a word that implies low-class aesthetic vulgarity (see Ivy 1995:236–37).

In general, Japanese residents expressed considerable unease and discomfort, if not a certain amount of fear toward groups of Japanese Brazilians in public. When the nikkeijin are in the factory wearing uniforms and working diligently, there is no problem,[12] but when groups of them cluster in the streets, especially at night, they are seen suspiciously, distrusted,

---

[11]Those Japanese who mention this latter problem seem to be using cultural stereotypes about foreigners in Japan and not their actual experiences with the Japanese Brazilians. Never did I see Japanese Brazilians enter Japanese apartments with their shoes on, and all of them maintain this Japanese cultural standard even in their own apartments.

[12]One doctor who occasionally receives Japanese Brazilian patients expressed a similar sentiment. When he encounters groups of nikkeijin in the streets, he is very wary of them, but when he sees them at his clinic, he feels safer because he knows they will not do anything bad while in his office.

and actively avoided by some. This reaction was shared by most of my informants and even by two Japanese workers who were generally quite open and friendly with the Brazilian nikkeijin on an individual basis and had gone out with them before. One young male worker remarked:

> When I see nikkeijin standing around in groups, it's no different from a group of Iranians. I don't like it—it's very suspicious (*ayashii*) and *bukimi* (unnerving, eerie, ominous), although it may be normal behavior for them. They tend to cluster in the dark and speak loudly.

"There's an image of crime associated with all foreign workers," an Oizumi resident remarked. "So we are scared when we see the nikkeijin cluster at night. It's a misunderstanding and prejudice arising from a lack of communication. But still, we don't cross the park at night if we see them hanging around."

A similar reaction was shared by Japanese residents in Machida city (near Tokyo) toward a group of Japanese Peruvians who played soccer matches at a local university playing field. Because they danced, drank, made noise, and played South American music on the radio after the matches until 10 P.M., local residents complained that the nikkeijin were "too frightening to pass by." As a result, the university stopped renting the grounds to the nikkeijin (*Nihon Keizai Shimbun*, October 14, 1992). There have been similar attempts to discourage Japanese Brazilians from congregating in public spaces (see Linger 2001:39).

One of my closest Japanese friends at Toyama, Nakayama-san, tried to explain his distrust of the nikkeijin:

> There's a lot of uncertainty and anxiety (*fuanshin*) because they speak a different language. We can't tell what they are saying, whether that are saying bad things about the Japanese. There's no way to really grasp their true nature (*shotai ga tsukamenai*). They seem easygoing and cheerful, but I also feel they will deceive and take advantage of me. So we can't even look them straight in the eye, and as a result, they become scary, eerie.

I once left my small camera in Nakayama-san's car when we went out. At work the next day, he told me that he had found the camera under the seat and agreed to drive over to my apartment later to drop it off. I thanked him and told him to leave it with my nikkeijin roommates if I was not there. He seemed surprised by my casual instructions. "Is that safe?" he asked. I told him that the Brazilian nikkeijin (at least the ones I lived with) could be fully trusted.

CONCEPTUAL ANOMALIES AND CULTURAL STRUCTURES OF IMPURITY: PSYCHOCULTURAL FEATURES OF JAPANESE PREJUDICE

When analyzing Japanese ethnic prejudice toward the Japanese Brazilians as a negative immigrant minority, we must consider not only the conscious attitudes directly expressed by individual Japanese but also negative reactions structured at the subconscious level. In fact, interethnic relationships can even be shaped by unconscious motives based on frustrated desires (Fanon 1967:chapter 6). I argue here that the Japanese Brazilians, as Japanese descendants born and raised abroad, have acquired a certain connotation of cultural impurity. In order to understand this aspect of ethnic prejudice toward the Japanese Brazilians, we must first briefly examine Japanese notions of purity and impurity, especially in relation to foreigners.

Foreign Migrant Workers as Impure

Emiko Ohnuki-Tierney (1984:chapter 2, see also 1990b) describes a Levi-Straussian symbolic conceptual structure in Japan based on a binary opposition in which the "inside" is associated with purity and the "outside" with impurity. Although the "outside" can be a source of pollution, impurity, and contamination, since its potentially dangerous power can also be harnessed and domesticated for beneficial uses, it has a dual, ambivalent meaning.[13] This cultural structure is best exemplified by the Japanese

---

[13]Such a dual symbolic understanding of the foreign outside is not unique to Japan but appears in many other cultures in various forms. Similar understandings of the "outside" have also been documented in the Fiji Islands, northern Sudan, India, the Americas, and the ancient western world (Boddy 1989; Dumézil 1988 [1948]; Frazer 1911–15; Sahlins 1985:chapter 3; Seeger 1981; Yoshida 1981). Although Ohnuki-Tierney claims (at least in the Japanese case) that the "outer margin" of society is associated with impurity while what is completely "outside society" has a dual meaning as the source of both destructive and positive power, this spatial distinction between the two different types of "outside" seems a bit contrived. For instance, the examples that she uses involving the classification of people into these two spatial

home, where shoes are removed at the entrance in order to prevent out-side dirt and pollution from contaminating the house.[14] It is also the basis for indigenous understandings of illness and germs. Ohnuki-Tierney claims that this type of historically developed symbolic classification sys-tem has persisted for centuries in Japan and has been deeply internalized by the Japanese, structuring not only their concepts of dirt, illness, and germs but also their classifications of and reactions toward people, espe-cially foreigners.

The function of foreign workers as beings from "outside" Japan con-forms to the dual and ambivalent symbolic meaning of beneficial and dan-gerous power. Although they have revitalized Japan's economy with their much-needed labor power, they have simultaneously introduced alien and impure cultural elements into Japan, thus threatening to contaminate and pollute its distinctive culture. As argued by Ohnuki-Tierney (1984:39–40, 42), because of the potentially dangerous nature of outside power, it must be properly and constantly harnessed and controlled to avoid polluting and disruptive effects. Therefore, as shown in public opinion polls, even those Japanese who are willing to accept unskilled foreign workers feel that they must be strictly controlled and monitored by placing restrictions on their length of stay, the number admitted, and the type of work al-lowed.[15] As Marilyn Ivy notes, the foreign has been acceptable in Japan only when thoroughly domesticated (1995:3).

When asked what their concerns and fears were if the number of non-nikkeijin immigrant workers continues to increase in the future, most of

---

categories are quite confusing. She claims that western foreigners, as people "outside society," have the dual meaning of destructive and beneficial power but that non-Japanese Asians are "marginal outsiders" and are thus considered impure (1984:42–43). However, from a spatial standpoint, non-Japanese Asians are just as much outside Japanese society as western foreign-ers. *Kikokushijo* (Japanese children reared abroad) and "overseas Japanese" are also lumped into this category as impure marginal outsiders, but again, they are not *spatially* located on the margins of Japanese society but reside completely outside Japan. In these later cases, Ohnuki-Tierney is confounding *spatial* marginality with *conceptual* marginality (i.e., the impurity of these people does not come from their *spatially* marginal position in Japanese society but from their *conceptually* marginal status as neither Japanese nor foreigners).

[14]Likewise, in Brazil, *a casa* (the house) refers to an inside social domain of control, order, and harmony whereas *a rua* (the street) is the outside world where disorder, unpredictability, and dangerous beings reign (DaMatta 1991:64, 66).

[15]In an *Asahi Shimbun* public opinion poll (November 6, 1989), 56 percent of the respondents claimed that they were willing to accept unskilled foreign workers under certain limitations and restrictions. In a Prime Minister's Office survey conducted 2 years later (1991), the pro-portion was a surprising 72 percent.

my Japanese informants tended to focus on practical concerns, such as increased crime, lower social stability, and the creation of foreigner slums. However, worries about outsiders as a source of cultural and racial impurity and pollution were also evident (cf. Douglass and Roberts 2000:11).[16] Some explicitly mentioned that they do not want the Japanese to become "mixed" with other races and to lose their distinctive culture. A few feared that foreigners would bring diseases (such as AIDS) to Japan. As Vera Mackie (1998:50) notes, Asian immigrant women working as bar hostesses in sleazy nightclubs are stigmatized as sexually impure.

Although the concern with purity is not often expressed, it does occasional come out, even in public statements. For instance, according to a Japanese academic opposed to immigration, "Foreign workers tend to have a higher birth rate, which will lead to a dilution of the original Japanese culture" (*The Japan Times*, June 18, 1989, 17, emphasis added). The threat of foreign contamination is even more evident in the comments of a right-wing student leader: "The relationship between our country and foreign workers is analogous to that between the human body and drugs. Once you take them inside, it changes the whole structure of the country, and when you want to get them out, it will be too late [i.e., you will be already contaminated]" (*The Japan Times*, October 16, 1989, 2). An advocate for foreign workers from a Christian NGO remarks, "Some people have the wrong idea thinking that Japan is a homogeneous society and has to keep its 'purity' " (*The Japan Times*, April 8, 1988, 3). At a conference I attended on foreign workers, one of the audience members complained that the panelists had addressed only practical economic issues and had not spoken about how foreign workers threaten the purity of Japan's Yamato race and spirit. Before this individual could continue ranting, his microphone was shut off, probably by a discreet technician.

Most of the Japanese I spoke with indicated that they can learn to tolerate the presence of large populations of racially and culturally "impure" immigrant foreigners in Japan. However, the tolerance of pollution has a lot to do with the spatial distance between the self and the polluting agent. Even if foreign workers enter Japan in mass numbers and ultimately "contaminate" the nation's pure culture, individuals can keep

---

[16]Likewise, in the Prime Minister's 1991 survey, most of those who opposed the acceptance of unskilled foreign workers were worried about such issues as the deterioration of social order and trouble in local communities, and only 6.7 percent of the respondents cited "the threat to Japan's unique culture" as a concern.

their social distance from such foreigners and thus psychologically protect themselves from pollution. Even in a place like Oizumi where foreigners of all types have become a common sight in the streets, residents
still actively avoid approaching or talking with them or sitting near them
on trains, especially at night and especially if the foreigner is dark-
skinned. Although my informants claimed that they keep their distance
because of a fear of foreigner crime, such reasons are also a sublimation
of a more basic and disturbing psychological fear of contamination.[17]
Therefore, when a protective spatial barrier is created through the social
separation of immigrant minorities, the individual's negative affective reaction toward their contaminating presence can be controlled by referring to popular ideologies that claim Japan must internationalize (*kokusaika*) because of "globalization" (*gurobarizeishon*). As Ivy (1995:3) argues,
such currently popular ideologies are not about opening Japan to different nationalities and ethnicities but about the controlled domestication
of the foreign.

The danger and threat of contamination become much greater when
these polluting foreigners enter more private and personal spaces or attempt to intermarry with the Japanese, leading to stronger psychological
reactions of revulsion because of their physical proximity. For example,
even my Japanese interviewees who expressed the most tolerant attitudes
and were willing to accept a permanent immigrant population in Japan as
an unavoidable necessity were notably less tolerant about the prospect of
racial intermixture between Japanese and foreigners, especially among *miuchi* (family and relatives). In other words, contamination of Japanese culture on a national level is begrudgingly tolerated, but not the contamination of one's own "pure" bloodline. This type of reaction is apparent in
the comments of one of my informants:

> I think it is unavoidable that the number of foreigners who do not look
> Japanese and are not of Japanese blood will increase. There is a fear that

---

[17]Of course, this type of defensive avoidance behavior is nothing peculiar to the Japanese but is
common in societies with low-caste groups that are regarded as impure, dirty, and defiling and
are thus avoided in daily interaction as well as socially segregated and excluded from society's
institutions. According to De Vos and Suárez-Orozco, "A caste barrier (or series of barriers) is
constructed to maintain and preserve the relative purity of segments of the population from
the danger of pollution and contamination that can result from indiscriminate contact with
those of a less pure nature" (1990:167).

Japanese culture and customs will break down and decline because of the introduction of foreign cultures, which is unacceptable for many because we need to continue our own history and traditions. However, when I think about the future, one thing I absolutely don't want is for Japanese blood to become mixed with that of foreigners. Even with Chinese and Koreans who look the same as Japanese, if they mix even 30 percent with the Japanese populace, it would be very disagreeable. It would be even more revolting if it happened within my own family.

A similar psychological reaction of disgust is evoked by foreigners who use public bathhouses, a sacred inner space of purity and cleanliness. In fact, some bathhouses experienced a dramatic drop in clientele after a few foreigners began using the facilities and have posted discriminatory signs refusing service to them. Although bathhouse owners claim that they refuse foreigners because of their different cultural customs of bathing, the fear of contamination by dirty outsiders is undoubtedly the main problem. A *Mainichi Shimbun* article on the subject (May 30, 1992) quotes one customer at a local bathhouse who says, "I can't enter the bath anymore. I think it's better not to go into a bathtub that [Asian foreigners] have used. Even if they say it's not AIDS [i.e., one can't get AIDS that way], you don't know what kind of diseases there are." Another customer who stopped using the bathhouse was even more direct. "It's because people with dark skin come," he said. "That's simply revolting." According to other bathhouses, clients frequently complain that "foreigners are filthy."

Another example in which defiling foreigners have been excluded from private spaces is the absence of immigrants who work as domestic maids, servants, and live-in nurses. In contrast to the heavy representation of immigrant women in the domestic service sector in other industrialized countries, non-nikkeijin foreign workers have not been hired for domestic jobs in Japan. Even the large number of Filipinas, who work as housemaids or nurses in many European and Asian labor-importing countries, are employed predominantly as "hostesses" in bars and nightclubs in Japan. Of course, there are various reasons for this, including the small size of Japanese houses and the fact that many Japanese women still remain at home and do the housework themselves. Yet, despite such reasons, the complete absence of demand for immigrants as domestic workers is quite remarkable given the increasing need for housekeepers, cleaners, baby-sitters, and caretakers of the elderly in Japan as women have begun to pursue full-time careers while men remain unwilling to do household work.[18] On the subconscious psychological level, to allow a potentially polluting foreigner into the house (the last bastion of purity) would be particularly egregious, even if it is to technically clean and "purify" the home.

The Japanese Brazilians as Impure Foreigners and Conceptual Anomalies

The symbolic meanings that the Japanese Brazilians (as a special type of foreigner) acquire in this binary conceptual structure where the inside is equated with purity and the outside with impurity are important for understanding the nature of Japanese ethnic prejudice toward them. As Ulf Hannerz (1996:159) notes, "return migrants" can be viewed by their former compatriots as a cultural resource or be branded as culturally polluted. The latter tends to occur in countries such as Japan where the concern for cultural purity and homogeneity is great.

Although the bloodline of most of the Brazilian nikkeijin remains pure Japanese and "untainted" by foreign blood, they have become culturally contaminated abroad (i.e., by the outside) because of their Brazilian birth and upbringing. One of my Japanese informants was the most explicit about the cultural impurity of the nikkeijin when she said: "We feel culturally superior to the nikkeijin because we have real Japanese culture while they have only contaminated Japanese culture. They aren't pure Japanese anymore, even if they look just like us." Children of Japanese businessmen who have resided in foreign countries for a certain period of time and have returned to Japan (the kikokushijo) are received in a similar manner, although the Japanese reaction to them is obviously much milder than toward the nikkeijin. Although the kikokushijo may be seen as a cultural asset who contribute to Japan's "internationalization" (Goodman 1990b), because they have acquired certain cultural differences while abroad, they are more likely to be seen as contaminated by foreign cultural influences and as requiring reassimilation to Japanese culture (that is, cultural "purification"),

---

[18]According to the Prime Minister's Office survey conducted in 1993, the percentage of Japanese men who are responsible for various household duties is as follows: 2 percent for housecleaning, 1.4 percent for laundry, 2.5 percent for shopping, 0.9 percent for cooking, 1.7 percent for cleaning dishes, 8 percent for supervising children's schoolwork, 0.7 percent for taking care of the baby, and 2.6 percent for taking care of parents. However, even such abysmally low rates of participation may be a recent improvement. The same survey conducted 13 years earlier (1980) found that husbands *whose wives were also working* spent only an average of *six minutes* per day on household work (reported in Cornelius 1994:385).

sometimes in special schools, before they can be properly reintegrated into Japanese society (see Kidder 1992; White 1988).[19]

Because of this foreign cultural contamination, the Japanese Brazilians have become anomalous and ambiguous beings who are racially Japanese but culturally foreign. They are liminal beings, in Victor Turner's terminology, who are "betwixt and between" the social categories of "Japanese" and "foreigner" and thus "elude or slip through the network of classifications that normally locate states and positions in cultural space" (1985 [1969]:95). According to Mary Douglas (1966), conceptual anomalies and marginal beings that defy classification are generally seen as impure and are feared as polluting (cf. Leach 1964 and Tambiah 1969). In other words, not only have the Japanese Brazilians become culturally defiled abroad, this contamination makes them liminal beings who acquire meanings of impurity by virtue of their unclassifiable status.[20] Indeed, other marginal groups in Japan have connotations of pollution as well (see Valentine 1990).

The Socialization of Impurity and the Japanese Brazilians

Since ethnic prejudices based on feelings of impurity and pollution are fundamentally a psychological reaction of disgust, their emotional force cannot simply be explained by rational thought or the logics of structural classification. Therefore, certain negative minority groups are seen as impure not only because they occupy a marginal position in a preexisting cognitive system of classification but also because individuals have been socialized and psychologically conditioned to react to them with feelings of revulsion and avoidance.[21] In this manner, socialization explains how

---

[19]Likewise, Graburn (1983:51–52) in his analysis of Japanese tourism also argues that tourists who leave their own country to travel the outside world can be potentially dangerous because they become ambiguous and polluting people.

[20]As marginal beings, the Japanese Brazilians can also serve as effective mediators between Japanese and foreigners (cf. Ohnuki-Tierney 1990a; Yoshida 1981), as shown by those who work as translators and ethnic liaisons in local government offices and Japanese companies. These ethnic mediators properly harness the foreign labor power of nikkeijin workers by helping the Japanese manage them while ensuring that the nikkeijin do not disrupt Japanese society by taking care of problems and conflicts that occur. This again relates to the previously mentioned dual meaning of the "outside" as a source of power that can be dangerous but can also produce positive effects if properly controlled.

[21]De Vos has also similarly criticized Douglas's exclusively structural explanations of impurity for ignoring psychological motivation grounded in socialization processes (see De Vos 1975b; De Vos and Suárez-Orozco 1990:chapter 5).

cognitive cultural structures of meaning evoke certain affective and emotional states within the personality, which ultimately influence behavior (D'Andrade 1995:chapter 9).[22]

Within the Japanese home, for example, negative feelings of impurity and pollution can become associated with what is outside the home through repeated socialization practices designed to prevent pollution from entering the house.[23] These include instructing children to always remove their shoes at the entrance, not to bring dirty things back home, and to keep pets such as dogs outside.[24] Parental injunctions, warnings, and punishment for bringing outside dirt into the house create an association of impurity with negative affect. The psychological experience of the outside as polluted also results from children's experience of purification practices within the home such as constantly washing one's hands and body (as well as clothes) to remove dirt accumulated while outside, cleaning the house, and taking the garbage "outside." Children are also constantly encouraged to wash, change clothes, and even to gargle when they return home to eliminate the dirt and germs they have picked up, thus demarcating the "outside" impure from the "inside" pure.

At a more primitive and panhuman level, the "outside" comes to be associated with dirt and pollution from early childhood by the experience of basic biological functions and behaviors in which impure substances within the body are eliminated (i.e., taken outside the body) through such acts as excretion, vomiting, spitting out contaminated food (or saliva), and blowing the nose.[25] At the same time, the child is told not to introduce unwashed

---

[22]By serving as the link between an abstract system of cognitive structures and emotion, socialization also explains why individuals tend to conform to the rules of cultural structures in their behavior without always being aware of what these actual structures are. As Levi-Strauss (1966) claims, such "deep structures" are unconscious and are ultimately the modified projection of the innate and unconscious functioning of the mind. In other words, although the natives may not be directly aware of the underlying structure of relationships and system of classifications they use to organize their experiences, they have been conditioned by socialization to associate certain cultural meanings and symbols with certain objects and people and thus to react and behave in accordance with the cultural structure.

[23]As Bourdieu notes, inhabited spaces such as the house objectify cultural systems of classification that underlie the social order, and therefore inculcate these principles (1977:89).

[24]In contrast to the United States, dogs are almost never brought into the Japanese home and are certainly not allowed to sit on sofas and beds. This again shows the Japanese cultural concern of maintaining purity in the home.

[25]It is interesting to note that the impure substances that are removed from the body are eventually taken out of the house either by flushing the toilet or by wiping up human excrement and putting it in the garbage, which is then taken out of the house.

and unclean foreign substances into the body, such as by putting toys, fingers, and other objects into the mouth. Food can be taken into the body only after it has been properly washed, peeled, processed, and cooked and thereby purified. Again, a negative biological reaction is aroused by eating (i.e., taking in) dirty or contaminated substances that should have been kept "outside." In this way, a basic schema of perception is developed in the child in which the outside is seen as the potential repository of psychologically revolting contaminants that arouse negative affect.

In a somewhat analogous manner, the psychological feeling of impurity toward the Japanese Brazilians originates from a socialization and educational experience in which Third World countries such as Brazil come to be regarded as backward and poor, its residents living in dirty and filthy houses in cities that abound with disease and bad hygiene, low sanitation and standards of cleanliness, contaminated food and water, and environmental and industrial pollution, all of which evoke a strong emotional reaction of disgust. As a result, the nikkeijin come to be regarded as polluted people because they have become culturally contaminated and defiled through prolonged contact with an impure and unclean Third World country and have acquired its "low culture."

The limitations of a purely structural and symbolic perspective that equates the "outside" with impurity become quite evident when we attempt to explain why certain foreign ethnic groups in Japan are considered less contaminating than others. Although both Asian immigrants and Caucasians from the United States and Europe are from outside Japanese society, the connotations of impurity are much stronger toward the former in contrast to the latter. Likewise, although both Japanese Americans and Japanese Brazilians occupy the same anomalous structural position in Japan's system of ethnic classification as people who are neither completely "Japanese" nor "foreign," the American nikkeijin are not considered as impure as their counterparts from Brazil. Undoubtedly, foreigners who originate from "clean" First World, Euroamerican countries seem not to evoke negative feelings of pollution as do those from Third World countries.[26]

---

[26]A few of my Japanese informants told me that they could "trust" the Japanese Americans more and felt "safer," "more relaxed," or "more familiarity and friendliness" with them in contrast to the Japanese Brazilians, who are regarded with a certain amount of fear. Although the American nikkeijin are just as culturally and linguistically different from the Japanese as the Japanese Brazilians (if not more so), the more familiar "culture" of the United States does not evoke such feelings of impurity, contamination, and danger as the more alien and "low" culture of Brazil.

Although the Japanese Brazilians are subject to such prejudiced emotional reactions from majority Japanese society, their impurity is not strong enough to warrant calling them "caste-like minorities" (see Ogbu 1978:23). Despite their exposure to contaminating foreign influences, because the Japanese Brazilians are of the same bloodline and retain some cultural and linguistic similarities with the Japanese, they are less polluting than other foreign workers. Asian and Middle Eastern immigrants in Japan are not just more culturally polluted because they have absolutely no trace of Japanese culture, but are racially defiled as well, especially those who have darker skin. This also partly accounts for why a good number of nikkeijin women have been employed as domestic nurses (*tsukisoi*)[27] in contrast to other immigrants, who have been excluded from the home. However, although feelings of impurity toward the Japanese Brazilians as a negative immigrant minority group has never reached caste proportions, their cultural pollution is still quite disturbing for the Japanese because they demonstrate the extent to which any Japanese, if they live abroad too long, can become culturally contaminated.

ETHNIC PREJUDICE WITHOUT DISCRIMINATION?: A SOCIAL VENEER OF ETHNIC POLITENESS

This chapter so far has demonstrated that the Japanese Brazilians are a target of some pejorative attitudes because of their perceived low socioeconomic status and their stigmatized cultural differences. Of course, negative minorities not only are subject to prejudice from the majority but also suffer from ethnic discrimination—the expression of ethnic prejudices in actual behavior through the negative and unequal treatment of the minority group (cf. Allport 1979:51). Ethnic discrimination can be separated into two types: personal discrimination, in which members of the ethnic minority are treated in a derogatory manner on an individual level in daily social interaction; and institutional discrimination, in which they are partly or completely excluded from participating in certain institutions because of their ethnicity.[28]

---

[27]According to the 1995 Japan Institute of Labor study, 4 percent of the nikkeijin surveyed were working as nurses in hospitals or in homes. Even in 1988, when the immigration of nikkeijin to Japan was just beginning, 3,000 of them were already working as nurses or housekeepers (Miyajima 1993:83).

[28]This is analogous to Pincus's (1994) distinction between individual and institutional discrimination.

The existence of ethnic prejudice on the cultural level, regardless of how ingrained or complex, does not necessarily entail ethnic discrimination (Merton 1982; Simpson and Yinger 1972:28–29). In the case of the Japanese Brazilians, what was most notable during my fieldwork was a remarkable discrepancy between prejudice and actual discrimination. Although many Japanese who are in contact with the nikkeijin harbor various ethnic prejudices, these seem to rarely surface in actual discriminatory behavior where the Japanese Brazilians are treated worse than the Japanese because of their ethnicity. Instead, a social veneer of politeness is generally maintained. In this sense, most of my Japanese informants can be classified as "prejudiced non-discriminators" in Robert Merton's terms (1982).

The treatment of the Japanese Brazilians by the Japanese at the workplace varies considerably by company. However, a good proportion of the nikkeijin work in larger companies such as Toyama, where politeness and courtesy are generally the behavioral norm and negative ethnic reactions are conspicuously absent. On the surface, the workers at Toyama did not show any type of dislike or disrespect toward the Brazilian nikkeijin, nor did they make any disparaging remarks. Although I was always on the lookout for any possible signs of discriminatory behavior, I never witnessed or heard of cases of mistreatment or abuse. Despite serious communication barriers and ethnic social separation, friendly and cordial interactions were sometimes initiated by the Japanese through the exchange of a few words, gestures, jokes, and smiles. In fact, almost all of the instances of social interaction between the two ethnic groups were started by the Japanese, not by the nikkeijin. On rare occasions, Japanese workers would initiate a more sustained exchange in Japanese, even if it was apparent (as it was in most cases) that the nikkeijin did not understand very well.

Social interaction related directly to assembly line work was also polite and well mannered, without traces of negative behavior or mistreatment. Work instructions (both verbal and physical) were repeated patiently until the nikkeijin workers understood. New, inexperienced nikkeijin workers were patiently taught their jobs; their slow work pace, mistakes, and problems were all tolerated. Except for a reluctant few, the Japanese were willing to assist nikkeijin workers, especially when they fell behind on the assembly line, and sometimes gave them friendly advice, even when not specifically asked. Most Japanese workers (such as those moving forklifts and carts) apologized when they got in the way of the Japanese Brazilians and passed by with a "*tan kyu*" (thank you) when the nikkeijin made way for them, even when the incidents were too insignificant to require apologies or thanks. The Japanese workers at Toyama never expressed discontent or even a slight hint of irritation at having to deal with foreigners who were inexperienced and did not speak Japanese very well.

In fact, the Brazilian nikkeijin were sometimes treated with a certain amount of politeness, indulgence, and courtesy that was not always given to fellow Japanese co-workers. When Japanese supervisors gave instructions to the Japanese Brazilians, they used a politer form of Japanese (*teineigo*) that was generally not used for Japanese workers. Since most nikkeijin have no experience with physical labor in Brazil, some have considerable trouble adjusting to the grueling pace of factory work at first.[29] When such individuals complained (excessively on occasion) about the speed and difficulty of work or about the physical pain, they were moved to another (easier) job or simply given less work instead of being told to be quiet and endure it, as would probably have been the case with Japanese workers.

The treatment of the Japanese Brazilians was also at times indulgent. Even when a few of them made serious mistakes or were clearly slow and clumsy on the job, they were not chastised or reprimanded; nor were any ethnically derogatory remarks made. Instead, the behavioral norm among the Japanese workers was to stay completely calm and tolerant without showing any sign of annoyance or exasperation. This placid social veneer was even maintained under the most extreme situations, when a tongue-lashing was obviously in order. I will never forget the Toyama supervisor who showed infinite patience toward an incompetent nikkeijin worker who simply could not master a simple task even after repeated demonstrations, instructions, and guidance. Despite the frustration he must have been feeling, the supervisor's face remained emotionally blank during the entire ordeal.

In fact, the anthropologist himself (as a nikkeijin worker) was not immune from occasional acts of incompetence. Once I absentmindedly removed a utility cable from an air conditioner (operating at a very high current) without first unplugging the machine. Not only did this short-circuit the machine and cause an electrical explosion (I felt the electrical shock go through my body), but it shut down the entire assembly

---

[29]This is especially true among some Japanese Brazilian housewives who were not working before in Brazil. I personally knew of two cases where such individuals had considerable difficulty adapting to the demands of physical labor.

line and set off the alarm. Although I was obviously distraught (besides wrecking the machine, being electrocuted by an air conditioner is not the most pleasant experience), I was surprised to find that neither the group leader nor the foreman nor the two section supervisors got angry at me. Instead, the reaction was one of sympathy and concern. "Are you all right, Tsuda-san? Did you hurt yourself?" they asked before anything else. When I apologized profusely for the egregious error, I was simply told, "Don't worry about it. As long as you are O.K." The closest thing to an admonishment I received was from my kumicho, who simply said, "Please be more attentive when you work with these machines." The damaged air conditioner was removed from the assembly line and sent off for repairs. Such negligence by a Japanese worker would undoubtedly have resulted in a firm scolding or warning, as I had witnessed a few times.

Therefore, the "worst" type of treatment the nikkeijin received from Japanese workers at Toyama was a general unwillingness to interact or associate with them. It was clear that those Japanese workers who seriously disliked the Japanese Brazilians simply stayed away from them instead of causing conflicts and problems. Even those Japanese who were willing to talk to them on occasion never socially accepted them at the group level. However, this type of ethnic segregation could be partly overcome through the personal initiative of those few nikkeijin who spoke good Japanese and were willing to talk to Japanese workers. On those rare occasions where they attempted to start conversations with the Japanese, they were greeted with interest.

This generally courteous treatment of the nikkeijin was even more noticeable outside the Toyama factory in Japanese stores, restaurants, banks, and other local businesses where politeness and courtesy backed by ritualistic use of honorific language is a norm that is impeccably maintained regardless of whether the customer is a Japanese businessman dressed in a dark suit and carrying a briefcase or a dark-skinned and unshaven Iranian worker dressed in oversized jeans and a T-shirt. Because retail and other businesses benefit from Japanese Brazilian immigrants as new and prominent consumers, it is obviously to their advantage to welcome the nikkeijin courteously. This is especially true for Japanese long-distance phone companies, whose salesmen are ultracourteous, polite, and even obsequious when they visit the apartments of nikkeijin with special discount offers. Workers from local gas, water, and electric companies are also quite courteous and patient with the nikkeijin when they appear for installation or repairs. In areas with high immigrant populations, local and municipal governments have also generally been very supportive, open-minded, and sympathetic to their Brazilian nikkeijin residents, partly because they support the regional economy as both workers and consumers.

A number of Japanese Brazilians reported being treated rather curtly or in an unfriendly manner by the Japanese on the streets when asking for directions. This probably occurs because the Japanese (especially in areas with low nikkeijin populations) are estranged by Japanese-looking individuals who cannot speak the language properly and sometimes assume that the nikkeijin are uneducated or illiterate Japanese. In most cases, however, when the nikkeijin properly introduce themselves as "foreigners" (and even if they do not), the treatment is reported to be understanding, helpful, and courteous.

Although relationships between the Brazilian nikkeijin and Japanese in apartments are considerably more strained and problematic, most Japanese residents do not openly voice their complaints and prejudices about their nikkeijin neighbors. Even those disgruntled Japanese residents who do not like to live near the nikkeijin generally avoid conflicts or confrontations and simply move out of the apartment complex. As a result, certain buildings are gradually taken over by the nikkeijin in residential districts where they are highly concentrated.[30] Recently, however, there have been an increasing number of incidents between suspicious Japanese residents and foreign workers, some even including the nikkeijin. In June 1999, complaints from local Japanese residents about Japanese Brazilian residents in the Homi public housing complex of Toyota City (Aichi Prefecture) over improper garbage disposal, noise, driving-related problems, theft, and vandalism triggered a campaign by a right-wing group to expel the nikkeijin from the neighborhood, leading to an incident where a campaign vehicle was set on fire. There was a serious threat that the tension between the Japanese and the nikkeijin would escalate into violence and

[30]For example, many of the Japanese Brazilians in Oizumi live in apartments consisting predominantly or exclusively of nikkeijin residents. Most employers claim that this occurs because entire apartments are sometimes bought out by companies and labor broker firms employing nikkeijin and not necessarily because Japanese residents leave when the nikkeijin begin moving in. However, it is clear that most apartment buildings are progressively taken over by these companies because units are vacated by previous Japanese tenants partly in response to the increasing number of nikkeijin residents.

retaliation before the situation was defused, partly with the deployment of police officers (Sellek 2001:215–16; Tsuzuki 2000).[31] Such serious tensions have not arisen in Oizumi/Ota and Hamamatsu cities, where the local government openly accepts the nikkeijin and has procedures to resolve problems between them and Japanese residents.

Despite the lack of personal discrimination on an individual level, however, ethnic prejudice can surface in institutional contexts. Although the immigrant settlement process is already well under way, many Japanese Brazilians remain temporary sojourners (at least in consciousness and intent) and have not begun to extensively participate in Japanese social institutions. Therefore, Japanese institutional discrimination has not yet become a serious problem and few nikkeijin have experienced it. In fact, some Japanese institutions openly welcome the Japanese Brazilians. For instance, those with families have been strongly encouraged to enroll their children in Japanese schools, and in areas with high concentrations of nikkeijin, special "Japanese classes" for nikkeijin immigrant children have been created and special teachers have been hired to tutor and assist them. The Brazilian nikkeijin also enjoy full access to medical care, even though some do not have medical insurance. Local governments have also been very receptive to the Japanese Brazilians, providing many services including national health insurance, international exchange offices, Japanese language classes, guidebooks in Portuguese, and counseling as well as assistance with alien registration and even job placement. There is no solid evidence of the Japanese Brazilians being ethnically barred from stores, local businesses, or public facilities as has happened occasionally with other foreigners.[32]

The only area where institutionalized discrimination currently exists is in housing. Although most Japanese Brazilians are provided with housing by their brokers or employers, an increasing number have begun searching for housing on their own (Kitagawa 1997:122). Even in Oizumi, there are landlords who refuse to rent to nikkeijin, usually citing differences in

---

[31]The most serious incident between nikkeijin residents and Japanese occurred in 1997, when a gang of Japanese youth randomly assaulted more than 10 Japanese Brazilian youth in a park near Komaki station (Aichi Prefecture) as an act of revenge. A 14-year-old nikkeijin youth was kicked, beaten, and stabbed, and died three days later in a hospital.

[32]Japanese newspapers have reported a number of cases of immigrant foreigners being barred from stores, public bathhouses, and even *pachinko* (pinball) parlors by owners who post signs refusing service to foreigners.

"customs" and communication problems. Yet, the Japanese Brazilians do not suffer as much ethnic discrimination on the housing market as other foreign workers, who are sometimes refused service by real estate agents or simply told that nothing is available. According to one Kawasaki real estate agent, those nikkeijin who "have a Japanese face" (i.e., are not of mixed descent) and speak the language usually do not encounter serious problems in finding housing.[33] In general, however, institutional ethnic discrimination against the nikkeijin is likely to become more pronounced in the future as more of them settle in Japan and attempt to participate in Japanese institutions to a greater extent.

Honne *vs.* Tatemae *and the Nature of the Japanese Self*

In order to understand the relative absence of both personal and institutional discrimination toward the Japanese Brazilians despite the presence of considerable ethnic prejudice, it is important to analyze how such a wide discrepancy could exist between Japanese ethnic attitudes and behavior. Although much ethnic prejudice is carefully hidden or not overtly expressed in many societies,[34] the Japanese Brazilians represent a somewhat unusual case of a negative minority that is rather poorly regarded but politely treated.

In Japan, the ethnic prejudices toward the nikkeijin are part of the *honne* (true inner attitudes and feelings) that remain concealed and normally do not appear in public behavior, which is regulated instead by the *tatemae* (socially proper and acceptable attitudes). Of course, there is nothing culturally unique about this general dynamic since all societies differentiate between attitudes and feelings that can be socially expressed

---

[33]Despite this, it is interesting to note here that even I had minor trouble during my housing search in Kawasaki because of my ethnicity. When the real estate agent told my landlord on the phone that I was a graduate student from the United States, the landlord hesitated and wanted to know whether I was a "nisei." Before he would rent to me, the real estate agent had to assure him that I "looked perfectly Japanese," acted and spoke just like a Japanese, and appeared to be a honest young man. The real estate agent assured me not to worry because once the landlord met me, he would realize that I was not "a real nikkeijin" and was "just like a Japanese." One Brazilian nikkeijin graduate student who could also speak Japanese well enough to "pass" as Japanese told me that when he looked for housing, he did not reveal the fact that he was nikkeijin until the deal was done.

[34]Pettigrew (1994) argues that most whites in the United States now conceal their prejudices toward blacks and do not engage in overtly discriminatory behavior.

and those that cannot.[35] In the Japanese case, this creates a division in the individual's subjective experience of the self. The *omote* self (the social self exposed to the public) represents the "mask" or "social façade" that the Japanese present in public social interaction (De Vos 1985; Lebra 1976:chapter 5) and therefore consists of socially approved tatemae attitudes. In contrast, the *ura* self (the private, inner self) consists of individual feelings, beliefs, and desires (the honne) that do not conform to such social norms and usually remain carefully concealed (Befu 1980:176; De Vos 1985:180; Doi 1986:56). This distinction is analogous to the Brazilian anthropologist Roberto DaMatta's concept of the "person" (a relational and stable social being submerged within a collective totality and wearing a rigid social "mask") versus the "individual" (an isolated, private, and inner being with unstable emotions and feelings) (1991:170–77). In western psychoanalysis, it is analogous to Winnicott (1965) and Laing's (1969) notion of a false self (a polite and well-mannered self that is socially revealed) versus the true self (a secret and hidden self of inner spontaneity and personal ideas and creativity) (see also Giddens 1991:58–61).

My intent here is not to invoke a conceptual opposition between a public social self and private inner self, which Rosaldo (1984:146) claims is merely an imposition of western notions of self on other societies that do not make such dichotomous distinctions. As Rosaldo and others note, the private ura self does not consist merely of a biological or psychic essence of drives and instincts completely divorced from the culturally conditioned omote social self. Indeed, the personal emotions and feelings of the inner self are also acquired through the socialization process (see Tsuda and De Vos 1997) and are therefore culturally constituted as well. The real issue is how much of the private, inner self is revealed and "out there" in public relationships (see Barth 1987:86). In Roberto DaMatta's words (1991:177–83), societies differ in the degree to which the socially constituted "person" is emphasized over the socially independent "individual." In Japan, the distinction between the omote and the ura self is stronger than in many other societies and the extent to which this private self remains hidden is greater.

Nowhere is this dichotimization of self-experience into omote and ura components more apparent than with ethnic feelings and attitudes. When

---

[35]In this manner, cultural variation across societies does not always consist of absolute differences in cultural *content* (as some advocating descriptive cultural relativism would suggest), but varying degrees of *emphasis* of certain fundamental cultural patterns commonly held by a number of societies.

talking about their prejudices toward the nikkeijin, some of the Japanese I interviewed mentioned how they do not reveal such inner honne feelings and personal opinions in public because they are considered improper and socially unacceptable:

> If we say that the Brazilian nikkeijin were poor farmers who couldn't eat in Japan so left for Brazil and that those who didn't even succeed in Brazil have now returned to Japan, we get lots of resistance and opposition (*teiko*). The Japanese don't let you say this now. Instead of saying what we really feel—that they are people who can't endure and persevere (*gaman*) and give up easily (*akippoi*) and that they are human failures (*dame na hito*)—we now call it "internationalization" (*kokusaika*). We don't want to think in such a negative way because it is considered bad, even if it is reality. So we say the nikkeijin are admirable (*rippa*) and courageous (*yuki ga aru*) for coming all the way from Brazil. This is the tatemae.

The other type of socially acceptable tatemae attitude about the nikkeijin is based on an expression of sympathy and pity—the Japanese Brazilian dekasegi are portrayed as hapless and unfortunate victims of circumstance (*higaisha*) who had to leave Japan when the country was poor, then suffered in economically impoverished Brazil, and therefore have had to return to a now rich Japan. In this sense, when talking about the nikkeijin, my informants frequently used words such as *kawaiso* or *ki no doku* (unfortunate, worthy of pity), *un ga warukkata* (they were unlucky), *taihen* (difficult), *kuro shita* (suffered a lot), and *aware* (sad, deserving compassion for their misery). A number of my informants spoke directly about such tatemae attitudes, in contrast to their inner, honne feelings. For example:

> We say that the nikkeijin went to Brazil because Japan was a poor country back then and that the bad Japanese government deceived them and encouraged them to emigrate. But this is not the honne of the Japanese. Inside, we feel they are human failures and poor people. If they had tried hard, they would not have been so poor.

As one Japanese worker mentioned, such socially proper tatemae attitudes are the basis for his polite treatment of the nikkeijin at work despite the fact that his honne tells him otherwise:

> We say the nikkeijin are kawaiso and have suffered a lot in Brazil. Since I feel bad for them, I try to treat them nicely in Japan and help them out

at work. But deep down, I feel that if they really had ability and had worked hard in Brazil, they would not be in such a miserable position.

Among Japanese workers, not only is the honne consisting of derogatory ethnic attitudes confined to the inner ura self, so are all types of resentments and complaints about the nikkeijin, such as having to work more to make up for slower nikkeijin workers, having favorite break areas taken over by the nikkeijin, and being unable to communicate even basic instructions to them. Despite these frustrations and disgruntlements, a number of workers at Toyama mentioned in interviews that they would take special care to treat the Japanese Brazilians well and not to do anything that would offend them. For instance, one of my supervisors confided to me:

> The Toyama management just orders us to use these nikkeijin workers, but we really resent that. If the nikkeijin can speak Japanese, it's O.K. But when we give them instructions and they tell us they don't understand Japanese, what are we to do? We can't use them like Japanese workers, and it just makes our lives more difficult. But we never say what we really feel about working with the nikkeijin. Never.

Therefore, because of the psychological separation of the self into the omote and ura, my Japanese informants at Toyama self-consciously controlled and concealed their various ethnic prejudices about the Brazilian nikkeijin under a courteous exterior of ethnic politeness. As a result, the Japanese Brazilians experience much less discrimination in Japanese society than negative minorities in other societies.

Social Superiority and Ethnic Prejudice

It is important to note that the ability to keep ethnic prejudice latent in this manner is not only a result of the psychology of the self but also a matter of relative social status. Prejudices toward the nikkeijin can be more easily contained and prevented from being expressed in behavior because the Japanese are in a privileged position of superiority and their social dominance is not in any way threatened by the presence of the nikkeijin. As one Japanese resident in Tokyo remarked:

> We always feel a sense of superiority in comparison to the nikkeijin. We are very conscious of how miserable the nikkeijin are and how they have

to come to Japan to do dirty jobs that the Japanese no longer want. Then we realize how privileged and fortunate we are as Japanese and a feeling of innate superiority is created.

This is true not only among white-collar Japanese who look down on nikkeijin because of their low social class position in Japan. Japanese factory workers also feel superior to their nikkeijin co-workers, who are seen as temporary migrant laborers earning low wages. A young Toyama worker said:

> I think we will be able to eventually accept the nikkeijin, but only through a sense that the Japanese are superior and by looking down on them as subordinate to the Japanese who do dirty work that we don't want to do. Although we obviously don't actually say this to them, we have a need to look down on them and see them as low class and inferior.

As long as the dominant majority's privileged social position remains uncontested and unchallenged by the ethnic minority,[36] there is no need to overtly denigrate the minority to maintain social superiority since the perception of them as inferior and less capable is naturally confirmed by their actual subordinate socio-occupational position. As Gordon Allport (1979:22) notes, when vertical mobility is restricted and lower-ranked groups are not actively menacing, expressions of prejudice are less prominent. This is especially true for new immigrant minorities who initially intend to live only temporarily in the host country and are thus content to remain socially and culturally marginalized and powerless. However, once the immigrant minority group settles in the host society, becomes socially mobile and better educated, and starts competing with natives for the same jobs, the previously snug position of power and dominance of the majority group is threatened and challenged. In order to defend and maintain that privileged position, previously latent ethnic prejudices suddenly emerge in discriminatory behavior in an attempt to keep members of the

---

[36]Again, this is true even among Japanese factory workers, who do not fear that the nikkeijin will threaten or take away their jobs. Because the Japanese Brazilians are part of the peripheral, casual labor force, they are always dismissed before regular Japanese employees. The only Japanese workers who probably feel competition from the nikkeijin are part-timers and other temporary workers.

minority group in their proper place by excluding them from majority institutions, reducing their opportunities, and reminding them of their inferiority. As Allport notes, "The effort to maintain a precarious position can
bring with it an almost reflex disparagement of others" (1979:371).

In this manner, a society that initially seemed "tolerant" toward immigrants gradually begins showing its true colors as previously hidden ethnic
prejudices and resentments surface. Public opinion surveys by Japanese
newspapers already show a significant hardening of attitudes toward foreign
workers in Japan in contrast to the surprising tolerance shown in earlier surveys.[37] A paradoxical situation is created in which the longer an immigrant
minority lives in the host society and the more its socioeconomic status increases, the greater the ethnic discrimination it experiences (cf. Hagendoorn
1993). Among my Japanese informants who spoke about the future of immigrants in Japanese society, an Oizumi store owner was the most eloquent:

> As long as foreigners work obediently for us in the factories doing jobs we
> don't want to do, there will be no problems. But once they decide to settle
> in Japan permanently and bring their families, they will begin demanding
> better jobs and housing and equal educational opportunities for their chil-
> dren. They may even want political rights. This type of self-assertion
> among foreigners will not be liked by the Japanese. People who were quiet
> until then will then begin showing their dislike for foreigners. Then others
> who feel the same way will join them. The honne will eventually come out.
> This is how things work in Japan—people don't say what they really think,
> but then something happens, and a few people speak out, and then every-
> one finds out that they were all thinking in the same way.

Variation in the Ethnic Treatment of the Japanese Brazilians

Of course, there is considerable variation in the manner in which the
Japanese Brazilians are treated by the Japanese depending on the social situation. Although a good number of the nikkeijin are employed in larger
companies like Toyama, many work in much smaller factories, frequently with a few dozen employees, where their treatment can be quite different and even discriminatory at times.

---

[37]Polls taken by the *Yomiuri Shimbun* (July 3, 1996) show that those willing to accept immi-
    grant workers declined from 72 percent in 1991 to 57.7 percent in 1996. Those who believed
    that Japan should not accept immigrants increased from 22 to 37.4 percent.

The reports from my Japanese Brazilian informants who had worked (or were working) in small firms diverged. One group stated that treatment was better in smaller firms because there was more interaction between the Japanese and the nikkeijin. In small companies with few nikkeijin, the Japanese pay more attention and talk to them, receive them with more warmth, and even sometimes establish personal relationships. At the same time, a smaller number of my nikkeijin informants felt that the treatment they receive in Toyama (and larger companies in general) is politer, more courteous, and less negative and prejudiced than in smaller companies where they are treated worse, forced to work faster and harder, and scolded for mistakes, and where supervisors are less tolerant and patient and use crass language, even yelling at them. Some nikkeijin claim that some Japanese workers at these firms even make ethnically derogatory remarks.

Relationships with Japanese are closer and more personal in small companies with fewer nikkeijin because they attract more interest due to their novelty and are scattered more widely on the factory floor, forcing them to directly interact with the Japanese. In larger firms with a greater proportion of nikkeijin workers, Japanese workers tend to be more accustomed and indifferent to them, and the Japanese Brazilians themselves tend to ethnically self-segregate because of their larger numbers. They are also more likely to be brought in by an outside labor broker firm and therefore work and eat lunch separately because they are not employees of the company. In contrast, because smaller firms are more likely to hire the nikkeijin directly as their own employees, their Japanese employees tend to interact and socialize with the nikkeijin to a greater extent. At the same time, Japanese Brazilians working at smaller firms tend to experience more negative treatment and ethnic discrimination because working conditions are worse at these firms, and the Japanese workers are less educated and tend not to be as well supervised or trained to deal with foreign workers as their counterparts at larger firms. In order to fully understand why the treatment of the nikkeijin is more intimate, yet less refined and more derogatory at smaller companies, we must examine the social situational characteristics that prevail at these firms.

The extent to which individuals suppress and conceal socially disapproved ethnic prejudices within the inner ura self does not remain constant but varies according to the social circumstances within which they are placed. According to Takie Lebra (1976:chapter 1), Japanese behavior is not based on universal and constant principles or values, but is highly dependent on specific social contexts and therefore socially relative. In certain situations, honne ethnic attitudes and prejudices can emerge in actual behavior.

Lebra (1976:chapter 7) identifies four domains of situational interaction in Japanese society based on the omote/ura distinction as well as the *uchi* and *soto* dichotomy. Uchi is a general cultural category that can refer to those inside one's social group, and soto refers to those who are outside the group. Therefore, social situations can be defined not only as either public (omote) or private (ura) but also by whether the social participants are within one's social group (uchi) or outside the group (soto). These two cultural dichotomies can thus be combined in a matrix fashion to produce four distinctive social situations, each with different characteristics and requiring a different type of behavior as shown below:

	omote ("public")	ura ("private")
soto ("out-group")	formal	anomic
uchi ("in-group")	restrained informality	informal

The soto-omote is a situation in which the people with whom the individual is interacting are outside his or her own group (soto) and the social atmosphere is public (omote). Since social interaction is under public scrutiny, the participants attempt to create a favorable impression by engaging in *formal* and courteous behavior regulated strictly by the tatemae of socially acceptable attitudes that conform to cultural norms and etiquette (see Lebra 1976:120–21).[38] As a result, the individual's honne of inner feelings and dispositions is strictly circumscribed and socially concealed.

In contrast, the uchi-ura domain of social interaction is a situation in which the interactants are among the same social group (uchi) and are in a private setting (ura). Since the individuals are socially intimate and are not exposed to public scrutiny or evaluation from outsiders, normal social inhibitions and constraints are lifted and they are permitted to freely divulge their honne feelings and opinions by engaging in *informal* behavior that violates usual norms of conduct.[39] The uchi-ura situation is analogous to DaMatta's concept of *a casa* (the house), an inside domain of social intimacy and closeness (1991:66).

---

[38]Using the theater metaphor, this is what Goffman (1959, 1967) calls the public "frontstage," where individuals are concerned about "impression management" and engage in ritualistic "face-work" behavior to maintain their reputations.

[39]This is the private "backstage" where the frontstage performance is "knowingly contradicted as a matter of course" (Goffman 1959:112).

This distinction between the soto-omote and uchi-ura domains of social interaction helps explain the differences in how nikkeijin workers are treated in large Toyama-type factories versus small-scale companies. Large factory settings such as Toyama are good examples of soto-omote social situations where the nikkeijin workers are not members of the company (the uchi in-group) but are indirectly employed as workers brought in from outside labor broker firms (soto). As a result, the treatment of the nikkeijin is not merely an internal company affair but a very public matter that involves the company's social reputation. In order to maintain the good name of the firm, behavior toward the nikkeijin "guest workers" must remain formal and polite and regulated by the socially proper tatemae, with negative ethnic attitudes (the honne) remaining carefully hidden.

This soto-omote nature of the social situation at Toyama is also enforced and regulated through management pressure, due to worries about public criticism and complaints arising from the mistreatment of foreign workers. Since most Toyama workers are instructed to treat the Japanese Brazilian workers politely and kindly and are warned if any mistreatment occurs, some of them mentioned to me that they make a conscientious effort to treat the nikkeijin well and avoid conflicts. The attentive management seems to be sensitive even to minor incidents and problems. For instance, although I saw no fault in the almost impeccable manner in which the nikkeijin were being treated at Toyama, my kumicho received a warning from the general management that behavior toward foreign workers was not good. As a result, he told his workers to talk politely to the nikkeijin, and even to avoid casual jokes that could be interpreted negatively by those who have trouble understanding Japanese. It is also clear that Japanese interaction with the nikkeijin outside the factory in such places as stores, banks, and restaurants occurs in a similar soto-omote frame of reference where the social setting is public and the nikkeijin are outside customers. Therefore, behavior is likewise formal and deferential since the social reputation of the business is at stake under the watchful eyes of the management.

In contrast, small firms that hire the nikkeijin directly operate more in the uchi-ura social situational frame. Although the nikkeijin are still outside foreigners, because they are employees directly belonging to the company, they are part of the uchi (the company in-group). Since outside broker firms are not involved, the interaction also occurs in a more private ura setting that is confined to the company and not publicly exposed. Therefore, not only is there greater social interaction between the Japanese and the nikkeijin as employees of the same firm (uchi), relationships between the two are closer and more intimate. Although this can lead to better treatment of Japanese Brazilian workers at smaller companies, since the social setting is also more informal and private, ethnic prejudice and resentments (the true feelings of the honne) are more likely to be expressed. If a company mistreats its own workers, it is simply an internal company matter and does not have greater public ramifications, as in the Toyama case. Therefore, negative and rough treatment, and even derogatory behavior toward the nikkeijin, can be more prevalent than in larger companies. However, even in smaller firms, overtly prejudiced remarks and discriminatory behavior toward the Japanese Brazilians occur only occasionally.

CONCLUSION: ETHNIC PREJUDICE AND DISCRIMINATION IN SOCIOCULTURAL, PSYCHOLOGICAL, AND SITUATIONAL CONTEXT

An analysis of Japanese attitudes and treatment of the Japanese Brazilians as the country's newest ethnic minority demonstrates the complicated and multifaceted nature of prejudice and discrimination. Ethnic prejudice can have both *social* and *cultural* components. The Japanese Brazilians as a negative minority are viewed in a pejorative manner in Japan because of their perceived low socioeconomic status as well as their disrespected "Brazilian" cultural characteristics. We have also seen how majority prejudice is a product of both negative *preconceptions* about the minority group and *present perceptions* of its actual behavior. The ethnic derogation of the Brazilian nikkeijin is partly the result of preconceived assumptions and stereotypes about migrants as impoverished, low-class people and demeaning images about Third World Brazil, which are not based on empirical observations or fact. However, Japanese ethnic prejudice is also based on current perceptions and actual observation of the cultural behavior of the Japanese Brazilians, which creates negative impressions among many Japanese. I have also argued that ethnic prejudice consists not merely of conscious perceptions and attitudes but also of subconscious feelings of cultural impurity and pollution. Such psychological reactions derive their emotional power not simply from abstract analytical categories of ethnic classification but also from ingrained socialization processes.

Although a rather complex set of ethnic prejudices exists, they are rarely revealed in actual discriminatory behavior by individual Japanese.

Since the nikkeijin are the most ethnically favored of all unskilled immigrant foreigners, prejudice toward them is not as pronounced. In addition, there is a notable psychological tendency among Japanese to conceal their pejorative ethnic attitudes in public behavior under a façade of cordiality because of a dual experience of the self based on a strong distinction between socially acceptable and unacceptable attitudes. However, the expression of prejudice is not just a function of its strength but depends on relative social status and immediate social situational pressures. The psychological suppression of prejudice is facilitated because most Japanese interact with the nikkeijin from a self-conscious position of social superiority. However, in certain small and less reputable Japanese companies, prejudice can be occasionally revealed because the greater privacy and social intimacy that prevail make psychological restraints less operative and the hierarchical relationship between the Japanese and the nikkeijin less salient. Even in such circumstances, those whose ethnic prejudices and dislikes are strong and cannot be submerged under a polite exterior simply avoid the nikkeijin and generally do not cause conflicts or actively engage in discrimination and disparagement.

In his psychosocial study of prejudice, Gordon Allport (1979:14–15) outlines five progressive stages in the discriminatory expression of prejudice: 1) antilocution (in which people talk about their prejudices to like-minded friends and other acquaintances, but no negative action is actually taken toward the members of the minority group); 2) avoidance (members of the disliked group are avoided but not treated in a derogatory manner); 3) discrimination (prejudice is actively expressed toward the minority); 4) physical attack; and 5) extermination. Viewed from this perspective, the expression of prejudice toward the nikkeijin occurs only at the first two levels and has not reached the third stage of actual ethnic discrimination in most cases.[40] As a result, the Japanese Brazilians can be considered a "weak" negative minority who do not suffer the overt discrimination and disparagement to which other negative minorities are accustomed.

---

[40]In Europe, where immigration is much more advanced and dislike toward certain immigrant groups much stronger, the expression of ethnic prejudice toward immigrants has even reached the physical attack level, for instance among neo-Nazi German youth groups. In fact, even immigrants of German descent have not always been spared from these xenophobic attacks (see Münz and Ohliger 1998:183).

Part 2

ॐ

IDENTITY

CHAPTER 3

௸

Migration and Deterritorialized Nationalism

The Ethnic Encounter with the Japanese and the Development
of a Minority Counteridentity

You know, it's interesting with these [Japanese Brazilian] youth who go to Japan and come back after a number of years. They aren't quite the same people they were when they left—they've changed. I see it in my daughter as well. I can't quite explain it, but their self-understanding is somehow transformed in Japan. This is something you should study for your thesis.

—a nisei business owner in Porto Alegre, Brazil

INTRODUCTION

THE DRAMATIC CHANGE from positive to negative minority status that the Japanese Brazilians experience when they migrate to Japan is accompanied by an equally significant transformation in their ethnic consciousness. As members of a negative immigrant minority, they confront considerable ethnic exclusion, socioeconomic marginalization, cultural difference, and "discrimination" in Japan. In response to such negative experiences, many of them distance themselves from their previous transnational ethnic affiliation with the Japanese and assert a much stronger Brazilian counteridentity in opposition to Japanese society. This nationalization of ethnic identity among nikkeijin return migrants in Japan has been noted by various other researchers as well (cf. Capuano de Oliveira 1999:292–301; Koga 1995; Linger 2001:chapter 6; Nishioka 1995:210, 214; Roth 1999:chapter 4; Sasaki 1999:268–69; Watanabe 1995b:99).

As Robert Lifton (1983:72–73) observes, identity formation and development is a dynamic balance between "centering" and "decentering." During periods when ethnic identities are relatively stable, they tend to remain implicit and unexamined and are usually not subject to conscious discourse and self-reflection. Ethnic consciousness usually remains dormant until individuals experience some external event or change that destabilizes or "decenters" their identities, causing them to actively question and reconsider their ethnicity as they confront new experiences and incorporate and integrate new forms of identification. It is this type of occasional identity decentering that enables the self to change and develop (as it is eventually "recentered").

Migration frequently disrupts and decenters the ethnic identities of immigrants as they are thrust into a completely different sociocultural environment (cf. Epstein 1978:100). Since ethnic identities are relationally defined through cultural contrasts with other groups, when immigrants are confronted by new ethnic groups, their former self-consciousness is challenged and problematized. However, the resulting transformation usually does not lead to the complete replacement of their previous ethnic identity by a new one. In the case of the Japanese Brazilians, return migration to Japan simply causes the dynamic balance between their dual ethnic identities to shift notably from the Japanese to the Brazilian side. In contrast to the maturational development of identity among children and adolescents, in which new identities are acquired and integrated into a previous identity structure (Erikson 1968, 1980 [1959]; Weinreich 1983b), the process of identity change for adults more frequently involves a readjustment of a preexisting identity configuration.

In this chapter, I analyze the impact of migration on the identity of the Japanese Brazilians by examining why it can cause a nationalization of ethnic consciousness. As migrants go abroad and become new ethnic minorities in the host society, they sometimes develop a much stronger sense of belonging and allegiance toward their home country than they had *before* migration, leading to a type of "deterritorialized nationalism,"[1] where national loyalties are solidified outside the territorial boundaries of the nation-state. In this manner, migration reveals one of the ironies of nationalism: it is precisely physical *absence* from the nation-state that enables national sentiments to be intensified, enhanced, and articulated.

---

[1]Deterritorialized nationalism is somewhat analogous to what Ernest Gellner (1983:101–109) calls "diaspora nationalism" among geographically dispersed ethnic groups. See Appadurai (1996) and Clifford (1994) for more recent uses of the term.

ETHNIC MARGINALIZATION:
THE JAPANESE BRAZILIANS AS "FOREIGNERS" IN JAPAN

Ethnic identity is not only internally developed through the individual's self-consciousness of racial and cultural differences but also externally imposed by dominant society onto the ethnic group (cf. Berreman 1982a; Comaroff 1987:309; De Vos 1982b:6; Weinreich 1983a:162–64). In Brazil, a strong inner awareness of "Japaneseness" among the Japanese Brazilians is further reinforced by external pressures from the surrounding society, which defined them as ethnically "Japanese." In Japan, however, they initially experience a conflict between internal and external pressures on their ethnic identity.

Immigrants often experience a discrepancy between their formerly held ethnic self-consciousness and the identity that is imposed on them by the dominant host society because the categories and understandings they bring from their home country are different from the system of ethnic classification in the host society.[2] Although the Japanese Brazilians had seen themselves as "Japanese" in Brazil because of their Japanese ancestral origins, distinctive racial appearance, and perceived cultural differences from mainstream Brazilians, the Japanese understanding of what it means to be ethnically Japanese is quite different and much more narrowly defined, based on an ideology not only of Japanese racial descent but also of cultural homogeneity in which complete Japanese linguistic and cultural proficiency is required. Most Japanese I interviewed did not recognize any significant "Japanese" cultural characteristics among the Japanese Brazilians and viewed them as quite culturally alien not only for their lack of Japanese language proficiency but also for their Brazilian attitudes and behavior. The remarks of one local resident in Oizumi were quite representative of this general Japanese reaction:

> There's a lot of *iwakan* (sense of incongruity) toward those who have a Japanese face but are culturally Brazilian. If they have a Japanese face, we interpret this to mean they are Japanese, so we initially approach the nikkeijin this way. But then when we find they are culturally different, we say they are *gaijin* (foreigners).

---

[2]For instance, see Basch, Glick Schiller, and Blanc (1994) and Charles (1992) for a discussion of the differences between the racial categories that Caribbean immigrants brought to the United States and the American racial category of "black."

Therefore, despite their Japanese descent, the nikkeijin are not accepted as "Japanese" in Japan but ethnically marginalized as foreigners because
of their Brazilian cultural differences (cf. Mori 1992:163). "The Japanese
don't care if we are Japanese descendants or not," one Japanese Brazilian
nisei remarked. "We are foreigners for them simply because we were born
in a foreign country and have cultural differences." Notions of cultural
(instead of racial) difference are frequently employed in dominant eth-
nopolitical contexts to marginalize immigrant or minority groups in this
manner (Medina 1997:776; Ong 1996:738–39; Verkuyten 1997:100–101).
For example, ethnic Germans from Eastern Europe who have return migrated to Germany are also marginalized as foreigners because of their cultural differences (Levy 1999; Münz and Ohliger 1998; Räthzel 1995).

The ethnic rejection of the Japanese Brazilians on cultural grounds
causes them to seriously question their previous assumptions of cultural
commonality with the Japanese. In other words, they realize that their
supposedly "Japanese" cultural attributes, which were sufficient to be considered "Japanese" in Brazil, are woefully insufficient to qualify as Japanese in Japan. The following statements summarize this type of experience:

> We think we are Japanese in Brazil, but in Japan, we find out that we
> were wrong. If you act differently and don't speak Japanese fluently, the
> Japanese say you are a Brazilian. To be considered Japanese, it is not suf-
> ficient to have a Japanese face and be a Japanese descendent. You must
> think, act, and speak just like the Japanese.

> In Brazil, we are considered Japanese because we speak some Japanese, eat
> Japanese food, and maintain some Japanese customs from our parents.
> This is Japanese enough for Brazilians, but for the Japanese, it means
> nothing. We appear quite Brazilian to them and are seen as foreigners.

A number of the nikkeijin therefore come to feel that what made them
ethnically different as "japonês" in Brazil was more their primordial racial
differences than any of their cultural attributes. "In Brazil, if you have
slanted eyes and a Japanese face, Brazilians say you are japonês," a young
sansei Japanese Brazilian woman observed. "But we come to Japan with
this same face, and the Japanese say you are a Brazilian, a gaijin. I have realized that being Japanese means much more than using chopsticks and
singing Japanese songs. In Brazil, this makes us 'Japanese'; in Japan it
doesn't." A Japanese Brazilian graduate student used an interesting analo-

gy: "I have Japanese blood and a Japanese appearance, but I've come to realize in Japan that my heart and culture are Brazilian. I like to say that my hardware is made in Japan, but my software is made in Brazil."

However, even those Japanese Brazilians who spoke Japanese quite well and did not manifest significant cultural differences from the Japanese seemed to be automatically classified and treated as foreigners because of their origins in a foreign country. For instance, Wilson, one of my nisei informants, spoke completely fluent Japanese and was even told by his Japanese co-workers that his personality is like a Japanese. However, he claimed that he was still always grouped together with other Japanese Brazilians as a foreigner, even though he had been working in the same factory for close to four years. Other culturally Japanese nikkeijin who were employed in local municipal and company offices or were graduate students at Japanese universities had similar experiences. One Japanese Brazilian nisei woman, who could not be culturally distinguished from the Japanese, claimed that she continues to be regarded as a foreigner at the office. Not only was she excluded from dinner outings by her co-workers, she had not been promoted despite her many years of service. In fact, even some *first-generation* issei, who were born and raised in Japan and had returned as dekasegi after living in Brazil for many years, claimed that they were no longer treated as Japanese by their former compatriots. Kenichi, an issei who emigrated from Japan as a teenager, described his experiences in this regard:

> I come back to Japan after all these years and find I am seen as a foreigner now by the Japanese, although I was born and raised in Japan and still have my Japanese nationality. I am not accepted as a Japanese but called *burajiru-san* (Mr. Brazil) or simply gaijin. Even though I speak Japanese just like them, they keep me separate. For them, I am simply a Brazilian dekasegi like all the rest.

Although I worked in the same section as Kenichi at Toyama, I hardly ever saw him talk with Japanese workers (except to translate), and he always spent break time exclusively with other nikkeijin.

When talking about their migratory ethnic experiences, the Japanese Brazilians frequently say "*Nós somos considerados japoneses no Brasil, mais somos vistos como estrangeiros aqui no Japão*" (We are considered Japanese in Brazil, but are seen as foreigners in Japan) (see also Yamanaka 2000:142). Indeed, although the Japanese Brazilians were always called "japonês" in

Brazil, they are constantly referred to as "gaijin" in Japan. At the Toyama factory, they were often directly addressed as *gaijin-san* (Mr. or Mrs. Foreigner), especially if they were recent arrivals or they were being referred to collectively or introduced to others. However, even when Japanese supervisors knew the personal names of their Japanese Brazilian workers, they frequently used such phrases: "Well, we'll put Mr. Tanaka here [on the assembly line], and then the gaijin here," or "Do you think the gaijin will be able to do this work?" The Japanese Brazilians are called gaijin not only in large factories like Toyama where relationships are more impersonal but also in smaller companies as well as in public, especially when they speak Portuguese in restaurants, stores, and trains. In addition, they are required to register as foreigners (*gaikokujin toroku*) at the local municipal office and are designated as gaijin for other public services as well. Of course, they are called by their personal names in more familiar contexts, but those instances when the gaijin label is used make them constantly aware of how they are ethnic outsiders in Japan. The irony is that the same term that they had always used in Brazil to refer to non-nikkeijin Brazilians as a means of ethnic differentiation and exclusion has now been turned against them in the hands of the Japanese for the same purposes.

Because of their ethnic marginalization as foreigners, the Japanese Brazilians experience considerable social isolation and separation from the Japanese as well.[3] According to a recent research survey, 44.3 percent of the Japanese Brazilians report that they have almost no social contact with the Japanese, and 15.8 percent have only minimal contact. Only 14.5 percent have active relationships with the Japanese (Kitagawa 1996), and even fewer have active contact with their Japanese relatives.[4]

Because many nikkeijin initially expect a certain level of social acceptance in their ancestral homeland as Japanese descendants, they are quite disillusioned by their ethnic exclusion. In fact, according to one research survey on nikkeijin conducted by Kitagawa (1993), when respondents were asked whether they were accepted in Japanese society more than *non-Japanese descent* foreigners, a substantial number (57.1 percent) claimed that they were accepted only about the same, while a surprising 13.1 percent said they were accepted *less*, and only 29.1 percent felt they were accepted more. Indeed, certain ethnic return migrants like the nikkeijin and

---

[3]For a detailed analysis of the social alienation of the Japanese Brazilians in Japan, see Tsuda (forthcoming 1, 2).

[4]Only 11.6 percent have active contact with their Japanese relatives, whereas 56.7 percent have almost no contact; 17.2 percent have occasional contact (Kitagawa 1997).

ethnic Germans in Germany are as ethnically segregated in the host society as completely foreign immigrants.[5]

Although the Japanese and Japanese Brazilians work in the same factories and live in the same apartment buildings and towns, there is little interaction between the two ethnic groups in most cases. At Toyama, the nikkeijin and the Japanese workers always remained apart during break and lunch hours, sitting in separate rooms or at different tables and conversing only among themselves. Sometimes if a group of Japanese Brazilians was sitting at a certain table during break, the Japanese would avoid that table, even if there was room. Interethnic interaction was limited at most to brief smiles or greetings in the morning and short exchanges of a few words or simple questions. Although they worked side by side on the assembly line and occasionally together on the same

[5]Although the German government grants citizenship to the ethnic Germans and has numerous measures to integrate them into German society, they are socially segregated and economically marginalized and have become an ethnic minority (Levy 1999; Münz and Ohliger 1998; Räthzel 1995:272–76).

Japanese Brazilian workers have lunch in a separate room at Toyama.

Japanese Brazilian and Japanese workers (in the lighter uniforms) sit at separate tables during lunch break. Notice the Japanese are also segregated by gender, whereas the Japanese Brazilians are not.

machines, conversation between Japanese and nikkeijin (beyond work instructions) was basically nonexistent. In fact, when Japanese workers had to give warnings to Japanese Brazilians working nearby, they would sometimes even go through their supervisors instead of speaking to the nikkeijin directly.

Outside the workplace, the social segregation of the Japanese Brazilians is also quite notable. Only a few have sustained social relationships with their Japanese co-workers, although some Japanese companies invite their nikkeijin workers to company parties and outings. Although the Japanese Brazilians do not live in immigrant enclaves, there is a certain amount of residential segregation, as noted in the previous chapter.[6] Even those who

---

[6]A third, 33.6 percent, live in apartments where over 25 percent of the residents are other nikkeijin and only 12.7 percent of them live in apartments with only Japanese residents (Kitagawa 1997). Residential segregation is even greater in communities with higher nikkeijin immigrant concentrations.

have Japanese neighbors do not interact with them or participate much in local community activities. As a result, their contact with Japanese outside the factory is generally limited to clerks and workers at local stores, banks, and municipal offices.

A number of my Japanese Brazilian informants emphasized the social exclusion they experienced as foreigners in Japan. An older nisei man living in Oizumi had this to say:

> Once the Japanese find out you aren't fluent in Japanese, they realize to their surprise that you aren't Japanese and therefore distance themselves. They completely sideline you and you can't become part of their group. As a foreigner, you are treated like an object in Japan. My [Japanese] neighbors have therefore decided not to say a single word to me and remain completely separate.

When my Japanese informants at the Toyama factory were asked about their ethnic reluctance to interact with the Brazilian nikkeijin, they commonly stressed the difficulty they have relating to foreigners who are culturally different. A young Japanese who worked next to me on the assembly line elaborated as follows:

> Because we live in an ethnically homogeneous society, the Japanese are simply bad at dealing with foreigners they don't know well and can't communicate effectively with. We don't cope well with ethnic diversity and are not used to people who are different, like the nikkeijin. We have no way to react and adapt to foreigners in our midst, so we just prefer to stay away. Some will stop to help foreigners if they need assistance, but most just look at them and ignore them.

Language was obviously the most significant cultural barrier that discouraged the Japanese from interacting with the Japanese Brazilians. At Toyama, many Japanese workers did not even attempt to speak with their nikkeijin co-workers because they were afraid of their inability to communicate. Others attempted to start conversations with the Japanese Brazilians but were quickly discouraged when faced with difficulties.

This social segregation of the Japanese Brazilians in Japan as Brazilian foreigners is personally disorienting to many of them because of the strong inner consciousness of their "Japaneseness" they had previously developed in Brazil.[7] Although this results in considerable tension and "affective dissonance"[8] between their internally experienced and externally ascribed ethnic identities, they eventually succumb to dominant Japanese ethnic understandings and redefine themselves as Brazilians in Japan.

Geraldo, a nisei who had been living in Japan for a considerable amount of time, recounted his initial experience in this regard:

> Before I came to Japan, I thought that the Japanese would accept us much better, although not completely. Therefore, at first, I hoped and wanted to be seen as Japanese here. Most have this experience especially because of the pride we have as japonês in Brazil. But here, we encounter the language and cultural barrier and are not accepted as Japanese. So we conclude that we are really more Brazilian than Japanese. Although this is difficult to accept at first, it doesn't help thinking that you are Japanese in Japan because we are outside of Japanese society in our way of thinking and acting. We can't really enter their system and be accepted, even if we try.

Rodney, one of my roommates in Oizumi, had a similar reaction:

> We are the children of Japanese, but this does not help in Japan. We are seen as gaijin completely. If the Japanese see we were born elsewhere and don't act like them, they don't accept us as Japanese. . . . I wanted to be accepted as Japanese and not as gaijin here because we have Japanese blood and we maintain the traditions and beliefs of the Japanese people in Brazil. But eventually we conclude that we have no choice but to be seen as Brazilians here.

Those who had stronger Japanese identities in Brazil react more negatively to their ethnic exclusion as "foreigners" in Japan, resulting in considerably greater inner conflict and identity dissonance. Although their refusal to accept hegemonic Japanese definitions of their ethnicity is more

---

[7] As Koga (1995:48) notes, few nikkeijin can readily accept being foreigners in Japan because of their inner sense of being Japanese.

[8] Affective dissonance is a term used by De Vos (1976a) to refer to a negative emotional arousal caused by inconsistency and incongruity and was formulated as a critique to Leon Festinger's (1957) famous concept of cognitive dissonance—a need to resolve the tension produced by cognitive and logical inconsistency.

prolonged, they also eventually begrudgingly conclude that they are indeed foreigners in Japan and more Brazilian than they were previously willing to admit. This type of experience is best illustrated in the personal accounts given by two middle-aged nisei women. It is worth quoting both at length:

> I had lots of pride in being Japanese in Brazil and was raised by strict parents who were real Japanese patriots. I was always seen and called Japanese. But here, they say I am a gaijin. At first, I would disagree and say that I'm Japanese. I would say, "Look at my face, I'm no gaijin." But then the Japanese would tell me that I was not born in Japan. I soon found out, however, that even if I didn't introduce myself as someone from Brazil, the Japanese could easily tell I was not Japanese because I speak Japanese differently. Then they would ask where I was from, and I would say Brazil. They would then understand and the situation would pass. After a long time, my thinking has changed and I now accept that I am a gaijin here. We have no choice but to be different because we think differently and talk differently from the Japanese. We are simply this way and there's nothing we can do about it. Although we were called japonês all the time in Brazil, I've realized that the only true Japanese are the Japanese of Japan.

The second account is from Michiko, a jun-nisei who had emigrated to Brazil at the age of four, spoke near-perfect Japanese, and had first come to Japan on a language traineeship:

> I thought I was completely Japanese in Brazil because I was born and raised in the colônia speaking only Japanese and received lots of pressure from my parents to act properly Japanese. The pressure was magnified when I entered Brazilian school and was respected for being so Japanese. . . . Before I came to Japan, I naturally assumed I would be welcomed as a Japanese and not as a foreigner. I was welcomed, but as a gaijin. In the family I was staying with, they didn't differentiate as much between Japanese and foreigners, but the Japanese around me at work reacted to me as a gaijin. It was really a big shock. I was really confused at first and kept asking myself, "Why can't I be seen as Japanese in Japan?" But then I thought about this and was finally able to acknowledge that it is obvious that I am seen as a foreigner because I didn't speak Japanese like a Japanese when I first got here, and there were also other differences in my behavior.

MIGRATION AND THE CHANGING
MEANING OF ETHNIC BEHAVIOR:
THE EXPERIENCE OF BRAZILIAN
CULTURAL DISTINCTIVENESS

The shift in ethnic identity among nikkeijin migrants from an initially stronger Japanese consciousness to an increased awareness of their Brazilianness is not only the result of migration from a society that saw them as ethnically "Japanese" to one in which they are seen as foreigners. Ethnic self-consciousness is rarely a simple product of externally imposed hegemonic constructs. For an ethnic identity to take hold, there must be some self-recognition among individuals of the qualities that distinguish them from mainstream society. In other words, not only do majority Japanese see the Brazilian nikkeijin as culturally foreign, the Japanese Brazilians themselves become acutely aware of their Brazilian cultural distinctiveness. Such self-perceived cultural differences are quite striking, if not disorienting for the Japanese Brazilians because of their previously assumed transnational ethnic affinity with the Japanese. Most did not expect their cultural foreignness to be so evident in Japan. In one study (JICA 1992), 95.7 percent of the South American nikkeijin surveyed felt significant cultural differences with the Japanese. The most important ones were in human relationships, followed by language, food, and household customs. Moral values and religion were lower on the scale.[9]

When the Japanese Brazilians migrate to Japan, they realize that their behaviors and attitudes, which seemed quite "Japanese" in Brazil in contrast to majority Brazilian culture, suddenly appear quite Brazilian when compared to actual Japanese culture and behavior. The ethnic meaning of a certain type of behavior therefore depends greatly on contrasts with the immediate cultural milieu. One of my informants summarized this experience as follows:

> When you are in Brazil, there [is] no standard of comparison. We just figured we were Japanese because we were always seen this way and we felt different from other Brazilians. But I found out here that I was mistaken. I am a typical Brazilian. Once you live in Japan, we come to the point where we compare ourselves with the Japanese and see big differ-

---

[9]Although most Japanese Brazilians are nominally Catholic and some of them attend religious services in Brazil, religion is not experienced as a major source of ethnic or cultural difference between themselves and the Japanese.

ences. In Brazil, we just form an idea of being Japanese, but in Japan, we discover that what we thought was Japanese about ourselves was not Japanese after all, but was actually quite Brazilian.

Likewise, Michiko explained:

> In Brazil, I felt really Japanese because my surroundings said so and because my parents, as well as everyone else around me, were Japanese. We thought we were all educated as Japanese and received lots of influence as Japanese descendants. I came to Japan with my Japanese cultural background but found myself very different from the Japanese in Japan. So we figure we must be less Japanese and more Brazilian. Now, my identity is more on the Brazilian than the Japanese side.

This process, where the cultural behavior of the nikkeijin is ethnically redefined as "Brazilian" when placed in a different, Japanese social context, is not limited to attitudes and interactional behavior but even extends to the perception of body comportment and dress. Although the Japanese Brazilians had frequently noted their more quiet and restrained, if not shyer "Japanese" demeanor in Brazil, they discover in Japan that their manner of walking, dressing, and gesturing is strikingly different from that of the Japanese. It was quite remarkable that virtually all of my informants claimed that it is extremely easy to tell the Japanese Brazilians apart from the Japanese in the streets because of such differences, although some mention that there are a few among them who cannot be readily identified (cf. Capuano de Oliveira 1999:295). The following statement by Tadashi, my best friend at Toyama, was typical:

> I can see a [Japanese] Brazilian coming from a mile away with about 90 percent certainty. I can tell by the way they walk and by their clothes. The Brazilians walk casually with a more carefree gait and glance around at their surroundings, and they are dressed casually in T-shirts and jeans. The Japanese are more formally dressed and walk in a more rushed manner with a purpose. The Brazilians also gesture much more than Japanese and walk around in groups, whereas the Japanese are usually alone.

This ability to differentiate the Japanese Brazilians from the Japanese simply by dress and comportment is shown by some nikkeijin ethnic business owners, who greet Japanese Brazilian customers in Portuguese with a *bom dia* (good morning) or *boa tarde* (good afternoon/evening) but say

Three Japanese Brazilians (left) sit on the train next to a Japanese passenger. Notice the differences in dress and body comportment. Another foreign worker sits at the far bench, next to the handrail.

"*irasshaimase*" ("welcome" in Japanese) when a rare Japanese customer appears.[10] As a result of such experiences, the Japanese Brazilians realize that even at the most basic level of motoric comportment and mannerisms, prominent cultural differences surface that clearly set them apart from the Japanese as people who have deeply internalized Brazilian ways.

In this manner, although the Japanese Brazilians are not racially visible in Japan,[11] they remain "culturally visible" and therefore experience their ethnic differences as a minority group.[12] Of course, those of mixed descent are an exception, since race continues to be salient for their identity experiences because they frequently appear phenotypically foreign in the

---

[10]Incidentally, I was greeted in Portuguese most of the time at these stores as a bona fide nikkei-jin. However, I seemed to have some Japanese Brazilian store owners baffled, since they greeted me in Japanese.

[11]It should be noted, however, that the Japanese Brazilians generally have darker, tanned skin because of their long exposure to the tropical sun in Brazil.

[12]In Frantz Fanon's words, they remain an ethnic group that is "overdetermined from without" (1967:116).

eyes of the Japanese. For instance, one of my mestiço informants, who was always called "japonês" in Brazil because of his appearance, was surprised to find that when he first started working in a Japanese factory, the Japanese workers asked: "Are you a Japanese descendant? You don't *look* Japanese." The same racial characteristics that identified them as "Japanese" in Brazil are seen as "foreign" in Japan, making them very aware that it is not only the perception of cultural characteristics that is dependent on the local social context but also the perception of race. Among the mestiço nikkeijin, therefore, the Brazilianization of their ethnic identity in Japan involves the experience of both cultural and racial distinctiveness.

In addition, cultural behavior that was not seen as particularly "Brazilian" when the nikkeijin were in Brazil becomes increasingly salient as markers of their Brazilian national identity when placed in a contrasting Japanese sociocultural milieu. For instance, when the Japanese Brazilians ate Brazilian food in Brazil, it was not strongly interpreted as something especially Brazilian or "ethnic," but was simply seen as a standard meal. However, when they go to a Brazilian restaurant in Japan and savor Brazilian food or when they have a *churrasco* (Brazilian barbecue) party, it is done with the strong awareness that the Brazilian food they eat is quite different from typical Japanese food.[13] Food suddenly becomes a means to culturally distinguish themselves, not only because the Japanese eat differently but also because the Japanese Brazilians frequently find Japanese cuisine bland, "weak," and cold in contrast to Brazilian cuisine, which is stronger and tastier (that is, very high in sodium, sugar, red meat, oil, and unsaturated fat).[14] Therefore, the simple act of eating acquires a new ethnic significance for the nikkeijin as a means to affirm and experience their distinctive Brazilian national identities.[15]

In addition, the Japanese Brazilians find themselves engaging more frequently and actively in traditional Brazilian activities and festivities in Japan than they ever did in Brazil through occasional ethnic events in which Brazilian music, dance, clothes, and food are featured. An increase

---

[13]Because of the rapid proliferation of Brazilian food stores and mobile food vending trucks in Japan, most Japanese Brazilians have ready access to Brazilian food.

[14]According to a Japanese Statistics Research Institute (1993) survey, after homesickness and difficulties with the Japanese language, the next most frequently cited problem was food (21.8 percent of all respondents).

[15]This accounts for the increased consumption of *fejoada* (the most prominent Brazilian national dish) at Brazilian restaurants in Japan.

A group of Japanese Brazilians enjoy a meal at a Brazilian restaurant in Oizumi town.

in such festivities occurs because of their renewed awareness of their "Brazilianness" in Japan and to *matar a saudade do Brasil* (literally, to "kill" their homesickness and longing for Brazil). At other times, such activities are sponsored by local governments to increase cross-cultural awareness and interaction among their residents. Since the Japanese are almost always invited to such occasions, they become opportunities for the Japanese Brazilians to display and demonstrate their Brazilian national culture. Some of the nikkeijin even feel obliged to participate as native "Brazilians."

A notable example here is the samba parades that are organized in areas with high nikkeijin concentrations. Although most Japanese Brazilians never bothered to participate in samba in Brazil (and a few even scorned it as a lowly Brazilian activity), they suddenly find themselves dancing samba in Japan as bona-fide "Brazilians" for the first time in their lives—and actually finding it a lot of fun. Such parades are effective as a means of experiencing "Brazilianness" not only for the participants themselves but also for the Japanese Brazilian spectators. When I attended the annual Oizumi samba parade, Tadashi, my nikkeijin friend from Toyama, expressed a common sentiment when he said, "I never bothered to go see a samba parade in Brazil. But here I am in Japan, watching samba for the first time in my life and feeling very Brazilian." After the parade ended, the Brazilian nikkeijin gathered in a nearby park, where the samba music continued and the spectators themselves were allowed to participate in the dancing until late at night. Such increased participation in ethnic activities through a type of Brazilian cultural revival in Japan intensifies their previously weaker national sentiments to an extent that was not possible in Brazil, where they were not interested and were not as conscious of how such behavior symbolizes Brazilian national identity.[16] This type of revitalization of traditional national festivities and ceremonies occurs among other immigrant groups as well (see Brettell 2000:117–18), including Brazilian immigrants in the United States (see Margolis 1994:187–90; Ribeiro 1999).

In this manner, when the Japanese Brazilians return migrate and are exposed to Japanese culture, they are forced to recognize their own cultural distinctiveness in relation to majority Japanese, making them feel quite Brazilian at the expense of their former transnational "Japanese" identification. This type of deterritorialized resurgence of national sentiments in the host society is a common experience among immigrants. In the home country, individuals are not as aware of the nationally distinct nature of certain behaviors or activities because they are socially shared by those around them as part of the country's culture. However, when they migrate to a different society and are subjected to a new cultural environment, the contrast brings out their cultural distinctiveness, thus creating an increased realization among them of the national differences that make them an ethnic minority in the host society (cf. Sasaki 1999:268).

SOCIOECONOMIC MARGINALIZATION: THE JAPANESE BRAZILIANS AS DEKASEGI IN JAPAN

Social Class Decline, Global Capitalism, and the Marginalization of Migrant Labor

The nationalization of ethnic identity among Japanese Brazilian return migrants is not simply a response to their ethnic marginalization and their

---

[16]Another national Brazilian activity that the Japanese Brazilians engage in actively in Japan is soccer. There are even nikkeijin soccer leagues and nationwide competitions in Japan (*Mainichi Shimbun*, February 29, 1992; November 14, 1992). However, soccer is not as distinctive and prominent as a Brazilian ethnic symbol because many Japanese also play and watch soccer, as shown by the tremendous popularity of the J-League in Japan.

recognition of cultural difference in Japan but also a product of the down-ward social mobility that accompanies their negative immigrant minority status. The sudden decline from their middle-class occupations in Brazil to working-class factory jobs in Japan is just as unsettling and shocking as the change from an ethnically respected "Japanese" minority to an ethni-cally excluded "Brazilian" minority.[17]

Some of my informants claimed that their loss of occupational status in Japan did not bother them, and others found ways to make it more bearable (see chapter 5). However, a good number of my informants spoke openly about their initially difficult experiences taking on such low-status, unskilled jobs and their feelings of shame and damaged pride. Although most Japanese Brazilians mentally prepare themselves before migration for the degrading jobs that they will have to perform in Japan, the actual ex-perience is still quite a shock. One nikkeijin wife I interviewed in Brazil spoke about her prior experience in Japan as follows:

> You go to Japan ready for the low-level jobs you have to do in the fac-tory. We know our social status will decline in Japan, and you accept this as a necessary consequence in order to earn money. But still, when you first put on that factory uniform and take your place on the assem-bly line, it really hurts. It damages your pride.

Others remarked that their factory jobs in Japan were more dirty, difficult, and demeaning than they had expected. "I knew it would be tough on my pride to give up my office job in Brazil and be a factory worker in Japan," one young man from Kawasaki remarked. "But I thought Japanese facto-ries were completely automated so I'd mainly be pushing buttons on a ma-chine. I didn't know I'd be getting my hands dirty and sweating all day."

The loss of occupational status is especially hard for those who had high-status professional jobs or previously held positions of authority as *chefes* (bosses) or *donos* (owners of a business) in Brazil but find themselves powerless subordinates in Japan who are forced to obey orders from less educated, Japanese factory workers. A nisei man in Oizumi who had been a bank manager in Brazil had this to say:

---

[17]Brazilian immigrants in the United States are also very conscious of their decline in social sta-tus from educated, white-collar workers in Brazil to lower-level factory workers in the United States.

Dirty, dangerous, and difficult: two Japanese Brazilian workers (right) in a noisy metal galvanization factory in Kawasaki city.

I really feel the loss of my former status here because I had a high-status job [in Brazil] and associated with only educated people of my level. I was the boss, giving other people orders. My first day in the factory, I remember my supervisor chastised me for not working fast enough. It got me mad and I felt like telling him, "How dare you boss me around? My social level is much higher than yours!" Now, I'm used to the factory work, but I still sometimes ask myself: "Why in the world do I have to do such work in Japan?" Only the salary is good in Japan, but the work is so demeaning.

Those who were well educated in Brazil are also left with a nagging feeling that their skills and ability are being completely wasted in Japan. "I studied twenty years in Brazil and now I am sweeping the floor in a Japanese factory," my friend Tadashi at Toyama once muttered as he passed by me on the assembly line, broom and dustpan in hand.

The social shock of downward class mobility is sometimes accompanied by considerable physical shock as well. Since most Japanese Brazilians have

no prior experience with manual labor, some have trouble adjusting physically to the rigors and strenuous pace of their factory jobs. Complaints
about the difficulty and even pain of assembly line work were frequent
among my nikkeijin co-workers at Toyama. One of my informants, who
had been a housewife in Brazil, told me she got sick and was even hospi-
talized for a month when she first started working in the factory. Even
those who do not suffer physically from the work complain that it is bor-
ing, repetitive, tedious, and dreary. One of my informants claimed that the
mechanical and robotic nature of the work in the factory bothered him
more than the loss in social class status it entailed.

Because of such experiences of downward social mobility or "declassing," the Japanese Brazilians feel not only ethnically excluded as foreigners in Japan but also socioeconomically marginalized as low-class migrant
workers, further solidifying their identity as Brazilian foreigners. In fact,
even within the working class in Japan, the Japanese Brazilians as foreign
migrant workers occupy a marginal position as a casual and irregular
labor force.

In order to fully understand the socioeconomic marginalization of immigrant workers such as the Brazilian nikkeijin, it is necessary to examine
broader national and global capitalist forces within which they are embedded (cf. Lamphere 1992). As the globalization of capitalist production
has intensified, advanced industrialized economies like Japan have come
to increasingly rely on migrant workers in order to cut production costs
in the face of intense competition from developing countries with cheap-
er labor forces. Although many Japanese companies have moved production to Third World countries, those that remain in Japan have been
forced to restructure. Because Japanese firms have been unwilling to
streamline production by downsizing and dismissing their regular workers
(Dore 1986:93), they have become dependent on an expanding informal
labor force of temporary and disposable workers, which serves as a flexible
economic "cushion" that enables them to adjust to business cycles and
temporary declines in production in a cost-effective manner.

As the supply of temporary and part-time domestic workers has dried
up,[18] Japanese companies have increasingly been using foreign workers
such as the Japanese Brazilians as a casual labor force in order to cut costs
and remain competitive in the global economy. Most nikkeijin workers

---

[18]For instance, in 1990, the demand/supply ratio for part-time workers was 4 to 1.

are employed by Japanese labor broker firms,[19] which allow various companies to "borrow" the necessary number of nikkeijin workers for limited periods of time when production increases and conveniently "return" them when they are no longer needed. The broker firm then transfers the excess workers to other companies that need their labor.[20] As a result, most Brazilian nikkeijin are *hi-seishain* (informal, temporary workers) and not regular company employees (*seishain*).

The Japanese Brazilians are very conscious of their marginality even within the Japanese working class. At Toyama, they were acutely aware that as temporary, casual workers, they had no job security in contrast to the regular Japanese employees of the company. Not only would they be the first to be dismissed during a production downturn, they could be transferred by their labor broker firm to another factory at any time. Some of them even claimed that the Japanese workers feel socially superior because of their permanent employment, greater experience, and ability to tell nikkeijin workers what to do.

The peripheral employment status of the Japanese Brazilians as dekasegi migrant workers also socially marginalizes them on the factory floor. Because they are temporary workers contracted from outside labor broker firms, they do not belong to the companies where they work. They are therefore socially separated from the regular Japanese employees at larger firms like Toyama, eat in separate lunchrooms, and are even sometimes segregated in nikkeijin-only work sections. In addition, because the dekasegi are constantly transferred from one company to another, most of the Japanese Brazilians at Toyama did not stay in the factory for more than a few months. Therefore, few Japanese workers bothered to associate with them since they were outsiders to the company who constantly circulated in and out. "You might try to befriend a nikkeijin worker," a Toyama employee explained, "but then they suddenly disappear the next day without warning. So I just don't bother with them anymore." On their side, the Japanese Brazilians found little use in establishing meaningful and long-term relationships with Japanese workers because of their status as transient outsiders who could leave at any time.

---

[19]A comparative study of immigrant labor in Hamamatsu, Japan and San Diego found that 74 percent of the nikkeijin were employed through labor brokers (see Cornelius 1998).
[20]See Tsuda and Cornelius (forthcoming) for further analysis of the utilization of nikkeijin migrant workers in Japan.

For those nikkeijin who previously felt considerable affinity to their ethnic homeland, such experiences of socioeconomic marginalization as foreign workers in Japan alienate them from Japanese society (see Tsuda forthcoming 1 and 2). Using the Brazilian anthropologist Roberto DaMatta's terminology, although they were fully integrated in Brazilian society as relational "persons," they become socially alienated and isolated "individuals" in Japan (DaMatta 1991:170–77). Not only does their ethnic segregation as "foreigners" in Japan make them realize that they are not Japanese, their socioeconomic exclusion makes them acutely aware of their status as Brazilian outsiders.

Liminality: Lack of Social Class Differentiation and Ethnic Identity

At the same time, however, the status of the Japanese Brazilians in Japan as dekasegi on the margins of the working class has become a collectively shared experience that differentiates them from middle-class Japanese society, thus serving as the socioeconomic component of their distinctive identity as Brazilian foreigners in Japan. Transnational migrants like the Japanese Brazilians who experience a significant drop in social class status in the host society frequently find themselves in a state of liminality characterized by a relative lack of hierarchical social differentiation within the immigrant community. According to Victor Turner, liminal periods are characterized by "society as an unstructured or rudimentarily structured and relatively undifferentiated *comitatus* [or communitas] . . . of equal individuals" (1985 [1969]:96). Since over 90 percent of the Brazilian nikkeijin migrants are employed as unskilled factory workers in Japan, they live in a relatively egalitarian and homogeneous community, performing the same type of manual labor, wearing the same uniforms, earning comparable wages,[21] and living in similar apartment complexes. In fact, even socioeconomic gender differences within the nikkeijin family are somewhat reduced as women become wage-earners with full-time jobs comparable to those of their husbands.' Although they still earn lower incomes in Japan,[22] their economic contribution to the family is notably increased in many cases, reducing spousal disparities in socioeconomic status within the family.

---

[21]The only notable difference in pay is between men and women. Also, those who have remained at the same company for a longer period sometimes receive slightly higher pay.

[22]According to the JICA (1992) survey of South American nikkeijin workers, the average hourly wage for men was 1,331 yen, whereas women received only 924 yen.

Of course, some significant differences have emerged among nikkeijin immigrants in Japan in terms of socio-occupational status and income. Not only are 3.5 to 10 percent of them employed as white-collar office workers in Japan, even some of those working in the factories have been promoted to high-status jobs with better pay (see chapter 6). However, an ideology of social equality continues to prevail in the immigrant community. Many Japanese Brazilians emphasized how previous social class distinctions between them in Brazil have receded in Japan and frequently remarked, "*Todos são iguais aqui no Japão*" (all of us are equal here in Japan). A second-generation nisei woman gave me her assessment, variations of which were reiterated by many:

> Regardless of your cultural level in Brazil and whether you were a doctor or engineer or manager, when you come to Japan, everyone becomes a manual laborer (*operário*) with the same wage and has to accept the same orders as subordinates of the Japanese. We are all equal here. We are all peons in Japan and we don't feel differences between rich and poor anymore.

However, this socially undifferentiated sense of liminality and communitas among nikkeijin immigrants is not only the result of apparent similarities in job and income levels. Prior differences in socioeconomic level, education, and occupation in Brazil lose their importance in Japan because they are virtually irrelevant for employment as unskilled immigrant workers (see Tsuda and Cornelius forthcoming). Gilberto, a well-educated Japanese Brazilian, spoke about the indifference of Japanese employers to the nikkeijin's previous socioeconomic status:

> Our educational level means nothing here in Japan, even if you have a Ph.D. This is not something that the Japanese demand of us, or even bother to ask, although sometimes they note such things when we apply for jobs. In the factory, no one knows or cares that you were educated and middle class in Brazil. For the Japanese, we are all just unskilled factory workers.

In fact, the author himself directly experienced the deprivation of former social class status that occurs in Japanese factories during the first day on the job at Toyama. The manager of the subcontracting firm that was employing the nikkeijin for Toyama had heard that the new nikkeijin who had entered the factory that day was actually an American graduate student conducting research. Just in case I had any intention of flaunting my former social status in the factory, the manager came all the way to my section and told me, "I don't care whether you are a student, or a researcher, or how educated you are. Here at Toyama, you are an unskilled factory worker, and all that concerns me is how productive you are as a worker. Is that clear?"

The consciousness among the Japanese Brazilians that they live in a socially egalitarian immigrant community is further reinforced by the dominant tendency among them not to talk about their previous middle-class status in Brazil. At Toyama, conversation among the Brazilian nikkeijin in the factory was focused exclusively on their present lives in Japan; almost nothing was divulged specifically about their former lives in Brazil. Some of my informants felt that talking about the past would stir up bad memories because of the economic problems they had faced in Brazil. However, even those who were relatively well-to-do in Brazil generally do not mention their former social status in order to avoid personal conflicts since speaking and boasting about how well-off they were back home evokes negative reactions from the others, especially those who were less privileged. Wilson, who was a large agricultural producer in Brazil, recounted his experiences in this respect:

> When I first got to Japan, I would boast a lot about how much land my parents owned and how we have a big house in the countryside, but I don't do this anymore. The Japanese didn't believe me, and among the nikkeijin, it made me look stupid. They would say, "if you lived so well in Brazil, why in the world did you have to come to Japan?"

Therefore, the behavioral norm among the Japanese Brazilians who enjoyed a higher social class status is to eventually stop speaking about their former lives in order to avoid resentment and jealousy from those less fortunate. "Those who are still talking about what nice middle-class lives they used to have in Brazil have not yet gotten used to living in Japan," remarked Gilberto. Therefore, it becomes hard to tell whether someone was a taxi driver or a doctor in Brazil or whether the person was rich or poor, educated or uneducated. This further reduces the consciousness of socioeconomic difference among the Japanese Brazilians, reinforcing their ideology of immigrant social equality.

As we saw in chapter 1, the experience of difference with majority society, which brings out the distinctive ethnic identity of a minority group, can also be of a socioeconomic nature if the minority is predominantly associated with a certain social class status that marks them off from the rest of society. Because the social status of dekasegi is so uniform and pervasive among the nikkeijin in Japan, it has become an effective ethnic emblem that identifies them as Brazilian immigrants. The commonly shared dekasegi identity among the Japanese Brazilians has become a basic ethnic attribute in the eyes of both the Japanese majority and the nikkeijin immigrant minority. The Japanese constantly use the word "dekasegi" to refer to the Brazilian nikkeijin both on a personal basis and in newspapers, mass media, and academic papers. The association is so strong that even those who are not factory workers in Japan are automatically seen as dekasegi. "If I don't introduce myself as different from other Brazilian nikkeijin, the Japanese always assume I'm a dekasegi," remarked one Japanese Brazilian graduate student in Japan. "They keep saying how difficult it must be for me in Japan. I have to constantly tell them that I did not come to Japan as a dekasegi for money." In turn, the word has also become a part of the common vocabulary of the Brazilian nikkeijin, who frequently refer to themselves collectively as "*os dekasseguis.*" Like so many other Japanese words, such as *zangyo* (overtime), *yakin* (night shift), *shigoto* (work), and *kyukei* (break time), "dekasegi" has become a common part of their everyday speech, as in "*Nós somos dekasseguis aqui no Japão*" (We are dekasegi here in Japan) or "*Tou fazendo dekassegui agora no Japão*" (I am doing dekasegi now in Japan).

Therefore, the collective experience of low socio-occupational status has become an integral part of the Brazilian identity of the nikkeijin in Japan because it ethnically differentiates them from mainstream Japanese. The nikkeijin frequently mention how they are in Japan to do low-class and undesirable jobs that the Japanese no longer want to do. Since middle-class social status has become an integral part of Japanese ethno-national identity (as it was for the nikkeijin in Brazil who identified as "Japanese"), the Japanese Brazilians acutely feel the difference in occupational status between themselves and what they perceive to be the predominantly white-collar Japanese populace. In this manner, their low social-class status again symbolizes their alienation from Japanese society as socioeconomically marginalized Brazilian foreigners.

The small number of Japanese Brazilians who work as bilingual liaisons in local government offices and companies or are studying in Japan as students do not feel the same social alienation as their compatriots working in the factories. Not only are they not marginalized as casual migrant laborers, they have close daily contact with the Japanese in their offices and universities and do not occupy a low social class that separates them from white-collar Japanese. Partly because their socio-occupational status in Japan does not serve as a strong means of ethnic differentiation, their identities as Brazilian outsiders are not as strong (see below).

NEGATIVE MEANINGS OF JAPANESE CULTURE AND SOCIETY AND THE DEVELOPMENT OF ETHNIC COUNTERIDENTITIES

In addition to experiencing ethnic and socioeconomic marginalization as "individuals" segregated from Japanese society, the Brazilian nikkeijin also develop some unfavorable attitudes about Japanese culture and society. Some of these negative perceptions are undoubtedly conditioned by their low social-class status in Japan, since immigrants who experience severe downward social mobility usually develop a highly critical perception of the host society (Portes and Rumbaut 1996:190). Such experiences challenge their previously positive images of Japan and further alienate them from Japanese society, thereby contributing to the "rediscovery" of their Brazilian national identity abroad in Japan.

"Japan-bashing" has by now become a prominent part of the nikkeijin ethnic experience in Japan and takes place during conversations in restaurants, at home, and at work. Non-negative or positive comments about the Japanese are rather rare and overshadowed by negative assessments. Some in fact engage in wide-ranging diatribes, such as Martina, a sansei woman who had returned to Japan for a second sojourn:

> I have no admiration now for Japan. The Japanese are false. They always appear friendly and smile in front of others, but when they turn their backs, they talk ill of the person. Brazilians are more sincere because they show all in their behavior. In Brazil, if you have friends, you always invite them over casually because you like them, but in Japan, a person goes to someone else's house to find out what his acquaintance can do for him. The Japanese are also very materialistic people and only care about money. There is no affection in Japan.

Negative Evaluations of Japanese Cultural Behavior

Among the many aspects of Japanese cultural behavior that are brought up for specific criticism, the Japanese Brazilians find the "cold," unreceptive, and impersonal nature of Japanese social relationships to be the most disappointing and deficient. As one individual succinctly stated, "Japan may be the First World technologically and economically, but they are the Fifth World when it comes to human relationships." "*Os japoneses são frios*," "*os japoneses são fechados*," or "*os japoneses têm um coração frio*" (the Japanese are "cold," "closed," or have a "cold heart") are among the most frequent negative comments made in Japan about the Japanese, especially in regard to their unwillingness to interact with strangers and foreigners.[23] Likewise, the Japanese are also commonly portrayed as people lacking *calor humano* (human warmth), who are less caring, affectionate, talkative, and willing to make friends in contrast to the Brazilians. This seems to be a universal complaint among Brazilian immigrants in other countries as well, whose receptions by host populaces seem "cold" compared to the warm acceptance and respect foreigners enjoy in Brazil (see Margolis 1994:173; Martes 2000:158; Ribeiro 1999:74–75; Sales 1998:99–100).

However, such perceptions about Japanese social relationships may be the product of differences not only between Brazilian and Japanese culture but also between office and factory work environments. In contrast to the more relaxed, quieter, and socially congenial nature of office work that most nikkeijin were accustomed to in Brazil, factory work is frequently fast-paced, noisy, and incessant, making any personal interaction on the job much more difficult and unlikely. Yet, the negative assessments of Japanese relationships made by the Japanese Brazilians are based on their observations of the Japanese outside the factory as well.

The perceived cold nature of the Japanese is frequently contrasted by the Japanese Brazilians with their own social relationships and makes them appreciate the warmth, friendliness, and openness of the Brazilians.[24] A nisei mestiço made some typical comments:

The Japanese are cold and don't have human warmth, even among themselves. It is because of their upbringing. In Brazil, we always invit-

---

[23]An older Japanese Brazilian woman in Kawasaki was one of the few who disagreed with her compatriots about Japanese coldness:
   All the [Japanese] Brazilians say that the Japanese are cold and racist and don't care about us, but this is not true. I work in a [factory] section where I am the only Brazilian and all others are Japanese. They treat me well, even if I don't speak Japanese, and help me out a lot. When my husband wounded his arm, the people at the hospital were kind, comforting, and very professional.
[24]A similar process occurs among Brazilian immigrants in the United States when they are confronted by the "coldness" and formality of Americans (Sales 1998:101).

ed people into our houses and we visited neighbors and friends all the time without hesitation. The Japanese don't have this custom and are very reluctant to have guests. They just go out to drink in bars, but then only with other men. Even neighbors don't have contact with each other here—they are strangers. In Brazil, neighbors always go out into the street, greet each other, and chat and go to each other's houses.

Similar observations are made about relationships between factory workers. The following is a representative statement:

In Brazil, people always talk to each other during work, unlike the Japanese who just work and don't say anything. Company employees in Brazil always go out together after work and go to friends' houses to talk. In Japan, even among the Japanese, I don't think this happens. The Japanese don't associate with each other outside the factory. Even when one of the workers from our factory comes to our apartment to tell us something, he doesn't come inside even when we invite him for coffee.

Another commonly noted cultural contrast is one of human emotion in which the Japanese are seen as lacking *carinho* (affection) and *sentimentos*. This was observed not only in general social interaction but also within Japanese spousal relationships, which are characterized by some nikkeijin as impersonal and distant and without the affection and love shown in Brazilian marriages. In general, the Japanese are described as introverted (*introvertido*) and restrained (*retraído*) and the Brazilians as extroverted, expressive, more outgoing, and happier in disposition.[25] Some of my informants felt that the Japanese insincerely and falsely hide their emotions, sentiments, and inner opinions, whereas the Brazilians are more open about their true feelings and attitudes.

Likewise, some of my nikkeijin informants characterized the Japanese as workaholics who do not socialize with each other, spend enough time with their families, or have active and fulfilling social lives like Brazilians. The opinions of one young nikkeijin man touch upon some of these impressions:

The Japanese were born to work and don't know how to have fun. They just go back and forth between the company and home and don't have

---

[25]Brazilians frequently characterize themselves as more emotional, passionate, and sentimental than others (see Scheper-Hughes 1992:433–34).

enough time for travel or leisure. Even when they go out on weekends with their wives and children, they have to plan things out weeks in advance. This is very strange for Brazilians. In Brazil, social gatherings would be spontaneous. People would just call each other up and simply get together.

"I asked a Japanese worker the other day what he did during the weekend and he said he just slept," my friend Tadashi once told me during break at Toyama. "The Japanese just concentrate on their work. Brazilians never think like this—they always enjoy life and would never kill themselves working."

In these cases and many others, there is a tendency for the Japanese Brazilians to interpret negative behavior by individual Japanese as a cultural characteristic and therefore to overgeneralize it to all Japanese as an ethnic trait. This is another example of "ethnic attribution" in which the behavior of individuals from a different and less familiar ethnic group is explained simplistically as an ethnic/cultural trait instead of a product of particular personalities or situational circumstances.

Japanese work habits and gender attitudes toward women were also frequently singled out for special criticism. Again, Japanese standards of behavior are given low marks and negative meanings by the Japanese Brazilians; in contrast, their own "Brazilian" cultural characteristics are seen as positive attributes. Although some Brazilian nikkeijin feel that the Japanese spend all their time working at the expense of their family and social lives, they also generally have negative evaluations of the actual ability and work ethic of their Japanese counterparts (cf. Tajima 1998:191). In contrast, they see themselves as working harder, better, and more conscientiously (cf. Capuano de Oliveira 1999:294–95). Tadashi recounted his experiences at Toyama:

> The [Japanese] Brazilians are much more precise and certain about their work. The Japanese do bad work but don't care. It's really regrettable. If a screw falls into a machine, they let it be and forget about it. When something like this happens, I always tell my hancho, who comes over to remove the screw, but the Japanese don't care. They don't work very effectively and just push stuff out of the way when they need more space. I am much more careful in my work.

"The Japanese think they are superior to us because they have been in the factory for much longer and have more experience," one nisei woman claimed. "But the Brazilians work better. In my workplace, I do the work of three Japanese and do it more efficiently and seriously. The Japanese workers don't want to contribute to quality. If the [Japanese] Brazilians do better work, the Japanese get jealous."

The lack of creative intelligence among the Japanese and their inflexibility are also frequently noted, in contrast to which some of the nikkeijin portray themselves as more innovative and effective:

> The Japanese have ability in what they do because most work at least five years doing the same job, but they have no creativity. Foreigners have more ability in this respect. The Japanese meticulously follow rules and just do exactly as they are told by their supervisors. But the Brazilians have more intelligence and try to work more practically by finding efficient ways to do things.

In terms of gender attitudes, some Japanese Brazilian women had harsh words for the manner in which they felt women are treated in Japanese society. The most frequently noted inequality was discrimination on the job, in which women receive less money for doing the same type of work because of a traditional gender gap in wages that persists despite Japanese antidiscrimination laws. A few Japanese Brazilian women even felt that they were paid less but are forced to do *more* difficult work than men in the factories. Others complained about how they were treated at work by their male supervisors. A typical response was given by Martina, who was more outspoken about this issue than the others:

> If I make a mistake at work, my supervisors tell me and I apologize. But if I am warned about something that is not my fault, I argue directly to my supervisor, who always tells me to be quiet since I am a woman. They say women shouldn't disagree but need to accept their lot with a bowed head. I can't accept this, so I argue. Japanese women are too submissive. It is cultural—lots of them see themselves as inferior to men.

Another nikkeijin woman was even more denunciatory and remarked, "In my factory, they use vulgar gestures to women and treat them like trash. Women are just there to have sex with and to clean the house and cook. We find this to be an outrage."

Gender relationships in Japanese families were also viewed negatively by a number of Japanese Brazilian women.[26] Again, Martina was quite critical in her assessment:

> Japan is really outdated when it comes to women and traditional behavior still continues at home. The woman stays in the house and takes care of the kids and the cleaning while men work outside. When the husband comes home, he never enters the kitchen and does zero work around the home. He sits at the table, tells his wife to bring the beer, then crosses his arms and waits for the food to come. Japanese women should change this situation if they think it is wrong. But they accept their submission.

However, it was not simply women who had a negative opinion of Japanese family relationships—some Japanese Brazilian men would also occasionally express their disapproval. One of my roommates in Oizumi, Umberto, came home from the local supermarket one day and spoke about an incident he had just witnessed:

> I was really surprised with what I saw at Iseya [Oizumi shopping center]. There was this poor Japanese mother struggling with all these bags of groceries and trying to get her children onto the escalator while the husband had already gotten on and was waiting at the top. I felt so bad for this woman that I went over and helped her with her groceries. This is typical behavior between husband and wife in Japanese families.

The treatment of women in Japan is again criticized from what is seen as the much better position of women in Brazilian families, as was evident in the reflections of Ivone, a nisei woman in Oizumi:

> Discrimination against women is big among the Japanese here. In Brazil, men and women receive equal wages for equal work. Behavior in the family is also different and there is more care and affection between husband and wife. Brazilians split their lives more evenly between work and the home and men do lots of the household chores. Women are not submissive and don't simply obey what men tell them to do. Although

---

[26]In the JICA survey of nikkeijin (1992:39), one of the most frequently cited differences between Japan and Brazil was Japanese machismo and the privileging of men over women.

the Japanese are coming to accept western ways, they still do not even
have the freedom to choose their spouses here.

In this manner, not only are differences in gender relationships in Japanese and Brazilian families accentuated, they are imbued with a strong
moral value in which the more equitable position of women in the Brazilian family is favorably viewed as right and proper compared to the negative situation in Japan. This simple contrast between patriarchal Japanese
families and more egalitarian Brazilian ones becomes especially stark for
nikkeijin women because of the above-mentioned reduction in gender inequality within their own families caused by migration. In contrast to the
greater hierarchical status differences that prevailed between spouses in
Brazil, where the husband was usually the principal breadwinner, both
spouses perform similar types of assembly line jobs in the factories and
work similar hours.[27] This leads to more egalitarian patterns of household
decision making, authority, and distribution of household duties and
chores (Grasmuck and Pessar 1991:93–94; 148–56; Margolis 1994:238–40;
Repak 1995:160–61).

The contrast is especially stark for women who did not work much outside the home and were mainly housewives in Brazil. A number of Japanese Brazilian women in Japan told me that they were able to make more
demands on their husbands in terms of household chores because they now
worked outside the home, make a substantial financial contribution to the
family, and therefore enjoyed greater economic and social power. In order
to emphasize this point, one of my female informants during a joint interview dumped a basketload of laundry in front of her husband, who dutifully began folding the clothes before putting them away. I remember other
male informants taking care of babies or even finishing their cooking when
I visited them while their wives worked during the evening. This greater
egalitarianism within their own families undoubtedly increases their negative perception of gender inequality in Japanese families.

There were other aspects of Japanese behavior that were negatively eval-
uated by the Japanese Brazilians as unfavorable cultural attributes. A number of my informants, on several occasions, characterized the Japanese as

---

[27]In many factories, including Toyama, there is no notable difference between the types of jobs
men and women do on the assembly line, since none of the work requires much physical
strength. However, factories with more physically demanding work (like automobile assembly) hire predominantly men or assign men to these types of jobs.

imitators lacking creativity. Images of Japanese as group conformists who think in homogeneous ways were also prevalent in some of the comments. Likewise, the Japanese were also frequently criticized as people who are very insular in thinking and limited in knowledge and familiarity with people from other countries (cf. Tajima 1998:191). They also received low marks for not living up to their reputation for respecting elders. A number of Japanese Brazilians expressed disappointment at what they perceived as improper and discourteous treatment of older Japanese both within and outside the factory. The opinion of Tadashi was representative:

> My father told me in Brazil that elders are respected in Japan, but I see old people doing worse jobs in the factories and getting paid less. Even if they are old, they still have to work. In some sections, older workers are not helped when they can't keep up with the work. In Brazil, you wouldn't have such behavior. When older people enter buses and trains, Japanese youth don't stand up to give up their seats like Brazilian youth always do. They keep sitting, or pretend they are sleeping.

Finally, the Japanese were described as materialistic, wasteful, and overly consumer-oriented (*consumista*) a number of times. A few noted how the Japanese simply throw things out without bothering to fix them and dispose of new cars after two years. Indeed, it is quite remarkable what some resourceful Japanese Brazilians can salvage from piles of Japanese "garbage" (large items for disposal, called *sodaigomi*, can be left out for pickup by the city). I have seen Japanese Brazilians bring home functional TVs, vacuums, fans, space heaters, portable boom boxes, and bicycles, all of which had been discarded by the Japanese (cf. Linger 2001:38; Yamashita 2001:30). "The Japanese are the most wasteful people in the world," one of my roommates in Oizumi concluded as he dragged home a vacuum cleaner. "All it needed was a new plug." In fact, it seems that Americans are equally wasteful, according to Brazilian immigrants in the United States, some of whom have literally furnished their entire apartment with what they call American "garbage decor" (Margolis 1994:72).

Such unfavorable evaluations of the Japanese people are quite a contrast to the perceptions the Japanese Brazilians had in Brazil before migration, where their positive and overly idealized images had been the basis of their transnational ethnic identification as a "Japanese" minority. In Japan, however, they discover many negative aspects of Japaneseness. As a result, many of them are quite disappointed and disillusioned as they

find that the Japanese do not live up to their previous ideals and expectations (cf. JICA 1992:38; Watanabe et al. 1992:79) and realize that the positive qualities they associated with the Japanese in the past were exaggerated, inaccurate, or simply not true.[28] The following excerpt from one of
my interviews with a middle-aged nikkeijin man illustrates the disillu-
sionment and loss of respect in the Japanese that a good number of my informants experienced:

> When we were in Brazil, we put lots of value in Japanese culture, not
> just in terms of attitudes and behavior but philosophically, and even
> spiritually as well. We emphasized our Japanese characteristics and
> would always say that we were different and that the Brazilians do not
> act as we do. But then we come to Japan and are shocked and disap-
> pointed because we see that reality is so different here. What we valued
> as "Japanese" in Brazil was only an image and it has died here in Japan.

The Discrepancy Between Expectation and Reality: Unfulfilled Images of the Primeiro Mundo

The Japanese Brazilians come to Japan with rather idealistic conceptions
not only about its people and culture but also about Japanese society as a
highly developed First World nation of ultramodern cities, advanced industrialized development, high technology, and luxurious living standards. Because of such expectations, the Japanese Brazilians are quite disappointed when they actually experience the country's narrow streets,
small houses, poorer neighborhoods, and relatively low living standards
and find that Japan is much less developed than they had previously imagined. Statements such as the following by a nisei man are abundant:

> I thought Japan would be highly developed, but there is a part that is de-
> veloped and not developed. I imagined that everything would be new
> and modern and beautiful, but you have old, ugly areas that look like
> *favelas* (Brazilian shantytowns) with badly made wooden houses. I was
> surprised by this. They would always show advanced Japanese technol-

---

[28]In fact, a compilation of letters written by Japanese Brazilians to one of the Portuguese newspapers in Japan (the *International Press*) is appropriately entitled *A Quebra dos Mitos* (The
Breaking of Myths).

ogy on Brazilian TV, but I don't see this technology in the day-to-day lives of the Japanese. Japan has technology and is rich, but the people don't live comfortably.

Other Japanese Brazilians realize that only Japanese cities are modern, while most of the vast expanses of countryside appear backward and underdeveloped. Some were also surprised by the small and dingy factories where they are frequently employed, in which much of the work is still done manually, in stark contrast to images of highly mechanized and modernized factories in Japan. One Japanese Brazilian woman working next to me on the assembly line at Toyama said, "I thought in Brazil that everything was modernized in Japanese factories with lots of high-tech robots doing the work. But working here, I don't see a robot in sight."

Frequently, specific examples of Japanese backwardness were cited by various informants, such as primitive dental treatment among elders, inefficient garbage collection, lack of sidewalks, poor street lighting, and old bicycles. Martina noted another aspect of Japanese backwardness that other informants also mentioned with some shock:

> They show things from Japan in Brazil, and it's always modern, high-tech buildings and beautiful houses. But here in Oizumi, they still have houses without flushing toilets. They just have a hole in the floor and it smells up the entire place when you open the door. You don't have this in Brazil. No flushing toilets in the First World? Japan is not as advanced as one thinks.

Indeed, those who were not disappointed in the material aspects of Japanese society were quite rare. This is not to say that most Japanese Brazilians do not appreciate the positive aspects of living in Japan. The country's socioeconomic stability, low crime rate, efficient transportation system, practical conveniences, and disciplined school system are among the positive social aspects of Japan that are frequently mentioned (cf. Yamanaka 2000:143). Some also enjoy its consumer culture, especially with the greater purchasing power they have in Japan. In general, however, the reaction of disappointment toward Japanese society prevails. As a result, a number of Japanese Brazilians realize that Brazil is not as underdeveloped as they previously thought and that urban living standards in Third World Brazil are not that low in comparison to First World Japan and are indeed more advanced in many ways. Despite the economic opportunities that

Japan offers, most conclude that from a purely social standpoint, Brazil is indeed a better country in which to live.

A minority of the Brazilian nikkeijin also had an antiquated perception of Japanese society based on nostalgic images of traditional Japanese culture, epitomized by ancient Japanese shrines, *samurai*, *kabuki*, and *kimono* (traditional Japanese dress). Such images are received both from their parents, who are familiar only with the old and rural Japan, and from some of the traditional Japanese festivities and practices that are maintained in Japanese ethnic associations and colônias in Brazil. In addition, some nikkeijin have seen old Japanese films in Brazil that are either historical or portray life in prewar or immediate postwar Japan. Others have looked at books and vacation guides that emphasize the historical beauty of Japanese shrines and temples as well as national parks. Although the Japanese Brazilians realize that such images of Japanese tradition are outdated, some still migrate with the nostalgic expectation and hope that some aspects of old Japan have been properly preserved. Again, they are disillusioned when they fully realize how completely westernized Japan has become, without any semblance of the traditional Japan that they had savored in Brazil. One nisei whose parents are from Okinawa related his experiences as follows:

> I always saw programs about Japanese folklore and beautiful rural areas. I also saw videos in Brazil about traditional Japanese culture such as *shamisen* [a traditional Japanese string instrument] and kabuki and felt a certain longing for Japan. My parents told me a lot of Japan, and Japanese traditions were a source of pride in the colônia in Brazil. I thought Japan would be less westernized but when I first arrived, I was surprised. Japan is too westernized, even more than Brazil, and there is nothing of the old, traditional Japanese culture left.

Another informant had similar impressions:

> I thought Japan was more traditional. I thought that many Japanese still walked around in kimonos because of what they show in films and [on] TV. But in Ueno or Shibuya (Tokyo), you see strange youth who just copy American ways. Houses, I thought were more traditional, but today, it's all modernized. I thought signs and ads in Japan would be written only in Japanese, but they use lots of English. I was surprised and disappointed because Japan was nothing like what I had imagined.

In fact, such reactions are similar to those of foreign-born ethnic Germans who return migrate to Germany and discover that the reality of modern (Americanized) Germany clashes with older German traditions and customs they had inherited from their parents and grandparents (Münz and Ohliger 1998:181).

Because of the disappointment arising from the discrepancy between prior expectations about Japan and actual reality, the initially positive images that the Japanese Brazilians had of Japan in Brazil suddenly worsen and are replaced by a much less favorable understanding of what it means to be Japanese (cf. Tajima 1998:188, 190–91).[29] As the cultural meaning of Japaneseness switches from positive to negative after migration, the Japanese Brazilians experience a profound alienation from their previous transnational "Japanese" identity. At the same time, however, when compared to the perceived negative aspects of Japan, the positive value of Brazilian culture and society suddenly emerges to a much greater extent, in contrast to the more negative meaning it previously had for them in Brazil (cf. Capuano de Oliveira 1999:297; Koga 1995:44; Mori 1992:148–49). Although the Japanese Brazilians in Brazil had frequently spoken of the negative aspects of Brazilian society and had maintained a critical distance as a "Japanese" minority, I observed a notable tendency among those in Japan to praise Brazil, even to an exaggerated extent, which was rare among them back home. Brazil is still characterized as a country with serious political, economic, and social problems, but other aspects of it are spoken of highly and contrasted favorably with Japan, such as its people, culture, material living conditions, sheer size, agriculture, natural resources, beautiful scenery, sports heroes, and food.

Because of this positive reconceptualization of Brazil in Japan, the Japanese Brazilians also develop very strong feelings of *saudade* (homesickness and emotional longing) for their natal homeland. "*Eu me sinto muita saudade do Brasil*" (I feel a lot of longing/homesickness toward Brazil) is a

---

[29]A questionnaire survey (Nishioka 1995) also documents the generally negative shift in opinion about the Japanese that occurs among the Japanese Brazilians in Japan. Respondents were asked both before and after migration whether they agreed with certain positive characteristics attributed to the Japanese. In all cases, there were significant negative shifts in perception after migration. The percentage of those who felt that the Japanese are honest fell from 61.6 to 43.8 percent, those that thought the Japanese are *majime* (serious, dedicated, studious) declined from 46.5 to 32 percent, those who believed that "the Japanese are hard working and diligent" fell from 63.7 to 43.4 percent, those who felt "the Japanese are smart" fell from 50.7 to 31.4 percent, and those who thought "the Japanese are kind" fell from 40.4 to 23.4 percent.

sentiment commonly heard among Brazilian nikkeijin migrants in Japan. In fact, 60 percent of them cite saudade as the biggest social problem they experience in Japan (see Kitagawa 1997). Such emotional feelings of nostalgia and longing for the home country are experienced by Brazilian (as well as Portuguese) immigrants in other countries as well (see Feldman-Bianco 1992; Margolis 1994). In this manner, migration and travel abroad enable positive feelings toward one's country of origin to be articulated in contrast to a negative foreign context and then infused with sentiments of nostalgic longing, so it can be experienced as an object of desire worthy of a true "homeland."[30] The result for the Japanese Brazilians is a greater identification with the Brazilian nation through an increased realization and affirmation of those positive qualities that make them ethnically Brazilian (cf. Roth 1999:147–48). One of my informants spoke about this positive reassessment of Brazil in the clearest terms:

> Brazilians think other countries are much better. The Japanese Brazilians always looked to Japan this way. But today, I realize we Brazilians were wrong. We didn't know what we had in Brazil. There is no better place than Brazil to live, especially because we were born there and have no linguistic or cultural problems. The people are better there and so are the conditions of living. I value Brazil much more now.

Since their understanding of Japanese society becomes laden with negative affect, not only do the Japanese Brazilians distance and disassociate themselves from the majority Japanese in Japan, but the resurgence of their Brazilian national sentiments takes on an oppositional quality as a minority "counteridentity" that is affirmed as a reaction against what is seen unfavorably as Japanese. Ethnic counteridentities are formed when minority groups refuse to identify with a negatively perceived dominant culture by asserting and maintaining a sense of ethnic difference in opposition to majority society.

Índios, Amazonia, Favelas, e Crime: *Japanese Brazilian Perceptions of Negative Japanese Images About Brazil*

The development of a Brazilian nationalist counteridentity is also a response to the unfavorable images of Brazil that many Japanese Brazilians

---

[30]See Tsuda (forthcoming 2) for a more detailed analysis.

believe prevail among the Japanese. Virtually all of my informants claimed that all the Japanese know about Brazil is the Amazon jungle, Indians, poverty, crime, drugs, political corruption, and samba (cf. Linger 2001:163). The comments of an older Japanese Brazilian woman were very typical of this dominant perception:

> All that they show in Japan about Brazil is the Amazon, poverty, crime, and carnaval, and they never show the good or developed parts of the country. Few know about São Paulo or Avenida Paulista [the central business district in São Paulo]. The Japanese also think Brazil is a very violent place with lots of crime.

The Japanese Brazilians also frequently claim that they (or their acquaintances) are asked whether Brazil has electricity, cars, TVs, and telephones. Other questions include how close they live to the Amazon, whether they wear shirts and shoes in Brazil or carry guns, or whether Indians walk naked in the streets. Similarly low images of Brazil seem to be prevalent in other First World countries as well. In fact, Brazilian immigrants in the United States have the same complaints as the nikkeijin about the American perception of Brazil (Margolis 1994:249–50).

Because of such negative Japanese images of Brazilian poverty and underdevelopment, a good number of my informants were aware that they are seen as poor and low class in Brazil. One sansei man's reactions to such Japanese perceptions were quite representative: "The Japanese think we were really poor in Brazil and were suffering from hunger. They have no idea that we had sufficient conditions to live in Brazil, or that many of us are educated." Another alleged, "Some Japanese believe we live in the *favelas* (shantytowns) and have to struggle just to live and eat." Others went further: "The Japanese think we live like wild Indians in the Amazon in a shack without toilets and that we bathe in the river nearby," one nisei woman claimed. "I get this impression from the questions that they ask about Brazil." A common story told by the Japanese Brazilians is about how they (or an acquaintance) showed photographs of their houses and possessions in Brazil to Japanese workers, who were surprised and amazed at their relatively high middle-class living standards back home and wondered why they had come to Japan as dekasegi if they had lived so well in Brazil.

The uniformity of opinion among my informants about Japanese perceptions of Brazil and images of nikkeijin poverty was quite surprising. In fact, only two of them felt that the Japanese have positive images of Brazil or know about their middle-class status back home. A few mentioned that the Japanese image of Brazil is improving with the increased prominence of Brazilian soccer in Japan.[31] Undoubtedly, many of the nikkeijin encounter some naive and outrageous images about Brazil and its living standards because they are mainly in contact with Japanese unskilled workers, generally the least-informed and -educated sector of the populace.

However, the Toyama factory workers I spoke with did not have the simplistic understandings of Brazil that many nikkeijin attribute to them. Although Brazil did evoke images of poverty, crime, and jungles, some had brighter and cheerful perceptions, and few thought the country was without large cities or seriously believed the Japanese Brazilians live without electricity or plumbing in shantytowns or in the Amazon wilderness. In fact, most had a very low awareness of Brazil and only had scattered impressions, such as of soccer, coffee, beaches, natural resources, tropical fruit, Rio de Janeiro, hot weather, music, and ethnic and racial intermixture.

Most of my nikkeijin informants alleged that unfavorable images of Brazil are passed on by the Japanese media, which report only on the negative aspects of Brazil because only such types of news attract attention as *novidades* (novelties). However, the few programs about Brazil I did see on television were not merely lopsided portraits of crime, poverty, and Brazilian primitiveness, although there are specials about nature in the Amazon. The documentaries and clips about Brazil tended to provide many different images of the country and covered a wide range of topics ranging from religious cults and Rio de Janeiro to politics and Brazilian industry. One long documentary focused on the modernist capital of Brasília, even claiming that "long before a single skyscraper existed in Japan, Brazil was already constructing a great futuristic city of the twenty-first century."

Therefore, some of the negative accounts and claims that the Japanese Brazilians make about what the Japanese think of Brazil seem to be exaggerated and partly conditioned by their own strong self-consciousness of Brazil's low image in the world. In addition, some of the supposedly outrageous questions that the Japanese ask about Brazil are put in a joking manner, but are frequently taken seriously by the Japanese Brazilians. More important, upon closer questioning, it became clear that many of my informants' accounts about outrageous Japanese perceptions of Brazil

---

[31]Japanese professional soccer teams (the J-League) are increasingly using a good number of prominent Brazilian soccer players, including World Cup stars such as Leonardo. One of the players, Ramos, has even married a Japanese, naturalized, and learned to speak some Japanese, and has become a prominent Japanese celebrity.

were based not on their own experiences but on what they have heard from friends and acquaintances. Frequently, even these acquaintances had heard these stories secondhand. In this manner, an experience limited to a select number of individuals is widely disseminated through the ethnic community until it becomes a prototypic experience in its collective consciousness, despite the fact that few of its members have actually had the experience. Often, the extent to which an experience is disseminated is not based on its statistical frequency but simply on its "shock value."

It is also true that some of the perceptions and experiences that immigrants have in the host society are preconditioned by rumors that they have heard back home. Even before migrating, some Japanese Brazilians have heard negative stories about the Japanese from previous dekasegi who have returned from Japan. For instance, during one orientation session I attended in a Japanese colônia in Brazil, a group of Japanese Brazilians preparing to leave for Japan was advised by their dekasegi predecessors not to get annoyed when the Japanese ask them whether Brazil has electricity or cars. The most illustrative example of a Japanese Brazilian migrating to Japan with such preconstituted negative experiences occurred when one of my former informants in Kawasaki, Dirce, introduced me to her nikkeijin friend who was accompanying us on a trip to downtown Tokyo. While we were walking to the station, her friend went into a standard discussion of how the Japanese have a low image of Brazil. I naturally assumed Dirce's friend had been in Japan for quite some time, judging from the experienced and authoritative manner in which she spoke, and was quite surprised to find out that she had just arrived in Japan for her first sojourn five days before.

The questionable empirical basis for such perceptions does not reduce their impact on the ethnic identity of Japanese Brazilian immigrants, since self-consciousness is a matter of subjective perceptions that are often not tempered by objective verification. Although many of the nikkeijin did not previously identify strongly with Brazil or have much pride in being Brazilian, when they experienced such outrageous and derogatory images of their country in Japan, a majority of them reacted quite negatively. When describing their reactions, they frequently used words such as *chateado* (irritated, annoyed), *raiva* (anger), or *revoltado* (upset, outraged). Such experiences, therefore, bring out their previously latent Brazilian national sentiments to a much greater extent as they feel a sudden need in Japan to "defend" Brazil by refuting such negative images and inaccurate stereotypes and emphasizing their country's positive aspects. One of my nikkeijin friends at Toyama expressed this common sentiment quite well:

When I realize how the Japanese think Brazil is just Indians and the Amazon and how they treat us as *coitados* (miserable, poor fellows) who live in shantytowns, it really makes me angry and annoyed. If I spoke Japanese better, I would explain to them that Brazil is not like this. I would tell them about the good aspects of Brazil and how developed and rich certain parts of the country are and what we have back home. I would show the Japanese that *they* are the coitados living in their miserable, tiny apartments and houses. But the Japanese don't believe you when you say these things of Brazil. They think it's a lie. Next time I come to Japan, I will bring photos of São Paulo.

Therefore, the greater value and appreciation for things Brazilian that the Japanese Brazilians feel in Japan is based on both their negative perceptions of Japan and their defensive reaction to Japanese negative perceptions of Brazil. Among a number of my informants, this was even connected to an increase in national pride and patriotism as they discovered a strong allegiance to the Brazilian nation that they had not previously fully acknowledged. "In Brazil, I never gave too much value to the Brazilian country, but now I do," a sansei man said. "I feel more patriotism toward Brazil." Another declared: "My sentiments for my homeland of Brazil and my love for the country will never leave me no matter how long I stay in Japan." This greater sense of Brazilian national allegiance among the nikkeijin in Japan is also symbolized by the prominent display of the Brazilian flag in their ethnic stores and restaurants, although the flag is hardly ever displayed in Brazil.[32] When analyzing the change in ethnic identity that the Japanese Brazilians experience as a result of migration, this resurgence of Brazilian nationalism in a deterritorialized, Japanese context cannot be ignored.

THE SUBJECTIVE EXPERIENCE OF ETHNIC "DISCRIMINATION"

The negative ethnic experiences that the Japanese Brazilians have in Japan are not limited to their exclusion as foreigners and their unfavorable assessment of Japanese behavior and culture. Their ethnic encounter with

---

[32]The only exception is during the World Cup when the Brazilian flag is sold by the thousands and is literally plastered on every store, office, home, car, and T-shirt.

the Japanese is loaded with subjective interpretations of "discrimination." Migrant groups frequently respond to negative experiences of discrimination by psychologically distancing themselves from the host country and renewing their feelings of attachment to their home country (cf. Clifford 1994:311; Joppke 1999:18). This type of deterritorialized migrant nationalism therefore becomes a counteridentity that is asserted against a negatively experienced host society (Simpson and Yinger 1972:198). The emergence of similar "resistance identities" in the face of exclusion and discrimination has also been noted among migrants in Europe and Arab Americans (Castells 1997:20; Naber 2000). In fact, the greater the level of discrimination, the more migrants will maintain a strong minority counteridentity as a form of resistance and active opposition.[33]

Objective and Subjective "Discrimination"

It is important to note that despite all their complaints about Japanese ethnic exclusion and lack of human warmth, the Japanese Brazilians do not feel mistreated or derogated in Japan. In one questionnaire survey, up to 86 percent of the respondents felt that their relationships with Japanese workers were good (Kitagawa 1997). Although a number of them cite certain incidents or factories where they have experienced negative treatment or encountered Japanese who do not like the nikkeijin, these were seen as isolated cases and not as a general pattern. Outside the factory, many Japanese Brazilians appreciate the polite and courteous treatment they receive as customers in Japanese stores.

Despite this, however, many of them continue to feel ethnic "discrimination" to a considerable extent. This is well documented in various research surveys. Kitagawa's 1997 survey found that 79 percent of the respondents felt discrimination from the Japanese and only 16 percent did not feel discriminated against. In Nishioka's (1995) survey, about 80 percent reported discriminatory treatment.[34] Only a minority of my informants did not mention discrimination or explicitly stated that they do not feel discriminated against in Japan. In one of Kitagawa's surveys, 36.5

---

[33]The situation is quite different for second-generation immigrant minorities, which may attempt to assimilate to majority society to avoid discrimination (see Tsuda 2001).

[34]Other surveys report lower rates of discrimination. The Japan Statistics Research Institute survey (Mori 1994) and the 1992 JICA study report that a little over 30 percent of the nikkeijin feel discriminated against.

percent of the Japanese Brazilians said they were *more* likely to become targets of discrimination in Japan than other immigrant foreigners, despite their Japanese descent (Kitagawa 1993).

Such seeming contradictions between reports of favorable treatment in Japanese society and experiences of ethnic discrimination among the Brazilian nikkeijin show a fundamental ambivalence that perhaps illustrates the tension many feel when encountering both the polite external behavior of the Japanese and the uneasy sense that ethnic prejudice probably lurks under the surface. In my interviews, a good number of my informants would make blanket statements about how they were treated well or experienced no real problems with the Japanese. However, as the conversation progressed, it would become evident that many of them viewed aspects of their experience with the Japanese in a negative way, even calling the Japanese "*racistas*" (racists).

Regardless of the actual objective levels of discrimination against immigrants in the host society, the manner in which they *subjectively* perceive discrimination is what directly influences their ethnic identity as a form of subjective self-consciousness. This distinction between "objective" and "subjective" discrimination is important because at times, there can be considerable discrepancy between discrimination as objectively measured on the *etic* level and subjectively perceived on the *emic* level. Even if "objectively" observable discrimination seems relatively low, an oversensitive minority group can continue to feel discriminated against.

In the previous chapter, I argued that despite the presence of relatively strong Japanese ethnic prejudice toward the Brazilian nikkeijin, there was relatively little objective and measurable ethnic discrimination shown toward them in actual behavior both within and outside the factory. Despite this, however, they experience considerable subjective discrimination, as they perceive, and at times even imagine, that they are being discriminated against (see also Ishi 1994:43).

The Japanese Brazilians seem to be sensitive to Japanese ethnic "discrimination" for a number of reasons. Those who are unable to communicate effectively or understand Japanese well undoubtedly experience uncertainty and even anxiety about what the Japanese are saying about them. However, a number of them know enough Japanese to pick up the gist of what is said without precise comprehension. Unfortunately, this also leaves considerable room for inaccurate negative interpretation of the remarks made by the Japanese as well as misunderstanding of certain linguistic nuances. Once during break time in the Toyama factory, one of the Japanese Brazilians from our section was telling the others that the ku-micho during the morning assembly seemed to be blaming the nikkeijin for product defects. Although the problem was mentioned and all the workers had been told to be careful about a certain procedure, nothing had been said about the nikkeijin workers specifically. Another factor that makes the Japanese Brazilians sensitive to ethnic "discrimination" is the severe decline in social class status they experience from their middle-class occupations in Brazil to the lowest level factory work in Japan. In contrast to the position of social authority that some of them enjoyed as managers and business owners in Brazil, they experience a sudden sense of power-lessness in Japan as they become "*peons*" subordinate to the Japanese, and their vulnerable and subservient position makes them sensitive to being victimized by possible derogation, exploitation, and discrimination. As a result, some of them seem to experience a mild form of what Takeo Doi (1974) has called *higaisha-ishiki* (victim consciousness). Finally, some are sensitive about their inferior status in the eyes of the Japanese because of their origins in a Third World country and are on the lookout for any signs of derogatory Japanese attitudes.[35]

Lack of Social Intimacy as "Discrimination"

For many of my informants, their ethnic marginalization as foreigners in Japan was not merely seen as Japanese "coldness" but also took on a stronger negative connotation as ethnic "discrimination." In Kitagawa's 1993 survey, "lack of social acceptance by Japanese" was the fourth most chosen response out of 14 possible reasons why the Japanese Brazilians feel discriminated against in Japan. Among those who spoke about this issue, only a small number felt that the Japanese tendency to avoid them was not necessarily discriminatory behavior based on Japanese prejudice. In fact, the affectively loaded terms of "*discriminação*" and "*racismo*" were used much more often by the Japanese Brazilians to describe how the Japanese

---

[35]A number of my informants told me how they feel that they have to work extra hard to demon-strate to the Japanese that they are people with ability. For example, one nisei woman said:
  The Japanese think we are uneducated in Brazil and don't have much ability, or even think we are stupid. I work really hard at Toyama because I feel we have to prove to them that we are people with ability. We have to show them that Brazil is not the back-ward country that they think it is. Of course, if I came from the First World, I would-n't feel this pressure.

exclude them ethnically than more neutral terms such as *"diferenciar"* or *"fazer diferenças"* (to "differentiate" or "make differences"). Consider the comments of Roberto, one of my friends in Oizumi who, like some others, even connected the Japanese reluctance to interact with him directly with "racism":

> I don't experience bad treatment from the Japanese at Toyama. But lots of Japanese look down on the Japanese Brazilians and so they don't mix with us at all. There was only one factory I worked at where the Japanese cared for me—the others showed no interest. When I first got to Japan, my friend would say that the Japanese are racist, and I spoke out against him at the time. But now, I agree with him.

A female sansei informant had similar remarks:

> The Japanese always keep us separated from them because of the prejudices that they have. I was almost offended when I first saw the separation at Toyama. There are some Japanese who simply don't like us and don't trust us because we are culturally different. So they don't try to talk with us or make friends—they don't even speak one word to us. Therefore, most [Japanese] Brazilians experience discrimination here. In Brazil, this type of discrimination exists only toward blacks.

Some Japanese Brazilians read further negative meanings into the Japanese tendency to keep their ethnic distance by also interpreting it as "fear" of them as an ethnic group. *"Os japoneses têm medo de nós"* (the Japanese fear us) is another frequently used expression among them. One of my co-workers at Toyama elaborated on this point:

> The Japanese are scared of us because we don't speak Japanese. I notice that they are afraid to remain near me. I see this fear in the trains. When a [Japanese] Brazilian sits near a Japanese on the bench, the Japanese leaves and moves to a different seat. Japanese women especially avoid sitting close to Brazilians.[36]

---

[36] This tendency of the Japanese to avoid the Japanese Brazilians on trains was mentioned by a couple of other individuals. However, in the trains that serviced the Oizumi/Ota area, I never witnessed Japanese actively avoiding sitting near Japanese Brazilians.

The Brazilian nikkeijin have such negative reactions partly because a majority of them cherished their "Japaneseness" in Brazil and expected a sort of ethnic "homecoming" as Japanese descendants in Japan. As a result, when such expectations are sorely disappointed by the Japanese refusal to ethnically accept them, some are quite shocked and interpret it as ethnic discrimination (cf. Mori 1992:162). One of my more perceptive informants, Fabio, also felt that some nikkeijin experience such ethnic exclusion as a discriminatory personal affront because it makes them feel inadequate:

> In Brazil, we have lots of pride in being Japanese and the Brazilians always call us Japanese and respect us for it. But when we come to Japan, the Japanese separate us as foreigners and we feel really disoriented. Those that can't speak Japanese well enough find they can't be accepted in Japan. They realize that learning more Japanese is very difficult here and this makes them feel inferior. So they search for some justification for why they can't adapt here in Japan. Therefore, if you say that the Japanese don't accept us simply because they are racist, it becomes easier to accept oneself. So calling the Japanese racist is more a means of self-defense.

In this manner, although the Japanese reluctance to interact with the nikkeijin as ethnic outsiders is not by itself an expression of prejudice, it is negatively interpreted as evidence of ethnic dislike and derogation by some Japanese Brazilians because of their sensitivity to discrimination. Indeed, some Japanese probably do refuse to interact with the nikkeijin because of ethnic prejudice, but such avoidance is motivated by a diverse set of other factors, including exclusive notions of Japanese ethnic identity, the language barrier, the closed dynamics of Japanese social groups, the temporary nature of the nikkeijin workers, and a labor broker system that socially marginalizes the Japanese Brazilians as casual migrant workers. Also, the Japanese Brazilians contribute substantially to their ethnic isolation through their own strong reluctance to interact with the Japanese (see Tsuda forthcoming 1 and 2).

The Experience of "Discrimination" on the Job

The Japanese Brazilians subjectively experience discrimination most often on the job (see also Watanabe 1992; Watanabe and Teruyama 1992), as shown by various surveys (JICA 1992; Kitagawa 1993). There was a general perception among my informants at Toyama and elsewhere that they were given the more difficult and worst jobs and were forced to work harder than the Japanese. This sense of discriminatory ethnic exploitation is expressed by the following statements:

> Yes, there is discrimination against the [Japanese] Brazilians on the job. The Japanese have the power to decide who does which task, so they always choose the easiest work for themselves and the worst jobs come to the Brazilians. But we can't argue. So the Japanese always get the jobs where they can work sitting down, and the Brazilians always work standing up.

> There's lots of easy work in the factory, but the Japanese never give us this work. I hear my supervisors saying, "If the work is hard, give it to the Brazilians." They figure they can give us the hardest and dirtiest work because we are from a different country and are in their land. I feel exploited working at the factory.

Some of my informants further expanded on their feelings of discrimination by observing that if they mastered certain tasks and worked efficiently in the factory, the Japanese would simply burden them with more and more work. Others claimed that the Japanese Brazilians were blamed for mistakes made on the assembly line and for product defects, as well as other problems that arise in the factory. "If the Japanese do something wrong at work, they keep it to themselves and cover it up," one of my informants on the Toyama assembly line claimed. "But if a nikkei does something bad, the rumor gets out and the whole factory finds out." Only a small minority claimed that there was little or no job discrimination and that Japanese and foreigners were treated more or less equally.

This general perception that the Brazilian nikkeijin have of unequal work distribution and treatment is a complicated issue. Based on observations of how my supervisors and those employers I interviewed allocated assembly line duties, it seemed unlikely that they were motivated by any ethnically prejudiced ill intent to burden the Japanese Brazilians with the most difficult and worst jobs. When assigning specific tasks, the most important criterion was the language ability of individual nikkeijin. Those who do not speak Japanese cannot be given complicated duties that require extensive explanation and are therefore frequently assigned only tasks that can be explained physically through movements and gestures, which tend to be the jobs that are more physically strenuous. In addition, when new Japanese Brazilians begin working in the assembly line or are assigned new tasks, they are first given less work than is usually allocated to one person because of their inexperience. When the nikkeijin worker becomes more used to the task, he or she is given more duties until the workload reaches the amount normally performed by one worker. This accounts for the perception of exploitation among some Japanese Brazilians that the Japanese are out to simply burden them with more work the more efficiently they labor. Although it is quite possible that in some Japanese companies, there is a tendency to discriminate by assigning worse jobs and more work to the foreigners, my observations in various assembly lines indicated that this was generally not the case at Toyama. Yet, my nikkeijin co-workers felt discriminated against just as much as workers from other companies.

In this manner, the nikkeijin seem to be perceiving and experiencing discrimination on the job even though the Japanese themselves do not necessarily intend such treatment. In some instances, the Japanese actually feel they are treating the Japanese Brazilians *favorably* by easing their workload. This is best illustrated by the reaction of one Japanese worker, Morita-san, who was one of those very rare individuals who spent a lot of time with the Japanese Brazilians and had even learned a certain amount of Portuguese. During one of our long conversations, Morita-san described his surprise when he first realized how his nikkeijin friends regarded their treatment in the factory as discrimination:

> I noticed early on that the nikkeijin would frequently use the word "*discriminação.*" When I checked it in the dictionary, I was surprised to find it meant *sabetsu* ["discrimination" in Japanese]. I do not think that we discriminate at all against the nikkeijin but treat them favorably. Of course, they are given bad work by the hancho sometimes, but the Japanese experience this too. The Japanese Brazilians call this "discrimination," but it is only their point of view. I guess when such experiences accumulate, they perceive it as discriminatory.

This subjective experience of ethnic discrimination among the Japanese Brazilians is shown by what happens when the Japanese, instead of giving them *too much* work, give them *too little*, sometimes in an effort to ease their workload. It was quite remarkable that some Japanese Brazilians at Toyama sometimes interpreted this as "discrimination" as well, albeit of a completely different type. In contrast to the strenuous jobs on the assembly line, when they were assigned easy sweeping or cleaning jobs, they sometimes considered this personally demeaning and an ethnic denigration of their abilities. One of my first interviewees, Keiko, who was planning to return to Brazil after a long four-year sojourn, gave a poignant account of her first day at work at Toyama:

> My first day was really difficult for me. I arrived on the factory floor all ready to work hard, but the Japanese told me there wasn't any work for me on the assembly line that day. So they gave me a bunch of rags and told me to wipe the oil off the factory floor. I was shocked. As I got down on my hands and knees to start wiping, I felt so humiliated and belittled that I couldn't stand it. I kept saying to myself: "Do the Japanese think that this is the only kind of work I am capable of doing?" I almost felt like crying. In the afternoon, it got better because they finally put me on the assembly line. I worked really hard the rest of the day, just to show the Japanese that I wasn't an imbecile, but could do the work. I was thoroughly exhausted by the end of the day.

A similar experience occurred for Regina, one of the Japanese Brazilian workers in my section who was temporarily transferred to a different assembly line soon after I first started working at Toyama. She came back in a week claiming that the Japanese in the other line were "racists." Since this was the first time I had heard the nikkeijin calling the Japanese racist, I was a bit surprised by her strong choice of words and asked why she considered them racist. "They made me sweep all the time!" she replied.

Therefore, when an ethnic minority is very sensitive to discrimination, individuals of the majority group are put in a double bind—their behavior is liable to be branded as "discriminatory" by the minority group regardless of which course of action they take. In other words, if the Japanese give the nikkeijin too much work, it is considered exploitation of foreigners, but if they give too little work, it is also ethnic discrimination because it means the Japanese disparagingly think the nikkeijin lack ability. Jorge, an older nisei who sat at my lunch table for a few weeks at Toyama, showed this type of double-edged ethnic logic when he said:

> The [Japanese] Brazilians are discriminated [against] at work. Those who need to show their ability to the Japanese and work really hard end up getting exploited because they are given more and more work that the Japanese are supposed to do. But those Brazilians who don't have

much ability or don't show it on purpose get easier work. The Japanese say, "Look at these Brazilians. They are stupid and can't do anything." So these people just get sweeping jobs.

An analogous situation occurs with those who feel stigmatized not because of their discrediting ethnic attributes but because of physical incapacities. For instance, a handicapped person may react negatively toward those who are unwilling to help as cruel and unsympathetic, if not prejudiced. However, if others are all too willing to help, it can also be interpreted negatively as condescending, patronizing, and based on a demeaning assumption that the handicapped person is too incapacitated to even support him- or herself (see Goffman 1963).[37]

Another type of treatment that the Japanese Brazilians receive that is considered ethnically denigrating and demeaning are the repetitive and careful explanations of work duties from Japanese supervisors. This was noted by my co-worker Tadashi, who understood Japanese to a certain extent:

> Sometimes I think that these Japanese must think that we have no brains or something because they treat us like kids at work. Maybe it's just the Japanese system, but they explain simple things to you that are obvious and not necessary. They tell us how to work with one type of machine, and when the same set of machines comes around 30 minutes later, they explain the whole procedure to us again, as if we can't figure out that it's the same as the first time around.

Jorge, who also could speak Japanese, had a similar impression: "The Japanese think we were not well educated in Brazil and don't understand even basic things," he claimed. "So they talk to us as if we were stupid. They give us easy instructions over and over again, like they were teaching little children to read."

Contrary to the negative interpretation of these two individuals (and some others I knew), this type of behavior among Japanese supervisors at Toyama was not based on any ethnic denigration but arose from a simple

---

[37]Lifton (1969) notes a similar reaction among Japanese *hibakusha*, victims of the atomic bomb, who both crave and resent special attention. If they are not given sufficient attention, they feel abandoned, as if their past suffering and close encounter with death is being ignored. However, if they find themselves the focus of attention, they view the concern as inauthentic and a confirmation of their weakness and stigma of being tainted with death.

concern that the Japanese Brazilians would not understand work instructions in Japanese unless they were explained meticulously and repetitively. In fact, I too was also given tedious and repetitive (and yes, "childish") explanations of my work duties by my Japanese supervisors until they realized that I had no trouble understanding Japanese, at which point this type of treatment abruptly ended. For members of negative ethnic minorities, self-conscious and well-intentioned attempts by majority individuals to treat them kindly and sympathetically may be interpreted as patronizing and condescending and therefore, just as offensive and demeaning as the overt expression of ethnic prejudice (cf. Fanon 1967:28–33).

Other issues that the Japanese Brazilians cite as evidence of "discrimination" include being fired during a recession before Japanese workers, receiving lower bonuses (or none at all) and fewer benefits, being assigned less desirable hours (night shift or more weekend work), and not being invited to company outings with Japanese workers at some firms (see also Ishi 1994:45). Even small issues, such as the handing out of *bentos* (box lunches or snacks) after overtime only to Japanese workers was seen by a few as discriminatory. However, such inequalities are again caused not by ethnic discrimination but by the fact that most of the Japanese Brazilians are employed indirectly through outside labor broker firms as informal, temporary workers (*hi-seishain*). As a result, they do not receive the same benefits as Japanese *seishain* (regular, permanent workers) and are the first ones to be dismissed during a production downturn. In addition, because they are not employees of the companies where they work, they are not generally invited to company parties and social events. The Japanese Brazilians have been confined to the less desirable, peripheral sector of the work force not specifically because they are ethnically nikkeijin but because they are migrant workers. In fact, *Japanese* seasonal and contract workers who are also part of the casual labor force experience the same type of socioeconomic marginalization. When both the nikkeijin and certain Japanese are subjected to similar negative treatment, it is hard to argue that this is ethnic discrimination directed specifically against the nikkeijin. Among companies that hire nikkeijin workers *directly* as their own employees, I saw no evidence (in interviews with Japanese managers) that the Japanese Brazilians were treated differently from Japanese workers and excluded from the company's social activities.[38] In this manner,

---

[38]In fact, even a few Japanese companies that employ the nikkeijin *indirectly* invited them to the firm's social events.

there is a tendency among the nikkeijin to rush to judgment by labeling any inequalities that they observe on the job as "discriminação" without fully realizing that such differences in treatment are motivated by other factors than pure ethnic prejudice.

The final example of discrimination at work cited by a few of my informants was the rough language and treatment that they sometimes received in certain smaller and less reputable companies. In Kitagawa's survey (1993), 9.6 percent of the respondents chose "spoken to in a derogatory manner" as an example of Japanese ethnic discrimination. Martina recounted her past experiences in a certain factory where rude treatment would occur:

> At the Saitama factory, they would treat me like an animal, saying "Oi!" (Hey you!) to get my attention and would even yell at me at times. Once, the supervisor got nervous and angry at me for something I did wrong and threw away the machine part in frustration. I felt I was treated like an animal and just looked the other way.

Others reported similar coarse treatment in small factories in the past where they would occasionally be chastised or spoken to impolitely. Although I was unable to conduct direct participant observation in such factories, this type of crass behavior seems to be a general norm at these companies and is not ethnically derogatory discrimination directed specifically at the nikkeijin (see also JICA 1992:32). This was noted even by some Japanese Brazilians who were able to view the situation more or less objectively. Celso, a sansei who worked for a small factory where working conditions were rough, had this to say when I first encountered him at work:

> Lots of [Japanese] Brazilians get angry when they are sometimes treated impolitely by the Japanese and call it discrimination. Sometimes when the work gets busy and noisy, the supervisor may shout at you: "Hey you! Stop! Stop! Let me do that!" They may get angry at you for making mistakes. Some Brazilians really let this bother them. It is a shock when you first enter the factory, but this is how people behave in factories like this. We are treated badly not because we are Japanese Brazilians. It happens to the Japanese too.

Other Examples of "Discrimination" Outside the Factory

Although most Japanese Brazilians acknowledge that they are well treated and welcomed in Japanese stores, banks, and restaurants, some give accounts of discrimination there as well. The common experience of being "discovered" by the Japanese to be foreigners was also sometimes understood as "discrimination." Because of essentialist notions of ethnicity in Japan according to which those who look Japanese are naturally assumed to be culturally Japanese as well (see chapter 2), the Japanese Brazilians have become ethnic anomalies and sometimes receive strange glances from the Japanese when they speak Portuguese or broken Japanese despite their Japanese faces.[39] Although most of them are not bothered by this reaction, a few of my informants detected traces of prejudice or derogation. "Whenever we speak Portuguese, the Japanese always look at us as if they have never seen someone with a Japanese face speaking a different language," one sansei remarked. "It's fine when they just look at us to confirm that we are foreigners, but sometimes their expression is different. They look at us in a sort of ugly way, like they dislike foreigners." Henri, a sansei from São Paulo who does not speak much Japanese, shared similar impressions, although he remained fundamentally ambivalent about the issue:

> The treatment by the Japanese is polite. When I enter stores, I am always greeted with an *irasshaimase* (welcome) because I look Japanese. But when I open my mouth or don't respond properly in Japanese when something is asked, they realize I am a foreigner. It's not really discrimination because most of the time, they just maintain their politeness. But sometimes their demeanor changes and they become more distant. When this happens, I think they look down on me as a foreigner.

As Allport (1979:144–45) notes in his classic study of prejudice, minorities who believe they are the object of prejudice constantly feel a sense of insecurity and unease about possible majority derogation, and this sensitivity creates an alertness and vigilance so that "even the smallest cues may be loaded with [negative] feeling." In this manner, a gaze, a shift in demeanor, or a facial expression can be interpreted negatively as ethnic "discrimination" even if prejudicial attitudes are not being directly expressed.

A few of my informants also mentioned that they are seen suspiciously in some stores as potential shoplifters because they are Brazilian. In fact, un-

---

[39]Dorinne Kondo (1990) also describes how the Japanese reacted to her in a similar manner as a Japanese American (see also Befu 1993:116; Hamabata 1990). As George De Vos notes, "It is yet a basic incongruity [in Japan] to consider the possibility that one could be Japanese and maintain adherence to a [culturally different] background" (1984:13).

founded rumors about discrimination against nikkeijin in Japanese stores have been created and then quickly propagated within the nikkeijin community. Most notable was a rumor that the Japanese Brazilians were barred from stores and discos in Hamamatsu city, Shizuoka Prefecture, through the posting of signs refusing service to the nikkeijin and announcements over the loudspeaker at a certain supermarket warning customers to be careful because Brazilians were among them. The rumor was started by an article in the *São Paulo Shimbun* (a Japanese Brazilian community newspaper in Brazil) and was later picked up by national Brazilian dailies and then spread rapidly by word of mouth through the immigrant community in Japan. However, according to Angelo Ishi (1994:43), the original article in the *São Paulo Shimbun* was based on only one letter from a Japanese Brazilian who wrote about his *friend's* reported experience. Although Ishi conducted research among the Japanese Brazilians in Hamamatsu, he found no evidence of stores prohibiting nikkeijin customers; nor had any of his informants actually experienced such incidents. Among my own informants, a surprising number were aware of this Hamamatsu story and used it as an illustration of Japanese "discrimination," although they themselves admitted never having witnessed or experienced such treatment in Japanese stores. Because many nikkeijin are sensitive to being victims of Japanese discrimination, they seem more than willing to believe such unfounded rumors as confirmation of what they had suspected and feared all along.[40]

In fact, there is even a tendency among some Japanese Brazilians to explain treatment that is less than polite in Japanese stores and in the service sector as "discrimination." One of my informants recounted an incident that seemed to bother him:

> It is natural that the Japanese have prejudices just like we do in Brazil. I went to the barber the other day and asked how much a haircut is. I had

---

[40]As mentioned in chapter 2, overt discrimination toward non-nikkeijin foreigners in Japan is very real. The most famous case is of Ana Bortz, a non-nikkeijin Brazilian who was escorted out of a jewelry store in Hamamatsu because the store had a policy of refusing Brazilian customers (the owner supposedly feared crimes by Brazilians). Ana Bortz took the case to court, won the lawsuit, and was awarded $12,500 in damages. The judge ruled that the store owner's actions were illegal because they violated the United Nations Convention on the Elimination of All Forms of Racial Discrimination, which Japan had ratified in 1996. Although the Japanese Constitution prohibits all types of discrimination as well, it refers only to "*kokumin*" (Japanese nationals). This case (Hamamatsu's Rosa Parks) may encourage other foreigners to fight against Japanese discrimination as well.

only 3,000 yen, which was a little less than the actual price. The barber told me he couldn't cut my hair if I didn't have enough money. He could tell that I was a foreigner, so I figure he refused me because of his prejudices.

Jefferson, a sansei from Oizumi, was quite disgruntled by how he is treated as a foreigner at the local train station:

At the bank and city hall, they are obliged to treat you well, but the train station is different. I asked for directions from the ticket attendant once, and he just replied curtly and handed me the ticket. He can tell I am a foreigner because I always dress in a T-shirt and Bermudas when I go there. I felt like yelling at him. I never did anything bad to him, so why am I treated like this? One time I walked through the turnstile and forgot to show my ticket. The attendant stops me saying, "Ticket! Ticket!" I wanted to ask him: "Why do you not speak normally to me? Why don't you treat me as an equal person?"

It is possible that these examples of less-than-polite treatment are seen by the Japanese as "normal" behavior given the circumstances and not based on ethnic prejudice or dislike of the nikkeijin. This was most clearly evident on one occasion when I assisted my nikkeijin friend, Tadashi, who wanted to inquire at the local Oizumi post office about sending money to his sister in Japan. After we left the post office, Tadashi quickly noted that the postal worker had been impolite and acted like he just wanted us to leave. Although I had realized that the worker had been a bit terse and had not been polite or patient with my questions, it had not bothered me. Then came the inevitable conclusion from Tadashi: "It's because we were seen as Brazilians." Later, when I returned to the post office for my own business, I saw the same postal worker at the counter and had a chance to observe him more closely. I quickly realized that in contrast to the politeness of most Japanese employees in the service sector, this fellow was of an odd demeanor and treated all his customers in a rather brusque manner, showing that Tadashi's previous assessment of "discrimination" was seemingly unwarranted.[41]

---

[41]Ishi (1994:44) cites an analogous example in which a Japanese Brazilian was not allowed to enter a disco in Hamamatsu because he was wearing Bermuda shorts. The individual thought he had been barred for his Bermudas because he was Brazilian, but in actuality, the disco had a rule that no one wearing tennis shoes, jeans, and shorts could enter.

In this manner, some Japanese Brazilians seem to automatically interpret any negative treatment they receive from the Japanese as ethnic derogation without realizing that it may simply be the result of a generally impolite individual or the peculiar nature of the situation and that the Japanese may be subject to the same treatment under the same circumstances. Of course, this does not mean that there is no discrimination against the Brazilian nikkeijin in Japanese society and that they simply imagine it. There are cases when their claims of ethnic discrimination seem to be completely substantiated, for instance in the housing situation, which was the most frequently chosen example of Japanese discrimination in the 1993 Kitagawa survey.

Despite the controlled and polite demeanor of most Japanese when encountering nikkeijin at the workplace or in public and the general lack of discriminatory intent, since many Japanese Brazilians experience discrimination subjectively to a certain degree, this simply adds to the negative meaning that the Japanese come to have for them. Not only are the sociocultural aspects of Japanese society viewed in an unfavorable manner, the Japanese are seen as people who even discriminate against their own descendants. Because of such negative characterizations, it can be easy for the Brazilian nikkeijin to blame the Japanese for the inequalities and negative experiences they have as a socioeconomically marginalized immigrant minority confined to low-status factory jobs. As a sense of ethnic antagonism and opposition to the Japanese develops, the Japanese Brazilians respond by strengthening their anti-Japanese counteridentity as Brazilian nationals who share common experiences of prejudice, derogation, and discrimination in Japanese society. This is yet another factor that contributes to the development of deterritorialized migrant nationalism, which ironically causes most nikkeijin to feel much more Brazilian in Japan than they ever did in Brazil.

INDIVIDUAL VARIATION IN THE EXPERIENCE OF ETHNIC IDENTITY

Despite the general patterns I have outlined in this chapter, each individual's renegotiation of ethnic identity in response to the dislocations of migration is unique. As always, the inherent diversity involves a difference of degree as well as of kind. As indicated here, when confronted by negative ethnic and socioeconomic experiences in Japan, most Japanese Brazilians are alienated from Japanese society and experience an intensification of their Brazilian national identities to various degrees.[42] For some, the net change is simply an adjustment and reorientation in ethnic consciousness, while for others, the consequences are greater, causing a fundamental redefinition, if not a reversal in identity from Japanese to Brazilian.

However, to understand the degree to which migration "Brazilianizes" the ethnic consciousness of individual Japanese Brazilians, it is insufficient to simply measure the amount of ethnic and socioeconomic exclusion, negative cultural difference, and discrimination that each of them experiences in Japan. The ethnic reactions of migrants are not simply determined by external pressures prevalent in the host society but also internally conditioned by prior ethnic experiences in the home country. Therefore, the particularities of individual ethnic histories can lead to a diversity of identity outcomes in response to the same external social pressures.

Those nikkeijin who maintained a stronger "Japanese" identity in Brazil generally react much more strongly to their negative experiences in Japan than would normally be expected. Because of their considerable pride and investment in their "Japaneseness," they are in for a more intense shock and disappointment when they are confronted by an unfavorable ethnic reception in Japan, marginalization as low-class factory workers, and the negative characteristics of the Japanese. Therefore, their unfavorable experiences are more personally significant and the subsequent impact on their ethnic identity more profound. Their prior ethnic experiences in Brazil *magnify* the sociocultural pressures they confront in Japan, resulting in a stronger reaction against Japanese society through an assertion of their Brazilian nationalist counteridentities.

In contrast, those who had stronger Brazilian identities in Brazil are not as personally affected by their negative ethnic experiences in Japan and therefore do not perceive much of a change in their ethnic identities. Although these "Brazilianized" nikkeijin are exposed to a similar negative ethnic environment in Japan, because they felt less affinity with the Japanese before migration, they are not as sensitive to ethnic exclusion and discrimination as foreigners in Japan. Likewise, their prominent cultural differences with the Japanese are not particularly disorienting but are simply a confirmation of their Brazilianness, which they had already acknowledged in Brazil. Although they may feel socioeconomically marginalized

---

[42]According to the 1992 JICA survey, only a minority (a little over 25 percent) do not strengthen their Brazilian consciousness in Japan.

in Japan as unskilled factory workers, especially if they previously held prominent middle-class jobs in Brazil, because they never strongly identified with Japan to start with, they feel less alienated from Japanese society. Due to their greater indifference to their "negative" experiences in Japan, such individuals simply feel a slight increase in or reinforcement of their Brazilian consciousness. Although they are a small minority (14 percent of my interview sample), since they have qualitatively different experiences from the others, they deserve special attention.

Roberto, a sansei who never firmly asserted a Japanese ethnic identity in Brazil, was one of the individuals with this type of experience:

> In Brazil, I didn't speak any Japanese and felt pretty Brazilian. I never thought about what the Japanese would be like and didn't have a firm idea or any expectations. It also didn't bother me that I would not be socially accepted in Japan. So I just came to see how the Japanese are and wasn't shocked like the others when I observed that they were so different, although there are things I don't like about them. I just came to know their differences. My identity has not really changed.

The best example of this type of individual was Celso, a sansei from Mato Grosso do Sul whom I first met during a factory tour in Kawasaki and came to know quite well. "I never felt very Japanese in Brazil and hung out with more Brazilians than Japanese [Brazilians]," he recalled. "Of course, like all the Japanese [Brazilians], I felt a little different from the Brazilians, but I completely accepted my Brazilianness." As a result, Celso did not mind when he was seen as a foreigner in Japan, since he did not expect to be treated as "Japanese" from the beginning. "The truth is, I *am* a Brazilian foreigner here," he said. Since he did not have a strong desire to be accepted as "Japanese," he did not interpret the Japanese reluctance to interact with him as discrimination:

> When the Japanese do not become friendly with us and treat us warmly, many [Japanese] Brazilians let it bother them and say the Japanese are cold and call it discrimination. But it is simply a matter of cultural differences and not ill will on the part of the Japanese. Personally, I don't feel that the Japanese are cold.

Although he worked in a small and dingy metal galvanization factory where conditions were harsh, noisy, and dangerous and the treatment from the Japanese could be quite crass, he was able to detach himself from the situation instead of accusing the Japanese of ethnic discrimination:

> At first, my supervisor would get angry at me when I made a mistake, or in desperation, would yell at me not to do something because he thought I would mess it up. If I had gotten angry or offended about this type of treatment, I would have left the factory like the others. But for me, I knew it wasn't a personal attack so it didn't really affect me, and I remained patient without worrying about it. Other [Japanese] Brazilians were very offended. They had an eye-for-an-eye attitude so that if they were yelled at, they would yell back and they forever remembered bad moments with the Japanese.

In addition, because of his stronger awareness that he is fundamentally Brazilian, Celso did not find his cultural differences with the Japanese to be surprising or disorienting like his compatriots; nor did those differences mean much for his ethnic identity. He claimed he did not have many expectations about the Japanese but just came to see how they are different from him. Finally, he did not react as negatively to the low images that the Japanese have of Brazil. In fact, he took these in full stride and realized that the demeaning questions that the Japanese sometimes asked of the nikkeijin were not ill intentioned.

> Some Japanese joke with you about Brazil. One person at work once asked me when I would return to Brazil. I told him I don't know. Then he said, "Ah, you don't want to return because you will have to live in your jungle huts again, right?" It doesn't bother me when they ask you things about Brazil in a joking manner. Sometimes they ask stupid questions, but they are just curious since they have no knowledge of Brazil.

Celso succinctly summarized his ethnic experiences in Japan as follows: "Some [Japanese] Brazilians come here and they really revolt and get angry at Japanese treatment. But then there are those who are indifferent. I am one of those who is indifferent." As a result, he felt his identity had not changed much in Japan. "It's continued more or less at the same level," he noted. "I was Brazilian in Brazil and am Brazilian in Japan. My friends say this too—that I haven't changed much since I started living here." When we met for dinner before I left Japan, Celso did admit that he felt "*um pouco mais brasileiro*" (a little more Brazilian) living in Japan than he did in Brazil, but he did not share the migrant nationalism of his ethnic peers. "If there existed some gauge that could accurately measure my identity, I would say the arrow has moved a little more toward the Brazilian side," he remarked. "But it is not nationalism toward Brazil or a feeling of greater patriotism. I just compare Brazil and Japan and think Brazil can be much better without so much misery. I just feel this more in Japan now than I did in Brazil."

The other group of individuals whose ethnic identities are relatively impervious to the disruptions of migration and who did not follow the normative pattern of identity nationalization are those who were the most "Japanized" of all the nikkeijin. They comprised about 8 percent of my sample and generally felt that they had maintained or even slightly increased their Japanese consciousness in Japan.[43] Not only did they have strong Japanese identities in Brazil, they were fluent in Japanese and could not be behaviorally differentiated from native Japanese. As a result, they felt ethnically accepted in Japan and did not perceive major cultural differences between themselves and the Japanese. In addition, most of them were white-collar employees who worked in a more congenial Japanese social environment in company or local government offices and therefore did not experience the loss of their previous middle-class status and the resulting socioeconomic alienation in Japan. Because they are spared the ethnic and social exclusion of their peers, they do not react against Japanese society and their ethnic consciousness remains relatively stable.

One individual who illustrated this type of experience was Keiji, a nisei from Paraná, who worked with the Japanese as a nikkeijin supervisor in the office of a company in Oizumi. Keiji was born and raised in a Japanese colônia and attended a half-day Japanese school. Partly because of the influence of his mother, he always believed that it would be embarrassing if he could not speak Japanese fluently. Since he always worked with Japanese in a Japanese multinational firm in Brazil, he was familiar with Japanese customs and food and claimed his behavior was already very Japanese in Brazil. As a result, he did not feel any real cultural contrasts with the Japanese in Japan. Both at work and outside the company, his social relationships were mainly with Japanese, and he even claimed his co-workers viewed him as completely Japanese, sometimes even asking him how to spell certain Japanese characters. As a result, experiences of Japanese ethnic

---

[43]The Nishioka survey (1995) shows that only 4 percent of the nisei and one percent of the sansei feel "more Japanese" in Japan.

discrimination were unknown to Keiji and he was even a bit scornful of nikkeijin who complained and criticized the Japanese, saying:

> I don't think there is discrimination against the Brazilians. The nikkeijin feel there is discrimination because they don't speak Japanese and therefore, they just think it up. There is negative treatment at times toward the Brazilians in certain factories, but the Japanese are treated the same way.

Although Keiji noted that he did not receive bonus pay like the Japanese employees at his company, he explained that this was simply because he was seen as a temporary employee and had not yet resolved to live in Japan permanently. Since he continued to feel "Japanese" in Japan as he had in Brazil, Keiji did not feel that his identity had changed much. If anything, his migratory experiences in Japan further confirmed his Japaneseness.

JAPANESE IN BRAZIL BUT BRAZILIAN IN JAPAN: THE SCOPE AND SIGNIFICANCE OF DETERRITORIALIZED MIGRANT NATIONALISM

The physical dislocation of transnational migration introduces a certain dynamism to ethnicity as identities are disengaged from a specific locality and renegotiated in an entirely different social context in response to encounters with new ethnic groups. The return migration of the Japanese Brazilians has resulted in a fundamental transformation of their ethnic consciousness. Their former identity as ethnic "Japanese," which they had developed in relation to mainstream Brazilian society, is subject to critical examination in Japan, forcing many nikkeijin to redefine themselves in nationalist terms as Brazilian vis-á-vis the Japanese.

When the Japanese Brazilians return migrate, they are excluded as foreigners and marginalized as casual migrant laborers, becoming alienated individuals isolated from Japanese society. As they recognize their cultural and socioeconomic differences from the Japanese, their Brazilianness emerges in a contrastive context. In addition, their previous positive understandings of Japaneseness are shattered as they experience various negative aspects of Japanese culture and society, confront derogatory Japanese perceptions of Brazil, and are subject to ethnic "discrimination." Not only do ethnic disaffection and social alienation in Japan replace their previous feelings of transnational affinity with the Japanese, their predominantly negative experiences in Japan highlight the positive sociocultural

aspects of Brazilian society. As a result, their dormant nationalist sentiments are revived in a deterritorialized context abroad as an ethnic minority counteridentity that is asserted in opposition to a negatively perceived Japanese society.

As Arjun Appadurai observes (1996:160–61), nationalism in the contemporary world has become increasingly diasporic and is no longer contained
within the territorial borders of a particular nation-state. However, it is important to note that nationalisms not only are carried across national borders
by territorially mobile groups but also can be further articulated and enhanced in the process. This ironic, deterritorialized consolidation of national identity outside the physical confines of the nation-state occurs precisely
because migration exposes individuals to experiences that recontexualize their
ethnicity in a foreign country and intensify national loyalties—experiences
that were not possible back home. In this manner, physical absence from the
nation-state enhances its presence in the ethnic consciousness of its citizens.

Although the Japanese Brazilians represent a rather unusual case of migration in that they are return migrating to their ancestral homeland and are
ethnically excluded because of particularly restrictive notions of what it
means to be Japanese, their experiences of ethnic and social marginalization,
cultural difference, and discrimination are shared by many other migrants.
Such negative experiences frequently cause migrants to react against the host
society and develop minority counteridentities by reaffirming and strengthening their feelings of affiliation to their country of origin. The deterritorialized resurgence of nationalist sentiment among migrants has been noted
among Portuguese in the United States (Feldman-Bianco 1992), migrants in
Indonesia (Jaspars and Warnaen 1982), Palestinians in Honduras (Gonzalez
1989:4), American Jewish students in Israel (Herman 1970), Caribbean immigrants in the United States (Basch, Glick Schiller, and Blanc 1994:109–14;
Charles 1992; Glick Schiller and Fouron 1990; Wiltshire 1992:175), Eastern
European émigrés (Verdery 1996), Southern and Eastern European immigrants who came to America earlier in the century,[44] and even the Japanese
who emigrated to Brazil (Maeyama 1982:33–35). Brazilian immigrants in the

[44]Europeans who immigrated to the United States became more conscious of their foreign national origins (Yancey, Ericksen, and Juliani 1982). Because of certain "structural conditions"
in the United States (institutional affiliations and residential concentration of immigrants by
nationality), there was a change from a previously local identification to a larger nationalistic
identification after migration (Portes and Rumbaut 1996:104). Portes and Rumbaut (1996:95)
argue that the tendency of American immigrant groups to identify predominantly with their
national origins was more a reaction to discrimination and their social situation in the United States than a linear continuity of the culture of their homelands.

United States, many of whom never thought about being Brazilian until they were confronted by American sociocultural differences, also experience an increased consciousness of their Brazilian national identity (see Margolis 1994). A rise in nationalist feeling occurs among diasporic groups (cf. Clifford 1994:307) and expatriates as well, including the Japanese temporarily residing overseas (Goodman 1990a:168; Reichl 1995:52–53).

Among the many factors that can arouse nationalist sentiments among a populace, migration to foreign countries probably has been the least considered. Migrant nationalism is not less effective than other types of nationalism simply because it is articulated in a deterritorialized context abroad. The power of national (or other forms of) identity does not presuppose the subject's physical presence in or proximity to the object of identification (i.e., the nation-state). In addition, deterritorialized nationalism is not merely an ephemeral phenomenon that is experienced only during the period of migratory dislocation and physical absence from the nation-state. When the migrants return home, their enhanced feelings of national allegiance acquired abroad persist and remain relevant for their self-consciousness. The Japanese Brazilian returnees I interviewed in Brazil continued to feel much more Brazilian than before migration, and some specifically mentioned that they now associate more actively with mainstream Brazilians. As a result, there was some indication that the Japanese Brazilian community in Brazil is becoming less ethnically exclusive and restrictive as a result of return migration.

The strength of deterritorialized nationalism among migrants seems to partly depend on the number of negative and discriminatory experiences they have in the host society. The more negative experiences they have as immigrants, the more they will assert their national sentiments and loyalties to their homeland as a defensive counteridentity and vice versa. For example, migrant nationalism is much weaker among Brazilians in the United States than among Japanese Brazilians in Japan because they do not perceive American society in a predominantly negative manner (see Margolis 1994:chapter 8) or experience as much ethnic discrimination.[45] In fact, although they are undocumented immigrants, Ana Cristina Braga

---

[45]In contrast to rates of perceived discrimination among nikkeijin that are close to 80 percent, less than 50 percent of Brazilian immigrants surveyed in the United States and Canada say they have experienced some type of discriminatory behavior (Goza 1994, 1999:775). According to a survey conducted by Ana Cristina Braga Martes (2000:157), only 23 percent feel that discrimination is one of the problems Brazilians face in the United States.

Martes (2000:chapter 5) reports that they feel *more* respected as residents in the United States than they did in Brazil for various reasons. In such cases, an increase in national awareness is mainly a reaction to the cultural differences immigrants encounter in the majority host society, which bring out their own national distinctiveness.

In addition, immigrants who have positive images and expectations about the host society tend to have more negative reactions because they are more likely to be disappointed and disillusioned by their actual experiences. Because ethnic return migrants frequently have nostalgic and favorable images of their ethnic homeland and expect to be welcomed to some extent as ancestral descendants, they are more likely to interpret their inevitable experiences of social marginalization and discrimination in the host society negatively than other immigrants. Therefore, they may ironically become more nationalistic in their ancestral homelands than those immigrants residing in a completely foreign country. For instance, although *non-Japanese descent* Brazilians who are admitted to Japan as spouses of the nikkeijin had similar experiences as the nikkeijin,[46] since they had very little emotional investment and personal affiliation with Japan and its culture in the first place, they were not as bothered by those experiences, which therefore had no major implications for their ethnic identity (see also Yamanaka 1997:24–25, 27). Interaction with a similar ethnic group can have a more profound impact on ethnic consciousness than contact with a completely foreign ethnic group whose characteristics have no personal relevance. The nationalization of ethnic identity is also more pronounced for ethnic return migrants because they were minorities in their origin country who frequently did not identify as strongly with the dominant national culture. As a result, they suddenly find themselves changing from former minority "ethnics" to "nationals" in the host society as they realize for the first time how much of the culture of their home country they have unwittingly internalized. In other words, as their national differences become "ethnicized" in a foreign country, their ethnic identity becomes more "nationalized."

---

[46]Although I did not systematically interview non-nikkeijin Brazilians in Japan, many of those with darker complexions felt discrimination in Japan. In contrast, the three Brazilians of Italian descent I spoke with claimed they were generally well treated and did not feel discrimination. Two of them mentioned how they are sometimes mistaken as Americans in Japan and are thus seen favorably. At Toyama, I was once asked by a Japanese worker whether a certain white Brazilian in the adjacent section was American. I had to tell her that there are Brazilians who are *hakujin* (whites) as well.

CHAPTER 4

☙

Transnational Communities Without a Consciousness?

Transnational Connections, National Identities, and the Nation-State

INTRODUCTION:
THE BRAZILIAN NIKKEIJIN AS NATIONALIZED
TRANSNATIONAL MIGRANTS

THE IMPACT OF MIGRATION on individual self-identity is undoubtedly complex and varied. According to Arjun Appadurai,

> As populations become deterritorialized . . . the results are surely con-tradictory. Displacement and exile, migration and terror create powerful attachments to ideas of homeland that seem more deeply territorial than ever. But it is also possible to detect in many of these transnations . . . the elements of a postnational imaginary. (1996:176–77)

Needless to say, my analysis has focused on the former consequence of mi-gration. In certain cases, migration undoubtedly makes transnational identities and "postnational imaginaries" possible. However, the Japanese Brazilian experience indicates that we cannot always assume that transna-tional migration involves a movement from the national to the postna-tional and from the modern to the postmodern.

The deterritorialized nationalization of ethnic identity among nikkeijin transmigrants is contradictory because it occurs not only in the absence of the nation-state but also in the presence of a transnational migrant community.[1]

---

[1]Roger Rouse defines transnational migrant communities as follows:
> Through the continuous circulation of people, money, goods, and information, the various settlements have become so closely woven together that, in an important sense, they have come to constitute a single community spread across a variety of sites, some-thing I refer to as a "transnational migrant circuit." (1991:14)

Ever since they left Brazil en masse, the Japanese Brazilians have established social and institutional networks between Japan and Brazil, allowing them to become increasingly engaged in the flow of information, goods, and people across national borders. In other words, the nikkeijin ethnic community has expanded beyond the territorial boundaries of the Brazilian nation-state to become truly transnational. In this chapter, I will first outline the various connections that have developed among Japanese Brazilians in the two countries. I will then consider why national identities continue to be maintained within these transnational migrant communities. This disjuncture between community and consciousness has significant implications for the ability of the nation-state to retain local hegemonic power amid the transnational forces that can threaten its integrity in the global ecumene.

THE SPATIAL CONFIGURATION OF TRANSNATIONAL MIGRANT COMMUNITIES

In addition to their greater geographical reach, how are transnational communities different from more localized ones? It is evident that communities can be defined and constructed without actual face-to-face interaction among its members, as popularized by Benedict Anderson's (1991) notion of "imagined community." Since most members of a national community never actually meet and become acquainted with one another, the sense of mutual group belonging among them is based on "imagined" social relationships.[2] Although it is tempting to distinguish imagined communities from "real" communities that are based on actual personal exchanges and interactions, this conceptual distinction is dubious (cf. Castells 1997:29) since social relationships in even small, local communities are imagined to a certain extent as well (cf. Anderson 1991:6).

Regardless of whether they are real or imagined, the social relationships that sustain a community can be maintained in two types of spaces (cf. Calhoun 1992): *contiguous* space, where actual face-to-face encounters and interactions occur, or *noncontiguous* space, where individuals can interact and communicate through telecommunications and electronic and broadcast

---

[2] It is unlikely, however, that communities can be completely invented or fabricated without any substantial historical or functional basis (see Anderson 1991:6; Castells 1997; Smith 1991, 1995).

media even if they are not in physical proximity. Through the visual, au-dial, and written transmission of information in noncontiguous space, a community's social relationships and institutional links can be sustained over great geographical distances and therefore transcend the limitations of contiguous physical space. This distinction between communities consti-tuted in contiguous and non-contiguous space is analogous to Arjun Ap-padurai's concepts of "spatialized" and "virtual" neighborhoods (1996:195).

Although "imagined" social relationships between individuals who have never actually met are constituted in noncontiguous space through the transmission of information and images via mass media (cf. Hannerz 1996:97), "real" social relationships based on actual interaction between in-dividuals do not have to be face-to-face encounters that occur in contiguous space. They can also be sustained over noncontiguous space since individu-als can directly communicate and thus "interact" by using telephones, fax machines, letters, and the Internet. Of course, the interaction is based on disembodied voices and messages transmitted over telecommunications net-works that lack the sensations of sight,[3] smell, and touch that accompany interactions in contiguous space.[4] In the case of fax machines and e-mail, the interaction is also usually not simultaneous but involves temporal delays. Despite their somewhat socially decontextualized nature, however, noncon-tiguous relationships based on telecommunications networks are just as "real" as those that occur in contiguous space because they still involve a mutual interactive exchange between actual individuals. In contrast, non-contiguous communication through the mass media (such as newspapers, radio, and television)[5] can only produce "imagined" social relationships be-cause it involves an asymmetric flow of information and images from pro-ducers to receivers (Hannerz 1996:97) who remain mutually alienated and cannot become personally acquainted through interactive exchanges.[6]

In the context of these distinctions, how are social relationships in transnational migrant communities spatially configured? Since social

---

[3]An exception is video teleconferencing.

[4]However, Hannerz seems to suggest that as the symbolic capacity of telecommunications in-creases through technological advances, information transmitted in noncontiguous space can overcome some of the deficiencies that make local face-to-face communication contextually su-perior (1996:28).

[5]The Internet has also become a form of mass media. Through Web sites and mass e-mailings, one individual can communicate with a large audience without actual interaction.

[6]Of course, there are a few exceptions such as radio and television talk shows, where audience members are allowed to call in and actually talk to the hosts or participants of the show.

networks that extend across national borders are maintained over long distances, they are usually more dependent on noncontiguous space than more territorially localized communities (cf. Hannerz 1996:98). In other words, transnational communities are not geographically restricted and confined to a single unified, contiguous space, but consist of individuals and institutions in a multitude of dispersed sites that are linked and interact in noncontiguous space through telecommunication networks.[7]

Transnational communities are thus "deterritorialized" in two different respects. First, they transgress the territorial borders of nation-states because they consist of social networks of individuals residing in more than one country. This is the sense in which transnational communities can cause nations to become territorially "unbound" (see Basch, Glick Schiller, and Blanc 1994). Second, transnational communities are deterritorialized because they are mainly constituted in noncontiguous space, thus superseding the territorial constraints of contiguous space and geographical distance. Of course, deterritorialization is not a unique characteristic of transnational communities. Subnational and even local communities can also become actively engaged in different locales and therefore consist of social relationships maintained in noncontiguous space to a certain extent. In fact, the only communities that are constituted primarily in contiguous, territorial space are local civic organizations and neighborhood associations, which are becoming increasingly rare in certain advanced industrialized countries as they are replaced by deterritorialized organizations that rely more on long-distance communication technologies and less on face-to-face interaction.[8] Undoubtedly, the differences between transnational and most other types of communities are a matter more of degree than of kind.

Although the advent and advance of global telecommunications has enabled individuals to imagine communities beyond the national to encompass the transnational (cf. Hannerz 1996:20–21), this does not mean that transnational communities are always based on imagined relationships, despite their predominantly deterritorialized nature. In fact, transnational social relationships frequently involve interactive exchanges between individual acquaintances in noncontiguous space that are no less real than face-to-face contiguous relationships. Although they extend across nation-

---

[7]This distinction between geographically confined and spatially dispersed communities has been made by scholars studying ethnic groups (Yancey et al. 1982:476).
[8]This is shown by the decline of civic engagement, local political participation, and neighborhood associations in countries such as the United States (see Putnam 1995).

al borders, they are frequently based on personal and intimate circles of kin, friends, and close colleagues (cf. Hannerz 1996:89). As Ulf Hannerz says:

> "Transnational communities" is not a contradiction in terms. This is a matter of kinship and friendship, of leisure pursuits, and of occupational and corporate communities. What is personal, primary, small-scale, is not necessarily narrowly confined in space. (1996:98)

Therefore, as Roger Rouse observes, transnational social relationships can be just as real, close, and personally significant as local communal relationships:

> Today, [migrants] find that their most important kin and friends are as likely to be living hundreds or thousands of miles away as immediately around them. More significantly, they are often able to maintain these spatially extended relationships as actively and effectively as the ties that link them to their neighbors. (1991:13)

Finally, transnational migrant communities are not simply based on deterritorialized, noncontiguous space. Individuals residing in separate nation-states also maintain connections over large geographical distances through the circulation of commodities and people over contiguous space. In other words, transnational migrant communities develop *deterritorialized* social and institutional networks that enable the *territorialized* exchange of commodities and people across national borders. In this manner, both telecommunications and transportation technologies have made geographical distance increasingly irrelevant to the closeness of transnational social relationships (cf. Rouse 1991:13–14). Although transnational communities have always existed in the past, it is only with the recent increase in the ease and speed of global communication and travel that they have become so extensive and cohesive (cf. Guarnizo 1997:288).

THE TRANSNATIONAL EXPANSION OF THE JAPANESE BRAZILIAN ETHNIC COMMUNITY

The Japanese Brazilian transnational migrant community probably consists of considerably less than a million people who are spatially dispersed in a multitude of different sites in both Brazil and Japan. Although the entire population of Japanese Brazilians in both countries is close to 1.3 million, only the 280,000 dekasegi currently in Japan and those back home who maintain relationships with them are transnationally involved. Various types of personal and institutional connections have developed among Japanese Brazilians in the two countries through the use of noncontiguous telecommunication (letters, telephones, fax machines, e-mail)[9] and mass media (newspapers, television, and Web sites) that enable them to establish both real and imagined social relationships across national borders that defy the limitations of contiguous space and keep the community cohesive over a considerable geographical distance. The transnational community is also maintained through the constant movement of commodities ranging from food and clothes to magazines and videotapes between Japan and Brazil and the circular migration of repeat sojourners. This constant transnational flow of information, images, goods, and people enables the Japanese Brazilians to remain simultaneously engaged in both nations.

Economic and Political Transnationalism

The economic ties that the Japanese Brazilians have established between Japan and Brazil are one of the most important components of their transnational migrant community. Most notable here are the remittances the nikkeijin dekasegi in Japan send back home to their families. Although anywhere from 60 to 80 percent of them live with their families in Japan, 12 to 24.7 percent of them send money home (Kitagawa 1993, 1997). Not only is this transnational flow of money to Brazil handled by Japanese banks, Brazilian banks have also opened branches in Japan.[10] Through such transnational economic transactions made possible by computerized banking networks operating in noncontiguous space, Japanese Brazilian migrants in Japan are able to economically sustain their families and communities in Brazil despite their physical absence. In fact, one survey found that 18 to 28 percent of nikkeijin households in two Japanese Brazilian communities in Brazil received 60 percent or more of their income from dekasegi earnings of family members in Japan (Kitagawa 1996). However, it is not only the sheer economic importance of monetary flows that keeps "transnational families" together but also their cultural meaning. Remit-

---

[9]Most migrant communities have not begun to extensively use e-mail as a form of communication and are therefore not involved in the production of "cyberculture" (see Escobar 1994).

[10]Most of the money the Japanese Brazilians transfer from Japan to Brazil goes through the formal channels of Brazilian bank agencies, in contrast to transfers by Brazilian immigrants in the United States (Klagsbrunn 1996:44).

tances are not purely economic transactions; they are a form of "symbol-ic capital" through which migrants abroad express and articulate feelings of familial responsibility and authority and therefore maintain close social and emotional ties with those back home. For instance, this was evident in the reflections of Umberto, one of my roommates in Oizumi:

> Sending money back to Brazil is the most important thing I do. It keeps my family alive, it sends my kids to school. It gives them what they need to live well. Because I'm not there, I can't do anything for them, to sup-port them emotionally, to act as a father for my children. But by send-ing money, at least I haven't given up one of my roles in my family as a provider. It reminds me that I'm still important for them, still part of my family.

The transnational scope of Japanese Brazilian economic activities en-ables them to simultaneously participate in both the Japanese and the Brazilian economy. By alleviating the acute Japanese labor shortage in the late 1980s and early 1990s, they rescued numerous small and medium-sized Japanese subcontracting firms in the manufacturing sector (and by extension, their parent companies) from imminent collapse. Although fewer companies are now suffering from labor shortages because of Japan's prolonged recession, they have become dependent on nikkeijin workers in order to cut production costs in an increasingly competitive global econ-omy (see chapter 3). As nonunionized, temporary migrant workers bor-rowed from labor broker firms, the nikkeijin can be quickly disposed of and removed from the payroll during a production downturn, unlike per-manent Japanese workers, and they do not receive costly bonuses and other employee benefits despite their relatively high hourly wages.

While playing a critical role in the Japanese economy in this manner, the Japanese Brazilians simultaneously influence the Brazilian economy through their transnational economic activities. According to various estimates, the amount of money the Japanese Brazilians send or take back annually to Brazil ranges from $2 to $4 billion.[11] In fact, a majority of the remittances

[11]In 1996, the Japanese Brazilians officially remitted $1.9 billion to Brazil through Brazilian banks and other financial institutions (including Japanese ones). However, the total amount of money the nikkeijin send annually to Brazil is considerably greater, since they also use un-official means to send remittances (such as through tourist agencies) and physically take money back with them when they return to Brazil as well. Some estimates are as high as $4 billion (Sasaki 1999:262–63).

sent by *all* Brazilian emigrants abroad to Brazil through formal financial institutions comes from Japan.[12] Not only do the nikkeijin financially sustain their families back home and thus contribute significantly to the Brazilian consumer economy, they also save an average of about $18,000 to $20,000 per year in Japan (see Japan Institute of Labor 1995:135; Sasaki 1999:262). Therefore, when they return home with their savings, significant amounts of money are directly infused into the domestic Brazilian economy as they open businesses, buy or build homes, and purchase cars and household appliances. As a result, local Brazilian merchants and communities have learned to cater to the nikkeijin. At the same time, Japanese Brazilian entrepreneurs in Brazil have migrated to Japan with their capital in order to open ethnic businesses in nikkeijin immigrant communities. Such business entrepreneurship among immigrants is becoming increasingly prevalent as an important component of the emergence of transnational economic communities (Portes 1998:46–50).

Despite their highly developed economic transnationalism, Japanese Brazilian immigrants have not been very transnationally engaged on the political front. This contrasts, for instance, with Mexican, Dominican, Cuban, and Filipino migrant communities, which have become powerful ethnic constituencies in the United States while also remaining engaged in political developments in their home countries through absentee voting, campaign contributions, and influencing voting patterns of relatives back home (see Glick Schiller, Basch, and Blanc 1995:57; Guarnizo 1997; Levitt n.d.:22–28, Portes and Stepick 1993). Since the Brazilian nikkeijin are relatively recent immigrants who retain a temporary sojourner mentality, they have not yet demanded any political rights in Japan or even representation at the local municipal level. In fact, immigrants usually do not get fully involved in the domestic politics of the host society until the second generation. Although prominent Japanese Brazilian associations and individuals were involved in pressuring Japanese bureaucrats when the Immigration Control and Refugee Recognition Act was revised in 1989 (chapter 1), the nikkeijin community has made no concerted political demands recently, despite the difficulties that some dekasegi continue to

---

[12]Remittances sent by all Brazilian emigrants to Brazil since 1991 ranges from $1.6 to over $3 billion annually. However, this is not an accurate figure since many Brazilian emigrants in countries other than Japan primarily rely on informal channels to send money (Klagsbrunn 1996:44–45).

have with Japanese visa requirements.[13] Nikkeijin immigrants in Japan have also been surprisingly apathetic about elections and important political developments back home. During the all-important Brazilian presidential elections in 1994, only 365 of them bothered to vote by absentee ballot (*International Press*, October 9, 1994). Brazilian immigrants in other parts of the world (mainly the United States and Europe) remain uninvolved in Brazilian politics as well. During the 1998 presidential elections, only 25,000 of them cast their ballots from abroad (Levitt n.d.).[14]

Transnational Personal Networks, Commodity Flows, and Mass Media Influences

The integrity of transnational communities also depends on direct personal relationships sustained across national boundaries in deterritorialized, noncontiguous space. Telecommunication technologies allow nikkeijin who are physically separated to interact and exchange personal information regardless of spatial distances and borders. As for most immigrants around the world (including Brazilians in the United States),[15] a considerable amount of this transnational communication is done through the telephone. Despite the high cost of buying a phone line in Japan (and the long wait to borrow a line), almost all the Japanese Brazilians acquire phone service in Japan. Since nikkeijin return migration began in the late 1980s, KDD (a large Japanese long-distance phone company) has experienced an exponential increase in calls to Brazil and by 1996, the entire Japanese Brazilian immigrant population was spending an amazing $50 million per month on international phone calls (Sellek 2001:137).[16] KDD aggressively

---

[13]One of my informants who had decided to remain in Japan indefinitely complained about Japanese nationality laws, which do not grant Japanese citizenship to children of foreign nationals born in Japan. Another was discouraged by the complicated naturalization process in Japan. However, it will be a long time before such complaints among permanent nikkeijin residents translate into direct political action.

[14]Among the more than 100,000 Brazilian immigrants in New York, only 800 voted for the presidential elections in 1989 (Margolis 1994:207).

[15]Like the nikkeijin, a vast majority of Brazilian immigrants in the United States phone Brazil on a regular basis and spend large amounts of money on long-distance calls (Margolis 1994:193).

[16]Twenty percent of all international phone calls from Japan are now made by migrant workers, with a growth rate of about 20 percent per year (Stalker 1994:32).

advertises within the nikkeijin immigrant community; the company's posters, ads, and logos are plastered everywhere in nikkeijin stores, restaurants, and other businesses, as well as on information pamphlets and in guidebooks. In addition to distributing brochures and other advertising materials, KDD sponsors nikkeijin immigrant organizations and Portuguese radio programs, and its representatives also campaign aggressively in the community, even recruiting Japanese Brazilian customers door to door with special discount programs. The Brazilian nikkeijin are also starting to use the Internet to stay in touch with family and friends back home. Some correspond through e-mail, whereas others use chat rooms catering to nikkeijin in Japan and Brazil or have even created personal Web pages with information on and photos of themselves (Roth 1999:153).

By using the phone and the Internet, many Japanese Brazilians stay in constant touch with family, relatives, and even friends in Brazil. Despite the geographical distances involved, these transnational interactions between individuals that take place in noncontiguous space are psychologically and emotionally "real" social relationships that can keep territorially dispersed families together. In fact, they can sometimes be more important and relevant than actual face-to-face, contiguous encounters. For example, Leonardo, one of my roommates in Oizumi, had this to say after he had spoken with his wife and children back home:

> Whenever I talk to my family on the phone, it really affects me emotionally. My kids are not doing very well in school—getting bad grades. My wife tells me that they always say they miss Daddy. I talked to them briefly and, as always, said I'd be back home soon. I always think about how I came to Japan for the economic gain, but how I've sacrificed my family because of it. These feelings always nag me.

Leonardo's fifteen-minute phone call to his family, despite its deterritorialized nature, had a much greater personal impact on him than the numerous conversations he had had that week with friends at work and at restaurants.

The social reality of such long-distance, transnational family interactions is shown not only by their ability to provide emotional support or cause personal anxiety but also by their practical influence on individual migratory decisions. Many nikkeijin immigrants decide whether to return to Brazil or to stay in Japan based on information they receive from family members at home about the Brazilian economy or the feelings of homesickness and loss because of family separation that are also transmitted through telecommunication in noncontiguous space. Such transnational family relationships also instigate considerable chain migration from Brazil because Japanese Brazilian migrants in Japan constantly attempt to convince family members and relatives in Brazil to join them. Many wish to alleviate the *saudade* (homesickness, nostalgic longing) they experience as a result of separation from loved ones (cf. Yamanaka 2000:142).

One of my close nikkeijin acquaintances at Toyama spent months attempting to actively recruit his family members (wife, children, and brother) over the phone and through personal letters to join him in Japan. He told me that he was so miserable and lonely living in Japan by himself that if he couldn't persuade them to migrate, he had no choice but to repatriate and face financial ruin. As a result, he had used every argument in the book for why they should migrate, including the need to alleviate loneliness, the economic benefits of living in Japan, the lack of crime and superior school system (for his children), and even the marvels of Tokyo Disneyland. The day his persistent efforts finally paid off, he appeared in the factory a changed man, visibly more happy and relaxed. "I've said so many nice things about Japan that I hope they're not disappointed when they actually arrive," he told me. "The other day, I even told them the Japanese are the friendliest people in the world!" My interviews revealed that most chain migrants would not have come to Japan had it not been for the personal exhortations of family, relatives, and friends. Some of them even told me that they later felt somewhat "deceived" by their close acquaintances, who exaggerated the extent of possible savings and the benefits of living in Japan. "Japan is good for some [Japanese] Brazilians but not all," one noted. In this manner, the constant family communication and interaction that occurs in noncontiguous space between the two countries ensures the continuous flow of migrants from Brazil that is necessary to sustain a transnational migrant community.

The circulation of commodities across national borders also plays an important role in constituting the transnational community. Japanese Brazilian ethnic businesses have proliferated in Japan and include Brazilian food stores and restaurants as well as a much smaller number of snack shops, clothing stores, discos, and even boutiques, barbers, and beauty parlors. When I lived in Japan, the largest Brazilian supermarket was in Oizumi; it boasted 520 square meters of space and 1,800 products. In 1996, a Brazilian shopping center opened in the town, and the owner is reportedly thinking

Inside the largest Brazilian food store in Oizumi town.

about creating a Brazilian theme park in the future (Kitagawa 1997:75). In areas with high nikkeijin immigrant concentrations, such clusters of Brazilian stores and restaurants have come to be known as "Little Brazils." A number of mobile Brazilian vendors also operate in Japan, bringing Brazilian food and merchandise by truck to local areas with few nikkeijin. I was amazed at how one of these truck vendors, by simply parking on a Tokyo street, was able to do a brisk business with Brazilian nikkeijin customers who seemingly materialized out of nowhere.[17]

These various Brazilian ethnic businesses obtain their products from distributors located in Japan, which order goods directly from Brazil by fax or telephone, therefore creating an extensive transnational retail network sustained by noncontiguous telecommunications networks that provides nikkeijin immigrants with not only food from Brazil but also a vast array of products such as magazines, newspapers, T-shirts, music, books, and videotapes of Brazilian news and television programs. In fact, in areas

---

[17]These vending trucks operate on a routine schedule or circuit, and thus the nikkeijin locals know when they will be arriving.

such as Oizumi, even *Japanese* merchants have joined the transnational flow of Brazilian commodities and have begun to stock Brazilian products such as the famed Guaraná (a soft drink made from a tropical fruit) and Brazilian newspapers. It is important to remember that the cross-border traffic of commodities is not merely an economic exchange but also a transaction of commodified meanings and images that constitute a transnational culture (see Smith 1991:157). As will be described in the next chapter, the Japanese Brazilians appropriate the Brazilian cultural meanings attached to these products (especially food and clothes) to articulate their Brazilian counteridentities and consolidate their attachment to their home country, thus sustaining the transnational community.

This transnational culture also consists of media images and information that circulate between Brazil and Japan through noncontiguous space. An active ethnic mass media has developed among the Japanese Brazilians in Japan, centered around three weekly Portuguese newspapers: the *International Press, Folha Mundial,* and *Tudo Bem.* One survey found that 80 percent of nikkeijin immigrants read one of these papers all or some of the time (Nomoto et al. 1993). The largest and most extensive in coverage is the *International Press,* which was started in 1992. During my stay in Japan, the paper claimed to have an estimated circulation between 33,000 to 55,000 per week. These papers feature not only news from Brazil and Japan but also stories about activities, incidents, problems, and personal experiences among Japanese Brazilians in various parts of Japan. The papers also contain business and service announcements, entertainment guides, information about upcoming events, job ads, and a section in which readers' questions are answered. In addition, the *International Press* features a section containing letters from nikkeijin dekasegi about their impressions, experiences, and frustrations in Japan as well as a classifieds section where they can sell personal goods, send messages to each other, provide information about regional activities, and place ads seeking companionship, correspondence, or love. In addition to newspapers, Portuguese radio programs, broadcast from stations in Shizuoka, Tokyo, and Nagoya, have become part of the immigrant mass media (*Ryuku Shimpo,* September 6, 1991). These broadcasts include programs and news, Brazilian music, and replies to letters from Japanese Brazilians experiencing difficulties in Japan.

Brazilian television has also become part of the immigrant mass media in Japan by literally being transnationalized and then commodified. Brazilian news programs, soap operas, comedies, and variety shows are

Roberto sits next to some of the electronic goods he has purchased with
his dekasegi earnings in Japan. He is watching a popular Brazilian
television show.

recorded on videotape and sent to nikkeijin-owned stores in Japan, where
they are rented to the dekasegi. Starting in October 1996, Brazilian satel-
lite television has also become widely available for the nikkeijin in Japan
through a digital multichannel broadcasting service called "PerfecTV." By
March 1998, 19,000 nikkeijin households had subscribed to this service
(Sellek 2001:135). In contrast, Japanese newspapers and television have not
been actively incorporated into the nikkeijin ethnic mass media.[18] Brazilians in the United States also rely heavily on such transnational mass
media networks to stay connected with Brazil (see Martes 2000:153–54).

Since the Japanese Brazilians can have real relationships and interactions with only a small circle of kin and acquaintances in both countries,
the transnational culture produced by the deterritorialized flow of media
images and the circulation of commodities across borders enables them to

---

[18]According to one survey, only 22 percent of the respondents relied on the Japanese mass media
for information and entertainment (Kitagawa 1997:140–41).

imagine a wider transnational community. By reading and hearing stories, accounts, and letters from the nikkeijin in other parts of Japan through newspapers and radio programs, they can imagine relationships with individuals they have never met through these shared experiences. In addition, by consuming the meanings and images embodied in the commodities, news, and television shows they receive from back home, Brazilian nikkeijin who have been geographically dispersed and displaced by migration can remain encompassed within a transnationalized "Brazilian culture" that is collectively shared and experienced among their compatriots in both Japan and Brazil. This creates a sense of mutual affinity and cultural attachment with other Japanese Brazilians they do not know, providing the "imagined" social cohesion necessary to sustain a transnational community of individuals scattered across great distances.

Transnational Institutional Connections: Labor Broker and Recruitment Networks

Transnational migrant communities are also kept together by institutions and organizations. There are a number of nikkeijin organizations in Japan that offer assistance only to Japanese Brazilians in the local community and are not transnationally involved. These include the Nikkei Information Center (NIC), the Comitê de Assistência Trabalhadores Latino Americanos (CATLA), and the Comitê dos Latino Americanos Nikkeis (CLAN), which offer a number of services including counseling, job search and housing support, assistance in acquiring visas, informational brochures, and translation. They may also act as mediators in disputes between Japanese Brazilians and their labor brokers and help organize nikkeijin events. These organizations have been limited in scope with insufficient financial resources and usually rely on membership fees or corporate support (KDD supports NIC for advertising and promotional purposes). When I was in Japan, a new support organization had been started called the Fundo de Auxílio aos Trabalhadores Latino-Americanos (Assistance Fund for Latin American Workers), which collects contributions from Japanese Brazilians in Japan and provides financial assistance for immigrants who run into serious problems (such as work accidents) and must return to Brazil.

In contrast to these local nikkeijin assistance organizations, the Tokyo-based Overseas Nikkeijin Association (*Kaigai Nikkeijin Kyokai*) is a truly transnational organization that is funded by JICA (Japan International Cooperation Association) of the Japanese Ministry of Foreign Affairs and encompasses nikkeijin from all countries. However, it does not contribute significantly to the Japanese Brazilian transnational migrant community because the nikkeijin dekasegi do not participate in this organization or utilize the services it provides in Japan. Relatively few of them attend the association's annual *nikkeijin taikai* (conference), which brings together various leaders and representatives from nikkeijin communities around the world (Roth 1999:29).[19]

By far the most significant transnational institution supporting the nikkeijin community is the system of labor broker firms that has been established between Brazil and Japan (see Nishizawa 1995; Watanabe and Teruyama 1992; Watanabe et al. 1992). This highly organized employment network facilitates and sustains the constant movement of nikkeijin migrants between the two countries that makes the transnational immigrant community possible. On the Brazilian side, there are numerous agencies that recruit Japanese Brazilians for factory work in Japan through extensive personal contacts and advertising in the community. These recruitment offices (many of which pose as "travel agencies") then send the Japanese Brazilians to Japan, at which point they are turned over to a Japanese labor broker firm (called *assen gaisha*). On the Japan side, the system partly utilizes the existing Japanese system of labor brokerage, which has traditionally supplied Japanese companies with a disposable, marginal work force of part-time, temporary, and seasonal workers.

This transnational labor recruitment system is able to quickly and efficiently transfer migrant labor over large distances because of telecommunications technology that makes the instant transmission of information possible in noncontiguous space. Data about potential Japanese Brazilian migrants from recruitment offices in Brazil is faxed to labor broker companies in Japan, who have contacts with Japanese companies in need of nikkeijin workers. The labor broker firms then fax information about job availability, wages, and working conditions back to recruitment agencies in Brazil. In a matter of days, the Brazilian nikkeijin can obtain information about the company at which they will work in Japan, what type of work they will do, how much they will earn, and where they will live.

These transnational labor broker networks not only provide direct access to a wide range of jobs in various Japanese companies but also offer a

---

[19]This annual conference has lots of activities conducted in Japanese and is primarily attended by issei.

vast array of additional services such as assistance obtaining visas and financing of all travel expenses. In Japan, they provide housing, transportation, insurance, and other social services (all in Portuguese). These brokers also hire bilingual Japanese Brazilians either as minisupervisors (called *tantosha*) who mediate between Japanese managers and nikkeijin workers on the factory floor or as liaisons and translators who assist the nikkeijin with job placement and housing, and even with personal problems. My roommate, Leonardo, who worked as a liaison for a local labor broker, frequently left during the evening to help Japanese Brazilians with public services, resolve conflicts with local residents, deal with internal family problems, and even translate for nikkeijin involved in traffic accidents.

The labor broker business is highly lucrative for those who run it. Broker agencies and firms charge nikkeijin migrants exorbitant fees for all their services. The one-time introduction or agent's fee can range from $1,000 to $1,600 (Mori 1992), and brokers also frequently overcharge their clients for airfare. Most notorious are broker kickbacks (*pinhane*), which are deducted from nikkeijin salaries and range from a low of 8 percent to a high of 50 percent of the hourly wage (Japan Institute of Labor 1995:83). Rent for apartments, as well as the costs of insurance, transportation to the factory, and lunches at work are also subtracted from salaries. Despite these financial drawbacks, because of the high hourly salaries most nikkeijin command in Japan, most are still able to earn from $2,000 to more than $3,000 per month.

A much smaller number of Japanese Brazilians have been brought to Japan through the direct recruitment and employment efforts of Japanese companies that do not rely on the transnational labor broker system. This direct employment system was created partly in response to the problems and abuses of the broker system and began functioning as early as 1989 (*Nihon Keizai Shimbun*, December 23, 1989). These Japanese companies rely on nikkeijin organizations, personal contacts, newspaper advertisements, or an employment agency sponsored by the Japanese government to recruit Japanese Brazilians in Brazil, who are then hired directly by the company on contracts that usually last from six months to a year, with the possibility of renewal. The abuses and excesses of the broker system are completely eliminated and the companies themselves incur housing, transportation, and other related costs.

By significantly reducing the uncertainty and difficulty of migration for the Japanese Brazilians, these transnational employment and recruitment networks have increased the volume of migration and are therefore one of the most critical factors in the development of a transnational nikkeijin community. Because of the extensive services they provide, the Japanese Brazilians do not need to obtain visas and find jobs and housing in Japan on their own in order to migrate; nor do they need a substantial amount of money since broker firms finance their travel expenses on advanced loans. Sometimes, the only thing that the nikkeijin really have to do is to visit a broker recruitment office in Brazil—the rest is automatically handled. One Japanese Brazilian described this common experience:

> It's so easy to come to Japan nowadays to work. All I had to do was go to a tourist agency in Liberdade [São Paulo] and they took care of everything from my plane ticket and visa to finding me a job and housing in Japan. I just filled out some forms and submitted some documents. Within a few weeks, I found myself working in a factory in Japan.

The ease with which the Japanese Brazilians can migrate to Japan is quite remarkable compared to the situation of other migrants, most of whom do not have access to such highly developed transnational labor broker and employment networks. For instance, Brazilians who wish to migrate to the United States must go through the increasingly difficult process of obtaining a tourist visa (which they plan to overstay) and finance their passage on their own. A minority even make the arduous and treacherous journey on land from Brazil to Mexico and attempt to slip through the heavily patrolled U.S.-Mexican border, sometimes falling prey to bandits and unscrupulous Mexican *coyotes* (immigrant smugglers).[20] Once they arrive in the United States, they must rely on friends and acquaintances or their own resourcefulness to find jobs and housing and obtain much-needed social assistance (see Margolis 1994:chapters 2, 3).

Transnational Migrant Circuits

Transnational broker and employment networks that facilitate migration contribute to the transnational scope of the nikkeijin ethnic community

---

[20]Undoubtedly, many of the difficulties that Brazilians migrating to the United States face are due to the generally clandestine nature of their migration. Even those who make it to the United States can be turned back by immigration authorities at the airport or apprehended by the U.S. Border Patrol.

not only by maintaining the migrant flow to Japan but also by enabling Japanese Brazilians to continuously shuttle back and forth between Japan and Brazil in a process of circular migration, a phenomenon that is also becoming increasingly prevalent among migrants in Europe and the Americas (Sassen 1999:142). A good number of nikkeijin who have returned to Brazil have remigrated to Japan for a second or even third sojourn, thus becoming true transnationals. As shown in table 4 below, the annual number of repeat entrants that Japan has received from Brazil more than doubled between 1991 and 1993, despite the country's prolonged recession.

In addition, these repeat migrants have come to represent an increasing proportion of the yearly Japanese Brazilian migrant flow into Japan: by 2001, 52 percent of all Brazilians who arrived were repeat entrants. As a result, circular migrants already make up a significant percentage of the Japanese Brazilian population in Japan. Even as early as 1992, a Japan Institute of Labor study (1995) found that 40.6 percent of the Japanese Brazilian respondents were in Japan for a second time and 20.8 percent were there for a third time (with 21 percent not responding).[21] Undoubtedly, circular migration has already become a prominent part of the Japanese

TABLE 4   Numbers of Repeat
Entrants from Brazil 1989–1994

1989	1,422
1990	3,841
1991	12,552
1992	23,921
1993	25,915
1994	26,446
2000	42,936
2001	42,267

Source: Japanese Ministry of Justice,
Immigration Bureau Statistics

---

[21]These high rates of return migration may be a bit deceptive because these surveys may also be counting Japanese Brazilians who return to Brazil only briefly for a vacation, to make contacts for a future business, to acquire necessary documentation, or for family reasons.

Brazilian migrant experience that constantly replenishes their transnational community.

When the Japanese Brazilians leave Japan after their sojourn, many declare that they will never again migrate to Japan, or at least do not intend to return.[22] However, as one labor broker in Kawasaki observed: "When these [Japanese] Brazilians leave Japan, they all say, 'I'm never going to come back to this country to work again.' But then a year or so later, they appear at our doorstep again saying, 'Hi, I wonder if you could find me another job here in Kawasaki.'" Although the convenience of transnational labor broker networks certainly increases the nikkeijin propensity to remigrate, they would not constantly circulate between the two countries unless they were responding to considerable economic pressures.

When the Japanese Brazilians return to Brazil, they experience considerable difficulty reestablishing themselves occupationally and economically. In fact, many find that returning home and readapting economically to Brazil is the hardest part of their migration experience (Sasaki 1999:255; Yamanaka and Koga 1996:20–21; cf. Capuano de Oliveira 1999:301). Although the Brazilian economy has stabilized since the implementation of the Plano Real, the outlook remains highly uncertain for most returnees because migration has seriously disrupted their previous careers. Since most either quit their jobs in Brazil or closed their private businesses before migrating, few are able to resume their previous occupations.[23] In addition, few of them have any specific plans or viable future prospects when they leave Japan (cf. Ishi 1991:147–48; Yamanaka and Koga 1995:20–21). Indeed, surveys indicate that close to 70 percent do not even know what kind of work they will do once they return to Brazil (Kitagawa 1997:149). Among those who do have plans, over half state that they would like to open some kind of business in Brazil (Kitagawa 1997:150), but few can specify what type of business or how they intend to go about it. Undoubtedly, most choose to become self-employed because they are fed up with the diminishing returns of being a wage-earning employee in Brazil's previous hy-

---

[22]Indeed, when the Japanese Brazilians are still in Japan, relatively few plan to remigrate in the future for another sojourn (only 23.7 percent and 13.3 percent had such intentions in Kitagawa's 1993 and 1997 surveys). However, after they return to Brazil, the number of those who begin to consider remigration to Japan rises significantly, as shown by the Japan Institute of Labor survey (1995).

[23]In fact, according to one survey, only 6 percent of the nikkeijin in Japan intended to return to their previous occupations (Kitagawa 1997:149).

perinflation economy.[24] However, since many of them were previously white-collar office workers, only a minority have personal experience running a small business, which is a risky prospect at best, especially in an unpredictable economic environment.[25] A good number of those who attempt to start businesses fail (see Sasaki 1999:255; Yamanaka 2000:145).

Those who search for new employment sometimes discover not only that satisfying jobs are again in short supply but also that employers are less willing to hire them because they are now seen as unpredictable workers who may quit their jobs and leave for Japan at any time (see Hiromi Mori 1994:54; Kuwahara 1993:24; Sellek 1996:259). Economic uncertainties are especially acute for young Japanese Brazilians, who never had a job or profession in Brazil and therefore do not have the experience and discipline to succeed economically back home. Many of those who were university students when they migrated to Japan never resume their studies and receive their degrees.[26]

Because of the disruption in their previous careers and the difficulties they experience in regaining their economic footing in Brazil, an amazing 24.8 percent of the nikkeijin migrant returnees remain unemployed in Brazil, according to one survey (Japan Institute of Labor 1995). Many Japanese Brazilians find that their savings accumulated in Japan are quickly depleted if they cannot find a steady source of income in Brazil (especially if their savings have also been used to buy homes and consumer items). Even those who are fortunate enough to have found a steady source of income in Brazil earn less than they did before migration (see table 5). Because their monthly Brazilian incomes can sometimes be earned in just several days in Japan, some of these migrant returnees lose their motivation to work in Brazil, given the comparatively minuscule economic returns.

As a result, when the Japanese Brazilians return to Brazil, they eventually confront the same problems of economic insecurity, insufficient job

---

[24]Gmelch, in a review of the literature on return migration, notes that lots of migrants, after returning from their temporary stay abroad, invest in small businesses, preferring to be self-employed (1980:150).

[25]In his study of one Japanese Brazilian community in Brazil, Hiromi Mori notes that the nikkeijin returnees do not have enough savings to successfully start a new business and that competition is stiff (1994:54).

[26]Among the four Japanese Brazilians I interviewed in Japan who were university students, only one intended to return to the university.

TABLE 5 Monthly Salary Distribution of the Japanese Brazilians in Brazil

Returnees from Japan		General Population	
Salary Level	*%*	*Salary Level*	*%*
under $100	11.9	under $80	4.3
$100–400	37.6	$80–400	26.4
$400–800	28.1	$400–800	27.2
$800–1,500	10.6	$800–1,600	21
over $1,500	10.7	over $1,600	21.4

Source: Derived from São Paulo Humanities Research Center (1987–88) and Japan Institute of Labor (1995)

Note: These wage statistics are not entirely reliable because a relatively high number of those surveyed by the two studies from which these figures are derived did not respond to salary questions.

opportunities, and low wages that caused them to migrate to Japan in the first place. Indeed, a number of them find that their employment and income situation back home has been worsened instead of improved by migration. For many, remigration to Japan to earn more money becomes the only alternative, thus initiating a pattern of circular migration. A similar process has occurred among Brazilian immigrants in the United States, who face the same economic problems as the nikkeijin upon returning to Brazil and have also become repeat migrants (see Margolis 1994:263–67). In this manner, migration breeds further migration by perpetuating, if not exacerbating the economic conditions that initiated it in the first place.

In addition, the temptation to return to Japan becomes greater for migrant returnees because their personal experiences from their first sojourn make the prospect of a second one considerably less daunting. They already know how to obtain visas, jobs, and housing and are better prepared to deal with the practical, social, and emotional problems of living in Japan as well as the physical difficulties of unskilled factory work. They also will not experience as strongly the shock of ethnic marginalization and downward occupational mobility in Japan typical of first-time migrants. In addition, since they have established cohesive transnational personal networks, they can be assured that their personal acquaintances in Japan will assist them in locating jobs and housing while also providing emotional and social support. As a result, they can migrate with much greater confidence and security while avoiding the major problems and pitfalls they experienced during their first sojourn.

In this manner, once they migrate, some Japanese Brazilians are caught in a self-perpetuating cycle in which they become dependent on continued migration for financial subsistence. As a result, many Japanese Brazilian families have come to rely completely on migration for economic survival.[27] This is sometimes true even for those who went to Japan not because of financial difficulties in Brazil but as "opportunity migrants" (see chapter 1) lured by promises of instant riches and easy social mobility. One of my informants in this category who was in Japan for a second sojourn with his spouse spoke to me about how much they deeply regretted their initial, rash decision to quit their stable jobs in Brazil and come to Japan with unrealistic financial dreams. He insisted that if they had remained in those jobs, they would now be living without any economic problems in Brazil instead of working in Japan again as unskilled migrant laborers.

A marginal group of Japanese Brazilians is therefore emerging who have become vagrants trapped in a transnational migrant circuit[28] or a circular diaspora (Yamanaka 2000) between Brazil and Japan and are seemingly destined to repeat a pattern of earning money in Japan, spending it in Brazil, then returning to Japan to earn more (cf. Linger 2001:135). These circular migrants have ironically been caught in a double marginalization that prevents them from becoming stable residents in either country—they cannot remain in Brazil because they have become economically marginalized but do not wish to remain in Japan because they are ethnically marginalized. This is precisely what keeps them moving and makes them transnationals who continue to transgress national borders.

TRANSNATIONAL COMMUNITIES, NATIONAL IDENTITIES: WHAT CAUSES THE DISJUNCTURE BETWEEN COMMUNITY AND CONSCIOUSNESS?

As the Japanese Brazilians have return migrated to Japan, their ethnic community has become territorially unbound from the confines of the Brazilian nation-state, allowing them to be simultaneously engaged in two

---

[27]For instance, in two rural nikkeijin colônias in Brazil, Hiromi Mori found that 40 to 90 percent of the families relied 100 percent on migrant savings to subsist (1994:48).

[28]Rouse (1991:14) uses this term more broadly to refer not just to the transnational circulation of people but also to goods and information.

countries. Deterritorialized, transnational communities can now be sustained over such enormous geographical distances because of the increasing compression of space-time in technologically mediated noncontiguous space (cf. Harvey 1989:266), enabling communications and information to be transmitted across national borders over great distances in an instant. As a result, individuals scattered in various different countries can maintain cohesive and "real" transnational economic, personal, and institutional relationships while imagining a sense of belonging to a broader transnational community beyond their limited personal network. Transnational communities are also consolidated by the constant circulation of commodities and people across borders, facilitated by the greater speed of modern transportation as well as the efficiency of transnational retail and labor recruitment networks.

It is frequently assumed that the formation of transnational migrant communities is linked to the development of new transnational ethnic *identities* that do not conform to the territorial boundaries of one nation-state. According to Roger Rouse, as migrants become involved in transnational circuits of capital, labor, and communications, it becomes increasingly difficult for them to delimit a singular national identity (1991:16–71). The Aguilillan migrants in Redwood City he examines establish transregional identities that are maintained through their transnational networks. In her study of the Chinese diaspora, Aihwa Ong claims that "postcolonial transnational subjects [call] into question not only stability in cultural identity, but also ties to a single nation-state, or even to a single imagined community" (1993:747). Likewise, Luis Guarnizo argues that Dominican transmigrants adopt flexible identities that cannot be subsumed in bipolar national terms as either Dominican or American (1997:289). In this manner, dual national loyalties among migrants are invoked as a form of transnational identity (Glick Schiller and Fouron 1990:341). Castles and Miller make a similar claim:

> Immigration may be able to make a special contribution to the development of new forms of identity. It is part of the migrant condition to develop multiple identities, which are linked to the cultures both of the homeland and of the country of origin. Such personal identities possess complex new transcultural [transnational] elements (1993:274).

For others, transnational migration produces not only multiple national identities but also common ethnic bonds that transgress national affiliations. According to Kearney, when the Mixtecs, a Mexican indigenous minority, migrate to the United States, they construct a transnational identity based on their minority ethnicity that links them to Mixtecs in Mexico. This is a response to their exclusion and exploitation in both countries and therefore serves as an alternative to a nationalist consciousness (1991:62–63). Basch, Glick Schiller, and Blanc (1994:268) also implicitly associate the creation of transnational migrant communities and "deterritorialized nation-states" with the development of common ethnic identities among members of different nations. For example, they mention the emergence of transnational pan-ethnic identities among immigrants from different Caribbean as well as Asian nations in the United States (1994:276), and transnational racial identities among American blacks and Afro-Caribbean immigrants (1994:283–86).[29]

However, the Japanese Brazilian case demonstrates that the relationship between community and identity is not always so simple. The emergence of transnational migrant communities is not always accompanied by a corresponding transnationalization of identity in which migrants develop a simultaneous allegiance and sense of belonging to two or more nations. In fact, the ethnic experiences of the Japanese Brazilians are characterized by a prominent *disjuncture* between community and consciousness. Before return migration, when their ethnic community was still confined to the Brazilian nation, they had already developed *transnational* hybrid identities as Brazilians who simultaneously remained very conscious of their ancestral ethnic origins and identified to a considerable extent with Japan. However, as their ethnic community has been expanded by migration to become truly transnational in scope, their identities have moved in the opposite direction to become more national and restrictive in orientation. As shown in the previous chapter, instead of expanding their ethnic consciousness by strengthening their dual, transnational allegiance to both Brazil and Japan, they distance themselves from the Japanese and come to identify more exclusively with one nation than before through a greater consciousness of their Brazilianness. In this manner, the return migration of the Japanese Brazilians has resulted in a greater nationalization of a previously strong transnational identity.

The result is a contradiction between migrant practices and identity in which the increasing transnational scope of migrant activity produces a

---

[29]However, Portes and Stepick (1993:chapter 8) emphasize the significant socioeconomic cleavages that exist between Afro-Caribbean immigrants and American blacks despite a sense of racial solidarity and unity in the face of American racism.

resurgence of national sentiment at the level of self-consciousness. In other words, we have a transnational migrant community without a transnational consciousness. This lack of an identity seems to be one of the distinguishing characteristics of some transnational migrant communities, in contrast to most national and subnational communities, in which members strongly identify with the community to a certain extent. Why does a disjuncture between community and consciousness occur at the transnational level?

Although transnational migration frequently leads to marginalization and negative experiences in the host society that can produce a deterritorialized migrant nationalism, why cannot the emergence of transnational communities instill a corresponding transnational consciousness that can counter this nationalization of ethnic identity? Why do national influences on self-consciousness remain more powerful than transnational influences? Territorially displaced migrant groups continue to frame their experiences in nationalist terms not only because they lack a political language necessary to articulate their transnational and postnational aspirations (Appadurai 1996:165–66) but also because transnational communities are unable to challenge the hegemony of the nation-state.

Of course, my nikkeijin informants were obviously aware that the Japanese Brazilians are now spread across two countries and connected to one another in various ways, and that their activities and movements are no longer restricted to one nation-state. Yet, almost no one expressed a strong consciousness of being part of this deterritorialized transnational community. Very few of my informants spoke of an emerging transnational identity that simultaneously incorporates aspects of both Brazil and Japan. Although Koga (1995:50) argues that those Japanese Brazilians who have lived in Japan for an extended period move beyond a Brazilian nationalist identity and develop a synthetic "nikkeijin" consciousness that combines the good aspects of both Japan and Brazil (cf. Tajima 1995:186–87), I did not find this to be the case even among my informants who had been in Japan for a long time.

However, when talking about how the dislocations of migration had changed their identities, a couple of my informants did state that they now felt *neither* Brazilian nor Japanese and identified themselves as "nikkeijin" who do not truly belong to either nation. Indeed, having been treated as a Japanese minority in Brazil but rejected as foreigners in Japan, they were conscious of this double marginalization and mentioned that they are a people without a homeland (*um povo sem pátria*).[30] However, such negatively defined *non-national* identities characterized by a lack of belonging to either nation are not necessarily based on a positive identification with the transnational migrant community.

Transnational migrant communities generally do not have a strong impact on the ethnic consciousness of their members because they remain formless, enigmatic entities that cannot be clearly defined, located, and identified in contrast to the nation-state. Fundamentally, they consist of fragmented, unorganized, and spatially dispersed collections of personal networks and institutional connections as well as decontextualized media images, scattered commodities, and territorially unattached migrants who move back and forth. This conglomeration of transnational connections and movements has no overarching institutional unity or internal organization like the nation-state. Although the flow of information, images, and commodities may constitute a transnational "culture," it is a culture without coherence and stability that lacks clearly definable and enduring values and beliefs with which individuals can identify (as is the case with national cultures).[31]

More important, the transnational migrant community lacks centralized political institutions and an ideological state apparatus that can consolidate and present it as a coherent source of identity and impose a sense of belonging, commitment, and loyalty upon its members. It has no official representatives or spokesmen, no propaganda system, no educational system to teach its values and history, no military or police force to impose its collective will on its members, and no laws of citizenship or nationality (i.e., transnationality) that would outline criteria for community belonging.[32] It seems that the ethnic mass media is the only institutional mechanism that enables individuals to imagine themselves as part of a transnational community. Because transnational migrant communities are not coherent, collective entities that evoke strong feelings of belonging

---

[30]However, even these individuals realize that they belong much more in Brazil than in Japan since they can at least be socially accepted and culturally integrated back home, whereas in Japan, they are totally outcast (Tsuda forthcoming 2).

[31]Hannerz (1996:90) also agrees that the nation and its culture are not being replaced by any single transnational culture.

[32]Gupta (1992:68–69) notes that certain transnational *political* communities, like the movement of nonaligned states, also lack many state and media apparatuses. This is less true for the European Community.

or allegiance, they remain unable to challenge the prevailing influence of the nation-state.[33]

Indeed, the Japanese Brazilians who have become transnationalized continue to see most of their experiences in nationalized terms. Their ethnic and socioeconomic marginalization, as well as cultural differences, in Japan that delineate their identities are regarded as products of their Brazilian national, not transnational background. Even most of the components that constitute the transnational community are seen as "belonging" to one nation or the other and not to some abstract entity that somehow encompasses or transcends both nations. For instance, the personal networks between Brazil and Japan are not regarded by the nikkeijin as "transnational" but are seen as "Brazilian" relationships with specific relatives and friends in Brazil (to be distinguished from relationships with Japanese workers or acquaintances in Japan). Likewise, the transnational labor recruitment and employment network is thought of separately by its national components. It consists of Brazilian recruiters in Brazil who then send nikkeijin migrants to Japanese-owned labor broker firms in Japan.

The transnational culture that the nikkeijin migrants have generated consists of distinctly Brazilian and Japanese parts. Much of it is based on the traffic of Brazilian media programs, and even news and information that are transnationally exchanged in the nikkeijin ethnic media are about either Brazil or Japan. Virtually all of the commodities that circulate between the two countries are Brazilian, whether they are videotapes, food, clothes, music, newspapers, or magazines, and are clearly distinguished from Japanese commodities that originate and are manufactured in Japan. Even food that is eaten in both countries (namely rice) is nationally identified and differentiated. Most Japanese Brazilians in Japan prefer the taste and texture of imported Brazilian rice (drier with smaller grains) to Japanese rice (moist with larger grains).[34] So far, the migration of the Japanese Brazilians and the creation of a transnational nikkeijin culture has involved little hybridization or creolization between Brazilian and Japanese culture[35] based on the emer-

---

[33]This may also be a reason for the difficulty that some transnational political communities have in creating strong bonds of solidarity and identity as an effective means of political mobilization (see Gupta 1992:69–70).

[34]See Ohnuki-Tierney (1993) for a discussion of the relationship between rice and national identity.

[35]See Hammarlund (1994), Hannerz (1987), and Gilroy (1993) for discussions of migration and cultural hybridization.

gence of new synthetic forms that can no longer be nationally distinguished. The only notable examples are the infiltration of Japanese words into the Portuguese that the nikkeijin speak in Japan and some of their ethnic festivities like samba (see the next chapter), which sometimes appropriate both Japanese and Brazilian symbolic representations.

The national takes priority over the transnational as a locus of identification in this manner precisely because of its territorialized nature. Usually, things are understood to originate and belong to a certain contiguous space—a geographically enclosed territory (like the nation-state). According to Hannerz, "even the transnational cultures have to have physical centers somewhere, places in which, or from where, their particular meanings are produced and disseminated" (1996:107). However, as analyzed above, the transnational community is deterritorialized—its social relationships are configured in noncontiguous space and do not remain anchored to any particular territory. Therefore, it is hard to conceive of things being located and originating in a deterritorialized transnational space that is not grounded in any sense of place. Guarnizo and Smith make a similar point:

> Transnational practices do not take place in an imaginary "third space" abstractly located "in between" national territories[36]. . . . Transnational practices, while connecting collectivities located in more than one national territory, are embodied in specific social relations established between specific people, situated in unequivocal localities, at historically determined times. (1998:11)

In fact, even circular migrants do not reside in some deterritorialized transnational space or "hyperspace" (see Kearney 1995:553) between the two nation-states. They are in Brazil at one moment and in Japan at another and are "deterritorialized" only when they are on the plane. Indeed, most transnational activities remain territorially grounded in local, national spaces. As a result, the transnational community continues to be experienced in national terms.

Therefore, it seems that the transnational migrant community does not possess the political, ideological, institutional, and cultural coherence

---

[36]This is a term that Homi Bhabha (1990) invented to refer to a hybrid space that displaces the histories that constitute it.

as well as the spatial integrity to challenge and subvert the hegemonic influence of the nation-state on individual consciousness, even when its citizens spatially escape its territorial confines and hegemonic apparatuses. As a result, the experience of nationality remains much more immediate, articulate, and powerful than the experience of transnationality. Because the transnational community is not consciously recognized as such but is construed in more local and national ways, it is not sufficiently "imagined" by its members as a source of identity and affiliation.

This disjuncture between transnational communities and national identities indicates that self-consciousness is not simply a direct function of migrant practices. Because the transnational practices of the Japanese Brazilians do not have much of an impact on their identity, they are overshadowed by the much more powerful experiences of discriminatory exclusion and sociocultural difference the nikkeijin have in Japanese society, which force them to define themselves in nationalist terms as Brazilians. Therefore, just because migrants engage in transnational activities does not mean they develop a transnational consciousness. When anthropologists analyze identity, they must be careful to listen well to what informants actually tell them and not make facile conclusions that conflate the observed behavior of individuals with their identities.

In this manner, even when they are transnationalized, people continue to think in terms of the nations from which they originally came (see Joppke 1999:182). This is especially true for migrants such as the Japanese Brazilians, who were born and have resided in the same nation-state for their entire lives before being territorially displaced. In contrast, the experience of transnationality would be quite different for those who have never been bound to any one nation because of a lifetime of dislocation. However, most migrants are of the nikkeijin type. Although the recent interest in flexible and multiple citizenship (see Clifford 1992, 1997; Ong 1993, 1999) focuses on constantly mobile and "deterritorialized" people who have lived in several countries, rely on global networks, and have obtained residential rights in several nation-states in order to adapt to the vicissitudes of global capitalism and politics, we must remain very aware that such true cosmopolitans are only a small economic and intellectual elite (which includes the academics who write about them) (cf. Fabricant 1998:29).[37]

---

[37]In fact, even in this age of increasing globalization and transnational movement, a vast majority of people in the world still do not even migrate. Only a mere 120 million out of the world's population of 5 billion live outside their country of origin or citizenship (Joppke 1999:270).

UNABLE TO EMERGE:
"NIKKEIJIN" AS A TRANSNATIONAL IDENTITY

Although the Japanese Brazilians do not articulate a transnational consciousness in response to the development of their transnational migrant
community, certain experiences inherent in the migration process may
produce other kinds of transnational ethnic identities that transgress the
boundaries of the nation-state.[38] In addition to identities based on multinational allegiances to two or more countries, there are *diasporic* transnational identities, which are created when similar ethnic, religious, or racial
groups that reside in different nations maintain a sense of commonality
based on shared historical experiences, ethnic origins, or affiliation to an
ancestral homeland. In contrast, transnational *pan-ethnic* identities can be
developed when immigrants originating from different countries in the
same geographical region are confronted by shared experiences of discriminatory ethnic exclusion, cultural difference, and economic marginalization
in the host country, which cause them to unite and assert their ethnic commonalities (cf. Clifford 1994:311–12; Lopez and Espiritu 1990). Examples
include the "Latino" identity among Latin American immigrants in the
United States and the "Asian American" identity among those from various Asian countries (see Lopez and Espiritu 1990; Mato 1997:193).

Among the Japanese Brazilians in Japan, however, these other types of
transnational identities have not emerged either. Few Japanese Brazilians
have developed a pan-ethnic, transnational consciousness by identifying
with nikkeijin immigrants from other South American countries, most
notably the Japanese Peruvians, who are the second largest group of
nikkeijin in Japan. Despite their shared ethnic experiences, the Japanese
Brazilians I interviewed did not strongly affiliate themselves with the
Japanese Peruvians as ethnically similar "nikkeijin." Instead, they continued to feel significant cultural differences and always contrasted themselves with the Peruvians, frequently in a derogatory manner that smacked
of ethnic prejudice. Consider the following statement from an older
Japanese Brazilian:

> The Peruvians are lazy and only a minority work really hard. They also
> talk too much at work and are disobedient, although there are some

---

[38]See Mato (1997:172–73) for a discussion of different types of transnational identity.

good ones among them too. Very few of them speak any Japanese or
know anything about Japan. Therefore, the Japanese don't like them
and prefer the Brazilians.

Even Tadashi, who had a couple of Peruvian friends at Toyama, was not
free from prejudice:

> Older nikkei-Brazilians have more prejudices toward the Peruvians than
> youth. Peruvians are much more unpredictable and temperamental.
> They get angry too fast and give up on the work. If the Japanese tell
> them to do something, they resist and say, "Screw this."
>   The Japanese Brazilians feel ethnically different from the Peruvians
> not only because of such self-perceived cultural contrasts but also because
> of national differences. The Brazilian nikkeijin in general tend to look
> down on Peru as a poor and less developed country in contrast to Brazil.

This sense of difference is externally reinforced by Japanese employers
who clearly differentiate between the two groups for employment purposes instead of perceiving them collectively as similar or identical
"nikkeijin." Except for a couple of employers I interviewed who claimed
not to discriminate between the Brazilian and the Peruvian nikkeijin,
most preferred to hire the Japanese Brazilians because they speak better
Japanese, are supposedly more culturally "Japanese," and cause fewer
problems. In addition, many of the Peruvians are of mixed or non-Japanese descent, and some enter Japan as "fake nikkeijin" with false documents. In fact, some reputable labor broker firms avoid the Peruvians altogether. As a result, the Peruvians receive lower salaries than the
Brazilians and are much more likely to be laid off during a recession or a
decline in production (Kitagawa 1993). As Aihwa Ong (1996) notes in her
study of different groups of Asian Americans in the United States, even
immigrants from the same pan-ethnic category are differentially and hier-
archically positioned within institutional structures depending on their
national origins (see also Portes and Rumbaut 1996). Since the Japanese
Brazilians were very aware of such ethnic preferences among Japanese employers and their own privileged status in the labor market, they had very
little economic incentive to identify with their fellow Peruvian nikkeijin.
    This consciousness of ethnic difference is reflected in the social separa-
tion between the two groups in daily interaction. At Toyama, they generally did not mingle with or talk to each other, even when they had been

working in the same section for quite some time. Except for three Peruvians I knew who mixed with Japanese Brazilians, the Peruvians and Brazilians sat at different tables or in separate sections of the same table during breaks and lunch and conversed only among themselves (cf. Roth 1999:54). In fact, Kitagawa's (1993) survey found that social interaction between different groups of nikkeijin outside the workplace was notably lower than their interaction with the Japanese.[39] This ethnic segregation is especially remarkable since the difference in language is not a barrier to communication, as it frequently is with the Japanese. Most Japanese Brazilians are able to understand a good amount of what is said in Spanish and communicate reasonably well with the Peruvians. A few of the Japanese employers I interviewed even reported that the two groups sometimes do not get along very well when placed in the same section in the factory. However, I did not witness or hear of any overt conflicts between the Japanese Brazilians and Peruvians at Toyama.

At the level of ethnic associations and businesses, however, there was more inclusion. Assistance organizations such as NIC, CATLA, and the Fundo Mútuo de Auxílio dos Trabalhadores Latino-Americanos provide services for both Japanese Brazilians and Peruvians in Portuguese and Spanish. Although most of the nikkeijin ethnic restaurants and food stores are owned by Japanese Brazilians and have an almost exclusively Brazilian clientele, some of them have a few Peruvian dishes on the menu or stock a few Peruvian food items. The Japanese Brazilian newspaper, *International Press*, now prints an edition in Spanish. However, large social events organized by the nikkeijin still seem to be ethnically exclusive. I attended two: the samba parade in Oizumi, which involved only Japanese Brazilian (and Brazilian) participants, and a dance party for Peruvians to which only a few Brazilians showed up (in fact, more *Japanese* attended than Brazilians). The other social activities planned by the nikkeijin, such as soccer tournaments and karaoke competitions, tend to be dominated almost completely by the Japanese Brazilians or divided along ethnic lines.

Therefore, instead of identifying pan-ethnically as "nikkeijin" and developing a sense of transnational affiliation, the Japanese Brazilians and

---

[39]This is partly due to the fact that there are relatively few nikkeijin from other South American countries in Japan, so most Japanese Brazilians do not encounter them frequently. Despite this very low level of interaction, however, there have been a number of marriages between Brazilian and Peruvian nikkeijin in Japan.

Peruvians continue to differentiate themselves as members of separate nations. In fact, this is a common experience among immigrants from different countries in the same geographical region. Despite an awareness of common linguistic, cultural, and regional roots, national loyalties and differences are too strongly embedded to yield to a common transnational identification. In the United States, for example, immigrants from different Latin American countries continue to reaffirm a sense of national pride in actual or symbolic confrontations with each other (Portes and Rumbaut 1996:135). This is especially true among Brazilian immigrants, who constantly differentiate themselves from other Hispanic immigrants because of linguistic differences, national distinctiveness and pride, and their own ethnic and class prejudices about Hispanics (Margolis 1994:243–45; Martes 2000:163, 172–74; Sales 1998:184–85). Pan-ethnic identification and political mobilization among immigrant groups with common regional origins usually does not occur until the second or third generation and is frequently caused by the tendency of majority society to group them together and treat them in a similar manner (see Portes and Rumbaut 1996:136).

The reason a transnational nikkeijin ethnic identity does not take hold among the Japanese Brazilians in Japan is also partly related to their "voluntary" minority status in Brazil. As argued in chapter 1, the Japanese Brazilians are not barred from assuming a majority Brazilian identity by ethnic discrimination and marginalization, but self-consciously prefer to retain their "Japanese" minority status and identity. Therefore, when they are ethnically excluded in Japan and their "Japanese" identity is denied, they are able to appeal to the Brazilian side of their ethnic identity and do not have to resort to some new transnational identification as "nikkeijin" people who do not belong to either country. In this manner, migration causes most of them to realize that Brazil is their true *pátria* (homeland) where they really belong (see Tsuda forthcoming 2).

In contrast, migrants who are denied their national identities in *both* the sending and the receiving country are much more likely to develop a transnational identity. This seems to be the case among the Japanese Peruvians (most of whom are descendants of the Japanese Okinawan minority). In contrast to the Japanese Brazilians, they tend to maintain an identity as "Japanese" in Peru not because of their status as a positive minority but in partial response to the much greater discrimination and negative perceptions they experience from Peruvian society. As a result, when they return migrate to Japan and their Japanese ethnicity is rejected, it is harder for them to resort to their previous "Peruvianness" as a new ethnic identity.[40] Instead, they construct a transnational identity as "nikkeijin" or appeal to their ethnic ancestry as descendants of "Okinawans" who have maintained traditional cultural values that are neither Peruvian nor contemporary Japanese (see Takenaka 1996, 2000, n.d.; cf. Yamanaka 1997:28).

TRANSNATIONAL MIGRATION AND THE NATION-STATE

The inability of transnational migration to produce transnational ethnic attachments and identities has important implications for the continued salience of the nation-state amid increasing global migration. According to Michel Foucault (1995 [1977]), the power of the state to produce docile, disciplined subjects is predicated on their spatial confinement. In this sense, migration can be viewed as a means of escaping the disciplining surveillance and "gaze" of the state by refusing to remain in a fixed national space (cf. Ong 1999:chapter 4). As a result, transnational migration has been interpreted by a number of scholars as an act of defiance, resistance, and opposition by individuals to state hegemony (Basch, Glick Schiller, and Blanc 1994:290) that produces new transnational (or postnational) forms of identification and belonging that subvert and supersede the nation-state. According to Kearney, "members of transnational communities . . . escape the power of the nation-state to inform their sense of collective identity" (1991:59; see also Clifford 1994:307). Hannerz claims that the transnational experience of discontinuity and rupture and the development of deterritorialized social relationships that cross national borders may weaken personal involvement with nations and national cultures, compromising the legitimacy of the nation-state (1996:89). Likewise, Appadurai (1996:169) argues that global processes such as migration are producing transnational forms of social organization and identity (i.e., "postnational imaginaries")[41] divorced from territorial states, therefore eroding their ability to monopolize loyalty and making them increasingly obsolete. Similar claims have been made about migrant diasporas (see Appadurai 1996:172–74; Clifford 1997:250–52; Rouse 1991:16).

---

[40]According to Takenaka (n.d.), the Japanese Peruvians also have negative images of Peruvians of non-Japanese descent who are in Japan illegally or as "fake nikkeijin." This also precludes a nationalist identification as "Peruvians."

[41]Ong (1999:chapter 4) uses the term "postnationalist ethos."

However, as the Japanese Brazilian case demonstrates, migration does not necessarily produce new forms of identification that transgress national boundaries and thereby challenge and resist the hegemonic power of the nation-state to shape individual consciousness.[42] Instead of being counterhegemonic, transnational migration can consolidate and increase national loyalty among migrants toward their home country, as shown in the previous chapter, thus contributing to the state's hegemonic objectives and nationalist agendas. Usually this intensification of national identity in a deterritorialized context is an unintended consequence, especially when the nation-state does not actively encourage emigration.

In the Japanese Brazilian case, the Brazilian government has regarded nikkeijin emigration as a potential threat to national integrity and has discouraged it in the past by cracking down on nikkeijin labor brokers in São Paulo, which were illegal under Brazilian law until recently. President Fernando Henrique Cardoso has even made informal appeals to the Japanese Brazilians to stay home for fear of a brain drain of highly skilled workers from the Brazilian nation. But the unexpected result of nikkeijin return migration has been an intensification of the national loyalties and sentiments of the Japanese Brazilians, a persistent ethnic minority that not only was called "sulfur" until recent decades because of its refusal to assimilate despite government efforts (Saito 1978:223; Smith 1979:58) but also is still regarded as ethnically exclusive by many mainstream Brazilians.

Therefore, we see a process whereby the state's hegemonic intention of producing loyal citizens is being furthered without active hegemonic domination by the state itself. When confronted with the apparent threat of increased emigration, governments have responded by creating "deterritorialized nation-states" (Glick Schiller 1997:160–61; Guarnizo 1997:305, 309) that encompass not only those who live within the country's territorial borders but also those who have migrated abroad. In other words, the nation-state attempts to expand its political influence beyond its borders in order to retain some control over its citizens overseas and ensure their continuing loyalty. For the Brazilian government, this has involved passing dual nationality laws and increasing services among consulates abroad (see Levitt

---

[42]Frequently, a more transnational ethnic consciousness emerges only among members of the second immigrant generation, who may embrace a multinational identity based on an affiliation with both their country of birth and the country where their parents originated (cf. McKeown 1999:326–27).

n.d.; Martes 1997; Ribeiro 1999:67).[43] In this manner, although transmigrants escape the territorial confines of the nation-state, they remain subject to its controlling "gaze" (Foucault 1995 [1977]) because its institutional power structures cross borders and transnationalize along with them.

However, the Japanese Brazilian case indicates that the nation-state's hegemony over its geographically dispersed population can be maintained without a corresponding projection of its political power beyond its borders because the very nature of migratory experiences can frequently cause a deterritorialized resurgence of national allegiances abroad. Using Appadurai's terms (1990), the increasing globalization of ethnoscapes (the distributions of people and ethnic groups around the world) does not necessarily have to be accompanied by a simultaneous globalization of ideoscapes (images that serve as ideologies to consolidate state power) in order for the nation-state to retain control over its emigrants in other countries at the level of self-consciousness.

Since the global migration of peoples in this manner can generate a contradictory process that reinforces the integrity of the nation-state, it cannot be simply assumed that the nation-state is always threatened and eventually overtaken by the unrelenting forces of globalization. Even if its power is being challenged by increasing economic, political, and informational globalization, national loyalties are being consolidated in unintended and unexpected ways (cf. Panagakos 1998:54). Therefore, it is a bit premature to declare, as Castells (1997:274–76) and Appadurai (1996) do, that the nation-state is losing its legitimacy to constitute self-consciousness in the modern world and will eventually be superseded by transnational and global entities.

CONCLUSION:
THE TRADITIONS OF TRANSNATIONALISM

The recent disciplinary interest in transnational processes has led some critics of the approach to openly wonder what is so new about transnationalism (see Foner 1997; Mintz 1998). Of course, the constant movement of peoples,

---

[43]Other governments have used such measures as extending political representation to emigrants abroad, creating stronger transnational economic ties with them, creating agencies to protect their interests abroad, and encouraging them to lobby for policies in their host societies that are beneficial to their homeland (Glick Schiller 1997:160–61; Glick Schiller, Basch, and Blanc 1995; Glick Schiller and Fouron 1998; Portes and Rumbaut 1996:108–109).

commodities, and information across national borders as well as the development of transnational relationships between migrants and their home
countries has been occurring for centuries (Glick Schiller, Basch, and Blanc
1994; Foner 1997; Mintz 1998; Portes and Rumbaut 1996). Undoubtedly,
transnational communities have been fundamentally reconfigured by the
advent of better communications and transportation technologies, which
have increased the speed, efficiency, and volume of flows across national
borders (cf. Foner 1997:362). As a result, transnational relationships have become more cohesive, extensive, and "real" than ever before as the ability of
geographically dispersed individuals to effectively transcend the constraints
of contiguous space has been enhanced. Although this does make current
transnational communities appear different from past ones (cf. Mintz
1998:124), the difference is mainly a matter of degree and not of kind.

Thus, it may seem that what is qualitatively different about transnational communities today is the potential emergence of new forms of
transnational identification that disregard national borders and thus subvert the nation-state's classical hegemony over individual consciousness.
However, I have argued that transnational migrant communities are not
too novel in this respect either, not only because the identification of individuals with more than one nation-state is also ancient (Mintz 1998:131)
but also because such communities are frequently unable to transcend traditional forms of national belonging. Ironically, the most distinctive aspect of a transnational migrant community is not what it has, but what it
does not have—a consciousness. In contrast to most national and subnational communities, which instill certain feelings of affiliation, dedication,
and loyalty among their members, the transnational migrant community
appears peculiarly disembodied.

The recent interest in transnationalism is part of a disciplinary shift in
anthropology and sociology in which traditional theoretical frameworks and
categories such as "nation," "ethnic group," or "nation-state" are viewed as
hegemonic constructions imposed upon subordinated populations (a
process to which social scientists have unwittingly contributed) that are increasingly inadequate for the study of transmigrants, whose experiences do
not always conform to such restrictive notions (see Basch, Glick Schiller,
and Blanc 1994; Glick Schiller and Fouron 1990:341; Rouse 1991).[44] Con-

---

[44]Likewise, Hsu (1996) argues that the concepts of "ethnicity" and "nation" are hegemonic, ideological constructs and discourses used to control and manage marginal minority populations
in the United States.

ventional sociological categories are therefore deemed too rigid and essentialized to adequately capture the fluidity and hybridity of a postmodern world and must be "deconstructed" in favor of new concepts and forms of representation such as transnationalism. However, I have argued that increased migration and the emergence of more cohesive transnational communities that extend beyond the confines of the nation-state are not making the nation obsolete as a source of identity and belonging (cf. Mintz 1998:118). Even in the field of transnationalism, studies are finally appearing that consider how national communities and loyalties continue to remain relevant in constituting transnational processes and how transmigrants do not always escape the disciplining power of the nation-state (see Glick Schiller 1997; Guarnizo and Smith 1998).[45] As shown by the personal experiences of my Japanese Brazilian informants, despite the increasing transnational scope of their activities, they remain quite parochial in their self-consciousness, with few of them considering themselves "transnationals."[46] With the increased movement of populations across national borders in the "postmodern" world, the traditional concepts of nation and nation-state will have renewed importance when analyzing the impact of migration on identity.

The emergence of transnational studies is also connected to the desire for an emancipatory politics. The literature frequently emphasizes the counterhegemonic potential of transnationalism as a source of agency, struggle, and empowerment that can provide individuals means to resist, subvert, and eventually escape the hegemonic forces of nation-states and global capitalism (see Basch, Glick Schiller, and Blanc 1994:290; Glick Schiller 1997:164; Glick Schiller and Fouron 1998:156; Kearney 1991). As Guarnizo and Smith observe (1998:5), this emancipatory potential is celebrated even if the transmigrants themselves do not have any political motives or conscious intentions to resist their subordination. Very few of my Japanese Brazilian informants regarded their return migration as a form of counterhegemonic resistance or were conscious of defying the

---

[45]In a similar vein, Ewing argues that the traditional boundaries of gender, ethnicity, and nation are not always subverted by territorial border crossings (1998:264).
[46]Basch, Glick Schiller, and Blanc (1994:16–17) admit that their Caribbean informants rarely thought of themselves as transnationals; nor did they use the word. The researchers explain this by claiming that immigrants have been influenced by the hegemonic context in which they live, where the terms of ethnicity, class, nation, and race have been imposed on their consciousness as a means of control.

wishes and agendas of the Brazilian state, although they frequently held the Brazilian government and economy responsible for their plight.[47] We should not allow our politics and sympathies with subaltern peoples to unduly influence our analysis and cause us to attribute motivations to our informants that do not necessarily exist or to ignore how transnational processes can reinforce, just as much as they can undermine, preexisting hegemonies.

---

[47]For instance, an ethnic business owner in Kawasaki remarked:

> I think it's absolutely absurd that the Japanese Brazilians have to come to Japan to do this kind of work. It just shows how incompetent the Brazilian government is when even well-educated and middle-class people have trouble surviving economically. If we were Japanese American, we would never have had to do this.

Part 3

ADAPTATION

CHAPTER 5

☙

The Performance of Brazilian Counteridentities

Ethnic Resistance and the Japanese Nation-State

COUNTERIDENTITIES AND ETHNIC RESISTANCE

ETHNIC IDENTITY as a form of self-consciousness is not simply a matter of internal experience but is actively displayed, demonstrated, and enacted in practice. In turn, such practices can either consolidate existing hegemonies or generate resistance to the dominant order (Comaroff 1985:5–6). Although the concept of hegemony is associated with Marxist social theory, Raymond Williams (building on Gramsci) expands it beyond ideological class domination to include relations between various types of dominant and subordinate cultural formations (including ethnic ones) that span the whole range of "lived experience" (see 1977:108–12). It is worth quoting him at length:

> [Hegemonic] forms of domination and subordination correspond much more closely to the normal processes of social organization and control in developed societies than the more familiar projections from the idea of a ruling class. . . . People seeing themselves and each other in directly personal relationships [including those among ethnic groups]; people seeing the natural world and themselves in it; people using their physical and material resources for . . . "leisure" and "entertainment" and "art" . . . can still be seen as elements of a hegemony: an inclusive social and cultural formation which indeed to be effective has to extend to and include . . . this whole area of lived experience. (1977:110–11)

If the true condition of hegemony is effective self-identification with hegemonic forms as Williams observes (1977:118), then the behavioral expression of *counter*identities can be regarded as a form of counterhegemonic resistance. In this manner, counteridentities are analogous to what Manuel Castells calls "resistance identities," which are "generated by those actors that are in positions/conditions devalued and/or stigmatized by the logic of domination, thus building trenches of resistance and survival on the basis of principles different from, or opposed to, those permeating the institutions of society" (1997:8).

This chapter further explores the implications of deterritorialized migrant nationalism by examining how the nationalist counteridentity that the Brazilian nikkeijin have developed in Japan leads to the behavioral assertion of their Brazilian cultural differences, enabling them to successfully oppose assimilative Japanese pressures and the stigma of their minority ethnicity.[1] Therefore, although this type of deterritorialized nationalism is a passive, secondary cultural nationalism (Befu 1993; Smith 1991; Yoshino 1992) that does not involve a struggle to establish a nation-state, it does result in a type of "identity politics" of resistance against Japanese ethnic hegemony and power.

In our constantly shifting and self-critical discipline, it does not take long for new paradigms to be questioned, problematized, and eventually deconstructed. Even the relatively new concept of resistance has been criticized in anthropology recently for oversimplification, ambiguity, reification, and romanticization. According to some critics, the analysis of resistance invokes simple binaries between domination/subordination and hegemony/counterhegemony, which cannot adequately deal with the ambiguous complexity of practices that both subvert and legitimate hegemonic meanings (see Kondo 1990:chapter 6; Ortner 1995; cf. Moore 1998). Sherry Ortner observes that the resistance literature also tends to ignore the internal politics and conflicts within subordinate groups, for instance between individuals who do and do not engage in resistance (1995:176–79). There is also ambiguity about whether resistance requires some degree of conscious articulation and agentive intentionality among those involved (Fegan 1986; Kaplan and Kelly 1994; Kondo 1990:chapter 6) or should be defined solely by the practical outcomes of individual or collective behavior. Abu-Lughod (1990) has even noted a tendency to romanticize resistance as a celebration of human resilience and creativity in the face of domination. Alternatives to the resistance approach have been

---

[1]Indeed, other ethnic return migrants like the ethnic Germans who have migrated from Eastern Europe to Germany seem to experience a similar process of minority identity assertion (Münz and Ohliger 1998:168).

suggested, such as the analysis of dialogic processes within contests of power and the analysis of decentered multiple selves and their contradictions and creative tensions (Kaplan and Kelly 1994; Kondo 1990:224–25).

In the context of minority ethnicity, I will use the concept of resistance to refer to behavior that demonstrates a refusal or unwillingness to assimilate to the culture of the dominant group. Such a practice-oriented approach acknowledges the diversity inherent in ethnic resistance, which varies from open acts of cultural defiance by minority groups to modest demands that their cultural differences be acknowledged and accepted. At the same time, since hegemonic cultural structures can only be transformed through redefinitions of cultural meanings in practice, a performative account of resistance (in contrast to textualist accounts) also enables us to assess the extent to which such small acts of resistance lead to incremental changes in the dominant power structure (Herzfeld 1997:30).

Also, ethnic resistance is not an unconscious or unintended act, but is motivated by a certain conscious intent to oppose dominant cultural norms. The degree of conscious articulation among individuals ranges from aggressive attempts to defy the dominant cultural order in public to a simple wish to maintain cultural differences, at least in the privacy of home. By focusing on ethnic identity as the motivation behind resistance behavior, I avoid the tendency in the resistance literature to "dissolve subjects" by ignoring the subjective experiences and intentions of individuals (Ortner 1995:183–87). Finally, in order to capture the full range of behavioral variation and illustrate the contested nature of resistance, I will also examine the significant internal conflicts that occur within the minority ethnic group between those who engage in various forms of resistance and those who comply with the dominant cultural order through assimilation-oriented behavior (see chapter 6). At the same time, since my account focuses on the diverse range of resistance and assimilative practices and intentionalities, it overcomes the simple binaries of resistance/assimilation and hegemony/counterhegemony.

Most of the resistance literature examines social groups that have already been subordinated and subjected to the hegemonic order through the imposition of dominant ideologies and belief systems in an act of symbolic violence. Since such groups have already been deprived of their own independent cultural patterns and basis for opposition, their resistance generally operates within the context of the hegemonic system and involves the subversion, manipulation, and redefinition of dominant cultural categories and meanings. As Williams observes, "nearly all initiatives

and contributions, even when they take on manifestly alternative or oppositional forms, are in practice tied to the hegemonic . . . the dominant
culture, so to say, at once produces and limits its own forms of counter-
culture" (1977:114). Since the subordinated share the same cultural ideologies as the dominant group, this type of resistance consists of actors
who maneuver within the confines of a script that the powerful have
written (Scott 1985:26). Therefore, the Malaysian peasants that Scott examines simply exploit the contradictions inherent in the hegemonic ideologies of the rich elite as a form of critique that enables them to make
demands against its members. Therefore, the "weapons of the weak" consist exclusively in elements of the dominant cultural order (cf. Vandergeest 1993:135).[2]

It is important to distinguish this type of "dominated resistance" from
the resistance of autonomous social groups that have not yet been subju-
gated and symbolically incorporated into the dominant ideological system. According to Williams:

> It would be wrong to overlook the importance of [oppositional forms]
> which, while clearly affected by hegemonic limits and pressures, are at least
> in part significant breaks beyond them, which may again in part be neu-
> tralized, reduced, or incorporated, but which in their most active elements
> nevertheless come through as independent and original. (1977:114)

Autonomous social groups retain their own cultural systems and generally resist and oppose dominant hegemony from an independent cultural
base by asserting their own system of values and defending their cultural
autonomy. In this case, it is not the specific meanings of dominant culture
that are contested but the imposition of this culture itself that is resisted
by rejecting and denying its power to constitute the experiences of the
subordinate group. Although the emergence of new social classes is one
important source of autonomous resistance to dominant hegemony,
Williams (1977:124–26) makes clear that oppositional cultures can emerge
from practices and consciousness that are outside of and excluded from

---

[2]However, Scott (1985:chapter 6) also examines how peasants undermine the moral authority
and symbolic hegemony of the dominant class by using their own social space where definitions imposed by the dominant group do not prevail. He also mentions peasant groups that
live outside the hegemonic system and are able to resist their symbolic incorporation (1985:321).

the dominant social class order, including those of ethnic groups.[3] New immigrant minority groups such as the Japanese Brazilians frequently engage in autonomous resistance since they bring independent cultures with them from their homelands and frequently defend them from encroachment in the host society. This contrasts with culturally dominated indigenous minority groups, whose resistance usually can only contest the meanings of hegemonic cultural ideologies that they have already been forced to adopt.[4]

The almost exclusive concern with the resistance of dominated groups in the literature partly explains the tendency to "thin culture" in ethnographies of resistance (Ortner 1995:180). According to Ortner, the culture of subordinate groups engaged in resistance is analyzed merely as a reaction to hegemony and not as an autonomous and authentic culture per se. In other words, such approaches consider only cultures of resistance that are constituted merely by subversive reinterpretations and manipulations of hegemonically imposed cultural meanings and categories. Even when cultural production in the act of resistance is considered, these cultures are seen as generated by oppositional reactions to domination and not as independent entities (see Willis 1981). In contrast, the autonomous resistance of new immigrant groups involves the analysis of independent cultural patterns that are not simply reactions to dominant cultural forms but exist in their own right.

Despite the autonomous nature of Japanese Brazilian ethnic resistance, their struggle for continued cultural autonomy as an immigrant minority in Japan is not an organized oppositional movement or an open ethnic rebellion against the Japanese. Therefore, it is an "everyday" form of resistance (Abu-Lughod 1990; de Certeau 1984; Scott 1985) in which they assert

---

[3]Williams explains as follows:

Cultural emergence in relation to the emergence and growing strength of a class is then always of major importance, and always complex. But we have also to see that it is not the only kind of emergence . . . there is always other social being and consciousness that is neglected and excluded: alternative perceptions of others, in immediate relationships [such as those among ethnic groups]; new perceptions and practices of the material world. In practice these are different in quality from the developing and articulated interests of a rising class. The relations between these two sources of the emergent—the class and the excluded social (human) area—are by no means necessarily contradictory. (1977:125–26)

[4]This distinction between dominated and autonomous resistance is somewhat analogous to de Certeau's concepts of tactics and strategies (1984:34–39).

their counteridentity and cultural differences in the routines of daily life. However, it still has the potential to challenge and disrupt dominant Japanese ethno-national ideologies.

RESISTANCE AND ETHNIC ADAPTATION: SOCIAL AND PSYCHOLOGICAL LEVELS

Because identities structure an ethnic minority group's behavioral responses, they also have a significant impact on its adaptation (cf. De Vos 1980, 1983; Fordham and Ogbu 1986; Hallowell 1955:75, 77). Social adaptation refers to a group's ability to cope with its "culturally constituted behavioral environment" (Hallowell 1955) by either modifying or maintaining its behavioral patterns. Although Anthony Giddens (1984:233–34) claims that the concept of adaptation is used too vaguely to refer to any type of social change, if we limit our consideration to *ethnic* adaptation— how a minority group responds to majority society by changing its behavioral patterns—it can be quite meaningful.

When assessing the ethnic adaptation of a minority group, it is important to keep in mind a distinction made by George De Vos between adaptation and adjustment (see De Vos 1982a:76–77; De Vos and Suárez-Orozco 1990:23–27). *Adaptation* is an assessment of *social* success and is usually measured in terms of occupational, educational, and social mobility in a given society (cf. Zhou and Bankston 1994:826). Therefore, judgments of the behavior of a minority group as socially adaptive or maladaptive are culturally relative and depend on each society's collectively held standards of social success or failure.[5] In contrast, *adjustment* refers to the *psychological* level of personality structure and self-consciousness. Minority behavior can be considered adjustive or maladjustive depending on whether it has positive or negative psychological consequences for individuals. Maladjustment occurs when behavior impairs psychological functioning in some way. It may range from various degrees of psychic tension to more serious forms of psychological disorder, mental disturbance, or illness. Although there are cross-culturally applicable *standards* of psychological maladjustment, the exact *content* of behavior that is considered maladjustive is culturally relative. In other words, all societies will agree

---

[5]As Ogbu (1978) mentions, each society has a model of social success, which he calls the "status mobility system"—a socially approved strategy for getting ahead.

that psychic tension or psychological distortion (whether cognitive, perceptual, or affective) is maladjustive. However, what constitutes psychological tension or distortion varies from society to society (cf. Spiro 1987:chapter 6). Of course, social adaptation and psychological adjustment are interrelated, with maladjustive behavior on the psychological level usually leading to maladaptive behavior on the social level. However, it cannot always be assumed that adjustive and adaptive behavior correspond. As will be shown in the Japanese Brazilian case, behavior that is psychologically adjustive for minority individuals may obstruct social mobility and thus be socially maladaptive.

The relative success of a minority group's ethnic adaptation and adjustment can be judged by certain "objective" indices in the context of each society such as rates of educational success, socioeconomic mobility, family cohesion, crime, and mental illness. Despite the dislocations of migration that the Japanese Brazilians experience and their negative minority status in Japan, they seem to be adapting and adjusting rather well to adverse social pressures without notable social or psychological disruption. Although marital discord sometimes accompanies migration,[6] nikkeijin families in Japan remain very cohesive and supportive, and I did not encounter any cases of separation or divorce.[7] Of course, it is still too early to assess the general educational and occupational success of the Japanese Brazilians in Japan since they are recent migrants and many still consider themselves to be sojourners. However, initial indications show that their children are doing relatively well in Japanese schools (see the epilogue). The crime rate among Japanese Brazilian immigrants is minuscule, with only 223 Brazilians caught for violations of the criminal law in 1993 (Police Agency 1994:93), which is equivalent to an annual crime rate of only 0.14 percent. In contrast, the Chinese and Peruvian crime rate is 7 times higher (but still only one percent) and the crime rate for Iranians in Japan is 12 times higher (1.7 percent). Even the mainly female Filipina immigrant population has a crime rate of 0.34 percent (2.5 times higher than the Japanese Brazilians).[8]

---

[6]See Grasmuck and Pessar (1991) for the case of Dominicans in the United States.

[7]There have been an increasing number of cases of Japanese Brazilians "missing" in Japan (*Wall Street Journal*, February 11, 1998, 1). These are usually husbands who migrate to Japan and then cut their ties with their families back home for some reason (usually inability to support them through remittances, falling in love with someone else in Japan, or some personal problem).

[8]The crime statistics for non-Brazilian immigrants do not include violations of the immigration law.

As expected, the incidence of mental disorder among the Japanese Brazilians increases in Japan with the psychological stresses of migration and the various social difficulties that they face, but the overall rate remains low. Although comprehensive statistics for mental illness do not exist, Dr. Décio Nakagawa, a psychiatrist in São Paulo, who specializes in the treatment of the Japanese Brazilian dekasegi, estimates that only 2 to 3 percent of them return from Japan with any kind of psychological problem.[9] Even these individuals show only minor psychological symptoms such as mild neurosis, persecutory delusions, slight paranoia, auditory hallucinations, anorexia, and insomnia, which can be cured with proper treatment (interview with Dr. Nakagawa).

ETHNIC COUNTERIDENTITIES AND CULTURAL PERSISTENCE

Earlier studies of internal migration and urbanization have shown that dramatic social changes need not necessarily be disruptive on an individual or group level (Bruner 1961, 1975; Inkeles 1976; Inkeles and Smith 1976). In such cases, adaptation is relatively smooth because a certain amount of continuity is maintained in the cultural patterns of internal migrants when they move within the same country (cf. De Vos 1976c:213).

However, even international migrants are frequently able to retain many of the cultural patterns of their home countries through a process of autonomous ethnic resistance based on the behavioral assertion of ethnonationalist counteridentities and a refusal to assimilate to the host society. The formation of a prominent Brazilian counteridentity in Japan prevents the Japanese Brazilians from identifying with the Japanese, creating considerable psychological resistance and reluctance to adopt and internalize Japanese cultural patterns. As a result, their Brazilian cultural patterns persist in Japan instead of being gradually replaced by Japanese ones through a personally disruptive process of cultural loss. This facilitates their adjustment to Japanese society.

In this manner, ethnic minority counteridentities frequently lead to what psychologists call "foreclosure"—a restrictive and premature commitment to a certain identity that creates an unwillingness to explore and in-

---

[9]Although the incidence of mental illness is relatively low among the Japanese Brazilians in Japan, the issue has received rather prominent coverage in Portuguese newspapers in Japan.

corporate new experiences into the self (see Erikson 1968; Weinreich 1983b). In fact, when an ethnic minority identity is constructed in opposition to a negatively perceived majority society, the internalization of dominant cultural norms can be threatening to the minority individual's self-identity and arouse considerable negative affect, ultimately bringing the person's ethnic allegiance into question. In this manner, counteridentities can become defensive mechanisms that lead to the selective exclusion and noninternalization of certain types of cultural material that are discordant to the self.

Numerous Japanese Brazilian informants affirmed that their thinking and cultural attitudes in Japan remained Brazilian and had not changed, even if their external behavior had sometimes become "more Japanese" as an accommodative response. However, the tendency for anti-Japanese counteridentities to subconsciously block the acquisition of Japanese cultural patterns was most evident in the difficulties that most Brazilian nikkeijin have in learning the Japanese language in Japan. Although language itself is affectively neutral, it can subconsciously take on negative connotations since it is directly associated with the dominant Japanese majority, which accounts for the linguistic "nonlearning" that the Japanese Brazilians experience.

Despite their ethnic similarities to the Japanese and their previous background in the language, most of the nikkeijin learn remarkably little Japanese in Japan. Only a few of my informants felt their Japanese had improved considerably during their sojourn, while a majority had learned only a relatively small amount. This contrasts with Brazilian immigrants in North America, who arrive with little English ability but learn the language relatively quickly (Goza 1994:148, 1999:774–75). Although various types of low-cost Japanese language instruction are readily available to the Japanese Brazilians through municipal governments, private institutes, nikkeijin assistance organizations, and personal tutors, only two out of my entire sample of 47 Japanese Brazilians were actively taking Japanese classes. In fact, one survey of Japanese Brazilians found that only 4.6 percent were attending Japanese language classes (Nomoto et al. 1993).

One of the greatest ironies of this situation is that the *non-nikkeijin* Brazilians, despite their complete lack of cultural and ethnic commonalities with the Japanese, are generally *more willing* to learn Japanese than the Japanese Brazilians.[10] Two of the nikkeijin I interviewed in Oizumi who

---

[10]This is also the case among Japanese Peruvians and Peruvians of non-Japanese descent (Takenaka n.d.:27).

offered private language instruction reported that they actually had more Brazilian than nikkeijin students and that the Brazilians tended to learn more. Both of these instructors were quite impressed with the eagerness with which they study the Japanese language.

In fact, I personally knew more than a few interethnic couples where the non-nikkeijin Brazilian spouse was actively studying Japanese while the nikkeijin spouse was making no such efforts. One of the most striking examples was my Brazilian friend at Toyama, Gesse, and his nisei wife, Olinda. Although Gesse had only lived in Japan a couple of years, he had learned to speak Japanese on a rudimentary level and had taught himself to read not only *hiragana* (the Japanese phonetic alphabet) but also a good number of complicated Japanese characters (*kanji*). I was most surprised to find he could read many of the signs written in advanced kanji posted around the factory. At other times, he would startle his Japanese supervisors by reading their names in Japanese off their name tags. In fact, he always kept a bundle of blank cards in his pocket and wrote down new Japanese words he encountered. I once asked him why he made such an effort to learn hundreds of difficult Japanese characters since it was not at all necessary for his daily life in Japan. "I just do it to pass the time," Gesse shrugged off the question. Later he told me that it is obviously important to learn the language when living in a foreign country. In stark contrast, Olinda told me she had learned almost no Japanese in Japan and could not even read basic Japanese characters. "When Gesse sits down with his kanji workbooks, I just watch TV," she remarked.

Another similar couple was Nelsa, a sansei, and her Brazilian husband, Osvaldo. Although Nelsa was in Japan for a second stay after an initial three-year sojourn, she still could not speak or understand much Japanese, whereas Osvaldo had picked up some basic communication skills. According to Nelsa, when both she and her husband attended a Japanese class for one year, he learned much more than she did. "It's really embarrassing when we ask the Japanese for directions," Nelsa told me. "The Japanese are always surprised to find that it is Osvaldo, not me, who asks the questions. But when they reply, they always look at me and not my husband, but I don't understand any Japanese. So it's always Osvaldo who thanks them for their help. The Japanese find this really strange." Nelsa planned to stay in Japan for possibly four years and had no idea when they would return to Brazil. Would she learn more Japanese her second time around? "I'll try harder this time," she promised.

In fact, it is generally known that foreign workers in Japan of other nationalities learn much more Japanese than the Japanese Brazilians.[11] I myself was rather surprised to meet a number of Iranian and Pakistani immigrants in Japan who had learned to speak Japanese proficiently. This is
quite remarkable given that non-nikkeijin foreign workers generally do
not have any previous background in the Japanese language and are apparently more ethnically segregated in Japan than the nikkeijin.

Of course, there are many reasons why the nikkeijin do not learn much
Japanese in Japan. In general, the long working day and their temporary
sojourner mentality prevent any serious commitment to learn the language.
Essentialized Japanese ethnic expectations that the nikkeijin, as Japanese
descendants, should know how to properly speak Japanese (see chapter 2)
are another disincentive since they are sometimes not sufficiently appreciated even if they do learn the language. In addition, most Japanese Brazilians live almost exclusively in a cohesive and enclaved social network of
nikkeijin relatives and acquaintances, supported by an increasing array of
ethnic businesses, labor brokers, and assistance organizations, all of which
provide extensive services in Portuguese. As a result, most of their economic, social, and practical needs can be met without speaking Japanese or
even interacting with the Japanese. This is especially true in regions such as
Oizumi and Hamamatsu, where nikkeijin ethnic communities are more
extensive, resulting in greater ethnic segregation.[12] Finally, because the
Japanese Brazilians are favored by Japanese employers over other immigrant workers for their privileged legal status and ethnic affinity (even if
they do not speak Japanese), they have less incentive to learn the language
to improve their employment chances.[13]

However, we cannot ignore how the unwillingness and inability of the
Japanese Brazilians to learn Japanese continues to be structured at a subconscious level by a minority counteridentity in which the self is defined
in opposition to the Japanese, producing considerable ethnic cultural resistance. Although non-nikkeijin Brazilians experience most of the same

---

[11]This was also shown by the results of a research project comparing the utilization of immigrant labor in the San Diego and Hamamatsu economies (see Cornelius 1998).

[12]As Yancey et al. (1982:474) observed among earlier European immigrants in the United States,
those living within concentrated ethnic communities tended to be considerably less assimilated than those who were residentially dispersed.

[13]Some of these reasons why the Japanese Brazilians do not learn Japanese are also mentioned
by Nomoto (1993) and Watanabe (1992:325).

practical "disincentives" to learning Japanese,[14] they show no psychological resistance to learning the language (and some are quite eager to do so) because they do not construct "anti-Japanese" ethnic identities in Japan. Therefore, the ethnic counteridentity that individual Japanese Brazilians develop in Japan can prevent the internalization of majority Japanese cultural patterns.

BRAZILIAN COUNTERIDENTITIES AS RESISTANCE TO JAPANESE ASSIMILATION

The premature foreclosure of the self to new cultural experiences from majority society can be considered a defensive form of psychological rigidity that can ultimately impede proper maturational development among minority individuals.[15] However, I argue that for negative immigrant minorities, a restrictive closing of their identities and the subsequent persistence of their cultural differences enables them to resist the ethnic hegemony of the dominant host society. The deterritorialized affirmation of a Brazilian nationalist counteridentity among the Japanese Brazilians allows them to avoid some of the personally debilitating effects of Japanese assimilationist pressures. As a result, this type of autonomous resistance becomes a positive form of psychological adjustment to Japanese society.

Migrant groups that are ethnically related to the host society confront more, not less, cultural pressure from that society, which complicates their adjustment. Although the Japanese Brazilians have been marginalized as foreigners in Japan, they have not been free from hegemonic Japanese ethnic demands. Unlike foreigners who are complete cultural and racial outsiders, the nikkeijin are expected to comply with Japanese cultural stan-

---

[14]It was mentioned to me more than a few times that because the nikkeijin are preferred by Japanese employers over non-nikkeijin Brazilians, the latter had more incentives to learn Japanese to improve their employment chances. However, I did not see strong evidence that the Brazilians had more trouble finding employment than the nikkeijin (frequently, they are automatically employed by the same broker firm as their nikkeijin spouses). In addition, since nikkeijin who speak Japanese well are given better jobs in Japan (see chapter 6), they have almost an equal incentive as the Brazilians to learn Japanese to improve their employment opportunities.

[15]In Piaget's terms (1967), individual maturation is a process whereby material from the external world is assimilated into the prior structure of the self as a form of accommodation to the external environment.

dards to some extent because of essentialized ethnic assumptions in which those of Japanese descent are supposed to possess a certain amount of cultural facility (Sasaki 1999:269). Therefore, the ethnic adjustment of the Japanese Brazilians in Japan is much more difficult and stressful when compared with that of other foreigners. Although they cannot escape the hegemonic ethnic constraints operative in Japanese society because they are not complete outsiders, they are unable to fully satisfy the ethnic demands made on them because they are partially foreign. Ironically, from the standpoint of ethnic adjustment, total marginalization is easier than partial marginalization.

The Japanese Brazilians were acutely aware of the unreasonable cultural demands the Japanese imposed on them as marginal beings trapped within the liminal space between native and foreigner.[16] The reflections of Jefferson, one of my younger informants, were quite typical:

> The Japanese make many more demands of us than of whites or other foreigners in Japan because of our Japanese faces. They think we should speak the language and understand Japanese ways because we are Japanese descendants. They must realize that we can't understand and act like them because we are from a foreign country. But the Japanese always demand this. They say, "You are nikkei, why don't you speak Japanese?" Our adaptation is harder because of this pressure.[17]

The greater cultural pressures placed on the Japanese Brazilians affect even their children in Japanese schools. One teacher noted that the pure nikkeijin students, because of their Japanese faces, have a harder time because they experience more pressure to culturally conform at school. In contrast,

---

[16]Of course, Japanese cultural pressure on the Japanese Brazilians varies according to region. Those living in areas with high Japanese Brazilian populations feel less pressure because the Japanese are used to them and know that they cannot be expected to speak and act Japanese despite their Japanese descent and phenotype. As one informant noted, "Here in Oizumi, I feel less Japanese pressure because it's like a little Brazil. The Japanese don't see you strangely because you dress differently, speak Portuguese, or don't act like the Japanese."

[17]Dorinne Kondo (1986:76–77) also recounts her experiences as a Japanese American in Japan who was expected to act Japanese:

> They . . . had every reason to make me over in their image, to guide me toward properly Japanese behavior, so that the discrepancy between my appearance and my cultural competence would not be so painfully apparent. I posed a challenge to their sense of identity. How could someone who *looked* Japanese not *be* Japanese? Their response in the face of this dissonance was to *make* me as Japanese as possible.

she claimed that the nikkeijin children of mixed descent tend to be more free and outgoing (cf. Hirota 1993:31). However, Japanese cultural standards are sometimes imposed even on the mixed-descent mestiços. Maria, a mestiça nisei, told me how the Japanese women at her factory during one outing told her not to sit Indian style on the *tatami* floor but in *seiza* style,[18] as is expected of Japanese women. "I just can't sit on my legs," she complained. "I'm simply not used to it. I always get leg pains after a few minutes." Maria was also reminded by her female Japanese co-workers not to use the rough Japanese to which she was accustomed, which is unbecoming of a Japanese woman.

Indeed, there are Japanese Brazilians who openly reflect on how their lives would be easier in Japan if they had a different skin color and did not look Japanese (*Asahi Shimbun*, January 6, 1992). In contrast to the nikkeijin, Brazilians of non-Japanese descent noted how they feel much more freedom in Japan because dominant Japanese cultural standards are not applied to them (cf. Sasaki 1999:269; Yamanaka 1997:24). The Brazilian husband of one of my informants reiterated this point:

> Unlike the Japanese Brazilians, I don't have the kind of problem where the Japanese expect you to speak Japanese well and behave Japanese. Since I look completely foreign, no one expects anything from me. I am free to behave the way I want here. In fact, when I speak even a little Japanese, the Japanese are impressed and treat me with interest. (cf. Linger 2001:89)

"Acting Brazilian" in Japan and Ethnic Self-Introductions

In this sense, the ethnic counteridentity that most nikkeijin develop in Japan facilitates their psychological adjustment because it creates a strong self-consciousness that they are not Japanese, but Brazilian foreigners, allowing them to effectively resist the cultural pressures placed on Japanese descendants in Japan. According to the psychiatrist, Dr. Nakagawa, "Those in Japan who say, 'I am different, I am not Japanese' tend not to have psychological difficulties. Their adaptation becomes similar to other [non-nikkeijin] foreigners."

---

[18] *Seiza* is when one sits upright with the knees together and legs folded. The sitting position is very uncomfortable for those who are not accustomed to it, and the anthropologist himself cannot endure seiza for more than several minutes, although men are allowed to sit Indian style on the tatami floor.

The Japanese Brazilians who had adopted this attitude in Japan were quite clear about their intentions to resist, if not defy Japanese ethnic expectations. Their oppositional behavior was by no means motivated by a Brazilian habitus of unconsciously structured, internalized dispositions that they were unintentionally reproducing in Japan by force of habit. My informants clearly articulated their wish to assert their Brazilian counteridentities and display their cultural differences by behaving in conspicuously "Brazilian" ways in order to demonstrate to the Japanese that despite their appearance, they are not Japanese and cannot be expected to conform to Japanese cultural expectations. This assertive and emblematic display of ethnic difference enables them to continue behaving according to their own cultural standards as Brazilians and therefore resist Japanese cultural assimilation.

For instance, Jefferson explained:

> I don't try to change my behavior in Japan just because the Japanese want me to act like them. Instead, I want to show my Brazilian differences. For the Japanese, such behavior is absurd, but I am who I am and cannot change this. So if I don't agree with the Japanese in their way of thinking, I always want to tell them.

Likewise, a few of my female informants told me how they would resist Japanese gender expectations by engaging in assertive behavior, thus demonstrating their identities as Brazilian women and intentionally differentiating themselves from what they saw as submissive Japanese women. Martina, a self-identified "feminist" in Japan, had this to say:

> I think it is wrong that we are expected to speak and act Japanese here just because we are Japanese descendants. It's especially tough on women. I tell people directly that I am not a Japanese woman even with my Japanese face and [last] name. I feel more Brazilian now and the Japanese will have to accept the differences in my behavior. They see me as too aggressive for a woman because I respond and tell them what I don't agree with. I don't lower my head by staying quiet like a Japanese woman—not saying anything and keeping my frustrations to myself. I don't change my behavior in Japan at all.

A common way through which the nikkeijin display their Brazilianness to the Japanese is through dress, which is among the emblems most frequently used to symbolize ethnic difference and identity. Although their manner of dress is naturally different from the Japanese, some deliberately wear distinctive Brazilian clothes to catch the attention of the Japanese. Jefferson was most explicit about his intentions:

> At first, I tried to dress like the Japanese. I knew that the Japanese manner of dressing was different from ours, so I went out and bought new clothes at the department store. But now, whenever I go to the bank or to stores, I wear Bermudas or Brazilian T-shirts. The Japanese never dress like this, so they can always tell I am Brazilian. I feel better this way because I don't want to be seen or mistaken as Japanese.

Interestingly enough, during our interview, Jefferson was plainly dressed and not wearing overtly "Brazilian" clothes.

The effectiveness of clothes as an identifying marker of Brazilianness has actually increased the demand for Brazilian clothes in Japan. As a result, Brazilian clothing stores have opened in places such as Oizumi. Of course, some Japanese Brazilians wear Brazilian clothes in Japan purely for physical comfort or out of habit, but others do so as a prominent ethnic display of cultural difference, if not defiance. The manager of a Brazilian store explained that the clothes she sells are generally more casual and tight fitting (for women), and have distinctive designs, fashions, and colors that cannot be found in Japanese department stores. Jeans have colorful ornamental features and those for women tend to be tighter around the hips (as the buttocks, not the breasts, are the primary locus of female sexual attention in Brazil).[19] Shirts have strong (even loud) colors and may have mosaic patterns, while T-shirts with the Brazilian flag, national colors, or the country's name prominently displayed are also popular.

Many of these "Brazilian" styles are undoubtedly exaggerated constructions that have conveniently appropriated stylistic images of Brazil without necessarily representing any particular dominant or subcultural style in Brazil itself. When national symbols are appropriated by migrants abroad, they are frequently culturally decontextualized and reconstructed so that they have ethno-national meaning only in a foreign context. Even if the symbolic forms are accurately transferred abroad, they are used in an

---

[19]According to Linger (1997:187), many Japanese Brazilians feel Japanese clothes tend to disguise more than reveal bodily figures (cf. Yamashita 2001:25).

A Japanese Brazilian woman working in a Brazilian clothing store in
Oizumi shows off her wares.

overly ostentatious manner that would be inappropriate back home. Few
Japanese Brazilians would wear T-shirts plastered with images of the
Brazilian flag and other nationalist symbols in Brazil. They are appropriate only in Japan because of the deterritorialized intensification of national sentiment among the Japanese Brazilians and their subsequent desire to
express their identities as Brazilians.

The performance of Brazilian counteridentities in Japan also involves
the use of language and greetings. Although some nikkeijin are sensitive
to Japanese opinions and social pressures and lower their voices when
speaking Portuguese in public areas, others take the opposite approach.
For instance, Martina told me that although she speaks Japanese well,
whenever she walks into a store, she makes a point of speaking Portuguese
loud enough so that the Japanese will notice. "I don't want to be confused
as Japanese," she said. "So I always show them I am Brazilian." Likewise,
the tendency of some nikkeijin to greet each other loudly and affection-
ately in public by embracing or kissing is similarly a display of Brazilian
behavior that is completely incongruous with Japanese culture and thus
serves as another means of ethnic differentiation (cf. Yamashita 2001:111).

Some individuals take their ethnic resistance further by exaggerating
their Brazilian behavior in Japan in a rebellious, exhibitionist manner,
purposefully acting more Brazilian in Japan than they ever did in Brazil.
As one of my informants observed a bit cynically:

> Some of these Brazilian youth have this attitude toward the Japanese:
> "Hey, I'm Brazilian and I am going to act Brazilian in Japan. And if you
> don't like it, screw you." As a result, they are seen less favorably by the
> Japanese. However, in Brazil, they would never have acted like this and
> do it only in Japan.

As Devereux (1982:53) in his study of ethnic identity remarks, "There is
often a tendency to exaggerate, with respect to foreigners [i.e., those outside the ethnic group], an ethnic identity trait that is less obvious in intra-
ethnic relations." Even among those who do not take such a rebellious approach, the public assertion of their ethnic counteridentity is frequently a
way to tell the Japanese that they are Brazilians and therefore cannot be
expected to act in Japanese ways and speak the language fluently.

Others engage in much more subdued displays of their Brazilian counteridentity. This is especially true among the more Japanized nikkeijin,
who are more accommodating toward Japanese cultural expectations and

feel more pressure to act in accordance with Japanese norms (see chapter 6). For such individuals, the assertion of their Brazilianness is much less ostentatious than their peers and is usually limited to introducing themselves as Brazilians or foreigners. Of course, the need to make self-introductions is not as relevant to those Japanese Brazilians who do not speak much Japanese, since it is quite apparent to the Japanese that they are foreigners when they open their mouths. However, for nikkeijin who can speak Japanese well enough to communicate, this issue becomes critical when they meet Japanese who are unfamiliar and who assume that they are native Japanese. In such cases, their imperfect Japanese leads to some confusion and disorientation among the Japanese. Indeed, when the Japanese Brazilians are mistakenly seen as Japanese, their Brazilian cultural characteristics become even more stigmatizing. Therefore, by introducing themselves as Brazilians when meeting Japanese for the first time, they implicitly excuse themselves in advance for their imperfect language ability and any cultural faux pas they may commit. Geraldo spoke about how he finds it beneficial in this regard to introduce himself as a Brazilian in order to avoid embarrassment or ill treatment:

> If I just ask simple questions at a store, there is no problem, but if they start using technical terms or the conversation continues, they are surprised at my lack of comprehension and find my accent really strange because they saw me as Japanese. So it's better to say from the beginning that I am Brazilian, so that the Japanese will understand and explain things to you more carefully without looking down on you. When I first got to Japan, I would try to act like a Japanese, but now I always say I'm Brazilian. It's a way to apologize beforehand for my inability to understand Japanese perfectly.

Once they have properly introduced themselves as Brazilian foreigners, the nikkeijin are able to act more freely without worrying about being stigmatized when traces of their "Brazilianness" are revealed. This relieves them of the pressure of being seen as Japanese and the resulting cultural expectations that are then imposed. Such concerns are most salient among those nikkeijin who speak fluent Japanese and are students or office workers in Japan. These individuals are the most likely to be mistaken as Japanese because of their cultural and linguistic abilities and their unwillingness to overtly display Brazilian behavior. Therefore, they sometimes find subtle ways to differentiate themselves as Brazilians and avoid being held to

the same cultural standards as the Japanese. This includes not only introducing themselves as nikkeijin but also writing out their Japanese last
names in *katakana* (a phonetic alphabet used for foreign names) instead of
using Japanese characters. Those who have both Brazilian and Japanese
first names sometimes intentionally use their Brazilian name in Japan, although they may have been called by their Japanese name in Brazil. "It is
my way of identifying myself as someone who is not Japanese," a Japanese
Brazilian graduate student remarked. "It is my way of asking the Japanese
to forgive me because I behave differently from them."

These individuals maintain ethnic independence by using not only
public symbols such as names and self-introductions but also personal
symbols. For instance, Marcos, a Japanese Brazilian journalist in Japan,
once told me that his peculiar goatee was his "little rebellion against the
Japanese," an idiosyncratic emblem of his ethnic differences with Japanese men, whom he believed do not like facial hair. Interestingly, he also
told me that he was clean-shaven in Brazil, again showing how his goatee
is a symbol of his Brazilian identity that only has significance in Japan. In
order to resist the cultural pressures of Japanese society, Marcos, like many
other nikkeijin, suddenly found a need to assert his Brazilianness—a desire he had not had in Brazil.

In this manner, there was considerable variation in the conscious expression of ethnic resistance, ranging from aggressive displays of cultural
difference in public to the subtle use of introductions, names, and other
personal symbols for proper identification in order to avoid Japanese cultural pressures and possible embarrassment. Yet, the motivation for engaging in ethnic resistance was similar. Marcos elaborated on the advantages of showing his Brazilian identity in Japan:

> It is easier to live in Japan if you see yourself as Brazilian and give up try-
> ing to be Japanese because this way, you can escape the pressure to act
> Japanese. I don't want to be Japanese here because it's too much of a
> hassle—you have to keep explaining to others why you act and think
> differently. So I always reveal my Brazilian identity when I communicate
> with the Japanese so they don't apply the same standards to me.

For Marcos, appealing to his Brazilian identity is also a way to preempt
negative evaluations based on Japanese cultural standards:

> If I try to be Japanese, they will judge me by their own standards and
> this will lead to discrimination [negative evaluations about his behavior].

But if I make it clear that I'm Brazilian, there is less discrimination because I can say: "I'm sorry, I'm Brazilian so I come late to appointments and am lazy." I can preempt Japanese discrimination before they come to the same conclusions.

"Samba" in Japan: Generative Cultural Schemas and the Practice of National Identity

The deterritorialized enactment of Brazilian nationalist counteridentities occurs not only in individual behavior but also in collective ritual performances. The most important example is the samba parades that the Japanese Brazilians organize in local communities with high nikkeijin concentrations. This is an example of the creative production of cultural forms often involved in ethnic resistance. However, nikkeijin samba is not merely a thin resistance culture generated simply as a reaction against Japanese ethnic hegemony. The motivations for its performance range from alleviating feelings of homesickness for Brazil to simple festive entertainment. Therefore, it has its own cultural basis and logic and is an appropriation and reinterpretation by an autonomous migrant group of a traditional Brazilian cultural form that acquires its own dynamics in the deterritorialized context of Japan. Because of the diverse intentions involved in its performance, the samba parade becomes a form of ethnic resistance only in the process of enactment.

The samba parade I observed in Oizumi was only one part of a day-long Japanese festival. However, it attracted far more attention and interest among the Japanese than any of the traditional Japanese floats, parades, or music. In fact, despite the efforts of its organizers to keep the parade moving, the nikkeijin dancers were frequently unable to progress because of the hordes of Japanese who clogged the street with their cameras and camcorders. Such enthusiasm makes the samba performance not only an internal experience of Brazilianness for the nikkeijin but simultaneously an externally oriented, ostentatious display of their Brazilian cultural differences.

However, as is the case with the emblematic use of "Brazilian" clothes, considerable decontextualization and distortion again occurs when national symbols from back home are appropriated for ethnically demonstrative purposes abroad. Since most Japanese Brazilians were not interested in participating in samba back home, they have insufficient cultural knowledge of this national Brazilian ritual. As a result, their ethnic performance in Japan is not structured or regulated by preexisting cultural models of samba but is a spontaneous cultural form generated by them in the context of enactment.

Therefore, the samba parade was a somewhat random cultural performance, improvised, haphazard, and casual. The costumes were randomly chosen and ranged from simple bathing suits, clown outfits, and festival clothes with Brazilian national colors (yellow and green) to T-shirts and shorts. One group even wore a strange mixture of Japanese festival outfits (with Japanese characters) with Brazilian national colors and symbols attached. Undoubtedly, few of the nikkeijin knew how to design or construct any real Brazilian samba costumes or had the resources to do so. As a result, only the two front dancers wore costumes that resembled those worn in samba parades in Brazil. In addition, most of the nikkeijin did not seem to know how to dance samba, and even if some of them were familiar with the dance form, almost no one had the experience or the will to execute it properly (cf. Yamashita 2001:144). As a result, instead of performing appropriately schematized body movements, most of the participants seemed to be moving and shaking their bodies randomly, some in a lackadaisical manner. After the parade, all the awards for the best dancers went to non-nikkeijin Brazilians, the only ones who danced samba properly and effectively. The general result was simply a potpourri of costumes and individuals moving their bodies without any pattern, definition, or precise rhythm that resembles actual Brazilian samba. The only parts of the parade that required any explicit cultural knowledge were the singer of the samba theme and the *bateria* (the drum section that beats out the samba rhythm), both of which were composed almost exclusively of non-nikkeijin Brazilians.

This lack of proper cultural knowledge about samba and the unstructured nature of the costumes and choreography indicates that instead of following any kind of well-defined, codified, and ready-made cultural model, the performance was based on a vague and ill-defined image of samba. Individuals rely on such imagined cultural schema when the actual cultural schema is unknown or unavailable. Since their behavior is therefore structured only on the most general and rudimentary level, the exact content of the cultural schema is elaborated and invented in the process of enactment itself. Therefore, participation in such spontaneous and unstructured collective practices is less an enactment of a preestablished cultural schema than the creation and active generation of a new one. The cultural model, to the extent that it exists, remains necessarily vague and general, so that its principles and specific content are filled in and elaborated as actors go along. As a result, the loosely structured spontaneity and generative nature of the performance actualizes and instantiates a new cultural schema, which is substantially different from original Brazilian samba and can be characterized as nikkeijin samba. In such instances, therefore, instead of cultural schemas generating practice, practice tends to generate cultural schemas. Spontaneous collective festivals and rituals are therefore based on what Marshall Sahlins calls "performative structures," in which the cultural structure is formed in the process of action itself instead of the act being strictly prescribed by a preexisting cultural structure (1985:xi, 26–28). This is what Swidler (1996) means when she claims that practices can "anchor" constitutive rules instead of vice versa. Using Geertz's (1973) terms, a "model of" behavior becomes culturally codified and collectively known as a "model for" behavior.

In this manner, new cultural forms and variations of established practices can be generated when individuals are forced to improvise as they attempt to enact a cultural tradition for which they have insufficient knowledge, understanding, and experience.[20] The final product that emerged through the nikkeijin performance had little in common with samba as it is practiced in Brazil and would have been barely recognizable back home.[21] Nonetheless, given the foreign and deterritorialized Japanese context in which it was enacted, it was seen as very "Brazilian" because of its cultural distinctiveness. As long as the nikkeijin could find some costume that looked vaguely Brazilian and could shake their body in one way or another, the performance remained effective as a collective assertion of their Brazilian nationalist counteridentity and a form of ethnic resistance.

This process of cultural authentication was also unintentionally supported by the presence of attentive Japanese spectators, who showed active interest in the unusual and different festivities of another nation. Since the

---

[20]Barth (1987) observes a similar process among the Ok in New Guinea. Because precise oral transmission of ritual practices is not possible, the cultural content of the performance is elaborated by ritual actors through such processes as metaphor. This generates a wide range of cultural variation in the performance of the same ritual.

[21]Ironically, the most professional samba parade in Japan occurs in Asakusa in Tokyo and is run almost exclusively by Japanese, with only one Brazilian samba school of 30 people represented in 1995. The Asakusa carnaval festival has a 15-year tradition and involves 30 schools of samba with 3,000 dancers and 500,000 spectators. In addition to the greater scale, the costumes are much closer to those used in Brazil and the dancing is much more professional and organized. The city of Kobe has an even larger samba parade, and there are also other samba groups in Japan (see Roth 1999:1, 3–4). These Japanese, who have carefully studied samba, provide a much more faithful reproduction of the Brazilian samba schema than the nikkeijin ever will. However, the nikkeijin have also created samba schools in Japan (Yamashita 2001:140) and may now be giving more culturally structured performances.

Japanese have even less knowledge about samba than the nikkeijin, they are unable to critique the performance as inaccurate or inauthentic the way a Brazilian audience would. For them, anything culturally different and novel is accepted and appreciated as bona-fide Brazilian "samba." Therefore, the implicit collusion between participant and observer in a deterritorialized context validates and authenticates the performance as a true display of Brazilian culture. As a result, the spontaneously generated samba performance is discovered as an effective means of asserting ethnic differences and resisting Japanese cultural assimilation during the process of enactment itself. The Japanese Brazilians can then use this newly created cultural schema for later performances as a way to express their ethnic counteridentities. As subsequent performances of nikkeijin samba are guided by the newly generated schema, they become more regularized and explicit as an act of ethnic resistance. However, the inherent collective spontaneity remains and always has the potential to further transform and modify the schema.

The front two dancers of the nikkeijin samba parade in Oizumi.

Interested Japanese spectators cluster around the samba parade.

COMMUNITIES AND COUNTERIDENTITIES: ETHNIC RESISTANCE TO NEGATIVE MINORITY STATUS

We have seen that the Japanese Brazilians assert their Brazilian resistance identities in Japan by various means, including speaking Portuguese in public, consciously "acting Brazilian," wearing Brazilian clothes, eating Brazilian food, introducing themselves as Brazilian, and dancing samba. By expressing and affirming their own autonomous culture, they successfully resist the pressure to act according to Japanese cultural standards. This allows them to continue living according to their own standards of behavior in Japan and avoid the personal difficulties and psychological stress of attempting to conform to a different system of cultural expectations. Therefore, this type of autonomous ethnic resistance as a form of adjustment to Japanese society has considerable psychological benefits.

The drum section of the samba parade.

The samba parade heads down Route 354 in Oizumi.

Immigrant Communities as "Ethnic Insulation" Against Japanese Prejudice
and Social Class Degradation

In addition to relieving them of assimilationist Japanese ethnic pressures
and demands, the Japanese Brazilians' maintenance of their cultural differences through ethnic resistance facilitates their psychological adjustment to their minority status in other ways as well. One of the most important considerations when analyzing the ethnic adjustment of negative
minorities is whether or not they internalize the negative images of them
prevalent in the dominant society (see De Vos and Wagatsuma 1966).
When negative minority group members are not only aware of but also
come to accept and adopt some of these unfavorable ethnic stereotypes,
they develop negative self-images and perceptions that can be psychologically debilitating to a considerable extent.

In contrast to some negative minorities who are acutely conscious of majority ethnic prejudices, relatively few nikkeijin had specific knowledge
about the derogatory ethnic attitudes the Japanese have about them. Although a good number of my informants detected ethnic "discrimination"
in Japanese behavior and claimed the Japanese have low images of Brazil and
their supposed immigrant poverty, more than half simply admitted that
they do not know what the Japanese really think about them. The awareness of Japanese ethnic prejudice among such individuals is therefore limited to a general sense of uncertainty and unease that the Japanese probably
perceive them in a derogatory way despite treating them in a generally polite manner. Pedro talked about such feelings in his day-to-day life in Japan.

> There aren't really instances when I actually perceive the attitudes that
> the Japanese have about us. Some of the others say that the Japanese
> look down on us or don't like us. There are lots of Brazilians who say
> this or that about the Japanese, but I don't have enough contact with
> them to actually know. But sometimes I feel this when I come in con-
> tact with Japanese. It's just the way they look at us, or behave in a
> strange way at times. But this may be normal, I don't know.

Some individuals, such as Martina, were a bit more certain about the existence of Japanese prejudice, but remained fundamentally unsure:

> The Japanese treat us really well and always smile and act pleasantly. But
> I feel it is a false type of politeness. I think that they probably don't like
> us, but don't show this in their behavior. This makes it difficult to tell

what their attitudes are, but I think they see themselves as superior and view us unfavorably.

Such underlying unease about Japanese ethnic attitudes remains even among those Japanese Brazilians who are able to establish friendships with individual Japanese. This is illustrated by the experiences of Roberto, one of the very rare individuals who actively spoke with Japanese workers at Toyama (despite his rudimentary Japanese) and had made friends with two of them. In fact, he always prided himself on his active contact with the Japanese and was very conscious that he was different from other Japanese Brazilians. When one Japanese friend, Shimizu-san, invited him for dinner for the second time, he was told that he could also bring along a friend and chose me. While we were bicycling to Shimizu-san's home, Roberto suddenly told me that he did not really know what Shimizu-san thought of him. I was a bit surprised at his sudden expression of doubt and told him that at minimum, Shimizu-san must like him if he was invited over for dinner twice. "I don't know," Roberto replied, still uncertain. "I can't figure out what Shimizu-san is really thinking. We haven't talked about this."

Indeed, because of their general lack of specific knowledge about Japanese attitudes, the Brazilian nikkeijin sometimes asked me whether *I* knew what the Japanese thought about them. Such questions put me in a difficult situation more than once. In turn, some of the *Japanese* workers at Toyama were concerned about what the nikkeijin thought of them and felt that perhaps the Japanese Brazilians have negative impressions of the Japanese and speak ill of them in Portuguese. I was also asked more than a few times by Japanese workers what the Japanese Brazilians think about the Japanese or what they talk about during break time. In this manner, the communicational and interactional barriers between the Japanese Brazilians and Japanese seem to be producing a certain level of mutual ethnic anxiety based on an ignorance about each other's attitudes.

There are a number of reasons why most Japanese Brazilians are not directly aware of Japanese ethnic prejudices. The language barrier is obviously an important factor. In addition, as discussed in chapter 2, prejudice toward the Japanese Brazilians itself is not very strong in Japan and is usually kept under tight control. In fact, some of my nikkeijin informants observed how the Japanese tend not to reveal their true feelings and ethnic prejudices. "The Japanese never express their sentiments, so I don't know how I am seen by them," one recently married sansei man noted. "I am never praised or criticized. The treatment is always the same. It is hard to

see what the Japanese are thinking." In addition, most Japanese Brazilians
are socially segregated from the Japanese and live in an internally cohesive
community of acquaintances and nikkeijin social networks. The relatively superficial contact that they therefore have with the Japanese (occasional interaction in the factory, encounters at stores or on the street) is
not extensive or deep enough in most cases for ethnic prejudice to truly
come out. In this manner, enclaved immigrant communities provide
"ethnic insulation" against majority prejudice and discrimination (cf.
Simpson and Yinger 1972:210–11).

However, a small minority of the Japanese Brazilians were quite aware
of pejorative Japanese ethnic attitudes toward them. Most notable were
those who spoke about how the Japanese see the issei as traitors who abandoned and fled Japan during difficult times when they were needed in the
country. Likewise, some Japanese Brazilians feel that ethnic prejudice is
the main reason they have minimal contact with their Japanese relatives.[22]
Such individuals claim that their Japanese relatives look down on them
and are ashamed to meet them because they are seen as having "returned"
to Japan as impoverished and low-class migrants despite the fact that their
parents or grandparents "abandoned" Japan decades ago with intentions
to succeed economically in Brazil (cf. Ishi 1992:70, 1994:39).

Japanese Brazilians who were proficient in spoken Japanese and had
more contact with the Japanese sometimes directly encountered prejudice.
A few mentioned occasions when they would overhear comments by individual Japanese with ethnically pejorative connotations. Ivone, one of
my informants who claimed to speak Japanese rather well, recounted such
an incident at a shopping center:

> I went to an open market they had at Iseya [Oizumi shopping center]
> and I overheard one Japanese retailer say, "The number of Brazilian
> nikkeijin has been increasing these days. How unpleasant." I became re-
> ally annoyed and so decided to have a talk with him in a civilized man-
> ner. I asked him, "Why do you say such things about us? Our parents
> left Japan because they were poor and now we come back to Japan and
> get this type of treatment just because we were born in a different coun-
> try." I told him that if he hates nikkeijin so much, he should put up a

[22]Seventy-four percent of the nikkeijin have little or no contact with their Japanese relatives
(Kitagawa 1997).

sign in his store refusing them service and I will tell all my friends not to buy anything from him ever again. The man ended up apologizing.

Even when the nikkeijin directly encountered such ethnic derogation, however, they were able to resist and protect themselves through the affirmation of a Brazilian counteridentity and the subsequent persistence of their own autonomous cultural standards. When immigrant minorities identify with the positively perceived cultural attributes of their own ethnic group in opposition to a negatively perceived majority society, they continue to judge and evaluate themselves from their own internal cultural standards instead of accepting and internalizing the negative perceptions of them prevalent in the host society (De Vos 1982b:34). Other researchers have also noted how disparaged ethnic or immigrant minorities that maintain positively valued minority identities are able to resist the negative effects of ethnic stigma, prejudice, and discrimination (see Castles and Miller 1993:33; Tajfel 1982:226).[23] In Goffman's words (1963:6), such individuals are stigmatized by dominant society but remain oblivious because they are insulated by their social isolation and protected by their own "identity beliefs."

As a result, there was little evidence that the Japanese Brazilians who had directly encountered Japanese ethnic prejudice had internalized such negative attitudes or had even become vulnerable and sensitive to them. Instead, they tended to reject such characterizations and stereotypes of them as misguided, misinformed, or simply inaccurate. Such thinking is evident in the comments of one of my nisei female informants:

> The Japanese think the nikkeis abandoned Japan because of poverty, but this is not true. The Japanese government also encouraged people to leave by saying what a great opportunity they would have abroad. Lots of people were deceived when they reached Brazil and found out how hard it was. Also, my parents were not poor. In fact, my father brought a considerable fortune with him to Brazil. He went to Brazil for the adventure.

---

[23]Likewise, Fanon (1967:chapter 5) describes how he attempted to liberate himself from the misery of being black in France by disregarding the prejudices of white society and emphasizing the positive value of his ethnicity. However, his attempts to find self-worth and pride in the achievements of ancient African civilization lacked personal and contemporary relevance and did not alleviate his ethnic alienation.

Celso gave an account of how he successfully countered an instance of similar prejudice from a Japanese co-worker by proving the individual wrong:

> One time, I was working next to this Japanese in the factory and he made some remark about how my parents had betrayed Japan by leaving after World War II when the Japanese were suffering. The first time, I remained quiet, but the second time he brought this up, I faced him directly and told him I am a sansei and that my grandparents had left Japan generations ago long before World War II. My *hancho* (group leader) was standing near me and he confirmed this.

A few of my informants also had experiences with individual Japanese who ethnically derogated them for being dekasegi. Geraldo gave an account of how he refused to accept such negative Japanese evaluations:

> There was one time I felt discrimination as a dekasegi in Japan. One of the Japanese at work almost accused me of this—he said, "You are a foreigner who came to Japan only for the money and don't care about anything else about Japan." He said when Japanese go abroad, they do so for vacation or company reasons, not just for money. I didn't bother to respond to this person, because I know it's not true. Lots of Japanese went abroad to Brazil and America in the past as dekasegi too.

Likewise, although a number of my informants were aware that the Japanese think they are poor and miserable people in Brazil who have to migrate in order to survive, they promptly dismissed such negative characterizations. The Japanese Brazilians frequently note that the Japanese simply do not know how well they lived in Brazil as part of the country's middle class.

In this respect, the cohesive and self-contained ethnic communities within which most Japanese Brazilians live are again critical because they enable the nikkeijin to collectively affirm the validity of their own independent cultural values and standards by asserting their counteridentities against the Japanese, allowing them to preserve their self-esteem and positive self-image in the face of majority prejudice. I witnessed (and participated in) a number of nikkeijin "ethnic pep talks" where they would criticize the inadequacies and negative attributes of the Japanese and reinforce their faith in their own cultural beliefs and attitudes.

Above all, the Japanese Brazilian family—the most intimate of all social groups in the ethnic community—is the most important form of ethnic resistance against any pejorative Japanese attitudes the nikkeijin encounter as a negative immigrant minority.[24] Although the Japanese Brazilians turn to each other to resolve various problems they experience in Japan, surveys indicate that a good proportion rely directly on their own families rather than friends and relatives (Japan Statistics Research Institute 1993; Kitagawa 1997). In addition to preventing loneliness and homesickness, the presence of the family eases the ethnic adjustment of the Japanese Brazilians to their negative minority status by allowing them to air complaints and grievances, thus relieving the frustrations that accumulate in their daily lives. One Japanese Brazilian in Kawasaki spoke of this crucial role of his family:

> I would have nothing here in Japan without my family. With them, it becomes much easier to neutralize the bad sentiments from the outside that we have living in Japan. We can separate out our Brazilian lives in the family from the outside and complain about the Japanese and help each other out. I spend a lot of time with my wife talking about the problems we encounter here in Japan.

Another individual had similar experiences:

> It is much easier to overcome our problems in Japan with the family. We can release our frustrations instead of keeping them inside and can talk about difficulties at work and what we don't like about the Japanese. We end up feeling that our problems have been alleviated. With the family, we can protect ourselves more. Without my wife here, I would be more influenced by the bad experiences I have outside [in Japanese society].

This function of the family as an independent ethnic space where the Japanese Brazilians can protect themselves from Japanese prejudice by asserting their own cultural values is also critical for nikkeijin children. A couple of nikkeijin parents spoke about how they consciously attempt to instill a sense of pride in Brazil among their children in order to counter negative Japanese peer pressures at school. "I tell my children they can't be made fun of at school because they are from Brazil," one father said. "I

---

[24]The importance of the family in the ethnic adaptation of the Japanese Brazilians is also mentioned by Watanabe and Teruyama (1992:58).

always need to tell them that Brazil is number one and describe to them the good aspects of the country. I tell them they should take pride in themselves regardless of what others say." On another occasion when I was interviewing a couple, their third grade daughter suddenly walked up to the dining table and announced (in Japanese) that she hides her Brazilian background from the kids at school. The mother quickly responded, telling her daughter that there was nothing shameful about being Brazilian in Japan and encouraged her to talk about Brazil to her friends.

The family, as a source of status, prestige, and respect, can also become a way for negative immigrant minorities to combat not only majority prejudice but also their low socio-occupational status. Regardless of their degrading social class status as factory workers in Japanese society, the nikkeijin can be treated with proper respect according to their own cultural standards of judgment within their own families, thus preserving their social self-esteem. Intact and cohesive families provide a context for the Japanese Brazilians to perform their respected social roles as parents, fulfill their duties and obligations as economic providers and caretakers, and serve as proper role models for their children, thus distancing themselves from their low social position as unskilled migrant laborers outside the home.[25] As the Brazilian anthropologist Roberto DaMatta notes (1991:64, 66), proper social roles and hierarchies based on respect and consideration are maintained inside the house (*casa*), in contrast to the struggle, work, and harsh reality of life in the outside world of the street (*rua*).

Because such positive and traditional family roles are available for the Brazilian nikkeijin through which they can define themselves, their disparaged ethnic and social class status outside the family is not internalized as part of their self-identity and does not adversely affect their self-image.[26]

---

[25]This contrasts vividly with negative minorities for whom the legacy of discrimination is so pervasive that it has completely disrupted the family. In such cases, minority individuals sometimes cannot maintain a respected social status even within the limited confines of the family. In this manner, the family, instead of protecting its members from outside ethnic and social class prejudice, can itself become an internal source of denigration and disparagement that can reinforce and exacerbate the degradation experienced in majority society. As a result, minority individuals are deprived of their last refuge of self-respect and self-esteem.

[26]De Vos (1982a) also observed a similar process occurring among Japanese American immigrant communities in which traditional criteria internal to the family and community, and not their low occupational position in American society, were used to define and evaluate individuals. This also shielded them from the prejudice and discrimination they experienced from majority society at that time (cf. Kitano 1976:132–33).

Therefore it is no surprise that those Japanese Brazilians who come to Japan without their families experience a much higher incidence of mental disorder. Among the nikkeijin migrants with mental disturbances that Dr. Nakagawa has treated, 63 percent were single, divorced, or widowed, and only 37 percent were married (Nakagawa 1994). This means that the rate of mental disorder is over four times higher among those without families in Japan.

Other researchers have also examined how the maintenance of separate ethnic identities, cultures, and social roles within cohesive ethnic communities and intact families can have positive effects on self-esteem by increasing a negative minority's resistance to majority prejudice and social class degradation (see Simpson and Yinger 1972:195; Tatum 1987:12–13).[27] In this manner, the development and behavioral affirmation of ethnic counteridentities among Japanese Brazilian immigrants and the subsequent preservation of autonomous cultural standards of self-evaluation within their communities is a positive form of psychological adjustment that enables them to avoid some of the potentially debilitating psychological effects of negative minority status. Although such ethnic resistance may not be sufficient if minority members are confronted by overt and sustained ethnic and social derogation (De Vos 1982b:34), this is not the case with the Japanese Brazilians, who experience ethnic prejudice and social discrimination in more uncertain and subtle ways as a "weak" negative minority.

Downward Social Mobility: Dealing with Degrading Immigrant Jobs

In addition to their low socio-occupational status in the host society, immigrants like the Japanese Brazilians who are predominantly of middle-class origins face additional difficulties because they must deal with the negative psychological effects of "declassing," or downward social mobility. Studies have shown that the most educated immigrants and refugees show higher levels of demoralization than those without education (see Portes and Rumbaut 1996:173–74). However, the Brazilian nikkeijin seem to be adjusting to their loss of occupational status in Japan without significant psychological malaise. Although some inevitably had difficulties

---

[27]In a completely different context, Obeyesekere (1982) examines how the affirmation of an ethnic identity among the Buddhist Sinhalese in Ceylon and the use of traditional images and symbols can help preserve ethnic pride when the unity of the group is threatened by political defeat and social degradation.

at first (see chapter 3), most of my informants had learned to cope with their low-class jobs in Japan.

It is quite evident that the Japanese Brazilians are able to avoid the worst effects of social class decline because they are fully cognizant of the demeaning factory jobs they must assume in Japan and thus migrate mentally prepared for their loss of social class status. My close friend Tadashi's attitude was illustrative:

> I don't see this [loss of social status] as a problem because we come prepared for anything, knowing we would be manual laborers in Japan, having to do jobs that the Japanese don't want to do. You may have been respected as a doctor in Brazil, but in Japan, you will be a mere laborer, a peon. I came with this attitude, so didn't feel incapacitated or inferior. I thought it was normal, and the work itself is actually not all that bad.

"When [Japanese] Brazilians come to Japan, they come with a consciousness that they'll take any work the Japanese offer, however bad, since we have no choice," Roberto from Oizumi explained. "There is no use complaining about how bad or hard the work is—you either do it or you don't. We can't make any demands because the Japanese will say, 'If you don't like the work, then please leave the factory.'" For Wilson, a former agricultural business owner, dealing with downward mobility in Japan meant constantly maintaining the right attitude:

> There are some who cry, get depressed, and even go neurotic in Japan because they never did this kind of work in Brazil, but 80 percent of us come with a proper attitude of resignation. I get yelled at in the factory, but don't care. I tell myself, don't get angry, it's no big deal. You need to constantly tell yourself, "I'm a mere peon here in Japan." You can't expect things to be like they were in Brazil.

In addition, the ideology of socioeconomic equality that has developed within the nikkeijin immigrant community (see chapter 3) also contributes to their successful adjustment to socio-occupational decline in Japan. Many of my informants took comfort in the fact that although they had to perform demeaning, low-class jobs in Japan, all other Japanese Brazilian immigrants were doing the same type of work and had experienced the same loss of social status. As my informants frequently repeated, *"Nós estamos todos no mesmo barco aqui no Japão"* (We are all in the same boat here in Japan). Jefferson elaborated on this sentiment:

> I was ashamed of doing this type of work at first, but now, I don't feel this way because all [Japanese] Brazilians are factory workers here. It would be difficult if I were the only person going through this, but we all have the same experience. We are all peons here in Japan. So there's no reason to be ashamed.

At certain times, I even noticed a tendency to celebrate this collective loss of socio-occupational status among the nikkeijin in Japan, since it has supposedly eliminated the unfair social class inequalities that existed in Brazil. Some of my informants, especially those who were less well-off in Brazil, emphasized how migration had leveled out and equalized previous differences in education, wealth, and occupation by reducing everyone (even rich nikkeijin who had been doctors and lawyers) to the low status of unskilled factory workers. By obscuring the actual socioeconomic inequalities and differences that have emerged in the immigrant community (see chapter 6), this ideology of equality becomes an effective way for immigrants to deal with their loss of occupational status through collectively shared experience and solidarity.

In contrast, those Japanese Brazilians who were of higher social class status in Brazil were less enthusiastic about the immigrant social equality that prevails in Japan. Instead of fully casting their lot with their fellow immigrant compatriots, these individuals dealt with their loss of social class status in Japan by emphasizing their higher socioeconomic background, thus implying that they were better than other nikkeijin immigrants, whom they portrayed as lower class than themselves. Although such individuals were rather rare, a former journalist from São Paulo was certainly one of them:

> I'm different from other dekasegi in Japan. The ones that come here are poorer and less educated. Some lost everything in Brazil and had no other option. I came here more to maintain a certain standard of living. I live in a large house in a good neighborhood of São Paulo and had a successful career, but unfortunately, was laid off because of the Brazilian economic crisis.

This is analogous to the reaction of some middle-class Brazilian immigrants in the United States, who repeatedly talk about other Brazilian immigrants who are low class, uneducated, and uncultured. By contrasting themselves with this "phantom lower class," they are able to maintain a sense of social superiority despite their own low class status in the United States (Margolis 1994:220–23, cf. Martes 2000:163).

The intention of most Japanese Brazilians to remain in Japan only temporarily as migrant sojourners is undoubtedly another factor that makes it relatively easy to reconcile themselves to their lowly immigrant jobs (cf. Margolis 1994:18, 229 for Brazilians in the United States). A middle-aged sansei man said:

> Because we're in Japan temporarily, we can adapt easier and our low status does not really matter. If I had to live permanently as a factory worker, I'd get depressed, but we always have the hope that we will return to Brazil. So we can endure difficult conditions here.

In this manner, the nikkeijin are able to distance themselves psychologically from their low-class jobs by viewing them as merely a temporary and instrumental means to improve their economic condition and thus eventually return to their former lives and higher-status occupations in Brazil (cf. Sales 1998:107). As a result, they do not internalize their degraded socio-occupational status in Japan as an integral and permanent part of their self-identity (cf. Piore 1979:54–55) and therefore avoid its adverse psychological effects.

However, the most prevalent way in which my informants were able to maintain their self-esteem in the face of a sharp decline in socio-occupational status was by focusing on their increased incomes and enhanced economic well-being in Japan. As is the case with Brazilian immigrants in the United States (Sales 1998:105, cf. Margolis 1994:78–79), the Japanese Brazilians did not feel they had actually suffered from downward social mobility because they had improved their economic position in Japan. "I don't feel a real decline in social status here because of the high incomes we earn," one of my female informants remarked, reflecting the opinions of many of her compatriots. "From a financial perspective, I'm actually better off in Japan."[28] As a result of their high immigrant in-

---

[28]One reason this type of adaptation to low immigrant status is effective among the Japanese Brazilians may be the greater tendency in Brazil to judge social status by economic wealth rather than occupational status and prestige per se, as is the case in Japan, where there is much less disparity between rich and poor.

comes, many of the nikkeijin I interviewed emphasized how they are able to maintain a middle-class lifestyle and standard of living in Japan. Celso was most explicit about his feelings in this regard:

> I'm not bothered about being a factory worker in Japan. I can earn enough money, live pretty well, and can go out on weekends, take trips to other parts of Japan, and buy what I want. It's not like in Brazil, where factory workers are very poor and live in *favelas* (shantytowns) at the lowest level of society. Factory workers earn well here and there isn't much difference in salary with other Japanese. I know a lot of Japanese don't respect factory workers, but I don't really care.

Like Celso, a majority of my informants who spoke about this issue emphasized how blue-collar workers in Japan are able to maintain decent incomes and middle-class standards of living because of the country's socioeconomic equality and do not suffer the social segregation, poverty, and illiteracy of the working class in Brazil, where income disparities are much worse. In fact, some Japanese Brazilians who were part of the lower middle class in Brazil take advantage of their greatly increased incomes in Japan by purchasing cars and other luxury items, which enable them to enjoy a higher standard of living than they had back home.

Beyond the Mundane: Religion and Negative Minority Status

When analyzing the ethnic adaptation of a negative immigrant minority, the importance of religious activity cannot be ignored. Although religion does not play a major role in the lives of most Japanese Brazilians in Brazil, when they are confronted with the stresses of immigrant life in Japan, a kind of religious "revival" occurs, a phenomenon that has been observed among other migrant groups as well (see Park 1989). Not only does the intensity of religious involvement increase, a number of agnostic nikkeijin become religious in Japan as well. Some of those who had hardly ever attended religious services in Brazil end up becoming frequent churchgoers in Japan. According to my informants, religious activity increases among Japanese Brazilian immigrants because they wish to alleviate their feelings of loneliness, homesickness, and social alienation in Japan through the social support and psychological comfort offered by religion.[29] Religious

---

[29]Brazilian immigrants in the United States attend church for similar reasons (Martes 1999:113–14).

groups seem to fulfill the need for social belonging and companionship more effectively than other ethnic gatherings, which are more ephemeral and are united only by cultural bonds and not by a commonly shared spiritual belief system. Although some Japanese Brazilians attend Japanese Christian churches, small churches have also been set up exclusively for them with services in Portuguese in areas where they are highly concentrated, such as Kawasaki city and the Oizumi/Ota area. Many of these churches are Catholic; Protestant denominations seem less frequent.[30] Some Japanese Brazilians from outlying areas travel long distances to attend services at these churches, some of which also have a full complement of social activities, including retreats, weekend camping trips, and parties during the Christmas and Easter holidays.

The active expression of ethno-religious identity and culture within the nikkeijin immigrant community becomes another way to deal with the negative psychological effects of minority status in Japan. In other words, religion offers a sacred plane of existence beyond the profane world with which immigrants can identify in order to somehow escape and transcend the travails of their daily lives. My attendance at a religious service at a local Japanese Brazilian Catholic church was quite illuminating in this respect. The priest at this church was, interestingly enough, a Japanese American nisei who had lived in Brazil for many years. As is true with all effective sermons, his made an attempt to relate religious teachings and principles to the immediate concerns and difficulties of everyday life in order to give them higher religious meaning.

One of the notable aspects of the sermon was the attempt to religiously transcend the cultural differences and segregation between the Japanese and the nikkeijin in order to soothe the ethnic alienation the Japanese Brazilians experience as a negative minority in Japan. In other words, through religious belief, the nikkeijin can find a sense of ethnic commonality with the Japanese at a higher spiritual level, since ultimately, as the priest kept emphasizing, *"Deus não faz diferenças entre os japoneses e os brasilerios"* (God does not differentiate between Japanese and Brazilians) and *"Nós somos iguais, nos olhos do Deus"* (We are all equal in the eyes of God). The priest went on to say:

---

[30]The author has not encountered any data about nikkeijin churches in Japan. Among churches in the United States that offer services in Portuguese for Brazilian immigrants, Protestant denominations outnumber Catholic churches, although most Brazilians are Catholic. This is because evangelical churches are smaller and tend to subdivide more easily (Martes 1999:88–89).

The Japanese you see in the factory—they are cold, distant, and don't talk or accept Brazilians into their groups. But religious faith and devotion can erase such differences, as people embrace the love of Jesus and become members of the same community. You can see this with those Japanese who convert and become Christians. They are different from other Japanese. They lose their cold and unfriendly Japanese ways and suddenly become warm and friendly and open. They stop bowing and begin to shake hands. They begin smiling and start talking even to strangers, just like the Brazilians [i.e., the true Christian is a Brazilian, just as God intended!]. All Christians find that they speak the same religious language.

This construction of an imagined religious community across ethnic boundaries through a shared Christian faith was reinforced by the presence of one devout Japanese Christian at the service, who could not speak a word of Portuguese but could still supposedly understand the word of God (with the assistance of a bilingual nikkeijin who sat next to her and constantly whispered in her ear). She was also the most emotional during the sermon and was one of the individuals who shared her own religious experiences in front of the congregation before the sermon. The attempt to build a shared spiritual community that transcends ethnic differences is even more salient in churches with a mixed Japanese/nikkeijin congregation. A few of my Japanese Brazilian informants who were part of such churches spoke about the universal religious bond between them and the Japanese despite the ethnic and linguistic barriers they feel in everyday life.

Religion can also help the Japanese Brazilians deal with their denigrated social class status as a negative immigrant minority in Japan. This was also a component of the priest's sermon when he mentioned the negative meanings attached to the word "dekasegi" in Japan. "The Japanese don't like foreigners coming to Japan just to earn money," he claimed. In response, the priest offered religion as a means to escape such a lowly status by justifying it as simply a means to a higher spiritual end:

Yes, we all come here as dekasegi for money, but we must remember that such objectives of our material lives are trivial compared to the greater plans that God has laid out for us. We are here to work and earn money, but this is only to sustain our material and physical lives so that we can search for a higher spiritual life and to ultimately be one with God. We must never forget this greater purpose in our lives.

Likewise, Hiromi, one of the nikkeijin members of the church who had been living in Japan for six years, emphasized how religion is a respite from the difficulties of life as a dekasegi worker focused solely on economic profit:

> All of the dekasegi come to Japan for financial fulfillment. But we find that money is not the solution to our lives. I came to Japan with this dream, and I fulfilled my wishes to a certain extent, but I still feel this emptiness in my life. So I search for the spiritual side of life through a closeness with God.

Finally, religion also offers a way to alleviate the loss of meaning the Japanese Brazilians experience because of the migratory disruption of their former lives and their subsequent ethnic and socioeconomic marginalization in Japan. Although many nikkeijin reaffirm their Brazilianness in an attempt to find new ethnic meaning when denied their previously cherished "Japanese" identity, some, like Hiromi, also turn to religion to help fill this void:

> When we were in Brazil, we were all "japonês" and had these Japanese values that we treasured. Now that we have come to Japan, we have lost these Japanese values since we are not accepted as Japanese here and don't know whether we are truly Japanese or Brazilian. So we search for higher religious values. We try to find new values to believe in.

The disruption of the nikkeijin's previous middle-class careers in Brazil and the marginal working-class jobs they subsequently perform as migrants in Japan can also lead to a profound loss of meaning and purpose among them. Not only do they lose their former professional status, some are overcome by a sense of insignificance in Japan as they find themselves working in large impersonal Japanese factories mechanically repeating a menial task over and over again, a mere cog among hundreds of unskilled workers on the assembly line. In addition, since most of them quit their previous occupations or closed their businesses in Brazil in order to migrate to Japan, they are unable to return to their previous careers. This future socio-occupational uncertainty simply exacerbates the personal anomie they experience. Again, religion can alleviate this sense of meaninglessness by providing a ready-made system of cultural beliefs and meanings that imbues mundane lives with spiritual significance and purpose. This is the sense in which religion functions as a "worldview" (Geertz 1973:87–125) or a "culturally constituted belief system" (Spiro 1987:201) that makes life comprehensible and meaningful (see also Weber 1946:281). In fact, there have been some cases of Japanese Brazilians who have saved themselves from the brink of suicide by joining a religious group in Japan and finding new spiritual purpose in their difficult and mundane immigrant lives.[31] By embracing religion and identifying with a higher spiritual plane of existence, the nikkeijin can transcend and neutralize the detrimental effects of their negative minority status in Japan.

OUTSIDE THE ETHNIC COMMUNITY: THE PROBLEMS CAUSED BY ISOLATION

Undoubtedly, the Japanese Brazilians are able to successfully adjust to their negative minority status in Japan because they can draw strength from the presence of their ethnic peers in both their families and their communities, which enables them to maintain their own identities, cultural values, and self-respect. In Roberto DaMatta's terminology, although they have become isolated and alienated "individuals" who are marginalized in Japanese society as ethnic outsiders and low-class workers, they are able to recover their "personhood" within their ethnic communities as socially integrated and constituted beings (DaMatta 1991:170–77) and use this social support to resist the degrading psychological effects of negative minority status.

Therefore, it is no surprise that those who are socially isolated from other nikkeijin and cannot rely on cohesive ethnic community support experience considerably more psychological difficulty in Japan.[32] As is true with most migrant workers, since the Japanese Brazilians use their social networks to migrate and find jobs in Japan, they tend to cluster in certain regions and cities. Even those who do not live in large nikkeijin communities such as in Oizumi or Hamamatsu have a well-knit network

---

[31]Such cases have been reported in the Portuguese language newspapers, *International Press* and *Folha Mundial*.

[32]The connection between solitude and mental illness among the dekasegi is also mentioned in an *International Press* article (February 12, 1995, 7a) in which a Japanese psychiatrist who treats nikkeijin patients mentions that living with a group of ethnic peers in Japan is critical for the mental health of the Japanese Brazilians.

of compatriots. Among my informants, the most isolated case I encountered was a family in Kawasaki where both spouses worked in factories with only Japanese workers and did not have any Japanese Brazilian acquaintances. The few nikkeijin relatives they had in Japan lived a considerable distance away.

However, because the Brazilian nikkeijin now live in more than 3,000 Japanese cities, towns, and villages all over the country (Kitagawa 1997:76), there are undoubtedly some living alone in Japan as ethnically isolated "individuals" who do not enjoy the benefits of membership as "persons" in a cohesive ethnic social group. Undoubtedly, such individuals suffer from acute loneliness and homesickness, which impairs their ability to ethnically adjust to Japanese social pressures and their negative minority status. The problem of loneliness is especially serious for nikkeijin who cannot communicate with the Japanese and can even lead to hallucinatory symptoms. There have been a number of cases where such individuals begin to hear voices in Portuguese and eventually construct an illusion that they have an imaginary friend with whom they begin to have conversations in the factory.[33] The make-believe friend provides them with a sense of companionship and is a way to deal with intense solitude. Although Foucault (1995 [1977]:193) claims that in modern disciplinary society, people who are deviant, abnormal, and mad are the ones who are most subject to intense social examination and control, it is also important to remember that those who are marginalized and alienated from society (and its control mechanisms) are the ones who tend to become mentally ill and abnormal in the first place. Thus, mental deviancy and social embeddedness do not always correlate.

This "imaginary friend syndrome" among socially isolated nikkeijin demonstrates the human capacity for symbolization as a means to adjust and cope with the adverse effects of social alienation. Most Japanese Brazilians who belong to cohesive ethnic networks and communities have a whole array of available "public symbols" that can be used to adjust to Japanese society. These include the negative cultural meanings of Japaneseness (coldness, social exclusion, discrimination, etc.), the positive concepts and meanings through which "Brazilianness" is understood (warmth, affection, friendliness), the use of the Portuguese language, and more spe-

---

[33]This "imaginary friend syndrome" is mentioned by Nakagawa (1994) and has also been described in nikkeijin Portuguese newspapers in Japan.

cific symbols such as Brazilian food, clothes, festivities, and the flag. Since the meanings of such public symbols are collectively held by the ethnic group, individual experiences expressed through them can be readily shared and understood by others, thus providing group support for the psychological adjustment of the Japanese Brazilians in Japan through a sense of common experience and mutual acknowledgment.

However, in order to adjust to their social environment, individuals also resort to the use of intensely personal symbols (sometimes on the imaginary level), which have completely idiosyncratic meanings that can be understood only by the person who constructed them.[34] This is certainly the case with the hallucinatory symbolic creation of an imaginary friend among socially isolated Japanese Brazilians. Since all symbolic and cultural forms are socially constructed to a certain extent and are not mechanical reflections of some type of objective reality, it is sometimes hard to determine when normal symbolization becomes hallucinatory. However, we can safely say that when a symbolic experience is perceived as a product of an actual external stimulus or occurrence that does not in fact exist, the person is hallucinating. In fact, hallucination and false sensory experiences are among the most frequent of mental disorders among the Japanese Brazilian dekasegi[35] and can lead to mild forms of schizophrenia in which individuals become unable to distinguish reality from fantasy in general (see Inoue 1994:75). This personal form of coping with intense solitude through symbolic hallucination may be psychologically adjustive for the particular situation at hand but can become *mal*adjustive when it becomes a general pattern that begins to affect other aspects of the individual's experience.

Solitude in Japan and the lack of an ethnic support group can on very rare occasions lead to more extreme forms of psychological maladjustment involving suicide and criminality. A number of Japanese Brazilian immigrants expressed considerable frustration at suddenly being placed

---

[34]However, Obeyesekere (1981) warns against a simplistic dichotomization between private and public symbols. Individuals give meaning and expression to even intensely personal and subjective psychic experiences, disturbances, and afflictions by using collectively held cultural forms (public symbols). In other words, culture is not only confined to collective, group processes but is also related to individual functioning, and the two should not be separated as mutually incompatible. Few symbols have exclusively personal meanings that are not at least partly derived from a collectively understood cultural system.

[35]Among the 95 percent of the patients that Nakagawa diagnosed as "paranoid," 88 percent were suffering from auditory hallucinations.

in a powerless position as subordinates of the Japanese who must dutifully comply with and submit to their orders and demands. One of the
recurrent motifs in my interviews with the nikkeijin were complaints that
they are unable to voice their opinions, suggestions, and complaints at
work and that even when they do so, the Japanese do not listen to or accept their opinions because they are seen as foreigners. As a result, some
of my informants felt that they simply had to keep quiet and "to swal-
low" (*engolir*) their problems and resentments, which can eventually lead
to the buildup of inner hostility. This pent-up aggression can become
quite overwhelming for those who do not have families, relatives, or
Brazilian social groups through which they can release their frustrations
(*desabafar*) by openly voicing their complaints and their problems with
the Japanese. In certain cases, such anger from interpersonal frustrations
can be turned inward, resulting in suicide. When inner constraints are
weak, such aggression can be turned outward as criminal behavior
(against the Japanese), and in the most extreme case, as murder. There is
one reported case of nikkeijin homicide involving a man who came alone
to Japan with hopes of earning an instant fortune but had to switch to a
difficult job after the salary for his first job was too low. His mounting
frustrations at work and the difficulties of dealing with the Japanese finally exploded, and he killed a Japanese neighbor who refused to assist
him with street directions because he could not speak Japanese well
(*Asahi Shimbun*, February 30, 1992).

ETHNIC RESISTANCE AND SOCIAL REPRODUCTION: JAPANESE NATIONALISM AND THE NATION-STATE

The considerable psychological difficulties experienced by those Japanese
Brazilians who are ethnically isolated in Japan demonstrate how critical
ethnic communities are as an independent space to counter both assimilationist Japanese pressures and the adverse affects of negative minority
status. Unlike culturally dominated minorities who have already been deprived of an independent basis for resistance and can only subvert and
contest the hegemonic cultural meanings that now constitute their lived
experience, the Japanese Brazilians, as a new immigrant minority with an
intact culture, can mount an autonomous ethnic resistance through the
deterritorialized assertion of their Brazilian counteridentities.

However, although the ethnic resistance of autonomous social groups may prevent their cultural assimilation and protect them from negative minority status, does it change or transform the hegemonic system? Does it allow minority groups to escape their subordination? Most analyses indicate that resistance usually does not lead to revolutionary change (cf. Kaplan and Kelly 1994:126). Although the resistance of dominated groups may generate new cultural forms such as spirit possession (Ong 1987), Zionist Christian rituals (Comaroff 1985), and oppositional youth culture (Willis 1981), these cultures of resistance are not analyzed as a serious challenge that undermines the hegemonic sociocultural order or helps emancipate these subordinate groups. In fact, the cultural production and creativity that accompany resistance and the subversion of hegemonic discourses can actually reinforce and reproduce dominant ideologies and perpetuate systems of inequality (Kondo 1990:213–14; Willis 1981).

The possibility of changing the social order appears quite slim especially for the resistance of dominated groups, whose appropriation and contestation of the ideological system does not threaten its integrity since their critical discourse ultimately remains dependent on hegemonic cultural meanings.[36] Although the resistance of autonomous social groups like the Japanese Brazilians may better illustrate its revolutionary potential, the prospects for true change in either the dominant ethnic or socioeconomic order do not seem very promising.

Instead of helping them to escape their socioeconomic marginalization, the ethnic resistance of the nikkeijin actually perpetuates and reproduces their subordinate social class position. In a society like Japan where cultural assimilation is a prerequisite for socioeconomic mobility, the refusal of the nikkeijin to assimilate and the subsequent persistence of their Brazilian cultural differences confines them to low-class jobs (see epilogue). Only those Japanese Brazilians who learn the Japanese language and deemphasize their Brazilianness are promoted to higher-status jobs in

---

[36]Scott (1985) suggests a number of reasons why the resistance of the Malaysian peasants he studied did not lead to revolutionary change. He argues that fear of reprisals and punishment prevented open acts of rebellion and that most resistance was focused on mundane issues and the meaningful realities of everyday existence, not on abstract revolutionary ideals and demands. In addition, resistance was also targeted at local rich elites, who were seen as the immediate cause of suffering, and did not question the larger state and capitalist structures that cause peasant subordination.

Japanese companies (see chapter 6). Therefore, although ethnic resistance may be psychologically adjustive, it tends to be *socially maladaptive* because it impedes social mobility.[37]

Although the ethnic resistance of the nikkeijin tends to reproduce their socioeconomic marginality, will the presence of a culturally distinct Japanese Brazilian immigrant minority that resists assimilation eventually change Japanese ethno-national identity[38] by forcing the Japanese to embrace a more inclusive identity that acknowledges and incorporates ethnically different peoples in their midst? Will the nikkeijin seriously challenge the power of the Japanese nation-state by undermining its dominant nationalist ideology of ethnic homogeneity?

One of the major shortcomings of the resistance literature (which its critics have not raised) is its tendency to completely ignore the experiences and practices of dominant groups and institutional power holders. Accounts of resistance examine only the subordinate or subaltern groups that resist some dominant ideology without considering how the power holders who create, legitimate, and perpetuate this ideology respond by reconsolidating the dominant cultural order.[39] By ignoring this process, the resistance literature therefore recovers agency for the "resisters" only to deny it to members of the dominant group, who are reduced to a faceless and passive ideological discourse. However, it is quite evident that members of the dominant group who perpetuate hegemonic discourses also display considerable agency and in turn "resist" the cultural challenge of the subordinated by defending and relegitimating the existing order. Therefore, only by examining how majority Japanese react to the nikkeijin and their continued defiance of assimilationist Japanese ethnic assumptions can we assess whether their resistance merely reproduces or successfully transforms dominant Japanese ethno-nationalist ideologies.

---

[37]This is not to deny that ethnic resistance has any socially adaptive advantages. As Zhou and Bankston argue (1994), the retention of ethnic culture can become an important form of social capital and community support that encourages and promotes academic achievement and future social success.

[38]Ethnic and national identity are considered synonymous in the Japanese case since the nation is seen as composed of one ethnic group (see also De Vos and Suárez-Orozco 1990:251; Ivy 1995:3–4; Yoshino 1992).

[39]As Raymond Williams notes: "new [oppositional] practice[s] [are] not, of course, an isolated process. To the degree that it emerges, and especially to the degree that it is oppositional rather than alternative, the process of attempted incorporation significantly begins" (1977:124).

Japanese national identity has been constantly articulated and redefined in response to encounters with peoples from foreign countries (first China and then "the West") (cf. Befu 1993:121–25; Ohnuki-Tierney 1990b).[40] In the last several decades, the Japanese have been affected by numerous foreign influences as they have become increasingly integrated into the global economy. Undoubtedly, the recent arrival of the foreign on Japanese shores in the form of labor migration is another historical moment that will cause many to reconsider what it means to be Japanese. Of course, the influence of the Japanese Brazilians on Japanese ethno-national identity is nowhere as significant or pervasive as the change in ethnic consciousness that the nikkeijin experience when they encounter the Japanese. Most Japanese do not have direct contact with the Japanese Brazilians, who remain only a minute fraction of the entire country's population, and even those who live in areas with high immigrant concentrations do not have enough personal interaction with the nikkeijin to really affect their ethnic self-consciousness.

However, because the nikkeijin are Japanese descendants, they are much more likely to cause the Japanese to reconsider their ethno-national identities than non-nikkeijin immigrants who are culturally *and* racially different and therefore have little ethnic relevance to the Japanese. As argued in chapter 3, ethnic identities are more likely to be modified when a certain group encounters those who are ethnically *similar* instead of those who are completely different. The presence of a new nikkeijin immigrant minority can potentially challenge essentialist notions of Japanese ethnic identity, in which racial descent is assumed to be closely associated with the possession of culture, by causing the Japanese to realize the cultural diversity that exists among Japanese descendants. Because the Japanese Brazilians are "racially" Japanese but "culturally" Brazilian, they are ethnic anomalies (cf. Kondo 1986) who defy classification by transgressing the traditional ethnic boundaries between "Japanese" and "foreigner."

Indeed, a number of my Japanese informants specifically described the surprise and personal disorientation they felt when they first encountered the culturally different nikkeijin, who so blatantly contradicted their previous assumptions that those of Japanese descent (that is, those who "look

---

[40]Likewise, Harootunian (1988) analyzes how Japanese nativist discourse and the construction of a distinctive Japanese national identity was a critical and oppositional reaction to the influence of Chinese thought and culture in early modern Japanese history.

Japanese") are culturally Japanese as well. A freelance journalist spoke the
most clearly about the ethnic incongruity of the Japanese Brazilians:

> When we first set eyes on the nikkeijin, our spontaneous reaction is one
> of confusion and shock. We think they are really strange. We assume
> they are Japanese, so we talk to them, and then wonder why they don't
> understand us and cannot communicate in Japanese. They look Japan-
> ese but speak in a strange tongue. Most Japanese do not have a concept
> of a nikkeijin. So we say, "Who are these guys?" We always expected
> those with a Japanese face to have a certain level of Japanese culture. But
> the Japanese are now changing this attitude as we realize that the nikkei-
> jin are different.

Therefore, the assertion of cultural difference through the ethnic resistance
of the Japanese Brazilians disrupts and disassociates the assumed correlation
between race and culture that is the foundation of Japanese ethno-national
identity, thus potentially leading to new ethnic attitudes (cf. Murphy-
Shigematsu 2000:211). In this manner, those on the margins of society reveal the basic assumptions and categories by which the society operates (see
also Valentine 1990:50) and frequently have more of a transformative impact on collective identity than complete insiders or outsiders.[41] Marginal
figures in Japanese history have served as metaphors for symbolic transformations in collective self-representations (Ohnuki-Tierney 1987, 1990a).

Despite the transformative potential of Japanese Brazilian ethnic resistance, however, it did not seem to cause my Japanese informants to
gradually expand the exclusive definition of Japaneseness to include those
who are of Japanese racial descent but are culturally different. As we have
seen in chapter 3, the result is exactly the opposite, as the nikkeijin are ethnically rejected and excluded as "foreigners." Because my Japanese informants experienced more negative cultural differences than positive similarities when they encountered the Japanese Brazilians (see chapter 2),
they obviously were prevented from identifying with them.

Therefore, instead of expanding their currently exclusive notions of
Japaneseness in ways that are more congenial to multiethnic accommoda-

---

[41]Rosaldo claims that those who live in the "border zones" of gender, race, ethnicity, or nationality are frequently most capable of creativity and change through transcultural blending
(1989:207–209, 215–17). According to Rutherford, the margin is a place of resistance that
threatens to deconstruct dominant and hegemonic forms of knowledge (1990:22).

tion, many of my informants seemed to experience a restrictive narrowing of ethno-national identity in which they acquired a greater awareness and appreciation of the distinctive national cultural qualities that make them Japanese by contrasting themselves with the culturally alien Japanese Brazilians. Individuals become most aware of their identity when they encounter groups that are culturally different, which bring out their own unique ethnic qualities. When my Japanese informants were confronted with those who are of Japanese descent but culturally Brazilian, they seemed to realize the importance of the cultural aspects of being Japanese to a much greater extent, which they previously took for granted as a natural consequence of being "racially" Japanese. In this manner, although the ethnic encounter with the nikkeijin *deessentializes* Japanese ethnic identity by problematizing the assumption that shared racial descent is the fundamental determinant of who is Japanese, it may produce a more restrictive cultural definition of Japanese identity based on an increased cultural nationalism. One Japanese worker spoke about such ethnic reactions most clearly:

> After encountering the Brazilian nikkeijin, I have become more conscious of my Japaneseness. This is something you ordinarily don't think about when you are just with other Japanese, but when I am with nikkeijin, although we are of the same blood, I see how different they are from us—in thinking, attitudes, the way they talk and dress—and I recognize what is Japanese about myself, my special Japanese cultural traits. I realize that I am a real Japanese, whereas they are not.

Indeed, it was quite notable how a majority of my Japanese informants engaged in homogeneous discourses of Japaneseness when reflecting upon the negative ethnic differences of the Japanese Brazilians, characterizing the Japanese as diligent, formal, quiet, polite, and restrained compared to the nikkeijin. This results in a heightened consciousness of their national cultural distinctiveness.

Of course, not all of my informants reacted negatively to the Japanese Brazilians or engaged in the same discourse of Japanese national uniqueness. It is also important to note that those who did tended to be from the working class and lived in rural industrial cities (i.e., Oizumi town and Ota city) and therefore were probably not as ethnically receptive and open-minded as more cosmopolitan and better-educated middle-class Japanese living in large metropolitan areas.

Even among the Japanese working class, however, there are rare individuals who are ethnically receptive and actively interact and socialize with nikkeijin immigrants. However, I was somewhat surprised that the three Japanese factory workers in Oizumi I knew who actively socialized with the Japanese Brazilians (either currently or in the past) still had rather strong ethnic prejudices about them. Nonetheless, I did interview a few Japanese informants of middle-class background (two of whom lived in the Tokyo area) who had positive impressions of the Brazilian nikkeijin, admiring their friendly openness, lightheartedness, and casualness. For instance, consider the remarks of one young Japanese woman, who had joined a nikkeijin assistance organization:

> I prefer being with the nikkeijin more than Japanese because they are so different. They are cheerful, lighthearted, and laid back, unlike the Japanese, who are too serious and gloomy. The Japanese are too sensitive and formal, but with nikkeijin, I don't have to use my nerves—I feel more open and less inhibited with them.

Another informant stressed how he likes the nikkeijin because they are openly friendly even to strangers, whereas Japanese keep to themselves, do not talk with people they don't know, and are simply bad at relating to outsiders.

It is important to note, however, that even these rare, socially receptive Japanese individuals are not ethnically accepting the nikkeijin as one of them. Instead, they like the nikkeijin precisely because they are foreign and therefore, culturally different from the Japanese. And like their more closed-minded compatriots, they also experience an increased sense of Japanese national cultural difference vis-à-vis the nikkeijin as they engage in a discourse of Japaneseness by homogeneously characterizing themselves as unfriendly and gloomy as well as overly formal, polite, and sensitive. The only difference is that Japanese national character is portrayed negatively in this case instead of positively. In this manner, even those Japanese who actively interact and socialize with the nikkeijin do not necessary broaden their ethno-national identities by collapsing the ethnic boundaries and distinctions between themselves and the nikkeijin.

Therefore, just as the Japanese Brazilians increase the consciousness of their Brazilian national differences when they encounter the culturally different Japanese, the Japanese seem to experience a strengthening of Japanese national identity in response to the nikkeijin. This mutual divergence in ethnic self-consciousness can be called "identity schismogenesis." Schismogenesis is a concept introduced by Gregory Bateson in his study of the Naven ritual among the Iatmul of New Guinea in order to understand progressive changes in behavior among individuals and groups. It refers to a "process of differentiation in the norms of individual behaviour resulting from cumulative interaction between individuals" (1958:175; see also Bateson 1972). The ethnic encounter between the Japanese Brazilians and the Japanese results in a type of "symmetrical schismogenesis"—a process in which two groups become progressively different in self-consciousness as they react to each other in identical ways. In other words, as the ethnic identity of the Japanese Brazilians continues to shift more and more toward the Brazilian side in response to the Japanese, the Japanese feel increasingly more Japanese in response to the nikkeijin. Although this resurgence of national sentiment is much less pronounced for the Japanese than it is for the Japanese Brazilians, it is strong enough to undermine their previous feelings of transnational cultural affiliation with the nikkeijin based on a consciousness of common racial descent.

Thus, by shifting the definition of Japaneseness from race to culture, the ethnic resistance of the Japanese Brazilians may simply produce a more explicitly articulated cultural nationalism among the Japanese that reinforces more than challenges and transforms the nationalist ideologies that support the hegemony of the Japanese nation-state. Since the power of the Japanese state has been consolidated by the effective use of an ideology of ethnic homogeneity and cultural assimilation, the massive influx of ethnically different foreigners has been strongly perceived by the Japanese government as a threat to social stability and national integrity (cf. Lie 2001:49). Although the migration of the ethnically related nikkeijin was initially seen as an exception, the government's opinion seems to have changed recently. Since Japanese immigration policy makers expected to receive only a small number of nikkeijin sojourners, they were unprepared for the explosive immigrant influx and did not realize that so many Japanese Brazilians would bring their families and settle in Japan (see also Kajita 1994:168). In addition, the nikkeijin were more culturally Brazilian than expected and have not smoothly integrated themselves into Japan's national cultural fabric. As a result, certain government officials seem to regret their decision to openly admit the nikkeijin. A former Ministry of Labor official was one of them:

> The nikkeijin that the Immigration Bureau [of the Ministry of Justice] intended to accept were different. We were expecting that they would

be more culturally Japanese and speak Japanese more. But those who actually came were not the type we expected. Sometimes, we look at some of these people and say, is this really a nikkeijin? I mean, they have no inkling about Japanese culture, and don't speak Japanese. . . . If we had known so many nikkeijin would come, we would not have allowed them to freely enter Japan.

In response to this unexpected increase of culturally foreign nikkeijin immigrants as well as the increase in "fake nikkeijin" who attempt to enter the country with false documents, the Japanese government has attempted to reduce the level of migration recently through more stringent enforcement of visa requirements at immigration bureau offices and the Japanese consulate in São Paulo as well as increased rejection of visa renewals. In 1993, the government even instituted a three-month job training program designed to persuade nikkeijin immigrants to return home (Sellek 2001:117).[42]

Therefore, as was the case with the Brazilian government, transnational migration is actively discouraged and restricted by the Japanese government because it is regarded as a serious challenge to the hegemonic power of the nation-state and its efforts to promote national unity among its citizens through ethnic homogeneity. One of the most prominently cited reasons among immigration policy makers for why Japan should not accept unskilled foreign workers has been the fear that public order will be disrupted by increased ethnic conflict and discrimination caused by ethnic diversity (Liberal Democratic Party 1992; Ministry of Justice 1994; Ministry of Labor 1991, 1992; Nojima 1989; interviews with government officials). However, my analysis indicates that the massive influx of nikkeijin immigrants may produce an intensification of cultural nationalism and create a greater awareness among Japanese of their distinctive cultural homogeneity (cf. Douglass and Roberts 2000:26, 30), thus implicitly revitalizing their sense of national allegiance.

---

[42]A similar pattern can be observed with ethnic Germans who have return migrated to Germany from Eastern Europe and the former Soviet Union. They were initially embraced by the German government because of their shared descent and presumed cultural similarities and are given German citizenship. However, when confronted with a massive influx of immigrants who were much more culturally foreign than expected, the German government recently took measures to restrict their entry and has cut back on generous social welfare benefits designed to integrate them into German society.

In fact, my Japanese informants responded to the presence of culturally alien Japanese Brazilian immigrants by advocating the same ideology of
ethnic homogeneity and national unity that the Japanese government has
been propagating, thus enhancing the control of the nation-state. When
asked about the future prospect of increased immigration to Japan, many
of them stressed the importance of Japan as an ethnically homogeneous,
island nation and felt that the disruption of this monoethnicity through
immigration would have negative consequences because the ethnically restrictive nature of Japanese society makes it difficult to incorporate large
numbers of foreigners. For instance, the reflections of Sasaki-san, a local
Oizumi store owner, were quite typical:

> Ethnic homogeneity is very important for the social framework of Japan.
> Japan has been this way for centuries and it has contributed to the na-
> tion's social stability and prosperity. It is in our national character—we
> all think similarly and can relate to each other, creating stability and har-
> mony. If we let a bunch of foreign workers into Japan with different cul-
> tures and consciousness, it will destroy this ethnic unity. Japan has al-
> ways had an island mentality and has been closed and unreceptive to
> foreigners for this reason.

My informants predicted dire future consequences if Japan was forced to
accept massive numbers of immigrants, including ethnic discrimination,
serious antiforeigner backlashes, increased crime, and ethnically segregated immigrant ghettos. In this manner, the discourse of Japanese ethnic
homogeneity has been remarkably resilient despite the influx of foreign
workers into Japan, as has been the case with past intrusions of the foreign into the country (Ivy 1995:9; cf. Lie 2001:50–51).

Therefore, nikkeijin return migration ultimately does not undermine
the hegemony of the nation-state over individual consciousness and loyalty either for the migrants themselves or for their hosts. Despite the potentially "subversive" impact of transnational migration, the transgression
of national borders by the Japanese Brazilians not only nationalizes their
own ethnic identity but also renews nationalist cultural sentiments among
the Japanese, thus reproducing and enhancing the hegemonic nationalist
projects of both the migrant sending and receiving countries. Transnational dislocation does not necessarily weaken involvement and commitment to the nation-state as Hannerz suggests (1996:89) but can promote
the consolidation and articulation of national identities.

CONCLUSION:
ETHNIC RESISTANCE AND THE STRUGGLE
FOR HUMAN RECOGNITION

Once ethnic identities are consolidated among an immigrant minority group, they can become the basis for collective mobilization for instrumental economic, political, or psychological purposes. For the Japanese Brazilians, as Japan's newest minority, the development of a Brazilian counteridentity has led to collective resistance against Japanese ethnic hegemony through the assertion of their cultural differences and a refusal to assimilate. In terms of ethnic resistance, recent immigrant groups must be distinguished from indigenous minority groups who have already been culturally subordinated. Since the experiences of the latter are structured by dominant ideologies, they have lost an autonomous cultural basis for opposition to a certain extent, and their resistance merely operates within the confines of the hegemonic system of the dominant majority. In contrast, the autonomous ethnic resistance of the Japanese Brazilians is more than a critical discourse that merely contests and subverts Japanese cultural values. It is an attempt to defend an independent cultural space from hegemonic encroachment by consciously engaging in behavior that is both a positive affirmation of an autonomous Brazilian culture and a rejection of Japanese cultural expectations.

Undoubtedly, when the Japanese Brazilians articulate their nationalist counteridentities in Japan, Brazilian culture itself becomes subject to modification as national Brazilian symbols (such as food, clothes, greetings, and samba) are appropriated in a foreign context for new and originally unintended purposes (i.e., to demonstrate their cultural distinctiveness to the Japanese). In addition, these cultural displays of difference in Japan are partly freed from Brazilian social constraints and concerns for authenticity. As Brazilian cultural meanings are thus revalued and reconstituted in a new Japanese context, the result is an exaggerated, decontextualized, and imprecisely reproduced version of Brazilian culture. However, as long as this new cultural form remains autonomous and distinct from the dominant Japanese cultural order, it continues to serve as an effective means of ethnic resistance. What emerges is much more than an impoverished and "thin" resistance culture created simply as an oppositional reaction to Japanese cultural hegemony. It is an independent culture in its own right, rich enough to ensure the continued persistence of the Brazilian nikkeijin as a culturally distinct ethnic minority in Japan.

The ethnic resistance of the Brazilian nikkeijin, however, does more to reproduce than to transform the dominant sociopolitical order. By ensuring that they remain a culturally different and unassimilated immigrant minority, it reinforces their socioeconomic subordination in Japan by confining them to the lowest-level factory jobs. Likewise, although their ethnic resistance deessentializes Japanese ethno-national assumptions, it ultimately seems to perpetuate hegemonic ideologies by promoting a more explicit cultural nationalism, thus ensuring the continuing marginalization of culturally different minorities.

Therefore, the ethnic resistance of the Japanese Brazilians does not improve their subordinated social or ethnic status and seemingly produces no tangible instrumental benefits. In this sense, Arjun Appadurai suggests that the assertion of distinct ethnic identities by marginalized groups may be an instrumental end in itself:

> [Ethnicity] may have a purely *identity-oriented instrumentality* rather than an instrumentality that, as is so often implied, is extracultural (economic or political or emotional) [italics mine]. Put another way, the mobilization of markers of group difference may itself be part of a contestation of values *about* difference, as distinct from the consequences of difference for wealth, security, or power [italics in original]. (1996:14)

However, I have argued that the identity-oriented instrumentality of the Japanese Brazilians is not merely a debate about cultural differences, because such ethnic culturalist movements always have significant and practical psychological consequences. The self-conscious assertion of a Brazilian counteridentity among nikkeijin return migrants is a positive form of ethnic adjustment that increases their psychological resilience to Japanese assimilative pressures, to which they are especially susceptible as Japanese descendants. In addition, by adhering to their own cultural standards within their communities, they are able to autonomously resist and counter the adverse effects of majority prejudice and socioeconomic subordination, thus preserving their self-image and self-esteem. If all else fails, their ethnic difficulties in Japan can be alleviated and transcended through the communal affirmation of their own independent religious values, which imbue their lives with spiritual significance and the promise of a higher form of existence.

According to Frantz Fanon, however, ethnic resistance among minorities is much more than an issue of successful adjustment. Ultimately, it is about being human.

> Man is human only to the extent to which he tries to impose his existence on another man in order to be recognized by him. . . . It is on that other being, on recognition by that other being, that his own human worth and reality depend. It is that other being in whom the meaning of his life is condensed. . . . [This] human reality in-itself-for-itself can be achieved only through conflict and through the risk that conflict implies. (1967:216–18)

Only through an active struggle for ethnic recognition from others can a truly independent and autonomous self-consciousness be attained (cf. Crapanzano 1982:200).[43] If individuals passively wait for recognition to be bestowed on them, they abdicate the right to actively define themselves and assert their self-worth, which is what makes them truly human. Through the performative enactment of their Brazilian counteridentities and the forceful display of cultural difference, the Japanese Brazilians in Japan have cried out, "I am Brazilian, not Japanese!" And the Japanese have been forced to listen, watch, and perhaps reconsider.

Consider the reflections of Morita-san, one of my closest Japanese informants, after his long and unusual association with a number of Brazilian nikkeijin:

> At first, I wanted them to become like the Japanese and tried to speak only Japanese to them, but I later realized that this is impossible. They can't become Japanese, nor do they want to. They want to remain Brazilian in Japan, and I came to respect them for that. After a while, I started teaching myself Portuguese and learning about Brazil. Now I want to travel to Brazil someday to experience the country.

This type of ethnic acknowledgment is the first step toward granting the Japanese Brazilians their humanity. It entails a recognition of their self-

---

[43]This presupposes an ability to see oneself from the perspective of the other so that the self becomes an object to itself (Mead 1977 [1956]). Therefore, the emergence of the self requires not only awareness of a contrastive world but also recognition of one's own otherness, which Crapanzano calls "possessive reflexivity" (1982:200).

definition and independent existence as a distinct ethnic group instead of merely constituting them through the hegemonic imposition of essentialized and assimilative Japanese ethnic understandings.

Yet, few Japanese I knew were willing to actively initiate the sustained contact and friendship with the nikkeijin that makes this type of ethnic recognition possible. For most, the nikkeijin are either persistent ethnic curiosities or temporary ethnic anomalies that should eventually be properly assimilated to conform to Japanese ethnic expectations. Morita-san was a very unusual individual and somewhat of a social outcast who was marginalized among his Japanese peers. Perhaps he himself sought some type of independent recognition from his compatriots by asserting his differences amid the assumed cultural homogeneity that constitutes Japanese ethnicity.

CHAPTER 6

ᡃ᠎ᡟ

"Assimilation Blues"[1]

Problems Among Assimilation-Oriented Japanese Brazilians

"JAPANIZED" NIKKEIJIN AND THE DIFFICULTIES OF ADJUSTMENT

THE HUMAN DESIRE for ethnic recognition sometimes involves not the display of cultural differences, but their downplay. Ethnic groups can also adapt to their minority status by seeking recognition of their ethnic unrecognizability. In contrast to the majority of Japanese Brazilians, who have insisted on asserting their Brazilian counteridentities as an act of ethnic resistance, a smaller number of individuals take a different approach and attempt a more assimilative type of ethnic adaptation by deemphasizing their cultural differences. In this manner, not only do individual Brazilian nikkeijin engage in ethnic resistance at different levels of intensity, some participate in it while others do not, leading to internal tensions within the ethnic minority group (cf. Ortner 1995:179). In this chapter, I will analyze the ambivalence and conflicts experienced by those nikkeijin who refuse to ethnically resist in Japan and instead turn toward more assimilative forms of minority adaptation. Despite its *socially adaptive* benefits in terms of class mobility, ethnic assimilation involves a number of psychological costs that make it less successful as a form of *adjustment*.

This points to an irony in the Japanese Brazilian ethnic experience. Although it would seem that those who have better Japanese cultural proficiency would have less difficulty in Japan, the "Japanized" nikkeijin who received a firm, Japanese-type socialization from their parents and speak

---

[1]The term is taken from a book about middle-class blacks living in a white suburban neighborhood in California (Tatum 1987).

the language well tend to have *more* difficulty psychologically adjusting to Japan than those who are more culturally "Brazilianized." I argue that because the Japanized nikkeijin attempt to accommodate themselves to Japanese cultural standards of behavior, they are more likely to experience stressful assimilationist pressures and more liable to be personally alienated from their ethnic peers. Such negative psychological consequences are more acute for individuals who retain an especially strong Japanese identification in Japan and even attempt to pass as "Japanese."

In fact, there is a greater incidence of mental illness among Japanese Brazilian immigrants who adopt an assimilation-oriented strategy of ethnic adjustment to their negative minority status in Japan. Although there are no conclusive statistics, it is remarkable that the dekasegi returnees whom Dr. Nakagawa treated for psychological symptoms had much better Japanese language abilities than the general nikkeijin immigrant populace in Japan (and thus by implication tended to be the more assimilation-minded, Japanized nikkeijin). A surprising 20.9 percent of his patients knew how to read and write Japanese, 66.1 percent could understand and speak Japanese, and only 12.9 percent could not understand Japanese (Nakagawa 1994). In contrast, in the JICA (1992) survey, only 10 to 13.4 percent of the nikkeijin immigrants in Japan could read and write Japanese and 27 to 33 percent generally could not speak or understand Japanese. The greater psychological difficulties experienced by those who attempt some form of assimilation have been shown in other studies as well. For instance, Hallowell (1955) found among the Ojibwa Indians that the most acculturated showed the poorest signs of psychological adjustment. Assimilation has also been linked to a greater incidence of psychological disorder among other immigrant groups (Portes and Rumbaut 1996:180–81; Rumbaut 1997).

ASSIMILATIONIST PRESSURES AND FEELINGS OF INADEQUACY

Undoubtedly, the more Japanized nikkeijin have greater trouble resolving their ethnic identities in Japan and are the most vulnerable to identity crises, or what Erik Erikson (1980 [1959]) calls identity "diffusion," in which individuals are unable to firmly commit to a certain identity (see also Weinreich 1986:318). Because the Japanized nikkeijin had a stronger affiliation and greater pride in being Japanese in Brazil and are able to speak the language quite well, they have a greater wish to be ethnically accepted by the Japanese in Japan and react more negatively to their exclusion (see chapter 3). In response to their ethnic and socioeconomic marginalization in Japan, they are less willing to embrace a Brazilian counteridentity than their ethnic resistance-minded compatriots since they had a more negative view of "Brazilianness" in Brazil and sometimes even constructed their "Japanese" identities through a denigration of what it meant to be Brazilian. The result may be a temporary inability to decide whether they are Japanese or Brazilian. Thus, because the Japanized nikkeijin have more psychological difficulty "recentering" their identities that have been "decentered" by migration, they are more likely to experience an "uncentered" or incoherent self. Although such individuals eventually come to acknowledge, if not assert their Brazilianness as well, the initial period of identity diffusion can be prolonged and difficult. For instance, consider the experiences of Fabio:

> At first in Japan, I did feel an identity crisis and didn't know who I was. Because I had convinced myself that I was so Japanese in Brazil, I wanted to be seen as Japanese in Japan. But the Japanese didn't accept me. The nikkeis always have this problem—of not knowing whether you are Japanese or Brazilian. Then you reach a point where you realize it is better to be Brazilian in Japan—you can resolve your difficulties more easily this way. After living here for five years, I can now say that I prefer to be Brazilian than Japanese.

This contrasts with the more Brazilianized nikkeijin, who more quickly resolve their identities without an extended identity crisis. The case of Rodney, one of my roommates in Oizumi, is a good example:

> I don't feel any confusion over my identity now, although it was quite a shock when I first got here because I thought we would be accepted as Japanese descendants. But now, I am certain I am Brazilian. If I spoke Japanese well and could act Japanese, I would feel some confusion, but I have realized that I can't be Japanese and acquire Japanese culture, starting with something as basic as my clothes. They even say we walk differently.

Since "Japaneseness" continues to retain a more positive meaning in Japan than "Brazilianness" for nikkeijin with assimilationist tendencies, they feel the need to adjust to Japanese customs and standards to a certain extent in an effort to avoid the stigma of being seen as ethnically Brazilian. In contrast to some of their compatriots, who intentionally display or even flaunt their Brazilian behavior in public, they attempt to speak Japanese properly, wear appropriate clothes, remain quiet on the streets and in their apartments, and even watch out for their gestures. Note the comments of Geraldo, a nisei who speaks pretty good Japanese and prefers to keep his Brazilianness to himself:

> I don't dress like some of these youth who wear Brazilian T-shirts, jeans, or clothes with loud colors. This is the way I always dress [in simple slacks and a plain shirt]. I also don't go around the streets talking loudly in Portuguese and always try to use proper Japanese when I speak to people in stores and banks. We are in the country of the Japanese, so we have to act in a way that does not offend their sensibilities. We have to conform to their way of living instead of expecting them to conform to ours.

Others expressed similar sentiments, frequently remarking that "*Nós temos que entrar no esquema deles*" (We have to enter into the Japanese scheme of things) or "*Nós temos que dançar conforme a música*" (We have to dance to the music).

Such individuals must not only self-consciously modify their behavior but also exercise self-control and restraint in order to avoid revealing their discrediting minority cultural differences. Because of the constant vigilance this requires, their ethnic adjustment involves considerably more psychological pressure and stress than is felt by those who remain less influenced by Japanese cultural standards. A few of my Japanized informants spoke of the lack of freedom they feel when in contact with the Japanese. Michiko, one of the most "Japanized" nikkeijin I knew, directly spoke about the considerable stress she felt from attempting to comply with Japanese cultural demands while somehow retaining her identity as a Brazilian. Since she was most explicit about her experiences, it is worth quoting her at length:

> It's tough being with Japanese because I constantly use my nerves with them. My thinking has become more and more Japanese and I've become a part of their hierarchical society. In Japan, you have to always elevate your superior and make sure you don't contradict him by know-

ing your position as a subordinate, especially if you are a woman. So with Japanese, I always act with proper *enryo* (reserve, deference) and restrain my Brazilian ways, but at times, I feel that I say inappropriate things and they probably see me as having too many opinions. I always have trouble with this and feel I voice my opinions and assert myself too much this way. So I have to always be conscious about myself. It's difficult because I always feel my freedom is restrained with the Japanese. With Brazilians, I don't have to worry about these things and can do what I want without censure. I feel more carefree.

It was apparent that a number of my Japanized nikkeijin informants had internalized the essentialist Japanese ethnic expectation that those of Japanese descent should be culturally Japanese. Of course, this orientation is not only a response to external social pressures in Japan but also based on their prior socialization experiences in Brazil, where they felt considerable pressure, prestige, and pride in maintaining the Japanese language and customs within their families and communities. Undoubtedly, such internalized ethnic expectations are magnified in Japan, making them quite sensitive to Japanese cultural pressures.

Although such assimilation-oriented Japanese Brazilians have a greater tendency to base their ethnic self-worth on their personal ability to act "Japanese," very few of them can actually live up to Japanese cultural standards and expectations because of their different Brazilian background as well as their inability to speak Japanese completely like a native. Even those who speak the language well frequently realize that the Japanese they learned from their parents is outdated or a regional dialect. Ultimately, this can leave them vulnerable to feelings of embarrassment, inadequacy, and even "inferiority." Similar experiences have been observed by Kardiner and Ovesey among American Indians and black Americans (1951; see also Simpson and Yinger 1972:193–94) and by De Vos among the Japanese Burakumin outcaste minority (De Vos and Wagatsuma 1966). According to Bruner (1975:43), this problem occurs among

[Minority peoples] who come to identify with the [dominant majority] group but who are unable to join or fully emulate it because of some barrier such as caste, color, or culture. . . . [They] incorporate the superordinate group's negative evaluation of themselves, which leads to feelings of shame, personal inadequacy, dependency, and hostility.

A good number of the Japanized nikkeijin spoke about their "embarrassment" and "shame" (*vergonha*) at not being able to speak proper Japanese. Nelsa, a young nisei woman, spoke about this issue in the greatest detail:

> I am ashamed of speaking wrong Japanese because I have a Japanese face. Even if they know you are a nikkei, the Japanese expect you to know the language, so they ask you questions. I can tell they become disappointed when they realize you can't speak as well as they thought. This happens in the factory all the time. Japanese workers sometimes come up to me and just talk normally, as if I were fluent in the language. It's always embarrassing when I can't quite understand what they tell me.

For some, this sense of "shame" associated with not being sufficiently Japanese was also caused by a lack of Japanese cultural knowledge, which sometimes led to acute public embarrassment. Tadashi's following account is a case in point:

> This is one of the greatest difficulties I have in Japan. Because I can't read Japanese and don't know some basic things about Japan, I always have to ask these obvious things in public and in restaurants because everything is in Japanese. When I ask, the Japanese quickly note that I'm a foreigner and explain it to you. But at times, it's really embarrassing and I end up feeling ashamed. One time, I was in a Japanese store and couldn't read the label on a product. So I went up to the store owner and asked if you can eat it raw. The owner replied in a loud voice, "No, no, you can't eat this raw!" I was embarrassed and felt like all the other Japanese customers were looking at me like I was some kind of idiot.

For Wilson, a Japanized nikkeijin who was especially concerned about mixing in with the Japanese, the embarrassment of his cultural differences even extended to body comportment and dress:

> In cities with few [Japanese] Brazilians like Tokyo, I feel ashamed if I am dressed like a Brazilian with sporty clothes. I try to pick up Japanese attitudes and forms of behavior as much as possible and talk softly in Portuguese with my wife in the trains. I don't want to be seen as a foreigner and looked at peculiarly by the Japanese in the train. I feel ashamed and out of place when this happens.

For some of these individuals, insufficient cultural assimilation in Japan was a source of not only ethnic insecurity and embarrassment but also feelings of inadequacy and even inferiority. My roommate, Leonardo, who worked as an ethnic liaison at a labor broker firm, was particularly sensitive to this:

> This feeling of inferiority is something the [Japanese] Brazilians are troubled with. Because we are [Japanese] descendants, most of us feel this pressure that we should be culturally more Japanese than we are. So I tried to learn as much Japanese here as possible. But we still feel inferior and deficient. This is another reason why we have psychological problems in Japan.

PANELAS AND PANELINHAS: INTERNAL CONFLICT WITHIN THE JAPANESE BRAZILIAN IMMIGRANT COMMUNITY

Those who retain a Japanese cultural orientation in Japan not only experience the difficulties of conforming to external Japanese assimilative pressures but also have to endure considerable negative social pressure from their nikkeijin peers. Although the immigrant community is critical for the successful ethnic adjustment of the Japanese Brazilians (as shown in the previous chapter), even the most cohesive and supportive community has its internal conflicts and cleavages that can cause problems for some of its members.

Because most of the Japanese Brazilians live in a socially egalitarian immigrant community where previous differences in social class, economic wealth, and educational level are not openly apparent (see chapter 3), some of my informants felt that there is greater cohesion and unity among themselves in Japan than in Brazil. Even outside the factory, over half of the nikkeijin have very close relationships with Japanese Brazilians living in their neighborhoods (Kitagawa 1997). However, other informants spoke of the fragmentation and conflict that occurs even within such a socioeconomically homogeneous community and how different groups of Japanese Brazilians create socially closed cliques (*panelas* or *panelinhas*).[2]

---

[2]Amazingly, one survey found that the number of respondents reporting "discrimination" among the Japanese Brazilians was almost as high as the number who felt discriminated against by the Japanese (Nishioka 1995).

This disunity and factionalism is reported to be greater in areas or factories where there are more Japanese Brazilians, in contrast to places where they are limited in number and therefore remain *bem unidos* (well united) (see also Ishi 1994:35). Frequently, the ethnic community is "cohesive" within each personal network of family, relatives, and friends, but between these cliques, social divisions and separations remain.

In fact, it seems that whenever any type of social class differentiation emerges among the Japanese Brazilians, it becomes the source of conflict and even animosity. As discussed in chapter 3, considerable resentment is directed toward those of previously higher social class status in Brazil who differentiate themselves in Japan from those who were less privileged. In addition, nikkeijin who lavishly spend the money they earn in Japan on cars and other consumer goods and display their instant wealth are sometimes resented by the others. Since a number of those who engage in such ostentatious consumption were poorer in Brazil and therefore wish to immediately indulge themselves with their suddenly enhanced purchasing power, richer Japanese Brazilians who are diligently saving money by maintaining a frugal and spartan lifestyle in Japan can find themselves materially less well-off than their formerly poorer counterparts. There is also some tension between nikkeijin who have been in Japan for an extended period and immigrant newcomers. Similar divisions and antagonisms have been observed among the Brazilian immigrant community in the United States (cf. Martes 2000:166–69).[3]

The Anatomy of an Ethnic "Ass Kisser": Negative Group Sanctions Against Nikkeijin Who Try to "Act Japanese"

In the Japanese Brazilian case, however, the most notable internal conflict within the immigrant community is between those "ethnic resisters" who remain "*brasileiros*" and openly assert their counteridentity and those who attempt a more ethnically assimilative approach by measuring their ethnic success in majority Japanese terms (cf. Ishi 1994:46). However, this is not only because the latter enjoy much better ethnic acceptance in Japanese society due to their greater cultural abilities. Such differences generate so

---

[3]Among Brazilian immigrants in New York, schisms have been created between those from different regions in Brazil and between powerless newcomers and oldcomers who have already started small businesses and employ their compatriots (see Margolis 1994:chapter 9).

much social tension because of the considerable instrumental socioeconomic advantages that result from culturally assimilative ethnic behavior. Those Japanized nikkeijin who openly display and demonstrate their Japanese language and cultural abilities are able to improve their social class status in Japan by obtaining higher-level jobs with better pay either as minisupervisors (*tantosha*) and translators for nikkeijin production workers or as liaisons and assistants in company or local government offices. As Pierre Bourdieu notes (1984), socioeconomic mobility requires a certain amount of accumulated cultural capital, which becomes a symbolic marker for class distinctions. The culturally Japanized nikkeijin are able to reap considerable economic and occupational rewards in Japan, in contrast to their less fortunate compatriots, who resist Japanese cultural incorporation and continue to be marginalized as low-class factory workers.

Although cultural assimilation is therefore much more *socially adaptive* as a strategy of class mobility compared to ethnic resistance, it entails considerable personal costs, making it a less successful form of *psychological adjustment.* The nikkeijin who have been promoted from assembly line jobs to become supervisory tantosha because of their "Japaneseness" become the target of much resentment and jealousy from their less assimilated peers, making them vulnerable to personal alienation from their own ethnic group. They are commonly referred to as "*puxa sacos*" (that is, "ass kissers") by other Japanese Brazilians and are usually portrayed as annoying and self-serving people who attempt to get ahead at the expense of their fellow nikkeijin through ethnically obsequious behavior toward the Japanese. The critical assessment of one of my informants in Kawasaki was rather typical:

> There are those who are Japanese speakers and obtain the confidence of the Japanese. Therefore, they are assigned as leaders of the [Japanese] Brazilians and receive better salaries not because they have more ability or have personal qualities, but just because they speak Japanese. So they try to get ahead by stepping on the others who don't speak Japanese. They make themselves look good to the Japanese by saying bad things about other Brazilians and distorting the situation when reporting to the [Japanese] supervisor. Such people are called puxa sacos because they defend the Japanese company at the expense of their fellow Brazilians so that they can get more money.

Indeed, the tantosha are sometimes subject to ostracism and even harassment from the Japanese Brazilians they have been instructed to supervise.

Attempts by Japanese employers to promote certain nikkeijin workers are sometimes thwarted by the serious internal ethnic conflicts that ensue. One manager of a company that employs female nikkeijin workers spoke about his experiences:

> One time, we put one of the experienced nikkeijin workers in a supervisory position because she spoke very good Japanese. However, we soon found out that she was being constantly harassed and mistreated by the other nikkeijin workers who refused to listen to her. We felt so sorry for her that we simply had no choice but to demote her and put her back on the assembly line again as a simple worker.

Another employer spoke more generally about this problem among his nikkeijin workers:

> If a Japanese supervisor gives them an order, they do what they are told without problems. But they refuse to accept each others' supervision. There are those nikkeijin who work better or have studied Japanese and can translate for us. But when we try to get them to assist the others, conflicts occur. Sometimes, they get angry at each other and we have to separate them. We have never had conflicts between Japanese and nikkeijin workers. Only among the nikkeijin workers have conflicts occurred.

"Brazilians don't want to take orders from other Brazilians," one of my nikkeijin informants observed about his co-workers. "If one person is privileged over the others, it becomes a reason to fight because of *inveja* (jealousy). I think the Japanese realize this." Fortunately, I did not witness such overt conflicts at Toyama because our tantosha was mainly a translator who worked in the manager's office and was not put in the difficult position of giving orders to her compatriots on the assembly line. Yet, even she was alienated from the other Japanese Brazilians, who never accepted her into any of their social groups during work breaks (despite her numerous friendly overtures). During lunch hour, she was forced to eat alone.

Of course, those Japanized nikkeijin who work as liaisons in labor broker companies or in local government offices because of their bilingual abilities have similar experiences. Fortunately for them, they are not in constant contact with nikkeijin workers in the factories. However, most of the "white-collar" Japanese Brazilians I spoke with were also quite conscious of the envy and jealousy directed toward them from their lower-status ethnic peers who are stuck in assembly line jobs. My roommate,

Leonardo, who worked as a liaison in the office of a labor broker firm, was very sensitive to such problems:

> People don't directly say it, but I always feel this jealousy. The others think I get paid much more for an easier and more comfortable office job just because I speak Japanese. My attitude toward those who are angry at me for having such a good job is: "Look, if you are so jealous, you should go out and learn Japanese yourself." If there are other qualified individuals, I would give them my job in a moment. In fact, I would rather work on the assembly line than do what I am doing now. A factory job is physically more difficult, but you don't have the stress that I constantly feel.

Such Japanese Brazilians are sometimes told by their employers never to reveal their higher salaries to other nikkeijin. Leonardo told me that when he is asked about his salary, he says he does not earn much more than those working on the assembly line. Even Debra, one of my informants who worked in the local Oizumi city office, reported that she is instructed not to speak about her salary to other Japanese Brazilians.

Not surprisingly, those Japanized nikkeijin who have been able to use their cultural and linguistic proficiency in Japan to become socioeconomically successful as ethnic business owners experience similar problems when they hire less-privileged nikkeijin as employees. Fabio, an owner of a Brazilian food distribution business in Kanagawa Prefecture, elaborated at length about this:

> When I first started hiring other [Japanese] Brazilians to work under me, I found that they were unwilling to take orders. I would tell them to do something and they wouldn't do it. Their attitude was: "You are Brazilian just like us. Why are you giving us orders?" I had lots of this until I was finally able to assert my authority. I sat them down one day and said, "Look, this is no way to run a business. Outside work, we can have normal relationships and socialize and have a good time. But on the job, you have to do your duty." After this, the problem receded.

Later on in the interview, Fabio spoke about the envy he receives from those Japanese Brazilians who work in the factories because of the higher socioeconomic status he has attained:

> Yes, I feel *ciúme* (envy) from the others. They don't like the fact that I am the same Brazilian as they are, but am in a higher status. They don't

like how I've succeeded in Japan by opening a business while they are still suffering in the factories. Sometimes they attack what I do, saying I am only a food peddler.

Those Japanized nikkeijin who have come to Japan as university students similarly face resentment from the nikkeijin dekasegi because of the social class disparities between them. One Japanese Brazilian graduate student described how he feels a lot of jealousy from his compatriots in the factories who tell him how nice his life must be in Japan because he receives money (from his fellowship) without working and does not face discrimination from the Japanese because of his higher middle-class status. In turn, he claimed that the nikkeijin who are graduate students are sometimes reluctant to interact with the dekasegi nikkeijin because they do not want to be associated with their low, working-class compatriots:

> The [Japanese Brazilian] *ryugakusei* (foreign university students) tend to cluster together and don't associate with the dekasegi. Consciously, we don't necessarily want to distance ourselves from them, but unconsciously, we do. It's not that we don't like the dekasegi. If you ask the ryugakusei whether they cluster together because they wish to avoid the dekasegi, they would quickly say, "Of course, not." But in actuality, it is because they do not want to be seen as low-class dekasegi in Japan.

Indeed, the tendency of higher-status migrants to distance themselves from their lower-status compatriots in the host society is rather common (see Glick Schiller and Fouron 1990:338).

Social class differences that arise in Japan because of differences in Japanese language and cultural ability are especially galling for those who were of higher socioeconomic status in Brazil but go to Japan and find that other nikkeijin who were previously of lower status can get better jobs there because they speak better Japanese. Postimmigration status differences are most galling when they represent an inversion of the premigratory class hierarchy. My roommate, Leonardo, gave an example:

> A person who was a doctor in São Paulo comes to Japan as a dekasegi and suddenly finds he is subordinate to this other fellow who was nothing more than a farmer in the countryside but gets a higher position in Japan because he happens to speak Japanese better. He says, "Look at this, a person who was uneducated in Brazil comes to Japan and is better off than I am!"

Such cases are not uncommon because those born and raised in rural Japanese colônias in Brazil (who are from an agricultural background) speak better Japanese than their middle-class counterparts in the cities, where Japanese ethnic communities are much less cohesive and the nikkeijin tend to be much more assimilated to Brazilian society (see also Maeyama 1996:22).[4]

Migration can invert previous class differences in this manner because the criteria that determine socioeconomic status in premigratory and post-migratory contexts are completely different. In contrast to the importance of educational and family background in Brazil, Japanese language ability and cultural competence have become the only significant determinants of socio-occupational status in Japan because the nikkeijin cannot advance to more "skilled" and higher-paid jobs unless they can speak Japanese. As a result, an intense socioeconomic status rivalry is initiated among them over their relative degrees of "Japaneseness." In fact, those nikkeijin who have some command of Japanese sometimes even show off their abilities,[5] contrasting themselves proudly with other nikkeijin in Japan who can only speak Portuguese. A couple times, I saw groups of Japanese Brazilians watching Japanese television and trying to "out-laugh" each other in order to demonstrate that they understood what was happening in the program, even when it was not particularly funny. My roommate, Leonardo, the bilingual employee of a labor broker firm, frequently told me that the nikkeijin in Oizumi are of a "lower level," meaning they are less "Japanese" than nikkeijin in other regions and therefore stuck in low-level jobs. One is reminded of Frantz Fanon's description of aggressive status competition among Antillean blacks based on comparative self-evaluations on a scale of relative whiteness (1967:211–15).

In fact, these status rivalries and resentments over who was more "Japanese" did not always involve visible differences in social class position. The stigmatic "puxa saco" label was used to refer not only to Japanese Brazilian factory supervisors and office workers but also to anyone who spoke Japanese well and tried to gain the cultural favor of the Japanese in the factory. Even if they had not actually obtained better jobs with higher

---

[4]This correlation between assimilation and socioeconomic status has been found among Japanese Americans as well (Levine and Montero 1973). It has also been noted by other researchers (Spiro 1955; De Vos and Suárez-Orozco 1990).
[5]Even when I conducted interviews in Portuguese with such nikkeijin, they would insert numerous Japanese phrases, demonstrating their command of Japanese to me.

incomes, the mere suspicion that they were trying to climb the socioeconomic ladder with their assimilation-oriented behavior was enough to cause tension and jealousy. Consider the following statement from one of my informants:

> Envy between the Brazilians is a very grave problem here and it causes fights among us and ruins friendships. For example, the [Japanese] supervisor talks only to certain [Japanese] Brazilians because they speak Japanese. Then the other Brazilians become angry, saying how that person is trying to get ahead at their expense just because he speaks Japanese, and they criticize him behind his back.

This type of status resentment can occur between nisei and sansei as well. Celso, a sansei who identified himself as ethnically Brazilian, was especially sensitive about this:

> In big factories with lots of [Japanese] Brazilians, you have nisei who think they are more Japanese because they speak the language and act more Japanese than the sansei. They try to affirm their Japanese descent, as if the sansei were inferior or something. So they want to pass on top of the other Japanese Brazilians by trying to work better and by getting the approval of the Japanese. Some engage in this kind of unfair behavior.

At times, it seemed that anyone with longer experience in the factories or who simply worked harder or showed some initiative on the job could be seen as currying favor with the Japanese and branded as a subservient, self-serving "ass kisser." For example, one nisei mestiço had this to say:

> Some people have been in the factory longer and want to stay on top of other [Japanese] Brazilians who are newer. So they kiss ass with the *hancho* (group leader) and the other Japanese to get their favor. This is especially true if they speak Japanese. Those Brazilians who have been in Japan longer think they are superior in the factory.

"Those nikkeijin who show self-initiative and responsibility, or do more than they are told get harassed by the others," one Japanese manager remarked. One of his nikkeijin workers confirmed this by saying, "If you do extra work in the factory, you are called a puxa saco. Such individuals are seen as trying to please the Japanese by doing more work than the other

Brazilians and trying to get ahead at their expense. So when we have free time, we just stare at the clock and do nothing." Undoubtedly, such is the "narcissism of small differences" that Freud once spoke about. Celso elaborated on this extreme sensitivity among his Japanese Brazilian peers at his factory:

> If you speak Japanese better than the others, you are a puxa saco. If you have more experience in the factory, you are a puxa saco. If you can do the job better than the others, you are a puxa saco. If you continue working two minutes after the factory bell rings, you are a puxa saco. This is how it is. It is just a human tendency.

Oreos, Bananas, Coconuts, and Ass Kissers: Negative Minorities and Ethnic Loyalties

Negative minorities in general frequently impose group sanctions against members who seek upward socioeconomic mobility through cultural assimilation (see Berreman 1964; De Vos 1992:233–65; Fordham and Ogbu 1986; Hagendoorn 1993:42; Simpson and Yinger 1972:208; Zhou 1997:989–90). In fact, each negative minority group seems to have colorful derogatory labels to ostracize such upwardly mobile individuals. Among African Americans, students who do well in school and attempt to succeed socially on majority white terms are accused of "acting white"[6] or simply called "brainiacs" (Fordham and Ogbu 1986). The other frequent term is "Oreo" (Tatum 1987:100), the analogy here being that like Oreo cookies, such individuals look black on the outside but are actually white inside. Asian Americans in the past who have tried to get ahead by adopting white American cultural behavior have similarly been labeled "bananas." Among Mexican Americans, such individuals are stigmatized as "coconuts." Of course, such negative sanctions operate not only among ethnic minorities but also among members of lower social classes. For instance, Paul Willis (1981) has observed how British working-class schoolchildren who study hard and succeed in school are teased by the other kids and called "ear 'oles" because they listen so attentively in class.

The strength of such sanctions against minority individuals with assimilationist tendencies depends on the level of ethnic antagonism that exists

---

[6]The "acting white" term may be used among some Native American groups as well (see Berreman 1964).

between the minority group and mainstream society. Among ethnic minorities that have experienced a long legacy of discrimination and social
disadvantage and have developed stronger counteridentities in opposition
to the majority society, the negative pressures and sanctions against such
individuals can be quite intense, significantly impeding their social class
mobility (see Fordham and Ogbu [1986] in the case of African Americans).
They may be seen as ethnic traitors who are willing to betray their own minority group by assimilating to majority society for their own selfish instrumental gain and socioeconomic advantage.

As a "weak" negative minority that does not suffer anywhere near the
ethnic denigration experienced by other castelike minorities, the nikkeijin
do not feel very strong antagonism toward the Japanese. However, as seen
above, the negative sanctions against assimilation-minded, upwardly mobile nikkeijin are so intense that they were sometimes seen not only as "ass
kissers" but also as antinikkeijin ethnic betrayers who have switched sides
and joined the Japanese.[7]

One reason socially mobile nikkeijin immigrants are ostracized and
generate such tension and conflict is that they overtly undermine the ideology of socioeconomic equality that has developed in the Japanese Brazilian immigrant community (chapter 3). As mentioned in the previous
chapter, one dominant way in which many nikkeijin cope with and psychologically adjust to their loss of social class status in Japan is by seeking
refuge in the shared consciousness that all of their fellow Japanese Brazilians suffer equally from a uniformly low and subordinate socioeconomic
position as unskilled dekasegi. Because this ideology of immigrant egalitarianism has become such an integral part of their ethnic experience and
adaptation in Japan, the fact that certain Japanese Brazilians have attained
higher socioeconomic status simply because of their better Japanese cultural abilities seems eminently unfair to those who remain economically
subordinated. As a result, even minor social class differences that have
emerged among them become a source of considerable resentment and so-

---

[7]In this respect, the tantoshas are subject to special vilification. One of my informants voiced
this sentiment most clearly:

> There is this sense that those [Japanese Brazilians] who become supervisors are no
> longer on the side of the Brazilians but work for the Japanese. All they care about is
> pleasing the Japanese because they work for the Japanese company now. So they no
> longer care about helping us and are willing to say bad things about us to show their
> loyalty to the Japanese.

cial tension. As one informant remarked, "We are not supposed to care about our low status in Japan because we are supposedly all equal in Japan as mere peons. Therefore, we don't like it when status differences begin to appear."

PASSING AND ITS PROBLEMS

As a result, the assimilation-minded Brazilian nikkeijin who adapt to their negative minority status by "acting Japanese" enjoy the instrumental benefits of better jobs and higher socioeconomic status, but at the risk of conflict and alienation from their ethnic peers, forcing them to forgo their expressive need for ethnic companionship and group belonging. In this manner, despite its socially adaptive advantages, the adjustment of assimilation-oriented individuals is fraught with a number of psychological difficulties.

Undoubtedly, these problems are exacerbated for Japanized nikkeijin who not only accommodate themselves to Japanese cultural norms but also adopt a more extreme form of assimilation by attempting to completely pass as "Japanese." Passing represents total behavioral assimilation where minority individuals attempt to be completely accepted by the majority group by concealing their different ethnic origins and cultural background.[8] Although passing was not possible for the Brazilian nikkeijin in Brazil because they were essentialized as an ethnic minority by their distinctive racial physiognomy, since race ceases to be a salient ethnic marker in Japan, their ethnicity is deessentialized, making it more eminently contestable through the active manipulation of cultural behavior.

The Anatomy of a Passer

There were four individuals in my interview sample who were passing as "Japanese" or had attempted to do so in the past. All of them had the ability to act and speak Japanese virtually like a native[9] and worked in the offices of municipal governments, Japanese companies, or ethnic assistance

---

[8]"Passing" is a term that was first used to refer to light-skinned blacks who passed as white (Lee 1955).
[9]It was no coincidence that three of the four had been born and raised in Japanese colônias in Brazil, where the Japanese language and customs tend to be better preserved than in the cities.

organizations. Because of their linguistic and cultural abilities and white-collar jobs, they were not ethnically excluded in Japan and were not alienated from Japanese society as socioeconomically marginalized migrant factory workers. Therefore, they had much more extensive contact and meaningful friendships with the Japanese. Since these individuals were performing the valuable function of cross-cultural liaison for the Japanese, they were appreciated and respected and were not seen by the Japanese in a prejudicial manner as culturally alien and impoverished migrant workers.

Therefore, none of the four "passers" (Keiji, Michiko, Marcos, and Yasuo) had negative ethnic experiences in Japan typical of the nikkeijin in the factories. In fact, they generally did not share the negative and critical attitudes toward the Japanese commonly held by their ethnic peers. They spoke about cultural differences between the two ethnic groups in a more or less neutral tone or with the assumption that Japanese ways are more refined or better. In fact, there was a tendency among these individuals to side with the Japanese by taking a critical perspective toward other Japanese Brazilians when speaking of problems between the two ethnic groups. For instance, Keiji dismissed the common nikkeijin claim of Japanese ethnic discrimination as a figment of their imagination and felt that their excessive complaining about the Japanese is a means to cover up their own feelings of ethnic inadequacy. In fact, he even suggested that they return to Brazil if they do not like Japan. Likewise, Michiko did not agree with her peers that the Japanese are "cold" and "racist" and gave an objective account of why the Japanese Brazilians feel this way despite the lack of ill intent on the part of the Japanese. Marcos portrayed his Brazilian compatriots as spoiled immigrants who constantly complain in Japan and do not know how privileged they are compared to other foreign workers.

Because of the lack of negative ethnic and social class experiences among these four passers, they did not develop strong Brazilian counteridentities in Japan. Instead, they continued to identify with the positive aspects of Japaneseness and maintained a "Japanese" ethnic consciousness to a certain extent. In addition, they perceived "Brazilianness" more negatively than did other Japanese Brazilians. Some of them had maintained their Japaneseness to a greater extent in Brazil than other nikkeijin because of their stronger negative perceptions of Brazilian society. In addition, because of their greater contact with the Japanese in Japan, they were more aware of derogatory Japanese attitudes toward the Brazilian nikkeijin and their Brazilian cultural behavior. Therefore, since they had the cultural ability to act completely Japanese, they not only complied with Japanese behavioral norms but also concealed their Brazilian nikkeijin background in order to avoid the stigma of negative minority status.

One of these individuals, Yasuo, spoke about why he tried to pass as Japanese in the past:

> When I came to Japan, I spoke Japanese well enough, but had an accent. So I was often asked who I was. They thought I was maybe from another region of Japan and was speaking a local dialect. When I told them I was a foreigner, their attitude would change and I would notice this resistance from them.

Because he was seen as a Brazilian foreigner, Yasuo felt that he was sometimes treated as a cultural imbecile:

> It was a real hassle when people saw me as a foreigner because they would figure I didn't know much about Japan and would ask things like whether I eat *natto*.[10] They would also instruct me like a child. For instance, I went to the house of my [Japanese] wife's friend and made some noise with the china when eating. Her friends told me that Japanese don't do this when they eat. I didn't like this kind of treatment because they would assume I behave differently because I'm a foreigner. If the Japanese do something wrong, they don't notice, but if it's a foreigner, they do. Also, sometimes I would be asked silly questions about Brazil.

In order to avoid such negative ethnic consequences, he decided it was more socially advantageous to simply act as if he were a native Japanese:

> I figured that it was easier to get along in Japan if I wasn't seen as a foreigner, so I hid my nikkeijin identity a lot at first. I was very Japaneselike from the beginning and could act like them. I realized that if I didn't tell people I was from Brazil, they would simply assume I was Japanese. Although they would notice my different accent, I would tell them I am from Fukushima, where my parents came from originally. I tried to copy Japanese behavior a lot.

---

[10]Natto are fermented soybeans that are eaten with rice. This is seen as one of the most distinctive of Japanese foods.

Keiji had similar experiences of passing, although he does not actively hide his Brazilian background if asked. This type of passing can be called "passive passing":

> I deal with the Japanese as if I were Japanese as well. When formal introductions are made, I just say my Japanese name and say "*Yoroshiku onegai shimasu*" [a standard Japanese greeting] but don't say I'm Brazilian unless I'm asked directly. The Japanese can't tell I'm Brazilian if I don't mention it. But if asked, I don't hide it. Sometimes, the Japanese can tell I'm not from Gunma Prefecture, so they ask where in Japan I'm from. At this point, I sometimes say, "Actually, I'm Brazilian."

When Passing Must Be Perfect

In this manner, passing as Japanese allows individuals to avoid the negative aspects of being treated as a Brazilian foreigner in Japan. However, those who adapt to Japanese society through this extreme form of assimilation face some serious personal difficulties.[11] Unlike other assimilation-minded nikkeijin, who simply accommodate themselves to Japanese ways for better social acceptance, those who pass must give a flawless Japanese cultural performance. Since they must suppress all visible signs of their Brazilianness by engaging in a constant and even obsessive process of ethnic self-monitoring, the stress associated with trying to "act Japanese" can be considerable. In addition to perfect command of the language and cultural behavior, total assimilation even requires self-control over the body. For instance, Marcos, one of the ethnic passers, mentioned to me that not only had he changed his clothes and demeanor in Japan to comply with Japanese behavioral patterns, he was even careful about the manner in which he walked in order to avoid being seen as a foreigner.

Therefore, those who pass continuously experience a sense of unease that their ethnic disguise will fail and face the constant threat of being "unmasked." As a result of such pressures, Marcos even told me that he used to experience severe nervousness about being ethnically detected as a

---

[11]The psychological problems of passing have been examined extensively by George De Vos (see De Vos and Suárez-Orozco 1990:chapter 7) as well as Erving Goffman (1963:73–91).

Brazilian foreigner in Japan. In fact, when he lived in a small town in the countryside without many other Japanese Brazilians, he developed an almost neurotic fear of being constantly "looked at" by the Japanese:

> When I walked around town, I always had this fear that other Japanese were looking at me strangely. They wouldn't look me straight in the eye but would just give me a sideways glance. I would wonder, why am I always being looked at? Can they tell I am a foreigner? Despite these efforts I made to appear Japanese, was there still something wrong or strange with me?

Indeed, there have even been reports of some Japanese Brazilians suffering from neurosis in Japan because of the cultural pressures they face to act and think Japanese (*Yomiuri Shimbun*, October 21, 1991).

Because of the strong desire to pass as "Japanese" among such individuals and the considerable amount of self-imposed pressure this generates, when their ethnic disguise eventually fails and they are discovered as "not Japanese," the sense of personal inadequacy can be quite intense. The most poignant case was that of Michiko, who did not have sufficient cultural skills to successfully pass when she first came to Japan:

> The first several months in Japan were really tough for me because I thought I would be welcomed here as a Japanese. I wasn't very emotionally stable back then. I would try to act as Japanese as possible. I would dress like them, try to speak just like them, and not reveal to them that I was from Brazil. But it didn't go smoothly and people could eventually tell I was a foreigner. I would go home deeply troubled and would get depressed. Sometimes I would even cry about this. I felt that something about my Japanese upbringing was inadequate because I couldn't be seen as Japanese in my parents' own country.

However, even when Michiko's Japanese became good enough to be indistinguishable from native Japanese, there would still be instances when her foreign origins would be revealed, to her chagrin:

> When I tried to become completely Japanese and didn't say I'm from Brazil, things I don't know that all Japanese should know always came up. The Japanese would be befuddled and wonder, "As a Japanese, why

> doesn't she know such a thing?" I would end up being embarrassed. This also happens when I cannot read certain Japanese characters that I should know.

The Consequences of Passing: Ethnic Alienation and Self-Hate

In addition to dealing with the pressures of assimilation and the constant threat of ethnic detection, those who attempt to pass are alienated from their own ethnic group like other assimilation-oriented nikkeijin. Although the four individuals examined here were in daily contact with Japanese Brazilians whom they assisted at work, they were partly or completely isolated from the nikkeijin immigrant community outside of the workplace and associated predominantly with the Japanese. Yasuo and Michiko were married to Japanese and hardly had any Japanese Brazilian friends. Marcos and Keiji mentioned that they occasionally associated with Brazilians, but their social activities were almost exclusively with the Japanese. Marcos also had a Japanese girlfriend. As Yasuo described, passing as Japanese required him to sever his former links to the Japanese Brazilian community because they would give away his true ethnicity:

> Once I decided I did not want to be seen as a Brazilian foreigner in Japan, I cut my relationships with other Brazilians and continued to associate only with Japanese so that I could learn Japanese and Japanese ways better. I knew that as long as I stayed with other Brazilians, I would be seen as a foreigner and not be accepted as Japanese.

Like other Japanized nikkeijin who were harassed as puxa sacos for assimilating to Japanese society in order to get ahead, the four ethnic "passers" also spoke about how other Japanese Brazilians envied and resented their privileged socioeconomic status or had simply stopped speaking with them. Again, the instrumental economic benefits gained from assimilation and passing were accompanied by the psychological costs of ethnic isolation and the loss of companionship (see De Vos 1992:chapter 7).

However, passing entails another negative psychological consequence—the implicit acceptance of majority society's derogatory images and attitudes about their own ethnic group. Because those nikkeijin who pass have adopted the cultural standards of the Japanese majority as positive, if not superior to their own, this can cause them to view the cultural characteristics of the Japanese Brazilians in a disparaging manner, ultimately leading to the internalization of Japanese ethnic prejudices about the nikkeijin.[12] In this manner, individuals who assimilate and pass sometimes become prejudiced against their own ethnic kindred, which may result in the development of a negative ethnic self-image and lead to a type of ethnic "self-hate" (Allport 1979:150–52; De Vos and Suárez-Orozco 1990:254; Tajfel 1982). This has been noted among other negative minority groups such as the Korean Japanese (Wagatsuma 1981) and American blacks (Allport 1979:29–46; Simpson and Yinger 1972:195), as well as Jews and Antillean blacks (Fanon 1967:182–83; 191–93).

In fact, even among those Japanized nikkeijin who did *not* attempt to pass, I noticed a tendency to criticize and even disparage other Japanese Brazilians from a Japanese cultural standpoint for being too "Brazilian" in Japan. This represents not only an awareness but a partial acceptance of Japanese ethnic prejudices about the nikkeijin. Some of my Japanized nikkeijin informants would mention how there are certain Japanese Brazilians who know nothing about Japan or the language and disobey Japanese customs by engaging in scandalous behavior and by *bagunçando o país* (messing up the country), thus worsening the reputation of all nikkeijin in the eyes of the Japanese.[13] Mestiços were sometimes singled out for special criticism, the implication being that they cause problems because they are less Japanese and even commit petty crimes in Japan (like shoplifting). Others blamed Japanese Brazilian youth who have no sense of responsibility on the job and do not work diligently or honestly. For instance, Jorge, an older nisei man, had this to say about the other Japanese Brazilians who worked in his factory section:

> I work with a bad group of young [Japanese] Brazilians who have no sense of responsibility and don't take their work seriously. For example, they let screws fall into the machines and don't care if the part is firmly attached or not. So the machines made in our section always have defects and this creates prejudices among the Japanese about us. They end up thinking that all of us are like this—lazy and irresponsible on the job.

---

[12]As De Vos (1976b:347) observes, "the closer a subordinate group gets to assimilation, the greater the degree to which the images (whether positive or negative) of the dominant group may be internalized" (see also Epstein 1978:102–103 and Tajfel 1982).

[13]This occurs among other negative minority and immigrant groups as well (Jaspars and Warnaen 1982; Mandel 1989; Tatum 1987). For instance, Mandel shows how Turkish guest workers in Germany point to less well mannered and educated Turkish rural folk as acting in ways that cause German prejudice and xenophobia against Turks in general.

Others made negative remarks about how their compatriots behave in the streets:

> There are those [Japanese] Brazilians who don't accept Japanese ways and behave in a scandalous manner. Even in Brazil, they don't behave this way, but they do in Japan, embarrassing other [Japanese] Brazilians who don't act like this. But the Japanese see this and it calls attention to all of us as Brazilians who behave badly in public. This really lowers the Japanese image of Brazil and increases discrimination against us.

Of course, this tendency to disparage members of their own ethnic group is simply taken to a greater extreme among those who attempt to pass as Japanese. Like the others, Marcos expressed strong disapproval toward his own ethnic kinsmen who flaunted their Brazilianness in public. However, the negative comments he made sounded like they could have come straight from the mouth of one of my *Japanese* informants:

> When I first got to Japan, I lived in a little country town with very few nikkeijin, but later on, there was an increase in the number of dekasegi. You had these groups of nikkeijin wandering around town who did not walk or dress like the Japanese. And they always moved around in big groups and took over the town. They would speak differently—really loud like Brazilians. The Japanese say the nikkeijin are really noisy—it's embarrassing. I think it's obvious that the Japanese are scared of them. Even as a nikkeijin, I found them scary.

Like other Japanized nikkeijin, Marcos distances himself from those Japanese Brazilians who supposedly act in such ethnically inappropriate ways, implying that the Japanese ethnic prejudices he has internalized apply to other nikkeijin and not to him, since he is much more "Japanese." By keeping his own identity separate from other nikkeijin, Marcos is able to protect his own self-image and self-esteem.[14] However, this is considerably harder to do in regard to Japanese ethnic prejudices that apply to *all* nikkeijin. In such cases, the development of a certain negative ethnic

---

[14]This contrasts with minority individuals who have accepted the ethnic prejudices of the dominant majority while their identities remain inextricably tied to their own minority group (cf. Herman 1970).

self-image may become unavoidable. The most striking example of this I encountered was Keiji. At one point, his tendency to judge his dekasegi compatriots from the standpoint of Japanese ethnic attitudes caused him to characterize them in a typical Japanese manner as low-class people without ability. However, since he was also a nikkeijin dekasegi, it was apparent that he partly saw himself in this derogatory manner as well. An excerpt from our interview is quite revealing in this respect:

> What the Japanese say about us is correct—about how the descendants of those Japanese who emigrated to Brazil but had no ability are the ones coming back to Japan as dekasegi. My high-status nikkeijin friends who were well educated and are company managers are obviously not coming to Japan to earn money. Only those who had no ability in Brazil and couldn't live well there do this kind of thing. If they had ability, they would work hard in Japan and would learn Japanese culture. But few do this. Instead, they cover up their own inadequacy by criticizing the Japanese. Most dekasegi are like this, although there are some good people. Only those who were good for nothings (*roku de nashi*) in Brazil become dekasegi. *Good for nothings like me.* I took it easy in Brazil and didn't like to study. [italics mine]

The Passing of Passing:[15] *Surface Assimilation Without Full Cultural Internalization*

Given these various negative psychological consequences associated with passing, it is not surprising that even the most Japanized nikkeijin eventually experiences "assimilation blues." As a result, attempts to pass as Japanese among nikkeijin immigrants seem to be relatively short-lived. As George De Vos (1982b:29) observes, "many individuals sooner or later find it psychologically more tolerable to drop their façade." Among the four individuals in my sample, three were no longer passing and had decided to properly reveal instead of conceal their Brazilian identities. Since the social advantages of passing are not very significant for the Japanese Brazilians, they realize that the negative psychological feelings that arise from attempting to become completely Japanese are not worth its marginal social

[15]Title taken from De Vos (1992:chapter 8).

benefits. Although passing definitely improves their ethnic reception and acceptance by the Japanese, it does not affect their employment chances. In fact, those who obtain the most privileged jobs as cultural liaisons in company and government offices do so not because they pass as "Japanese" but precisely because they are Brazilian nikkeijin who have bicultural abilities. In addition, openly revealing one's Brazilian origins does not lead to any overt ethnic denigration or social discrimination from the Japanese, which is not the case with some other negative minorities.

All three former passers emphasized how they eventually decided to affirm their Brazilian identities in Japan in order to avoid the psychological stress and pressure of conforming to Japanese cultural norms. Michiko explained:

> If I'm seen as a foreigner, I have more freedom in Japan and can behave without always worrying whether I am acting properly Japanese or not. Before, I wanted to be seen as Japanese, but now, I always introduce myself by saying "I'm Brazilian," and prefer to be seen as Brazilian rather than Japanese. That way, I feel I can make a mistake speaking the language or act in the wrong manner without being censured. I feel much less pressure in Japan now because I reveal my Brazilian identity.

By introducing herself properly as "Brazilian," Michiko also no longer has to worry about socially embarrassing and awkward situations when her attempts at ethnic disguise would fail:

> Before, when I related to people as if I were Japanese, it was difficult. When our conversation would deepen and I wouldn't understand some Japanese nuance, the Japanese would become troubled and confused. Eventually, when they found out who I was, they would feel deceived. But if I tell them from the beginning that I am Brazilian, I don't have to constantly worry about this. I feel much more secure simply being Brazilian.

Yasuo had similar reasons why he came to dislike concealing his true identity as a nikkeijin. Indeed, individuals like Michiko and Yasuo fully realize that true passing is indeed extremely difficult, requiring much more than the cultural ability to hide one's ethnicity by acting completely Japanese. Ultimately, their ethnic deception has to go further. As Michiko recounted:

> Even if I could successfully hide my Brazilian background, I found that I couldn't avoid talking about the past when having conversations with the Japanese, and for me, all of my past has been spent in Brazil. This simply meant I couldn't avoid talking about Brazil.

Therefore, passing for Michiko meant concealing her entire previous life and essentially becoming a person without a past. Otherwise, she would have had to invent a completely "false" past, a tall order for even the most imaginative and creative ethnic passer. Few are willing to engage in the extensive level of deception that true passing requires.

However, the assertion of a Brazilian "counteridentity" among these former ethnic passers is done in a less apparent and visible manner compared to some of their more Brazilianized compatriots and basically involves introducing themselves as "Brazilians" or "foreigners." In this manner, the decision not to pass as Japanese and the strengthening of their Brazilian self-consciousness do not result in a subsequent change to a more "Brazilian" type of behavior. Instead, their Brazilian identities are experienced and maintained primarily in internal consciousness and are usually not intentionally displayed or asserted in overt public behavior, which remains "Japanese" in appearance and demeanor. Such discrepancies between ethnic identity and behavior are quite common among minorities (see Mitchell 1974).

This type of ethnic adaptation, in which minority individuals conform to majority cultural patterns in their external behavior while internally retaining a separate and independent ethnic consciousness, can be called "surface assimilation."[16] Both Michiko and Keiji claimed that regardless of how much they acted Japanese, their inner thinking and self-consciousness would remain Brazilian.[17] Thus, behavioral assimilation is not always accompanied by the full internalization of majority cultural norms and attitudes and may not influence or affect the depths of the inner self, whose attitudes and beliefs remain independent of majority cultural pressures.

---

[16]Tajfel (1982:246–47) calls this type of surface assimilation "accommodation" and claims that it is the weakest of the four types of assimilation he identifies.

[17]However, Michiko told me that she sometimes found it difficult to maintain an independent Brazilian ethnic identity because her social contacts were only with other Japanese (including at home, as her husband was Japanese) and she therefore had few opportunities to experience and express her Brazilianness in Japan. She was even afraid that she would "lose" her cultural differences and consciousness as a Brazilian.

A conceptual distinction must therefore be made between cultural "internalization," in which the individual acquires external cultural values as personal beliefs because they are thought to be true, proper, and correct, and the simple "learning" of culture, where individuals acquire and obey cultural norms but do not agree with them, or truly understand their meaning and the personal emotions they are intended to evoke (Spiro 1984:326). Those Japanese Brazilians who have passed in the past as Japanese have simply "learned" to comply with Japanese cultural norms while disagreeing with and, in fact, disliking some of them. Indeed, as we saw in chapter 2, many *Japanese* adapt to their social environment in a similar manner—while conforming to cultural norms of proper conduct on the surface, they remain acutely aware of their inner ura self of personal feelings and opinions, which remains independent from external social pressures. In other words, those Japanese Brazilians who have decided to "act Japanese" on the behavioral surface while maintaining a separate Brazilian ethnic identity may find that they are psychodynamically more "Japanese" than they actually suspect!

Using Milton Gordon's (1964) classic terminology, surface assimilation is a type of "behavioral" assimilation without "identificational" assimilation. This contrasts with "full assimilation," where minority individuals not only "learn" but also completely "internalize" majority cultural patterns so that an awareness of ethnic difference and an independent identity are eliminated. In this latter case, not only behavior but also inner consciousness is assimilated. It is quite likely that most ethnic minorities who "assimilate" settle on a type of surface assimilation in which external behavioral compliance is not necessarily accompanied by inner consent or the adoption of a majority identity.

ADAPTATION THROUGH DUAL ETHNIC LOYALTIES: ASSIMILATION AND REFERENCE GROUP "DISTANCING"

Of course, the categories of ethnic assimilation and ethnic resistance are not mutually exclusive, since the same individual can sometimes adapt to Japanese society in both ways depending on the situation. Some Japanese Brazilians maintain their "Brazilianness" and their ethnic loyalties among their nikkeijin peers while displaying assimilative behavior in the presence of the Japanese in order to gain the acceptance and trust of both groups.

The performance of ethnic identities constantly shifts depending on the social context. A few of the Japanized nikkeijin who maintained relationships with both the Japanese Brazilians and the Japanese adapted to their minority status in Japan by manipulating the ambiguity of their ethnicity and dichotomizing their ethnic behavior accordingly. For example, one of my Japanese Brazilian graduate student friends had a conspicuous habit of "adjusting" his clothing depending on whether he was meeting with a group of Japanese or Japanese Brazilians. It was remarkable how a properly restrained and well-mannered "Japanese" graduate student wearing a dress shirt and slacks could transform himself into a merry and even raucous "brasileiro" on a moment's notice, wearing a nationalist Brazilian T-shirt and laughing while speaking in Portuguese. Likewise, Martina described how her friend, Alice, engages in such dual ethnic behavior in the factory by acting very differently in front of the Japanese than she does with her nikkeijin fellows:

I'm sometimes bothered by how Alice changes her behavior. In front of us, she complains and criticizes the Japanese and shares our grievances. But when she is with a Japanese group, she bows and stays quiet, afraid to contradict what they say. For instance, even if she dislikes a type of Japanese food, she says she likes it. Even if she doesn't like the Japanese in the factory, she never shows this in front of them.

Such ethnic adaptation through the maintenance of dual ethnic loyalties is probably quite common among individuals of stigmatized ethnic groups and has been observed by Harald Eidheim (1969) among the Lappish minority in Norway and by Gerald Berreman (1964) among the Aleuts, an indigenous North American group. In this manner, minority individuals can enjoy the socioeconomic benefits of assimilation while avoiding the personal alienation and antagonism from their ethnic peers that usually accompany such behavior. Some of the ethnic passers who had the cultural ability to act as both Brazilian nikkeijin and "Japanese" undoubtedly manipulated their ethnic identity this way for instrumental purposes. As Keiji remarked succinctly, "I use my identity conveniently in Japan. When I'm with Brazilians, I act and feel Brazilian. When I'm with Japanese, I act and feel Japanese." This is somewhat analogous to the "identity prostitution" I engaged in as a fieldworker at Toyama.

CONCLUSION:
RESISTANCE VERSUS ASSIMILATION AS FORMS
OF ETHNIC ADAPTATION

The ethnic adaptation of any minority group involves considerable tension between those who oppose and resist majority cultural incorporation and those who tend toward more accommodative forms of ethnic behavior. Those nikkeijin who have resolved to ethnically resist their way through Japan regard the ethnic assimilators as ass kissers willing to sell out to the Japanese for selfish economic gain. In turn, the latter resent the ethnic resisters, who publicly flaunt their Brazilianness and scandalize the image of the nikkeijin in the eyes of the Japanese. Such internal ethnic divisions have been observed among various negative minorities, including the Korean Japanese, Burakumin, and Ainu in Japan (Lee and De Vos 1981; De Vos and Wagatsuma 1966; Siddle 1997), blacks in the Antilles (Fanon 1967), and Haitian immigrants in the United States (Portes and Stepick 1993:chapter 8).[18]

When faced with Japanese prejudices about the Brazilian cultural behavior of the nikkeijin and their perceived migrant poverty, the ethnic assimilators attempt to escape their stigmatized minority status by acting ethnically Japanese and thereby overcoming their marginalization as casual and unskilled factory workers through upward social mobility. In contrast, the ethnic resisters, who were more Brazilianized in Brazil and do not have the cultural ability to assimilate, react to Japanese ethnic and socioeconomic exclusion by retrenching themselves within the immigrant minority community and asserting a Brazilian nationalist counteridentity against the Japanese in an act of ethnic resistance, if not defiance.

Undoubtedly, the social tension between the ethnic resisters and assimilators occurs because both forms of ethnic adaptation have distinct advantages, as well as disadvantages. The majority who insist on their Brazilian cultural differences by displaying their Brazilianness in Japan are able to psychologically adjust to Japanese society with a minimum of personal disruption. However, such ethnic behavior proves to be socially maladaptive since it traps them in their low-status factory jobs, thus repro-

---

[18]White (1988:98–102) has found that Japanese who return from a business sojourn overseas also readapt to Japanese society through these two different strategies. One group are the "reassimilators," who attempt to hide their overseas experience in order to avoid being stigmatized for the cultural differences they may have acquired abroad. Another group attempts to adapt by exhibiting their differences as "internationals."

ducing their negative minority status and socioeconomic subordination. On the other hand, the Japanized nikkeijin who choose a path of relative assimilation experience less discrimination, better social acceptance from the Japanese, and the possibility of advancement to higher-level jobs. However, they face a number of complications on the psychological level, which are generally avoided by the more Brazilianized nikkeijin who are content with being minority. These include greater vulnerability to identity crisis and diffusion, the psychological stress of conforming to unfamiliar cultural patterns, and negative peer pressure, if not harassment from other Japanese Brazilians for their ethnic betrayal. In addition, those few who choose to pass as Japanese experience constant unease about being detected and ultimately become susceptible to the internalization of a negative ethnic self-image. However, even most of those who initially attempt to pass come to eventually acknowledge and assert a Brazilian identity because it makes their adjustment to Japanese society psychologically easier. As a result, most Japanese Brazilians are able to avoid the debilitating psychological consequences that can be associated with negative minority status.

Like most social science categories (including positive and negative minorities), ethnic resistance and assimilation are only ideal types, not absolute categories under which individuals should be rigidly and simplistically classified. However, instead of eliminating these binary categories as static, artificial, and essentialized, I have attempted to dynamize them. Such conceptual distinctions are merely extremes on a continuous spectrum. Most individuals fall somewhere in between or simply tend toward one side or the other (cf. Gans 1997). The last two chapters have shown the tremendous diversity in the ethnic behavioral responses of the Japanese Brazilians, which range from defiant demonstrations of cultural difference against the Japanese to attempts to completely conceal these differences and pass as "Japanese." And differences in degree between individuals are sometimes just as important as differences of kind.

The degree of engagement among individuals in these modes of ethnic adjustment also varies over time and depends on the situational context. Even the extreme ethnic assimilators examined in this chapter eventually changed to a more resistance-oriented adjustment, but their "resistance" remained much less conspicuous than that of many of their ethnic peers. Also, as shown by those who demonstrated dual ethnic loyalties, some individuals are both ethnic resisters and assimilators, depending on whether they are in the company of their compatriots or their

Japanese hosts. And finally, there is an entire realm of behavior with ambiguous ethnic referentiality that cannot be categorized as either resistance or assimilation. Even with ethnically motivated behavior, individuals sometimes lack the distinct ethnic intentionality that anthropologists like to attribute to them. Not all Japanese Brazilian behavior was a self-conscious demonstration of ethnic loyalties or intended as a performative display of a particular ethnic identity. Therefore, the static categories of ethnic resistance and assimilation cannot be imposed on the constantly shifting and contingent nature of individual experiences without threatening to decontextualize and oversimplify the analysis to a certain extent. The artificial conceptual boundaries that we draw are constantly problematized and blurred in the actual lived practice of our informants. Ultimately, we must locate ethnic experiences in specific contexts, not in abstract and reified categories, which should serve only as analytical reference points for the conceptual contextualization of ethnic individuals.

CONCLUSION

ॐ

Ethnic Encounters in the Global Ecumene

WHEN MIGRANTS and their hosts are related through common descent, ethnic identity becomes increasingly salient as a factor that both motivates migration and constitutes the experience of the migrants. This introduces new complexities and paradoxes to the usual dislocations and discontinuities of migration. Indeed, the experiences of the Japanese Brazilians as well as the Japanese in the host society are shot through with numerous ironies, contradictions, and disjunctures.

The return migration of the nikkeijin means that a minority that was ethnically distinguished in Brazil because it was so "Japanese" is disparaged in Japan because it is so "Brazilian."Although the nikkeijin excluded majority Brazilians in Brazil for not being Japanese, they are in turn excluded in Japan for the same ethnic deficiency. As a result, the Japanese Brazilians and Japanese feel ethnically close to each other when they are geographically distant and ethnically distant when they come into close contact. This causes the Japanese Brazilians to feel "Japanese" in Brazil but "Brazilian" in Japan. As individuals migrate and become transnationals, their identities can therefore become more national, resulting in a transnationalized ethnic community that is accompanied by a nationalized ethnic consciousness. In this manner, territorialized loyalties to the nation can be realized in a deterritorialized context so that the presence of the nation-state is felt most acutely in its absence. However, the counterhegemony of ethnic resistance caused by such deterritorialized migrant nationalism reproduces the Japanese ethnic hegemony it opposes. Since the arrival of ethnic diversity in Japan is accompanied by an assertion of the nation's ethnic homogeneity, the continued opening of the country to increased "internationalization" through global population movements tends to lead to a "closing" of its ethnicity to such influences. Nonetheless, the

Japanese Brazilians, who were racially excluded in the ethnically inclusive country of Brazil, will eventually be culturally included in a country known for its ethnic exclusivity (see the epilogue).

GLOBALIZATION AND ETHNIC IDENTITY

In this manner, as previously stable ethnic meanings are territorially un-bound by global migration and travel across national borders in transna-tional contexts, the ethnic consequences for both the Japanese Brazilian migrants and their Japanese hosts are unexpected, demonstrating the often contradictory and divergent effect of globalization on individual ethnic identity. In this concluding chapter, I will contextualize the ethnic en-counter between the Japanese Brazilians and the Japanese within the glob-al ecumene. As Anthony Giddens (1991) observes, one of the characteristics of modernity is the intrusion of distant events and conditions into indi-vidual identity and self-consciousness. In other words, self-consciousness becomes truly modern when the sources of identification are no longer confined to the local but encompass the global. Modern identities are em-bedded and situated in wider contexts because global forces have increas-ingly penetrated particular localities, forcing individuals to respond to them when constructing their identities.[1] The interrelation of the self to the global milieu is especially important for individuals whose identities have become subject to migration processes.

Contiguous and Noncontiguous Globalization

Globalization can be defined as the movement and flow of goods, people, information, and images across national borders, which causes the world to become increasingly interconnected as a single place (cf. Featherstone 1996; Hannerz 1996; Robertson 1987; Wilson and Dissanayake 1996). Of course, we must distinguish between global processes, which actually ex-tend across the entire globe, and transnational processes, which simply in-volve two or more nations (cf. Levitt n.d.:15–16; Kearney 1995:548). Ulf Hannerz (1996:6) has warned against referring to *any* process or relation-

---

[1] In fact, with the advent of electronic mass media, this is the first time in human history that the "self" has become interrelated to the global milieu (Giddens 1991:4, 27, 32).

ship that somehow transgresses national borders as global, when it is quite clear that it is only a transnational process. For instance, most migration flows are not truly global but merely transnational, since they involve only a limited group of nations from particular regions. Therefore, when we examine the impact of globalization on local societies, it becomes quite apparent that most "global" influences are locally experienced and manifested only as specific transnational institutional or social processes. For instance, when we discuss the impact of "global migration" on Japan, we do not mean that a migrant flow that spans the entire globe is affecting Japan, but simply that Japan is being influenced by specific transnational migrant flows from certain countries (such as the Japanese Brazilians from Brazil). Since these migrations are all constituent parts of the larger global movement of peoples, they therefore represent the effects of global migration at the local level.

Two general types of globalization can be identified. The first can be called *noncontiguous* globalization—the flow of information and images across national boundaries in which the globalizing agent influences local societies over a geographical distance without being physically present. This type of globalization is analogous to what Arjun Appadurai calls mediascapes (1990) and does not involve the transfer of actual materials or peoples, but occurs in what Manuel Castells (1989) calls the "space of flows," the noncontiguous space of telecommunications and media networks that makes the exchange and transmission of information and images possible over long distances.[2] The other type of globalization is *contiguous*, involving the actual physical movement of people, goods, and capital across national borders, and is analogous to Appadurai's concepts of ethnoscapes and technoscapes. Examples include migration, international trade, and the transfer of production or service facilities abroad by multinational firms. In these cases, the globalizing agent (whether people, goods, or capital) actually moves to other countries and is physically present in the local society. Therefore, this type of globalization occurs in the contiguous "space of place" where actual human and material contact occurs in physical proximity.

Of course, in reality, both types of globalization interpenetrate and are mutually enabling, with one frequently acting as a prerequisite and conduit for the other. For instance, *noncontiguous* globalization is made possible

---

[2]As Sassen (1998:chapter 9) notes, telecommunications and electronic spaces "neutralize" distance.

only by the prior, *contiguous* global transfer of capital through the physical establishment of an infrastructure of telecommunications networks, multinational firms, news and media agencies, and publication and advertisement firms, all of which enable the flow of information and mass media to occur. On the other hand, *noncontiguous* global flows frequently facilitate and instigate *contiguous* globalization. For instance, migration, direct foreign investment abroad, and other forms of contiguous globalization are usually encouraged by the initial noncontiguous dissemination of positive images and information about the potential host country.

Local Responses to the Global

The Japanese Brazilian case demonstrates how these two types of globalization, when experienced by individuals at the local level, can have divergent impacts on their ethnic identities, depending on the highly variable meaning that the global can have in local contexts.[3] On the one hand, local societies can react favorably to global forces by identifying with the foreign societies from which these influences come, thus expanding their self-consciousness by developing transnational identities that supersede local loyalties and affiliations and transgress the territorial boundaries of the nation-state. However, globalization can also subject local peoples to unwanted foreign influences and can paradoxically instigate a counterreaction in which a consciousness of local differences and national loyalties is intensified to resist and challenge the threatening intrusion of the global (cf. Appadurai 1996:10; Wilson and Dissanayake 1996:5). Therefore, global processes do not always transnationalize ethnic identity but can also produce a localization of individual consciousness.[4] In this manner, whether local populations receptively embrace a transnational consciousness or experience a strengthening of localized, national identities in opposition to the global depends on whether global influences have positive or negative meanings for them.

Both types of local responses to globalization are relevant for understanding the ethnic encounter between the Japanese Brazilians and the

---

[3]In the globalization literature, the "local" frequently refers to subnational communities. However, as Featherstone (1996) argues, national communities can also be seen as a local entity in contrast to the global.

[4]Appadurai (1996:188–99) also discusses how globalization can either undermine or reinforce local identities.

Japanese. In Brazil, the *noncontiguous* global dissemination of *positive* images about Japan through mass media networks caused the Japanese Brazilians to identify transnationally with the Japanese. The Japanese also had developed transnational feelings of affiliation with the nikkeijin because of essentialist ethnic assumptions in which shared racial descent is understood to naturally produce similarities in cultural orientation. This perception is also reinforced by the mass media in Japan, which tends to portray the nikkeijin in a positive manner by emphasizing their cultural and ancestral ties to the Japanese. This development of a common transnational identity between these two geographically separated ethnic groups based on the noncontiguous global flow of information was eventually responsible for initiating a process of *contiguous* globalization that brought the nikkeijin to Japan as return migrants. Not only was a sense of transnational ethnic affinity with the Japanese critical for the decision of the Japanese Brazilians to migrate to Japan in response to an economic crisis in Brazil, it also made the Japanese government willing to openly accept them for its own economic purposes.

Of course, mutual feelings of ethnic commonality developed from afar are quite a contrast with what happens when the two ethnic groups actually encounter each other at close range under the auspices of contiguous global migration. Despite their common descent and ethnic origins, both groups discover a host of prominent and negatively perceived cultural and socioeconomic differences between them, causing their initial sentiments of transnational ethnic affinity to recede. For the Brazilian nikkeijin, their previously positive and idealized perceptions of Japanese culture and society are shattered when they are ethnically and socioeconomically marginalized in Japan, causing them to discover the negative aspects of Japaneseness. Likewise, the Japanese, who expected the nikkeijin return migrants to be ethnically Japanese, are disappointed by the culturally alien and supposedly low-class, impoverished migrants they actually encounter. Since the impact of the global is experienced in predominantly *negative* terms in both cases, it does not promote a mutual transnational consciousness but has the opposite effect: the consciousness of local differences and national identities is renewed as a defensive reaction against the influence of global migration. Nikkeijin return migration has therefore caused a transformation in the ethnic identity of both the Japanese Brazilians and the Japanese as a previously shared transnational ethnic consciousness based on presumed cultural commonalities has been divided into separate ethnic identities based on national cultural differences.

In this manner, globalization can by its very nature give rise to its op-posite—a resurgence of local consciousness through the increased asser-tion of national identities among both migrants and their hosts.[5] This "global production of locality"[6]—the paradoxical process whereby in-creased globalization intensifies local identities and nationalisms—is by no means restricted simply to those affected by migration but has been ob-served among a wide array of other social groups as well.[7] As Manuel Castells notes: "The age of globalization is also the age of nationalist resur-gence, expressed . . . in the widespread (re)construction of identity on the basis of nationality, always affirmed against the alien" (1997:27).[8] In fact, such disjunctures and contradictory tensions between "globalization" and "localization" are a characteristic of the global condition (cf. Appadurai 1996:chapter 2; Castillo and Nigh 1998:144).[9]

In this manner, local and national cultures endure despite the increas-ing permeability of territorial boundaries to global flows of commodities,

---

[5]As Arjun Appadurai argues, while global forces may erode local communities as territorial so-cial formations ("neighborhoods"), they also strengthen the conscious experience and identifi-cation with this local community ("locality") (1996:188–99).

[6]This term is borrowed from Appadurai (1996:188), although he uses it in a different context.

[7]For instance, Befu (1983) observes that the increasing relocation of Japanese abroad as part of the globalization of capital has been accompanied by a restrictive narrowing of Japanese ethnic identity and a rise in national sentiments. Castells (1989:349–50) describes how the deprivation of local meaning and sense of place caused by the impersonal global flow of information among power-holding corporations has given rise to resistance and mobilization among local commu-nities as they attempt to regain control and significance through the assertion of cultural iden-tities. Castells (1997) interprets a wide variety of social movements (religious fundamentalism, peasant uprisings, religious cults, environmentalism, feminism) as examples of such resistance to globalization. Frequently, national religious and cultural revivals are also direct responses by local populaces to the forces of global capital and the subsequent "westernization" of lifestyles. Brenner (1996) documents a case among Muslim women in Java in which a new Islamic move-ment has emerged as a "modern" alternative to westernization and a way to assert local differ-ences against the homogenizing forces of globalization. Rasmussen (1998) also examines active local resistance to global migration in terms of gender identity among the Muslim communi-ty of Tuareg in Niger.

[8]Chalmers Johnson also notes that despite increasing global economic and sociopolitical inte-gration, local ethno-national fragmentation continues in the modern world (1995:288–89).

[9]Likewise, Wilson and Dissanayake speak of "a new world-space of cultural production and national representation which is simultaneously becoming more *globalized* (unified around dynamics of capitalogic moving across borders) and more *localized* (fragmented into contes-tatory enclaves of difference, coalition, and resistance)" (1996:5).

media, and people.[10] This persistence, if not intensification, of national differences in culture and consciousness in the face of the homogenizing effects of globalization has been explained in numerous ways. Anthony Smith (1995) attributes it to the continuing strength of historical cultural legacies and ethnic ties, while Robert Foster (1991:236–37, 251–52) argues that local societies appropriate and reinterpret global forms in their own particular ways, thus creating indigenized hybrid meanings that produce distinct national cultures. Others claim that the disorienting deterritorialization of peoples under globalization frequently causes them to search for a stable and secure collective identity based on a sense of rootedness to a specific place, giving local nationalisms renewed meaning and relevance (cf. Massey 1992:7; Harvey 1989:300–301, 306). However, it is also evident that globalization can exacerbate the conditions that instigate national sentiment because of its negative effects and meanings at the local level, leading to a refusal to identify with global influences. In the case of migration, the increasingly global movement of peoples across territorial borders leads to encounters with ethnic others among local peoples that give contrastive, if not oppositional cultural meaning to national identities.

In general, noncontiguous globalization is more likely to elicit positive responses among local societies and produce transnational identifications than contiguous globalization, which can lead to negative local reactions and defensive nationalist identities. Because noncontiguous globalization frequently consists of fragmented and disembodied images about other countries that are detached from their original social contexts as they circulate around the world, they can be readily appropriated and favorably interpreted by local societies, making it easy to identify transnationally across territorial borders through positively imagined encounters with foreign peoples and countries. For instance, the mutual transmission of popular culture between the United States and Japan through the media (Japanese TV animation in the case of the United States) has generated considerable interest in Japan among American children (it "looks more cool" than the United States) and also caused Japanese children to yearn for America (Iwabuchi 1998:177–78; cf. Allison 2000:87). Because such

---

[10]Marilyn Ivy also notes that the inclusion of Japan in global processes does not mean that differences are collapsed in favor of an undifferentiated global modernity (1995:5–6).

popular cultural images are frequently divested of ethnic, cultural, and linguistic differences (Japanese animation characters on American television do not look, speak, or necessarily act Japanese),[11] they easily create transnational identifications while ignoring the real ethno-national barriers between the two countries. In contrast, when foreign ethnic groups actually encounter each other under contiguous global migration, it is much more difficult to surmount the linguistic and cultural differences between them, which frequently impede a mutual transnational identification.[12] Indeed, contiguous globalization can have a disillusioning effect that ruins the idealized images produced by noncontiguous globalization by forcing confrontations with the "reality" of foreign groups and societies.

Although global migration often does not produce transnational identities, as migrants disperse to various localities, they become increasingly engaged in the global traffic of information, commodities, and labor across national borders, which enables them to create close and cohesive social relationships over large distances through personal and institutional networks configured in noncontiguous space. As a result, transnational migrant communities emerge that are deterritorialized in two senses—they render both the borders of national territories and the barriers of contiguous space meaningless. However, the extension of an ethnic community across national borders is not subjectively recognized to a sufficient extent by the migrants themselves, who are unable to see past the lingering prominence of the nation-state to articulate a truly transnational consciousness. Deterritorialized transnational communities are unable to offer

---

[11]Since much noncontiguous global information about foreign societies is transmitted visually (through television and movie images), in extreme cases, individuals sometimes construct a transnational identity by mimicking foreign cultural practices with no real understanding of the actual meaning behind these practices. A good example are groups of Japanese youth who imitate American black rappers. These youth have adopted the clothes, styles (including hairstyles), and mannerisms of American blacks but have no inkling about the historical, cultural, and psychological motivations behind such behavior. In other words, such identities are without cultural content or are imbued with local cultural meaning that is alien to the original group that is being imitated.

[12]This can create a situation where people identify with the popular culture of a foreign country but not with its immigrants. Although Brazilian popular culture swept through Japan in the 1970s and Brazilian music (*Bolsa Nova*) and samba continue to be popular among some Japanese (Roth 1999:3), very few have embraced the Brazilian nikkeijin in the same manner or even expressed any interest in them. The situation is similar among Brazilian immigrants in the United States. Despite the current American craze for Brazilian popular culture, Brazilian immigrants remain an "invisible" minority in the United States (see Margolis 1994:17).

an alternative to a nationalist consciousness because they lack the ideological, institutional, and cultural apparatus as well as the spatial integrity that would make them a coherent source of identity and belonging.

The inability of transnational sentiments to emerge in deterritorialized transnational contexts also has paradoxical implications for the relationship between globalization and the hegemonic power of the nation-state. Although the Japanese Brazilians had eluded past efforts by the Brazilian nation-state to impose a unifying nationalist consciousness on them, it is precisely when they leave Brazil and join the global flow of migrants that they unintentionally come under its disciplinary power through the resurgence of national sentiments abroad. Therefore, globalization has enabled the Japanese Brazilians to escape the territorial confines of the Brazilian nation-state, but not its hegemony. The increasing dispersion of peoples around the world does not always require a commensurate global expansion of ideological state apparatuses in order for the nation-state to retain some control over the loyalties of its citizens abroad.

The deterritorialized migrant nationalism produced by globalization is also lived by individuals in actual practice. The performative enactment of nationalized counteridentities among nikkeijin migrants through the display of Brazilian cultural difference in Japan becomes a form of resistance against Japanese ethno-national hegemony and a means to defend themselves against assimilationist pressures and their low social class status. Although nationalist cultures are inevitably reformulated as they are articulated and reenacted by migrants abroad, they are effective as a means of ethnic resistance because they remain distinctive, autonomous cultural forms.

The presence of a large number of nikkeijin immigrants in Japan who resist Japanese ethnic hegemony by asserting a Brazilian nationalist counteridentity therefore challenges Japan's nationalist project of assimilating culturally incongruous minorities under an ideology of national homogeneity. While deterritorialized nationalism among migrants unintentionally reinforces the nationalist agendas of their *home* countries, it undermines those of the *host* country by threatening its national integrity (cf. Appadurai 1996:172–74). This type of "antinationalist nationalism" (see Clifford 1994:307) is one reason why transnational migration and the nation-state are frequently seen as antithetical—migrants who maintain strong transnational ties to their homeland do not develop any allegiance to their host country and therefore escape its assimilationist agenda, which is necessary for the consolidation of the nation-state.

However, even here, the effects of transnational migration can have unintended consequences. While the increasing presence of territorially mobile migrant groups that maintain transnational loyalties seems to threaten the national integrity of the receiving country, it can also renew nationalist feelings and allegiances among its own citizens as a counter-reaction. In the case of Japan, the return migration of the Brazilian nikkei-jin will eventually enhance its control over its people, who are becoming increasingly conscious of their distinctive national homogeneity as they encounter the ethnically foreign.

Thus, the unrelenting forces of transnationalism and globalization do not always weaken the nation-state as a primary source of identity in the modern world. Although the nation-state is being increasingly challenged by illegal migration, the rise of global capitalism, and the greater prominence of global mass media and information networks,[13] the relationship between globalization and the nation-state is not mutually exclusive nor a zero-sum game wherein one gains at the expense of the other (cf. Sassen 1998:chapter 10). Instead, increased globalization can reconsolidate local nationalisms, thus ironically enhancing the hegemony of nation-states. When faced with global challenges to national sovereignty, the power of the nation-state does not simply decline but is instead reconfigured and adapted, creating new forms of governance and hegemonic control (cf. Ong 1999:chapter 8; Sassen 1998:chapter 10). As Raymond Williams reminds us, hegemony is an active process that has to be defended and renewed and constantly reconstituted in response to oppositional and counterhegemonic pressures (1977:112–13).

---

[13]Whether transnational process and increased globalization will eventually undermine the power of the nation-state is an open question that has been frequently debated (Appadurai 1996:19–23, chapter 8; Castells 1997; Gupta 1992:69–70; Hannerz 1996; Sassen 1996; Wilson and Dissanayake 1996). It is undeniable that the power and salience of the nation-state has been threatened to a certain extent by various transnational and global processes. In terms of migration, the global movement of illegal immigrants has reduced the ability of governments to control national borders. In the economic realm, the increasing prominence of multinational corporations, global finance, and free-market trading blocs has made it more difficult for nation-states to regulate and control their own domestic economies. The globalization of communications and mass media is somewhat undermining governmental attempts to monitor and control the flow of information across national borders. Even at the political level, the gradual emergence of transnational political communities such as the European Union has challenged the previous sovereignty of nation-states over political and economic policy.

IDENTITIES AS THE DEESSENTIALIZATION
AND EXCLUSION OF DIFFERENCE

Deessentialized Ethnicity and the Contextualization of Identity

Undoubtedly, when the experience of ethnicity is influenced by the contingencies of globalization, the outcome is unpredictable and produces a number of unexpected disjunctures among globalization, identity, community, and the nation-state. However, the return migration of the Japanese Brazilians illustrates the contingent and contradictory nature of ethnic identities because they are also deessentialized in the process.

In Brazil, not only were the "Japanese" identities of the nikkeijin ethnically essentialized by their racial appearance, their distinctive cultural behavior was also racialized as a natural product of their Japanese descent. In turn, the Japanese Brazilians also understood their "Japanese" ethnicity through racialized notions of culture, laying personal claim to the positive images of Japanese culture in Brazilian society by virtue of their Japanese ancestry. When the perception of cultural difference is racially essentialized in this manner, it is removed from the contingencies of context and practice, rendering ethnic identities relatively immobile. The Brazilian preoccupation with racial appearance forever designates the nikkeijin as culturally Japanese regardless of their level of assimilation. On their side, many Japanese Brazilians continue to insist that the positive "Japanese" cultural qualities they have inherited from their parents and grandparents have persisted despite generations in Brazil, a claim made partly credible by symbolic ethnic reenactments and re-creations of "Japanese" tradition in their communities. As a result, both majority Brazilians and minority nikkeijin are somewhat blinded to their substantial cultural similarities, which greatly outweigh any lingering differences.

When the Japanese Brazilians return migrate to Japan, they are initially confronted by similar essentialized notions of Japanese ethnicity. Although race loses its power of ethnic differentiation, they are faced with a Japanese ethnic ideology in which culture is still closely related to notions of racial essence. Only this time, the nikkeijin's shared racial descent is understood by the Japanese to produce *similarities* in cultural orientation, resulting in a Japanese insistence that the nikkeijin be culturally Japanese. Such essentialist ethnic understandings are meant to forcibly incorporate them under an assimilation-oriented and homogeneously constituted Japanese ethnicity. It is important to remember that domination and control do not always involve portraying others as *different* and inferior, as the critics of Orientalism have emphasized (Said 1979; Gupta 1994). Perceptions of the other as *similar* also facilitate hegemonic projects of incorporation and assimilation based on efforts to remake the other in one's own image (cf. Todorov 1984 [1982]).

However, Japanese attempts at assimilation and control eventually fail as the Japanese Brazilians prove unable and unwilling to meet Japanese ethnic expectations, eventually escaping the racial essentialization of their ethnicity through assertive demonstrations of their Brazilian cultural differences. By disassociating culture from race in this manner, they effectively deessentialize racialist conceptions of Japanese ethnicity among both the Japanese and themselves, causing them to question their previous assumptions of cultural similarity based on shared descent. If anthropology has attempted to deessentialize the self by disengaging it from notions of biological or universal essence (Kondo 1990:34),[14] my nikkeijin and Japanese informants seemingly came to the same conclusion in their ethnic encounter, although few of them attained this level of theoretical reflexivity. Migration not only affects the *content* of identity, it can also create a different understanding among migrants of the *nature* of identity itself (cf. Rouse 1995). For the Japanese Brazilians, ethnic identity changes from something that is racially inscribed (essentialized) to something that is culturally contingent and actively negotiated in various social contexts (deessentialized).

Essentialized ethnic identities become harder to sustain under transnational migration because it disengages relatively static ethnic meanings from a certain locale and reengages them in a new social context, causing them to be challenged, renegotiated, and redefined. As a result, not only is cultural behavior understood to be "Japanese" in Brazil ethnically redefined as "Brazilian" in Japan, the meaning of Japaneseness switches from positive to negative. Likewise, the ethnic meanings of Brazilian food, symbols, and ceremonies are all reappropriated and reconstituted in ethnic performances of national identity in Japan. In fact, even race itself is deessentialized, as it becomes a culturally relative category subject to constantly shifting contextual redefinitions. This is best illustrated by those mestiço nikkeijin whose racial phenotype is designated as "Japanese" in

---

[14]This has also been emphasized by those studying the cultural construction of emotion as part of the self (see Lutz 1988; Rosaldo 1980, 1984).

Brazil but appears quite "foreign" in Japan. Therefore, as ethnic meanings are racially deessentialized by migration and subject to revaluation abroad, their contextually relative and contingent nature becomes more apparent, making ethnic identities more dynamic and much more contestable. As a result, the Japanese Brazilians in Japan are able to culturally negotiate their ethnicity on a continuum ranging from Brazilian to Japanese. This is especially true among the Japanized nikkeijin with bicultural abilities who conveniently manipulate their cultural behavior and maintain situationally shifting, dual identities.

Identities Over Time: Ethnicity Stabilized and Reessentialized

Since identities are subject to change whenever people migrate to a new society and enter into relationships with new ethnic groups, the increasing transnational movement of people made possible by globalization has undoubtedly accelerated the pace of identity change. However, the intensity of spatial movement does not always correspond to the magnitude of identity change since relocation to certain contrastive social contexts has more of a determinative influence on identity than relocation to others. As argued in chapter 3, those who migrate to an ethnically related host society generally experience a greater impact on their self-consciousness that those who migrate to an ethnically alien society.

In addition, transnational movement has a greater influence on identities when individuals migrate abroad than when they come home. The ethnic experiences that the Japanese Brazilians have in Japan change their identity much more than the ethnic experiences they have when they return to Brazil. In fact, dekasegi returnees in Brazil seem to have become relatively impervious to renewed Brazilian social influences on their ethnic identity. Although Brazilian society again designates them as "japonês," most of my nikkeijin informants claimed that they did not experience a shift back to their "Japanese" ethnic identities after developing a stronger Brazilian national consciousness in Japan. Many of them shared the experiences of my friend in Ribeirão Preto, São Paulo, who talked about how he continues to feel ethnically Brazilian after returning to Brazil:

> When I came back to Brazil, I was again seen and treated as japonês. This will never change. But it doesn't affect how I feel inside. Psychologically, I am now certain I am more Brazilian than Japanese—I found this out in Japan. My experiences here may chisel away at my identity,

but fundamentally, they don't influence me and my identity remains stable. Being seen as a foreigner in Japan despite my Japanese face was a shock that I will never forget.

The Brazilian social context now has less influence on the ethnic identities of the Japanese Brazilians because their encounter in Japan with the Japanese is much more ethnically "real" for them than the socially decontextualized images that majority Brazilians have constructed of their "Japaneseness." Having migrated to Japan and discovered that they are not in fact ethnically Japanese, the nikkeijin no longer attribute much significance to such external pressures from Brazilian society that define them as "Japanese."

However, what happens to the rate of identity change among those who remain in Japan for the long term? Initially, the Japanese Brazilians feel more and more Brazilian as they continue living in Japan, resulting in an identity schismogenesis with the Japanese. However, does the progressive strengthening of their Brazilian national identities stabilize after a certain period? All of the Japanese Brazilians with whom I discussed this issue felt that after residing in Japan for a certain period, they reached a point when they stopped feeling "more Brazilian." Consider the following statements:

> Because of the experiences I was having in Japan, I think my identity kept changing to the Brazilian side for a while, but it is now stabilizing. I've reached a point when the change in identity stops. I now know who I am here in Japan and how the Japanese think about me, and it doesn't have as much effect on me now.

> I discovered my Brazilianness in Japan and now feel much more Brazilian than I did in Brazil. But my Brazilian feelings do not continue to become stronger over time. After the first shock I received in Japan, I felt a sudden rise in my Brazilian consciousness, but then the confusion ended. Now, I can see both the Japanese and Brazilian sides of myself objectively.

What causes the eventual stabilization of the ethnic identities of the nikkeijin in Japan, preventing further identity schismogenesis with the Japanese? Why is a state of dynamic equilibrium reached? Gregory Bateson (1958) examined various factors that eventually control, restrain, and counteract processes of schismogenesis between two groups and prevent the eventual collapse of the social relationship.

As is evident in the case of the Japanese Brazilians, identity formation over an extended period of time is influenced more by the *quality* of experience than by the pure *quantity* of experience. When the nikkeijin migrate to Japan, they are subjected to various personal experiences with the Japanese that heighten their Brazilian ethnic consciousness. As similar experiences accumulate and continue to reinforce their ethnic status as a Brazilian minority in Japan, they experience a further strengthening of their Brazilian identity. However, after a certain period of time, they become accustomed to such experiences and are no longer shocked, seriously influenced, or bothered by them. As the initial novelty of the ethnic encounter with the Japanese is replaced by the monotony of its repetition, it ceases to have the same impact on the individual's self-consciousness as before. Having sufficiently adjusted to the new Japanese sociocultural milieu by changing their ethnic self-consciousness, the Japanese Brazilians are now able to cope with their continuing experiences in Japan by simply maintaining their identities at the same level without further need for modification.

In this manner, ethnic identity stabilizes as a new dynamic equilibrium between individual consciousness and the external social environment is established. In Ralph Lifton's words (1983 [1976]:72–73), the individual has successfully "recentered" his or her identity in response to new social conditions. Therefore, despite the continued increase in the *quantity* of the same experiences in Japan, we can expect the ethnic identity of the nikkeijin to remain stable until the *quality* of their ethnic experiences again changes, for instance through migration to another society. Transformations in ethnic identity over the long term therefore depend more on the changing nature of experience and less on the accumulated amount of the same experience.

As identities eventually stabilize, they also tend to recede from active consciousness. Individuals become most aware of their identities when external social changes, such as those caused by migration, suddenly problematize and transform their former self-consciousness. As Erik Erikson observes in the context of identity development during the life cycle, people are most aware of their identity when they are about to change it or acquire a new one (1980 [1959]:127). However, after they have ethnically adjusted to a new sociocultural milieu by adopting a stable identity, they are able to cope with similar social experiences on a daily basis without their identity becoming a prominent or frequent concern in daily life. Ordinarily, therefore, a stable sense of identity is experienced *preconsciously* and thus remains outside of constant awareness as an implicit and unexamined part of the "habitus" (Bourdieu 1977) of structured internal dispositions that do not reach the level of conscious discourse and self-reflection. A number of my informants who had been in Japan for a while said that they no longer think as much about their ethnic identities and just go about their daily business. A nisei woman was most explicit:

> At first, I was very conscious of my status as a Brazilian foreigner in Japan. I was very aware of how I dress differently, act differently, and don't speak Japanese very well and about how other people would see me as gaijin, or call me Brazilian. After a while, I resolved in my mind that I was indeed a Brazilian foreigner here and could not be considered Japanese. Now I don't worry about this anymore because I am used to it. I just live normally and usually don't think much about how I am a Brazilian here anymore.

In addition, as the Japanese Brazilians remain for a certain period in Japan as immigrant settlers, their Brazilian identities become culturally *re*essentialized. Because of the initial deessentialization of their ethnicity caused by migration, their ethnic identities are now culturally defined instead of determined by the primordial factors of racial appearance and descent. However, this does not prevent their identities from again becoming essentialized as they continue to live in Japan. Although culturally defined identities may seem more contestable and negotiable than those based on notions of racial essence (see Mason 1986:6), they can also appear to be ingrained and immutable since they are based on characteristics that have been "inherited" through years of socialization and cannot be easily changed in response to new social circumstances.

Indeed, a good number of Japanese Brazilians realize in Japan that their cultural attributes are so fundamentally Brazilian that they could never become ethnically Japanese. "Even if I remained in Japan for the rest of my life and made serious efforts to integrate myself into Japanese society, I would be unable to become culturally Japanese," my roommate, Rodney, once remarked to me, echoing the sentiments of a number of his compatriots. "I just can't change my Brazilian ways. The differences start with something as basic as the way we walk. It is simply impossible." In this sense, the Brazilian ethnic identity of the nikkeijin in Japan comes to be essentialized not by the barriers of racial difference but by the primordial differences of personal histories, lifelong socialization, and educational experiences that will forever confine them to a Brazilian cultural ethnicity. Since few Japanese Brazilians can act truly Japanese or speak Japanese fluently, most are immediately identifiable because of their prominent cultural and behavioral differences, despite their racial "invisibility." As Guarnizo and Smith note, identities forged from below by marginalized migrant groups are frequently no less essentialized than those hegemonically imposed from above by the nation-state (1998:23).

Although identities may be contextual, situationally contingent, and relationally defined, they are not as shifting and free-floating as some postmodernists tend to think. Identities are most subject to change when they are decentered, deessentialized, and redefined in a new social context through transnational migration. However, once migrants remain in the host society for a certain period of time, their identities become stabilized and reessentialized[15] until they are again disrupted by relocation to another foreign society. Therefore, only those who frequently experience transnational mobility to new societies have constantly shifting identities. Such dynamism may be lacking among individuals who remain territorially bound.

Processes of Ethnic Exclusion

In my analysis of the ethnic encounter between the Brazilian nikkeijin and the Japanese, I have been more interested in how ethnic identity is constituted by the experience of cultural and socioeconomic difference from other groups than in the experience of in-group similarities and common origins.[16] Since Frederik Barth (1969) urged researchers to shift their attention from the cultural *content* of ethnicity to how ethnicity functions as a form of social differentiation through the maintenance of ethnic "boundaries," a number of researchers have focused specifically on the construction of ethnic identities through the perception of difference (Comaroff 1987; De Vos and Romanucci-Ross 1982; Nagata 1981; Wallman 1986).

---

[15]Using Giddens's terminology, the temporality of identity shifts from transformative, irreversible time to reproductive, reversible time (see 1984).

[16]A number of classical definitions of ethnicity have emphasized commonly shared origins, culture, and heritage as the basis for ethnic groups (Berreman 1982b:17; Cohen 1974:ix; Gordon 1964). Some definitions have emphasized the importance of both differences and similarities in the formation of ethnic groups (Roosens 1994; Weber 1961).

An approach that emphasizes the experience of difference can be criticized for ignoring the actual cultural qualities and characteristics that constitute ethnic identities (see Cohen 1994:120). Yet, my work has demonstrated that a consciousness of difference and the content of identity are not mutually exclusive. The experience of difference enhances and articulates, instead of precludes, the understanding of the shared cultural content that constitutes the collective ethnic self. Only through a strong consciousness of differences with other ethnic groups do individuals become aware of the commonly held cultural qualities that define their own ethnicity. As a result, both my Japanese Brazilian and Japanese informants not only stereotyped the differences of the other but also stereotyped themselves in order to emphasize their own homogeneity.

When we examine *transnational* ethnic identities, however, the internal similarities in cultural content seem to take precedence over the consciousness of external cultural differences. As shown by the Brazilian nikkeijin and the Japanese, individuals identify with ethnic groups in other nations because of perceived commonalities in descent or culture. Even in such cases, however, an awareness of difference remains relevant as a primary component of ethnic identity. For instance, the "Japanese" transnational identity that the Japanese Brazilians construct in Brazil is meaningful only because it can be articulated and elaborated through comparisons with Brazilian culture, which enable the distinctive positive qualities of the "Japanese" ethnicity to emerge.

Since ethnic identities require a consciousness of cultural differences, they are constructed through the ethnic marginalization and social exclusion of others. Therefore, both the dominant majority and the subordinate minority group use notions of racial, cultural, and social class difference to exclude each other and delineate ethnic boundaries. Contrary to the usual pattern, the Japanese Brazilians as an ethnic minority in Brazil did more excluding of majority Brazilians than vice versa. Of course, in Japan, it is the Japanese who do most of the ethnic excluding. Ironically, the Japanese Brazilians find themselves victimized in Japan by the same Japanese exceptionalism that they used to ethnically exclude the Brazilians in Brazil. Even the terminology of ethnic exclusion is the same, with only a change in the referents. Although the Japanese Brazilians in Brazil defined themselves as the "Japanese" and designated majority Brazilians as "gaijin," when they return migrate to Japan, *they* become the "gaijin" who are deemed ethnic outsiders by the Japanese of Japan (the "real Japanese"). Yet, when the former ethnic "victimizers" become the victims of the same ethnic exclusion, they tend to forget their original victimizing. It was a rare, self-reflective young nisei man who said:

> The nikkeis don't like to be ethnically separated in Japan and complain of discrimination, saying the Japanese are racist. They don't realize that they had prejudices in Brazil too and excluded [non-nikkeijin] Brazilians from nikkeijin groups just as we are now excluded by the Japanese here. The nikkeis forget that in Brazil, they were the ones on top and looked down on others.

In fact, historical consciousness sometimes involves the same process of collective amnesia where former victimizing is forgotten by subsequent victimization. The atomic blasts in Hiroshima and Nagasaki that ended World War II overshadowed, if not erased, any vivid historical memory among the Japanese of their previous atrocities in Asia (cf. Weiner 1997b:81). Five decades later, a collective consciousness of their imperialist victimizing is still struggling to emerge (complicated by the increasing generational distance from the historical event). But it has been unable to overcome an overwhelming historical sense of *higaisha-ishiki* (victim-consciousness) at the hands of the Americans. The effects are still pervasive, creating problems ranging from education (the writing of history textbooks) to international relations with other East Asian countries.

Of course, when the past is left unreflected upon, it can be unwittingly reproduced. In reaction in their ethnic and socioeconomic marginalization in Japan, the Japanese Brazilians eventually revert to the ethnically exclusionary ways that characterized them in Brazil to a certain extent. The Brazilian counteridentities that they develop in Japan contain a certain amount of "anti-Japanese" feeling that makes some of them just as ethnically exclusionary as the Japanese. Of course, few Japanese wish to be ethnically accepted by the Brazilian nikkeijin. Yet, the issue is not completely moot, since those Japanese who do attempt to establish ethnic rapport with them for one reason or another frequently mention the difficulties they encounter. Japanese graduate students studying the Japanese Brazilians have had trouble with nikkeijin informants who are reluctant to be interviewed. Likewise, a rare Toyama worker who expressed some desire to associate with the nikkeijin related her experiences to me:

> The nikkeijin keep to themselves all the time. As a Japanese, I'm an outsider to them who doesn't belong. Maybe I'm imagining things, but

sometimes, I even sense some latent antagonism. It's not that I actively try to be accepted by them, but they remain distant, different. I just can't enter their groups.

As a result, even as identities are territorially unbound, disengaged from notions of racial essence, and subject to constant contextual redefinition under the effects of global migration, they do not necessarily become inclusive, expansive, and multicultural. In contrast to the assumptions of some in the recent transnationalism and globalization literature (see Appadurai 1996; Malkki 1992; Rouse 1991), I have argued that inclusion in the processes of global postmodernity does not ensure cosmopolitan, hybrid identities that encompass and embrace others (cf. Fabricant 1998:38–39). Therefore, a contradiction is created between migrant practices and self-consciousness wherein the global expansion of people's activities and movements across national borders is not necessarily accompanied by equally expansive transnational and globalized identities. Instead, their self-consciousness can frequently become more nationalist in orientation.

This is true even for the Japanese Brazilians who have decided to establish residence in both countries and constantly move back and forth in response to changing global economic conditions. Although they resemble Aihwa Ong's notion of "flexible citizens" (1999), they have not become cosmopolitan transnationals with hybrid identities and multiple attachments but remain primarily loyal to Brazil. They are drawn to Japan for the economic opportunities but do not integrate themselves into Japanese society and therefore, constantly return to their homeland. "Japan is only a country to work and earn money, not to live," a number of them told me (see also Rossini 1996:109; Yamanaka 1997:26). As Hannerz observes, most tourists, exiles, and labor migrants do not become "cosmopolitans" who directly immerse themselves in the cultures of the countries in which they stay but remain encapsulated in their own social relationships and cultures (1996:104–106).

Therefore, even in an increasingly borderless world where national boundaries are being transgressed and collapsed, local differences are not always transcended in favor of an undifferentiated global modernity. Although globalization involves the open inclusion of the foreign—whether migrants, commodities, or information—it frequently produces restrictive exclusions among those involved. As a result, people remain parochial and exclusionary even as they are being encompassed by global flows that seemingly disregard such local boundaries and differences.

In fact, identities sometimes are the most inclusive and receptive before people ever emerge from their specific localities to become part of the global migration process. As we have seen, it was precisely when the Japanese Brazilians were still a minority territorially bound to Brazil that they expanded their identities beyond national confines by ethnically encompassing the Japanese. However, once they crossed national borders and became globally engaged, their previous transnational identities were nationalized and became more restrictive. Likewise, the Japanese, who are on the receiving end of global migration, relinquished their initial feelings of transnational affiliation with the nikkeijin in favor of a more exclusively understood national consciousness. In this manner, contiguous global migration has caused the ethnic identities of both the Japanese Brazilians and the Japanese to regress to the very confines of the nation-states from which they had initially escaped.

As global migration has brought the Japanese and the nikkeijin geographically closer, they have become more ethnically distant. Although ethnic transnationalism brought them together, ethnic nationalism eventually pulls them apart. However, as the Japanese Brazilians become a permanent presence in Japanese society in the future, will this ethnic schismogenesis between them and the Japanese persist? Or will the pressures of ethnic incorporation eventually replace current processes of ethnic exclusion? Will the Japanese Brazilians eventually be included within a dominant Japanese ethnicity and integrated into the Japanese national community? Or will they continue to be ethnically and socioeconomically marginalized as a culturally foreign minority group? It is still too early to seek answers to these questions, since the Brazilian nikkeijin have barely been in Japan for a decade. Yet, we can already glimpse their eventual ethnic fate by examining the experiences of nikkeijin children, who represent the "second" immigrant generation in Japan.

EPILOGUE

⟡

Caste or Assimilation?

The Future Minority Status and Ethnic Adaptation
of the Japanese Brazilians in Japan

FROM SOJOURNER TO SETTLER:
THE PERMANENCE OF "TEMPORARY" MIGRATION

THE ISSUES OF MIGRATION and ethnicity outlined in this book will continue to be relevant for the future as the Japanese Brazilians become a permanent immigrant minority in Japan. Like Brazilian immigrants in the United States and Canada (Goza 1994:149, 1999:777; Margolis 1994:chapter 12), a good number of them will remain sojourners and "target earners" who will return in the near future to Brazil, but a sizable portion of the immigrant population is settling long-term and permanently in Japan. Although virtually all of the Japanese Brazilians arrive in Japan as temporary dekasegi sojourners and plan to return to Brazil in a couple of years,[1] research surveys indicate that 41 percent have already been in Japan for more than three years, 40 percent intend to remain in Japan for at least three more years or do not know, and roughly 50 percent wish to settle long-term in Japan (Kitazawa 1997:104, 142, 148). Surveys conducted in the early '90s show that perhaps 20 to 30 percent had already decided to remain indefinitely or permanently in Japan (Japan Statistics Research Institute 1993; Kitagawa 1992, 1993).

The economic and social causes of nikkeijin immigrant settlement in Japan are similar to those of other immigrant groups (see Tsuda 1999b for an extensive analysis). Although the Japanese Brazilians plan to make a

---

[1]Both of the questionnaire surveys conducted by JICA (1992) and the Japanese Institute of Labor (1995) report that only 2 to 3 percent of the Brazilian nikkeijin came to Japan because they wanted to make it their permanent home.

fortune in a few years and then quickly return home, most find it difficult to save money because of the high cost of living in Japan. In addition, the decade-long Japanese economic recession has decreased their incomes by reducing hourly wages and overtime, forcing many to extend their stays in Japan in order to save the desired amount of money. At the same time, the recession has not caused a significant number of nikkeijin to repatriate because they have not experienced any serious unemployment in Japan and their income levels continue to be much higher there than in Brazil. Meanwhile, despite overall improvement in the Brazilian economy since the late 1980s, economic uncertainty has remained, making many Japanese Brazilians rather pessimistic about their long-term economic futures back home. Surveys indicate that close to 40 percent have no hope for Brazil's political and economic future or do not know what the future will hold (Kitagawa 1997:148). A similar process has been observed among Brazilians in the United States, who are prolonging their immigrant stays partly because of the belief that Brazil is a country in perpetual economic crisis, an image that is reinforced by their ethnic mass media (Sales 1998:40, 141, 145). In the case of the Japanese Brazilians, their immigrant population in Japan has actually *increased* steadily during the recession instead of decreased.

Of course, immigrant settlement is not purely motivated by economic reasons. Over time, immigrants also gradually become "socially embedded" in the host country, making it less likely they will quickly return home. As the Japanese Brazilians have prolonged their stays in Japan for economic reasons, an increasing number of them have brought their families to Japan. Others (especially repeat migrants) are now migrating to Japan with their families in anticipation of longer stays. In 1990, 35 percent of the immigrants were already living with their families. A few years later, the figure had risen to 60 percent and it remains at that level.[2] Those Japanese Brazilians with their families in Japan no longer experience the psychological difficulties and social insecurities of living alone in a foreign country, while also becoming less emotionally and socially attached to Brazil. As they face the prospect of an extended stay in Japan with their families, the Brazilian nikkeijin are also less willing to endure long working hours and economic austerity in an effort to maximize their earnings

---

[2]These figures are from surveys conducted by Kitagawa (1992, 1993, 1997) and the Japan Statistics Research Institute (1993).

and have instead begun to desire more socially fulfilling lives in Japan (cf. Margolis 1994:178, 275 in the case of Brazilian immigrants in the United States). This shift from purely economic to social priorities therefore reduces their incomes and increases the cost of living, making it even more difficult to save the amount of money necessary to return home.

At the same time, many Japanese Brazilians have become quite accustomed to and comfortable living in Japan because of the presence of family and friends as well as the development of extensive immigrant ethnic communities. In addition, as their children attend Japanese schools and become increasingly assimilated to Japanese society (see below), their social connections and involvement in the surrounding Japanese community intensify and they become increasingly committed to the host country. Since a good number of these children have forgotten Portuguese and know nothing about Brazil (in fact, some even tell their parents they do not want to leave Japan), this increases the reluctance of some nikkeijin parents to repatriate since they realize their children will have serious problems readapting to Brazilian society. In general, nikkeijin wives were somewhat more reluctant than husbands to return home, perhaps because of their greater concern about their children.[3] In this manner, families are a significant factor that promotes immigrant settlement in the host society.

Despite such clear indications of settlement, however, many Japanese Brazilians continue to claim that they will return to Brazil soon. However, as is the case with their Brazilian counterparts in the United States (see Margolis 1994:chapter 12; Sales 1998:130, 132), their behavior belies such stated intentions and many continue to postpone their return for various reasons. When such clear indications of migrant settlement are combined with the rising amount of circular migration between Brazil and Japan (chapter 4), it is quite apparent that the Japanese Brazilians will remain a permanent ethnic presence in Japan, as repeat sojourners or as settlers.

So what will be the future ethnic status of the Japanese Brazilians as a permanent immigrant minority in Japan, and what will happen to their second-generation descendants? Will they eventually overcome

---

[3]Grasmuck and Pessar (1991:156) argue that Dominican migrant women in the United States are generally more reluctant to return home to a patriarchal society because they will lose the increased socioeconomic power and status they enjoy as wage-earners in the United States. Although I did not directly investigate this issue, such concerns seemed less prominent among Japanese Brazilian women (cf. Margolis 1994:259–60 in the case of Brazilian immigrant women in the United States).

their socioeconomic marginalization as low-status, unskilled migrant workers through cultural assimilation and social incorporation and disappear into the mainstream Japanese populace?

CONTINUED ETHNIC RESISTANCE AMONG FIRST-GENERATION IMMIGRANTS

It is quite apparent that the circular migrants who will continue to shuttle back and forth between Brazil and Japan will remain more or less ethnically unassimilated and confined to low-class factory jobs. However, even those Japanese Brazilians who have resolved to reside long-term or permanently in Japan maintain their Brazilian nationalist counteridentities and do not show a significantly greater willingness to culturally assimilate or socially incorporate themselves into Japanese society. Except for a few, they were not learning Japanese or adopting Japanese cultural patterns but remained Brazilian in both self-consciousness and behavior.[4] As mentioned in the conclusion, a majority of them essentialized their cultural differences as Brazilians in Japan and felt they could not become culturally assimilated as Japanese even if they were to spend the rest of their lives in Japan. Gradual assimilation is not the inevitable outcome for all immigrant minority groups since some continue to identify themselves by national origin and do not develop a strong affiliation with the host country.

As analyzed in chapter 5, although the ethnic resistance of the Japanese Brazilians to Japanese cultural assimilation facilitates their psychological adjustment as a negative immigrant minority in Japan, it also results in behavior that in turn reproduces their negative minority status by ensuring their continued ethnic exclusion and socioeconomic marginalization. If they continue to assert their Brazilian cultural differences in Japan, they will not be ethnically accepted by mainstream Japanese society, especially because Japanese ethno-national identity is not becoming more inclusive in response to the nikkeijin.

As a result, the refusal of the Japanese Brazilians to culturally assimilate may become increasingly socially maladaptive by permanently im-

---

[4]Margolis notes a similar experience among Brazilian immigrants in the United States. Although many are becoming immigrant settlers, they continue to think of themselves as Brazilian and maintain strong ties to Brazil.

peding their socioeconomic mobility and confining them to low-class factory jobs.[5] In fact, those Brazilian nikkeijin who have decided to settle permanently in Japan have already begun to express a desire to eventually leave their degrading 3K working-class jobs and move on to higher-level work, either through promotion within the factory or by finding white-collar occupations outside the factory. However, as discussed in chapter 6, only a few who have mastered the Japanese language to a certain extent have been promoted.

In addition, the stigma of migrant temporariness continues to disadvantage even those Japanese Brazilians who have made a permanent commitment to Japan, causing their employers to be reluctant to make them permanent and regular seishain who are placed on the usual promotion track. Also, as long as the nikkeijin continue to remain dependent on the labor broker system for jobs and other critical services, they will be restricted to the informal and marginal sector of the Japanese working class since brokers have always been used as a source of temporary workers for Japanese companies. Very rarely are those hired through labor brokers given permanent jobs with the possibility of regular promotion (cf. Nishizawa 1995). Therefore, even the social mobility of the assimilation-minded, Japanized nikkeijin has been restricted thus far to jobs as minisupervisors in the factory, ethnic liaisons in local company and governmental offices, and owners of small ethnic businesses. In this sense, the Japanese Brazilians may not be able to rise beyond what Blalock (1967) and Bonacich (1982) call "middleman minority" status, where immigrants escape the lowest rungs of society to occupy intermediate socioeconomic positions as brokers, middlemen, and merchants but do not advance to higher occupational positions, which are reserved for members of the dominant majority.

The other barrier to the social class mobility of immigrants who remain culturally unassimilated is simple employment discrimination, in which foreigners who are culturally different are not treated equally with domestic employees and properly promoted, regardless of their personal abilities and skills. Although the Japanese Brazilians enjoy superior access to the *unskilled* working-class labor market, they will likely face much more institutional discrimination as they attempt to enter middle-class occupations and come into direct competition with native Japanese for

---

[5]Piore (1979) notes that members of immigrant communities who do not culturally assimilate are unable to compete with native workers for higher-level jobs.

white-collar jobs, for which the labor market is much tighter and opportunities limited, especially during a recession.[6] Although ethnic discrimination and derogatory treatment of the nikkeijin will remain dormant as
long as they are seen as marginalized and "temporary" migrant workers,
once they begin to threaten the previously secure and dominant socioeconomic position of the Japanese, ethnic discrimination may begin to
mount (see chapter 2).

In addition to employment discrimination, general social and institutional discrimination may become more pronounced as the Japanese
Brazilians settle permanently in Japan and attempt to more fully participate in Japanese society. Although they have been adequately provided
with local government services in many cases and their children have been
fully accepted in Japanese schools, there has already been notable housing
discrimination because of their linguistic and cultural differences (see
chapter 2). This problem will gradually become more serious as those who
wish to settle in Japan attempt to find private housing on their own instead of living in temporary apartments and dormitories provided by their
brokers and employers. Another possible source of discrimination is in
marriage, as certain Japanese parents may object to their children marrying Brazilian nikkeijin.

Of course, this does not mean that cultural assimilation is the only way
for ethnic minorities to avoid discrimination and advance themselves socioeconomically. We must always differentiate between *cultural* assimilation and what has been called *structural* (or social) assimilation into a society's institutions and mainstream occupations (Gordon 1961; Spiro
1955:1244). In most cases, some level of cultural assimilation is necessary
for socio-occupational mobility to occur.[7] However, in some multiethnic
societies such as the United States with a pluralistic national ideology,
many minority individuals can frequently retain a certain amount of ethnic distinctiveness and cultural difference without jeopardizing their
chances of socioeconomic integration and class mobility (cf. Bun and

---

[6]Rohlen (1981) notes a similar pattern among the Korean Japanese in which those who compete
for higher-level jobs confront more discrimination from the Japanese.

[7]However, Portes and Stepick (1993:215–16) argue that the disappearance of cultural differences
among immigrant minorities is not always a prerequisite for social assimilation. Frequently,
ethnic political mobilization along lines of cultural difference socializes immigrants into the
functioning of mainstream institutions and facilitates their inclusion in them.

Kiong 1993:147), especially in cases where ethnic diversity within institutions is actively promoted.[8]

In contrast, a type of "hegemonic nationalism" (Medina 1997:760) predominates in homogeneously conceived societies like Japan where cultural assimilation to the dominant majority group is a necessary prerequisite for social acceptance and socioeconomic integration. In such cases, minority groups that remain culturally different continue to face institutional discrimination, impeding their social class mobility. This is most apparent with the Koreans in Japan, who have had to not only culturally assimilate but even hide their Korean names and identities in order to avoid institutional discrimination and perpetual socioeconomic marginalization in Japanese society (Lee and De Vos 1981). The Japanese Brazilians will eventually have to do the same if they wish to rise above their current low socio-occupational level.

In general, however, confinement to a marginal social class position is not as severe a problem for first-generation immigrants,[9] who tend to be less susceptible to its personally debilitating consequences partly because they are "voluntary minorities" who came to the host country of their own volition. Since their socioeconomic marginalization in the host society was brought on by their own autonomous decision to migrate, they do not develop strong feelings of resentment even if their degraded social class status persists. In addition, first-generation immigrants maintain a "dual frame of reference" in which they compare their present immigrant lives to the greater economic hardships they faced in their home country (Castles 1984:188; Ogbu 1978; Suárez-Orozco and Suárez-Orozco 1995b:53–56). As discussed in chapter 5, even if they remain confined to low-status immigrant jobs, they are able to view their lives positively and feel "better off"

---

[8]However, even in the pluralist-minded United States, those minorities who culturally assimilate obviously have a better chance of social success and upward mobility. For instance, a study by Levine and Montero (1973) found that among three generations of Japanese Americans, those who were more socially mobile tended to be more culturally assimilated and less likely to belong to Japanese American organizations or to speak and read Japanese. Even in cases where their ethnic minority status is an advantage in employment (such as with affirmative action programs), employers tend to prefer those minority individuals who have fully adopted the cultural patterns of majority society.

[9]Only a minority of first-generation immigrants generally attain significant social mobility. In the former West Germany (the most comparable case with Japan for many reasons), 40 percent of immigrant workers have enjoyed some job advancement, but only from unskilled to semiskilled jobs (Castles 1984:137–38). Few have experienced real upward mobility.

in contrast to the worse economic conditions under which they were suffering back home. In addition, since a good number of first-generation immigrants maintain a desire to return to their homelands, their current low class status is made more bearable because it can be rationalized as "temporary." Even if repatriation becomes no longer possible or desirable, they remain oriented toward a hopeful future because of the expectation that their children will eventually succeed in the host society and advance to a higher socio-occupational position than themselves. Therefore, occupational discrimination in the host society is not always seen pessimistically as oppressive but as something that can be eventually overcome through perseverance and hard work.

In this manner, voluntary immigrant minorities generally remain achievement-oriented with a positive attitude as they continue to strive for an improved life. As a result, they tend not to develop strong feelings of hostility and antagonism toward dominant society or suffer the type of personal despair that characterizes some indigenous "involuntary" minority groups, whose negative minority status has been forced upon them by conquest, colonization, or forced migration and who have been trapped at the bottom of the socioeconomic ladder as an underclass for generations.[10]

THE SECOND GENERATION:
THE PROBLEMS OF ETHNIC RESISTANCE

However, the situation is considerably different for "second-generation" immigrants who either migrated when they were very young or were born in the host society. If they remain a culturally unassimilated negative minority and therefore continue to suffer discrimination and low socioeconomic status,[11] they may begin to resemble "involuntary minorities" since their social subordination and negative minority status were literally forced upon them through their parents' decision to migrate (cf. Suárez-Orozco and Suárez-Orozco 1995b). Not having experienced the economic hardships of their parents in the ethnic homeland, they no

---

[10]The concepts of voluntary and involuntary minorities are similar to Blauner's (1982) notions of colonized and immigrant minorities.

[11]Many second-generation immigrants are unable to advance themselves socially and obtain better jobs than their parents. For instance, this is the case with immigrants in a number of Western European countries (see Castles 1984:187).

longer share a "dual frame of reference" but come to adopt the native populace's aspirations and expectations of socioeconomic success and upward mobility (cf. Perlman and Waldinger 1997:912). As a result, their low social class position makes them feel much more deprived than their first-generation parents because they fail to perceive the relative benefits of their lives in the host society. At the same time, second-generation immigrants become more vulnerable and sensitive to majority ethnic prejudice and discrimination because of their greater interaction with and involvement in dominant society, unlike first-generation immigrants, who remain socially isolated in ethnically enclaved communities and have not been in the host society long enough for the negative effects of discrimination and negative minority status to sink in (cf. Portes and Rumbaut 1996:182–86; Tajfel 1982:241).

As a result, second-generation immigrant minorities no longer see their discriminatory confinement to low-class jobs as a temporary negative social consequence to be endured for the promise of future socioeconomic success but as permanently oppressive discrimination against them, intensifying their antagonism toward the dominant society (see Portes and Rumbaut 1996:249). Rebellious ethnic counteridentities are strengthened as they refuse to conform to dominant cultural norms and resist pressures to succeed on the majority group's terms through educational achievement. This increased antagonism toward the dominant society can strengthen a negative attitude that equates social success and class mobility with ethnic betrayal, creating strong peer sanctions against individuals attempting assimilation-oriented social advancement. At the same time, the perception of permanent majority discrimination and a severely limited economic opportunity structure can lead to a sense of despair and hopelessness, causing minority individuals to literally "give up" and refuse to dedicate themselves to educational attainment because they believe that academic success ultimately makes little difference in getting ahead or that they will have to work much harder for the same socioeconomic rewards (Cornelius 1995:13; Fordham and Ogbu 1986; Ogbu 1974). Such resentment, rebellion, and resignation can lead to a rejection of majority cultural values and social standards of success[12] and are frequently accompanied by

---

[12]Some have argued that immigrant children adopt cultural patterns detrimental to educational success through contact with indigenous negative minorities (Perlman and Waldinger 1997:912; Portes 1995:73).

feelings of inferiority, lack of self-respect, mutual disparagement, internal frustration, and aggression.[13]

In this manner, although ethnic resistance through the refusal to assimilate has positive psychological effects for temporary and first-generation immigrants, its socially maladaptive consequences (discrimination from the majority society and restricted social mobility) can have a devastating negative psychological impact on second-generation immigrants. This causes them to behave in ways that can further increase their social maladaptation through the development of personal attitudes that preclude social advancement and perpetuate their low social class position. In this sense, minority ethnic resistance to dominant society eventually does not transform, but can reproduce precisely those forms of hegemonic socioeconomic oppression that are being actively opposed.[14] An initially voluntary immigrant minority with positive adaptational attitudes develops negative and maladjustive psychological patterns characteristic of many involuntary negative minorities, causing it to join the ranks of these socially marginalized, "castelike" minorities that have suffered a debilitating legacy of disparagement, social oppression, and low socioeconomic status (cf. Gans 1992). As a result, a process of segmented assimilation occurs (see Zhou 1997) where immigrant groups are incorporated into a low socioeconomic stratum.

Therefore, if the second-generation Japanese Brazilians do not culturally assimilate and continue to suffer from low socioeconomic status as a negative minority, it is possible they will come to somewhat resemble the Burakumin, an indigenous castelike minority, or the Korean Japanese. Like the Japanese Brazilians, the Burakumin are of Japanese descent, but they continue to experience discrimination as a culturally impure minority group because of their traditional association with ritually unclean occupations such as leatherworking, animal butchery, tanning skins, grave digging, and the handling of corpses. Although many of them have left

---

[13]Similar maladaptive patterns have been noted among negative minorities such as African Americans, Mexican Americans, Korean Japanese, and the Japanese Burakumin (Alvarez 1982; De Vos 1982a; De Vos and Wagatsuma 1966; Lee and De Vos 1981; Perlman and Waldinger 1997:913; Rohlen 1981; Suárez-Orozco and Suárez-Orozco 1995a,b; Zhou 1997:987).

[14]A number of earlier studies in the sociology and anthropology of education examined why negative minorities or working-class individuals continue to reproduce their low socio-occupational position generation after generation, despite their active resistance to dominant forms of oppression (Bourdieu and Passeron 1977; Bowles 1977; Ogbu 1974, 1978; Willis 1981).

such impure occupations and much of the socioeconomic basis for their ethnic disparagement has disappeared (and in fact, majority prejudice against them has decreased), they still suffer from considerable discrimination simply because of their descent[15] and manifest many of the problems traditionally associated with negative minority groups, such as poverty, welfare dependency, high crime rates and alcoholism, educational problems, mental illness, and disrupted families (see De Vos and Wagatsuma 1966), despite some improvement in recent years (Neary 1997:70–71). The Japanese Brazilians are also associated with a certain amount of impurity because of their close association with degrading and dirty 3K factory jobs shunned by most majority Japanese. Although their impurity is certainly much weaker than that of the Burakumin, their association with pollution is reinforced by their foreign origins and resulting cultural contamination.[16]

The Koreans migrated to Japan as laborers before and during World War II (many were forcibly relocated) and decided to remain in Japan after the war. Unlike the Burakumin, their stigmatized ethnicity in Japan is a result not of the continued impurity of past occupational status but of the impurity of race. Although most of the current generation of Korean Japanese have been born and raised in Japan and are culturally indistinguishable from majority Japanese (Onuma 1987), they continue to be subject to discriminatory barriers to social mobility simply because of their Korean descent and have not yet escaped their low socioeconomic status (Weiner 1997b:83). Many of them remain confined to the poorer and marginal economic sectors of society, and like the Burakumin, some of them have developed debilitating social and cultural patterns, including high delinquency, broken families, and inferiority in response to a history of colonization, discrimination, and economic exploitation (Rohlen 1981:186–87). Although a good number of them hide their Korean origins and attempt to pass as Japanese in order to avoid discrimination, their ancestry is usually detected during employment or at marriage when background checks of family registries are conducted (Lee and De Vos 1981).

[15]Neary (1997:55) notes that the basis for the impure outcaste status of the Burakumin changed from occupation to bloodline sometime around 1600.

[16]It is interesting to note here that although the Burakumin are an indigenous minority, they are sometimes associated with foreign ancestry as well (Neary 1997:53).

FROM STRANGERS TO NATIVES:
FULL ASSIMILATION AND LOSS OF MINORITY STATUS

The problems of negative minority status for second-generation immigrants outlined above will become serious issues for the Japanese Brazilians in the future. Over 30 percent of them now have children in Japan (Japan Statistics Research Institute 1993), most of whom are attending school. In 1993, there were already 4,075 Brazilian nikkeijin children enrolled in Japanese schools (Tajima 1995:177–78) and the number has risen to 7,000 (*The New York Times*, November 27, 2001, A4). In addition, the Japanese government estimates that 4,000 children are born to those of Brazilian nationality in Japan per year (Sasaki 1999:260).

Although it is still an open question what type of adaptational response most second-generation Japanese Brazilians will adopt, most nikkeijin children who came to Japan at a very young age face strong assimilative pressures in Japanese schools. Even schools with sizeable numbers of nikkeijin students make no attempt to provide any bilingual education (see Sellek 2001:203), preferring instead to linguistically assimilate the children as quickly as possible by having them take special Japanese language classes and placing them in ordinary classes for the rest of the day (sometimes with a personal tutor at their side). The Japanese teachers in Oizumi and Kawasaki I interviewed were generally quite optimistic about their nikkeijin students and reported that they learn to speak Japanese rather quickly, usually in about one year (although full comprehension of classroom instruction is much more difficult). According to these teachers, the children "graduate" from their special Japanese language classes within several months to a year, and most eventually reach an average academic level. Although the nikkeijin children initially cluster ethnically, they gradually get along well with Japanese children and participate fully in classroom and recess activities.[17] Japanese children usually interact with them openly and freely with less concern for ethnic differences than adults. Reportedly, students who refuse to study or attend school, or drop out, are rare. Some nikkeijin children have even excelled in the classroom, and only a minority are having significant learning problems or serious difficulty relating to the Japanese students.

---

[17]A couple of teachers mentioned that the nikkeijin children continue to prefer interacting with other nikkeijin children.

The next generation: a Japanese Brazilian student working on a math problem in class with a special Japanese tutor.

Although classroom instruction is usually prioritized as the primary form of learning at school, the peer group can also be very influential in ensuring the cultural assimilation of Japanese Brazilian children because many face strong pressure from their peers to conform to Japanese thinking and behavior in order to be socially accepted and avoid ostracism and rejection. As a result, Japanese teachers report that cultural differences among nikkeijin children in classroom behavior, styles of play, dress, food preferences, and study habits eventually disappear (see also Watanabe 1995a:56).

For many immigrant children, the assimilative cultural influence of the host society through secondary socialization in schools and through peer groups becomes much stronger and eventually overrides primary socialization in their families, where their parents attempt to retain the cultural and linguistic patterns of the home country. This is another example of how deterritorialization can cause generational conflicts within families by producing divergent and incompatible identifications and aspirations between parents and children (cf. Appadurai 1996:44). Japanese Brazilian parents report that they are generally unsuccessful in their attempts to teach their children proper Portuguese and to instill Brazilian patterns of thinking, or even to impart sufficient knowledge about Brazil. Even nikkeijin children who come to Japan at an older age begin to forget Portuguese and speak incorrectly.

The cultural influence of family socialization is especially impaired and weakened by migration because both parents frequently work long hours and do strenuous work, leaving them with relatively little time and energy to spend with the children during weekdays. This is exacerbated by the language barrier that develops between the immigrant generations, further lowering the level of interaction between parents and children. As a result, immigrant children increasingly turn to peer groups at school for emotional needs and social support (cf. Suárez-Orozco and Suárez-Orozco 1995a:186). In fact, Japanese Brazilian parents reinforce the assimilative pressures at school by encouraging their children to do well in their classes and make friends with Japanese children, thus helping to undermine the cultural power of the family that they seek to defend. In general, they spoke favorably of their children's performance and experiences at school and generally had a positive attitude, even heaping praise on the merits of the Japanese educational system at times.

The result of such pressures on nikkeijin children is rapid Japanese cultural assimilation and loss of their Brazilian cultural background (cf. Yamashita 2001:90). In fact, several of the nikkeijin children I spoke to who had been in Japan for several years could not be distinguished from Japanese children in speech, dress, or mannerisms. Some of them could no longer speak any Portuguese. As a result, most Japanese Brazilian children come to identify strongly with the Japanese and do not develop any notable Brazilian consciousness. Since there is no semblance of bilingual or multicultural education, not only are they unable to maintain their Portuguese, they do not learn about Brazil or develop any cultural appreciation for their homeland at school. Since they came to Japan at an early age, their experiences in Brazil are forgotten or are not strong enough to influence their ethnic self-consciousness in Japan. As a result, many nikkeijin parents are concerned about the serious linguistic, educational, and adaptational problems as well as identity crises their children will face after returning to Brazil,[18] and there

---

[18]According to a Nagoya University survey (reported in Nomoto et al. 1993), 80.3 percent of Brazilian nikkeijin with children in Japan indicated that their most serious concern was about their children's ability to adapt to Brazilian society once they returned home. The difficulties that repatriated nikkeijin children have are already becoming a serious social issue, and special assistance centers have even been set up for them in Brazil.

have been attempts to provide Portuguese instruction to nikkeijin children in Japan through private or community-organized language schools. However, one survey found that only 21 percent of nikkeijin parents are able to send their children to such classes (Kitagawa 1997:158), and although Brazilian educational materials are used, the children chat in Japanese (see Yamanaka 2000:143).

In addition, compared to their parents, Japanese Brazilian children do not have the negative ethnic experiences in Japan that would prevent identification with Japan and lead to the development of a Brazilian counteridentity. Not only are they spared the degrading experience of performing low-class immigrant jobs, they are in a receptive and encouraging Japanese educational environment relatively free from the overt social exclusion and ethnic "discrimination" that their parents take for granted. Also, since their cultural and linguistic differences with Japanese children are not as great at an early age, most are able to adjust to the behavioral patterns of their peers and gain social acceptance and friendship.

In fact, a number of Japanese teachers as well as Japanese Brazilian parents note that some nikkeijin children actually hide their Brazilian backgrounds at school and attempt to ethnically "pass" as if they were Japanese children. This is a result of an assimilative school culture where differences in ethnic background can lead to ostracism and bullying[19] and the resulting tendency of some nikkeijin children to internalize negative Japanese images of Brazil. One of my adult informants spoke about her older sister's experience in this regard:

> My sister's daughter now thinks completely like a Japanese. She doesn't want to return to Brazil because she thinks Japan is the best. Because of these images she gets from Japanese society, she thinks Brazil is a poor, backward country populated by armed bandits and is scared of the place. She even asked my sister the other day if Brazil has televisions, like Japan.

Therefore, some nikkeijin children are embarrassed when their Japanese Brazilian parents are invited to school and speak Portuguese in front of their classmates (cf. Yamashita 2001:90). One of my nikkeijin interviewees described how her child, who was passing as Japanese at school, even told

---

[19]A few Japanese Brazilian parents as well as Japanese teachers mention instances of bullying (*ijime*) of nikkeijin children by their Japanese peers.

her mixed-descent father that he did not have to attend a school reception for parents. "They teach these kids at school that Japan is the greatest country in the world," one Japanese Brazilian mother said, relating her impressions to me. "The Japanese Brazilian kids learn this type of thinking and begin to distance themselves from their Brazilian backgrounds. Some are even ashamed."

Given such strong assimilative pressures at school, the weakened cultural influence of the family, and the positive value of Japaneseness for these children (and the negative meaning of Brazilianness for some), there is little to prevent them from internalizing Japanese cultural norms and adopting a Japanese ethnic identity. As a result, a number of young nikkeijin children end up thinking, speaking, and acting Japanese outside and even inside the home. Although they may resist at first, as they continue to repeat such cultural patterns of thinking and behavior under the social pressures at school, they eventually internalize them.

This type of cultural assimilation affects not only individual behavioral patterns but ethnic identity and inner self-consciousness as well. Many of the younger children end up thinking that they are completely Japanese and come to identify exclusively with Japan, sometimes even telling their parents that they are "Japanese" because they live in Japan and speak Japanese. "My daughter has no consciousness of being born in Brazil," a Japanese Brazilian mother said, referring to her third-grade daughter, who had come to Japan when very young. "I tell her that she is not Japanese, but she asks me why. I tell her it's because our customs are different. She seems to understand, but I always have to explain this to her." This type of cultural assimilation is not "surface assimilation," as was the case with the few Japanized nikkeijin adults examined in chapter 6, but "full assimilation" in which Japanese cultural patterns are completely internalized and a Japanese ethnic identity is adopted.

Of course, nikkeijin children who come to Japan at a very young age must be distinguished from the much smaller number of older youth who arrive when they are in late elementary or junior high school (cf. Sellek 2001:204). In general, those who migrate during adolescence maintain their cultural affinity with Brazil and have more adaptive difficulties in contrast to those who migrate before adolescence (cf. Piore 1979:66; Taft 1973:113). Since the older nikkeijin children have already experienced a lifetime of Brazilian sociocultural influences and have completed much of their self-formation, they continue to identify with Brazil to a certain extent despite Japanese cultural pressures at school and do not completely assimilate to Japanese culture or assume a Japanese identity. This contrasts with their younger counterparts, who do not remember their Brazilian experiences very well and have not yet firmly developed a sense of self, and therefore are very impressionable and malleable to Japanese cultural influences. The older nikkeijin children also experience more prominent cultural and linguistic differences with Japanese students, which makes it more difficult for them to learn Japanese, keep up with school, and be accepted by their Japanese peers. In addition, they face more adultlike cultural pressures from the older Japanese students, who sometimes see them as strange because they do not speak Japanese properly and act and dress differently. Unlike younger children, who are not as concerned about such ethnic differences, these older nikkeijin students experience more social ostracism and rejection from their peers.

As a result, their mode of ethnic adaptation comes to resemble that of their parents to a certain extent. Because Japan and its culture are viewed with ambivalence, this causes some of them to develop a Brazilian counteridentity (albeit of a considerably weaker type than their parents'), which makes it harder for them to identify with Japan, learn the language, and internalize Japanese cultural norms of behavior. Japanese teachers frequently note problems in learning, academic performance, and sociocultural adaptation among their older nikkeijin students, even labeling a number of them as children "at risk."[20] Indeed, some of these older nikkeijin youth are already dropping out of school and are able to get only unskilled factory jobs because of their insufficient language ability (cf. Sellek 1996:258; Tajima 1995:180; cf. Yamashita 2001:92). A good number of nikkeijin who graduate from junior high school do not go on to high school, and very few enter Japanese universities because they have very little chance of passing Japan's difficult entrance exams (cf. Linger 2001:68, 134–35, 193; Sellek 2001:204). As a result, they are trapped in the low working-class jobs of their immigrant parents and are unable to improve their socioeconomic position.

Fundamentally, the problem that these older children face in Japan is ethnic identity diffusion (identity crisis). In general, adolescents are most vulnerable to identity diffusion when compared to adults, who have already resolved their identities, and children, who have not yet consolidated an identity and remain permeable to external influences. Japanese

---

[20]Some of the adaptational problems of Japanese Brazilian youth outlined here are also mentioned by Tajima (1995) and Watanabe (1995a).

Brazilian youth experience *more* conflict and dissonance between their individual sense of self and the external social milieu—which, according to Erikson (1968, 1980 [1959]), is the main source of identity diffusion—than nikkeijin adults. In contrast to the adult nikkeijin, who have insulated themselves in their ethnic communities and therefore function in a more or less "Brazilian" social environment that is congruous with their Brazilian counteridentities, the nikkeijin youth are exposed to an exclusively Japanese milieu at school in which they are subject to intense Japanese cultural pressures that clash with their inner Brazilian sense of self. Therefore, they remain unable to identify fully with Japanese culture because of some of their negative or ambivalent experiences with the Japanese and their conflicting Brazilian self-consciousness. At the same time, unlike the adult nikkeijin, they cannot reject Japanese society and identify completely with Brazil by confidently asserting their Brazilianness since their inner Brazilian identity is not as well developed and they face considerable external Japanese social pressure at school.

Since the formation of a firm ego identity is one of the important tasks of adolescence, the disruption of this critical stage of self-development by migration and the subsequent inability of these nikkeijin youth to properly resolve their ethnic identities may lead to a perpetual state of ethnic ambivalence that can have serious long-term social and psychological consequences. Because they are unable to properly identify with either the Brazilians or the Japanese, their Portuguese continues to deteriorate to the point where they can no longer speak properly, but they do not acquire sufficient Japanese linguistic or cultural skills. As a result, they are in danger of becoming ethnically marginal beings who no longer truly belong to the nikkeijin immigrant community but are not fully accepted by the majority Japanese either.[21]

However, except for the relatively small number of these Japanese Brazilian adolescents in Japan, it is likely that most of the second-generation nikkeijin children will eventually assimilate on a cultural level. Therefore, it seems that the ethnic resistance of the first-generation nikkeijin to Japanese cultural pressures will be relatively short-lived as their descendants gradually succumb to the essentialized logic of a dominant Japanese ethnicity in which the assumption of common descent has sustained an

---

[21]Other researchers have also observed adjustment and adaptational problems among immigrant children because of their inability to resolve their conflicting and confused ethnic identities (Suárez-Orozco and Suárez-Orozco 1995b:66–71; Taft 1973:112; Weinreich 1983a,b).

ideology of cultural homogeneity. Yet, at the same time, this will enable the second-generation nikkeijin to escape the low-class immigrant occupations of their parents and fully incorporate themselves into mainstream Japanese society.

Of course, full cultural assimilation among minority individuals is not always a guarantee of social acceptance and socioeconomic mobility if their simple membership in an ethnic minority group is a sufficient basis for majority discrimination. This is the case with both the Burakumin minority and second-generation Korean Japanese. Although they do not manifest any notable cultural differences with the Japanese, they continue to be socially marginalized and discriminated against as ethnically impure simply because they are of Burakumin or Korean descent.[22]

However, the future of the Japanese Brazilians will not resemble that of either of these minority groups because they have been ethnically constituted in Japan in a fundamentally different way. Unlike the Burakumin, the ethnic impurity of the Japanese Brazilians probably will *not* continue to linger into future generations because it has been temporarily *acquired* through cultural contamination abroad and their current assumption of dirty immigrant jobs in Japan rather than *inherited* through descent like that of the Burakumin, who were closely associated with unclean occupations for centuries. In addition, because the nikkeijin are of Japanese descent, they are fundamentally different from the Korean Japanese, who continue to suffer from discrimination simply because they are "racially" Korean. In contrast, the nikkeijin are exclusively a cultural minority. And unlike the essentialized ethnic stigma of race, which is inherited by birth and can only be diluted at best through intermarriage, cultural differences can disappear through assimilation, eventually expunging this source of ethnic impurity. One local city official in Oizumi expressed a common sentiment among my Japanese informants when he said:

> If the nikkeijin children eventually learn to speak the language fluently and to behave just like the Japanese, they will be accepted as Japanese. I believe the Brazilian nikkeijin are fundamentally different from the *zainichi kankokujin* (Korean Japanese) because they are of Japanese descent. The Japanese believe in *kettoshugi* (the principle of descent and blood ties). As we say, "blood is thicker than water."

---

[22]Minorities are made inferior especially when their members are socially rejected despite their efforts to culturally assimilate (cf. Fanon 1967:93).

In other words, in contrast to the inherited historical impurity of the Burakumin or the stigmatized racial descent of the Korean Japanese, the cultural and social class differences that currently mark the Japanese Brazilians as a negative minority are not irrevocable but are "temporary" characteristics. As a result, the nikkeijin can still be culturally and occupationally "purified" in Japan through cultural assimilation and subsequent social mobility to middle-class status.[23] In addition, most of the assimilated second-generation nikkeijin will probably conceal the Brazilian background of their parents. However, even if their ethnic background is revealed, it is unlikely to remain a significant source of discrimination or even of notable ethnic differentiation because they have met the racial, cultural, and social class criteria for being Japanese.

Despite the ethnic tolerance and diversity of Brazil, it is precisely there that the Japanese Brazilians will be perpetually seen as a minority group because of the mark of racial difference. In ethnically restrictive Japan, they will eventually disappear into the majority populace through cultural assimilation and social mobility because their ethnicity is not racially essentialized. As a result, future generations of Japanese Brazilians in Japan will not remain strangers in their ethnic homeland.

---

[23]In this manner, the Japanese Brazilians more closely resemble former *hinin* (i.e., literally "nonpersons"), who were impure outcastes only by occupation and social status, and not permanently by descent like the Burakumin (Price 1966). As a result, the hinin, unlike the Burakumin, have long since disappeared into the majority Japanese populace and have lost their former castelike minority status.

References

Abu-Lughod, Lila. 1986. *Veiled Sentiments: Honor and Poetry in a Bedouin Society*. Berkeley: University of California Press.

———. 1990. "The Romance of Resistance: Tracing Transformations of Power Through Bedouin Women." *American Ethnologist* 17 (1): 41–55.

Allison, Anne. 2000. "A Challenge to Hollywood? Japanese Character Goods Hit the U.S." *Japanese Studies* 20 (1): 67–88.

Allport, Gordon W. 1979. *The Nature of Prejudice*. Reading, MA: Addison-Wesley.

Alonso, Ana María. 1994. "The Politics of Space, Time and Substance: State Formation, Nationalism, and Ethnicity." *Annual Review of Anthropology* 23:379–405.

Alvarez, Rodolfo. 1982. "The Psycho-Historical and Socioeconomic Development of the Chicano Community in the United States." In Norman R. Yetman and C. Hoy Steele, eds., *Majority and Minority: The Dynamics of Race and Ethnicity in American Life*, 157–70. Boston: Allyn and Bacon.

Anderson, Benedict. 1991. *Imagined Communities: Reflections on the Origins and Spread of Nationalism*. London: Verso.

Andô, Zempati. 1973. "Cooperativismo Nascente" (The Rise of Cooperatism). In Hiroshi Saito and Takashi Maeyama, eds., *Assimilação e Integração dos Japoneses no Brasil* (The Assimilation and Integration of the Japanese in Brazil), 164–88. Petrópolis, Rio de Janeiro: Editora Vozes.

Appadurai, Arjun. 1990. "Disjuncture and Difference in the Global Cultural Economy." In Mike Featherstone, ed., *Global Culture: Nationalism, Globalization and Modernity*, 295–310. London: Sage Publications.

———. 1996. *Modernity at Large: Cultural Dimensions of Globalization*. Minneapolis: University of Minnesota Press.

Barth, Fredrik. 1969. "Introduction." In Fredrik Barth, ed., *Ethnic Groups and Boundaries*, 9–38. London: George Allen & Unwin.

———. 1987. *Cosmologies in the Making: A Generative Approach to Cultural Variation in Inner New Guinea*. Cambridge: Cambridge University Press.

Basch, Linda, Nina Glick Schiller, and Cristina Szanton Blanc. 1994. *Nations Unbound: Transnational Projects, Postcolonial Predicaments, and Deterritorialized Nation-States*. Amsterdam: Gordon and Breach.

Bateson, Gregory. 1958. *Naven*. Stanford: Stanford University Press.

———. 1972. *Steps to an Ecology of Mind*. New York: Ballantine.

Befu, Harumi. 1980. "The Group Model of Japanese Society and an Alternative." *Rice University Studies* 66 (1): 169–87.

———. 1983. "Internationalization of Japan and Nihon Bunkaron." In Hiroshi Mannari and Harumi Befu, eds., *The Challenge of Japan's Internationalization: Organization and Culture*, 232–66. Tokyo: Kwansei Gakuin University and Kodansha International.

———. 1993. "Nationalism and *Nihonjinron*." In Harumi Befu, ed., *Cultural Nationalism in East Asia*, 107–35. Berkeley: Institute of East Asian Studies, University of California Press.

Berreman, Gerald D. 1964. "Aleut Reference Group Alienation, Mobility, and Acculturation." *American Anthropologist* 66:231–50.

———. 1966. "Structure and Function of Caste Systems." In George A. De Vos and and Hiroshi Wagatsuma, eds., *Japan's Invisible Race: Caste in Culture and Personality*, 277–307. Berkeley: University of California Press.

———. 1972. *Hindus of the Himalayas: Ethnography and Change.* Berkeley: University of California Press.

———. 1982a. "Bazar Behavior: Social Identity and Social Interaction in Urban India." In George De Vos and Lola Romanucci-Ross, eds., *Ethnic Identity: Cultural Continuities and Change*, 71–105. Chicago: University of Chicago Press.

———. 1982b. "Race, Caste, and Other Invidious Distinctions in Social Stratification." In Norman R. Yetman and C. Hoy Steele, eds., *Majority and Minority: The Dynamics of Race and Ethnicity in American Life*, 15–33. Boston: Allyn and Bacon.

Bhabha, Homi K. 1990. "The Third Space." In Jonathan Rutherford, ed., *Identity: Community, Culture, Difference*, 207–21. London: Lawrence & Wishart.

Blalock, Hubert M. 1967. *Toward a Theory of Minority Group Relations.* New York: Wiley.

Blauner, Robert. 1982. "Colonized and Immigrant Minorities." In Norman R. Yetman and C. Hoy Steele, eds., *Majority and Minority: The Dynamics of Race and Ethnicity in American Life*, 302–17. Boston: Allyn and Bacon.

Boddy, Janice. 1989. *Wombs and Alien Spirits: Women, Men, and the Zar Cult in Northern Sudan.* Madison: University of Wisconsin Press.

Bonacich, Edna. 1982. "A Theory of Middleman Minorities." In Norman R. Yetman and C. Hoy Steele, eds., *Majority and Minority: The Dynamics of Race and Ethnicity in American Life*, 270–81. Boston: Allyn and Bacon.

Borjas, George J. 1989. "Economic Theory and International Migration." *International Migration Review* 23:457–85.

Bourdieu, Pierre. 1977. *Outline of a Theory of Practice.* Trans. Richard Nice. Cambridge: Cambridge University Press.

———. 1984. *Distinction: A Social Critique of the Judgement of Taste.* Trans. Richard Nice. Cambridge: Harvard University Press.

Bourdieu, Pierre and Jean-Claude Passeron. 1977. *Reproduction in Education, Society and Culture.* Trans. Richard Nice. London: Sage Publications.

Bowen, Elenore Smith (Laura Bohannan). 1964. *Return to Laughter.* Garden City, NY: Anchor Books, Doubleday & Company.

Bowles, Samuel. 1977. "Unequal Education and the Reproduction of the Social Division of Labor." In Jerome Karabel and A. H. Halsey, eds., *Power and Ideology in Education*, 137–53. New York: Oxford University Press.

Brenner, Suzanne. 1996. "Reconstructing Self and Society: Javanese Muslim Women and 'the Veil.' " *American Ethnologist* 23 (4): 673–97.

Brettell, Caroline. 2000. "Theorizing Migration in Anthropology: The Social Construction of Networks, Identities, Communities, and Globalscapes." In Caroline Brettell and James Hollifield, eds., *Migration Theory: Talking Across Disciplines*, 97–135. New York: Routledge.

Brown, Roger. 1986. *Social Psychology*. 2nd ed. New York: Free Press.

Bruner, Edward M. 1961. "Urbanization and Ethnic Identity in North Sumatra." *American Anthropologist* 63:508–21.

——. 1975. "Tradition and Modernization in Batak Society." In George A. De Vos, ed., *Responses to Change: Society, Culture, and Personality*, 234–52. New York: D. Van Nostrand.

Bun, Chan Kwok and Tong Chee Kiong. 1993. "Rethinking Assimilation and Ethnicity: The Chinese in Thailand." *International Migration Review* 27 (1): 140–68.

Butsugan, Sumi. 1980. "Participaçao Social e Tendência de Casamentos Interétnicos" (Social Participation and the Tendency of Interethnic Marriages). In Hiroshi Saito, ed., *A Presença Japonêsa no Brasil* (The Japanese Presence in Brazil), 101–12. São Paulo: Editôra da Universidade de São Paulo.

Calhoun, Craig. 1992. "The Infrastructure of Modernity: Indirect Social Relationships, Information Technology, and Social Integration." In H. Haferkamp and Neil J. Smelser, eds., *Social Change and Modernity*, 205–36. Berkeley: University of California Press.

Capuano de Oliveira, Adriana. 1999. "Repensando a Identidade Dentro da Emigraçao *Dekassegui*" (Rethinking Identity in the Context of Dekasegi Emigration). In Rossana Rocha Reis and Teresa Sales, eds., *Cenas do Brasil Migrante* (Scenes of Migrant Brazil), 275–307. São Paulo, Brazil: Boitempo Editorial.

——. N.d. "Migration and Identity: Brazilian Dekasegi in Japan." Unpublished mauscript.

Cardoso, Ruth Corrêa Leite. 1973. "O Papel das Associações Juvenis na Aculturação dos Japoneses" (The Role of Youth Associations in the Acculturation of the Japanese). In Hiroshi Saito and Takashi Maeyama, eds., *Assimilação e Integração dos Japoneses no Brasil* (The Assimilation and Integration of the Japanese in Brazil), 317–45. Petrópolis, Rio de Janeiro: Editora Vozes.

Castells, Manuel. 1989. *The Informational City: Information Technology, Economic Restructuring, and the Urban-Regional Process*. Oxford: B. Blackwell.

——. 1997. *The Power of Identity*. Malden, MA: B. Blackwell.

Castillo, Rosalva Aída Hernández and Ronald Nigh. 1998. "Global Processes and Local Identity Among Mayan Coffee Growers in Chiapas, Mexico." *American Anthropologist* 100 (1): 136–47.

Castles, Stephen (with Heather Booth and Tina Wallace). 1984. *Here for Good: Western Europe's New Ethnic Minorities*. London: Pluto Press.

Castles, Stephen and Mark J. Miller. 1993. *The Age of Migration: International Population Movements in the Modern World*. London: Macmillan.

Centro de Estudos Nipo-Brasileiros (Center for Japanese-Brazilian Studies). 1992. *Pesquisa de Comportamento e Atitude de Japoneses e seus Descendentes Residentes no Brasil*. São Paulo: Centro de Estudos Nipo-Brasileiros.

Charles, Carolle. 1992. "Transnationalism in the Construct of Haitian Migrants' Racial Categories of Identity in New York City." In Nina Glick Schiller, Linda Basch, and Cristina Blanc-Szanton, eds., *Towards a Transnational Perspective on Migration: Race, Class, Ethnicity, and Nationalism Reconsidered*, 101–23. New York: The New York Academy of Sciences.

Cicourel, Aaron V. 1964. *Method and Measurement in Sociology*. Glencoe, IL: Free Press.

Clifford, James. 1988. *The Predicament of Culture: Twentieth-Century Ethnography, Literature, and Art*. Cambridge: Harvard University Press.

———. 1992. "Travelling Cultures." In Lawrence Grossberg, Cary Nelson, and Paula Treichler, eds., *Cultural Studies*, 96–116. New York: Routledge.

———. 1994. "Diasporas." *Cultural Anthropology* 9 (3): 302–38.

———. 1997. *Routes: Travel and Translation in the Late Twentieth Century.* Cambridge: Harvard University Press.

Clifford, James and George E. Marcus. 1986. *Writing Culture: The Poetics and Politics of Ethnography.* Berkeley: University of California Press.

Cohen, Abner. 1974. "Introduction: The Lesson of Ethnicity." In Abner Cohen, ed., *Urban Ethnicity*, ix–xxiv. London: Tavistock Publications.

Cohen, Anthony P. 1994. *Self Consciousness: An Alternative Anthropology of Identity.* London: Routledge.

Cole, Robert E. 1971. *Japanese Blue Collar: The Changing Tradition.* Berkeley: University of California Press.

Comaroff, Jean. 1985. *Body of Power, Spirit of Resistance: The Culture and History of a South African People.* Chicago: University of Chicago Press.

Comaroff, John L. 1987. "Of Totemism and Ethnicity: Consciousness, Practice, and Signs of Inequality." *Ethnos* 52 (3–4): 301–23.

Conaway, Mary Ellen. 1986. "The Pretense of the Neutral Researcher." In Tony Larry Whitehead and Mary Ellen Conaway, eds., *Self, Sex, and Gender in Cross-Cultural Fieldwork*, 52–63. Urbana: University of Illinois Press.

Cornelius, Wayne A. 1991. "Labor Migration to the United States: Development Outcomes and Alternatives in Mexican Sending Communities." In Sergi Díaz-Briquets and Sidney Weintraub, eds., *Regional and Sectoral Development in Mexico as Alternatives to Migration*. Boulder: Westview Press, 89–131.

———. 1994. "Japan: The Illusion of Immigration Control." In Wayne A. Cornelius, Philip L. Martin, and James F. Hollifield, eds., *Controlling Immigration: A Global Perspective*, 375–410. Stanford: Stanford University Press.

———. 1995. "Educating California's Immigrant Children: Introduction and Overview." In Wayne A. Cornelius and Rubén G. Rumbaut, eds., *California's Immigrant Children: Theory, Research, and Implications for Educational Policy*, 1–16. San Diego: Center for U.S.–Mexican Studies, University of California, San Diego.

———. 1998. "The Structural Embeddedness of Demand for Mexican Immigrant Labor: New Evidence from California." In Marcelo Suárez-Orozco, ed., *Crossings: Mexican Immigration in Interdisciplinary Perspective*, 114–44. Cambridge: Harvard University Press.

Cornelius, Wayne A., Philip L. Martin, and James F. Hollifield. 1994. "Introduction: The Ambivalent Quest for Immigration Control." In Wayne A. Cornelius, Philip L. Martin, and James F. Hollifield, eds., *Controlling Immigration: A Global Perspective*, 3–41. Stanford: Stanford University Press.

Crapanzano, Vincent. 1977. "On the Writing of Ethnography." *Dialectical Anthropology* 2 (1): 69–73.

———. 1982. "The Self, the Third, and Desire." In Benjamin Lee, ed., *Psychosocial Theories of the Self*, 179–206. New York: Plenum Press.

DaMatta, Roberto. 1991. *Carnivals, Rogues, and Heroes: An Interpretation of the Brazilian Dilemma.* Notre Dame, IN: University of Notre Dame Press.

D'Andrade, Roy G. 1995. *The Development of Cognitive Anthropology.* Cambridge: Cambridge University Press.

de Certeau, Michel. 1984. *The Practice of Everyday Life*. Trans. Steven Rendall. Berkeley: University of California Press.

DeSantis, Grace and Richard Benkin. 1980. "Ethnicity Without Community." *Ethnicity* 7:137–43.

Devereux, George. 1967. *From Anxiety to Method in the Behavioral Sciences*. Paris: Mouton & Co.

———. 1982. "Ethnic Identity: Its Logical Foundations and Its Dysfunctions." In George De Vos and Lola Romanucci-Ross, eds., *Ethnic Identity: Cultural Continuities and Change*, 42–70. Chicago: University of Chicago Press.

De Vos, George A. 1975a. "Apprenticeship and Paternalism." In Ezra F. Vogel, ed., *Modern Japanese Organization and Decision-Making*, 210–27. Berkeley: University of California Press.

———. 1975b. "Dangers of Pure Theory in Social Anthropology." *Ethos* 3 (1): 77–91.

———. 1976a. "Affective Dissonance and Primary Socialization: Implications for a Theory of Incest Avoidance." In Theodore Schwartz, ed., *Socialization as Cultural Communication: Development of a Theme in the Work of Margaret Mead*, 73–90. Berkeley: University of California Press.

———. 1976b. "Conclusion: Responses to Change: Recurrent Patterns." In George De Vos, ed., *Responses to Change: Society, Culture, and Personality*, 342–59. New York: D. Van Nostrand.

———. 1976c. "Urbanization: Adaptation and Adjustment." In George De Vos, ed., *Responses to Change: Society, Culture, and Personality*, 207–13. New York: D. Van Nostrand.

———. 1980. "Ethnic Adaptation and Minority Status." *Journal of Cross-Cultural Psychology* 11:101–24.

———. 1982a. "Adaptive Strategies in U.S. Minorities." In Enrico E. Jones and Sheldon J. Korchin, eds., *Minority Mental Health*, 74–117. New York: Praeger.

———. 1982b. "Ethnic Pluralism: Conflict and Accommodation." In George De Vos and Lola Romanucci-Ross, eds., *Ethnic Identity: Cultural Continuities and Change*, 5–41. Chicago: University of Chicago Press.

———. 1983. "Adaptive Conflict and Adjustive Coping: Psychocultural Approaches to Ethnic Identity." In Theodore Sarbin and Karl E. Scheibe, eds., *Studies in Social Identity*, 204–30. New York: Praeger.

———. 1984. "Introduction: Trends Toward Social Democracy in Japan." In *Institutions for Change in Japanese Society*, George A. De Vos, ed., 2–19. Berkeley: University of California Press.

———. 1985. "Dimensions of the Self in Japanese Culture." In George A. De Vos, Francis L. K. Hsu, and Anthony J. Marsella, eds., *Culture and Self: Asian and Western Perspectives*, 141–84. New York: Tavistock Publications.

———. 1992. *Social Cohesion and Alienation: Minorities in the United States and Japan*. Boulder: Westview Press.

De Vos, George A. and Lola Romanucci-Ross. 1982. "Ethnicity: Vessel of Meaning and Emblem of Contrast." In George De Vos and Lola Romanucci-Ross, eds., *Ethnic Identity: Cultural Continuities and Change*, 363–90. Chicago: University of Chicago Press.

De Vos, George A. and Marcelo M. Suárez-Orozco. 1990. *Status Inequality: The Self in Culture*. Berkeley: University of California Press.

De Vos, George A. and Hiroshi Wagatsuma. 1966. *Japan's Invisible Race: Caste in Culture and Personality*. Berkeley: University of California Press.

Doi, Takeo L. 1974. "Higaisha-Ishiki: The Psychology of Revolting Youth in Japan." In Takie S. Lebra and William P. Lebra, eds., *Japanese Culture and Behavior*, 450–57. Honolulu: University of Hawaii Press.

———. 1986. *The Anatomy of Self: The Individual Versus Society.* Tokyo: Kodansha International.

Dore, Ronald P. 1973. *British Factory–Japanese Factory: The Origins of National Diversity in Industrial Relations.* Berkeley: University of California Press.

———. 1986. *Flexible Rigidities: Industrial Policy and Structural Adjustment in the Japanese Economy 1970–80.* Stanford: Stanford University Press.

Douglas, Mary. 1966. *Purity and Danger: An Analysis of the Concepts of Pollution and Taboo.* London: ARK Paperbacks.

Douglass, Mike. 2000. "The Singularities of International Migration of Women to Japan: Past, Present, and Future." In Mike Douglass and Glenda S. Roberts, eds., *Japan and Global Migration: Foreign Workers and the Advent of a Multicultural Society,* 91–120. London: Routledge.

Douglass, Mike and Glenda S. Roberts. 2000. "Japan in a Global Age of Migration." In Mike Douglass and Glenda S. Roberts, eds., *Japan and Global Migration: Foreign Workers and the Advent of a Multicultural Society,* 3–37. London: Routledge.

Du Bois, Cora. 1986. "Studies in an Indian Town." In Peggy Golde, ed., *Women in the Field: Anthropological Experiences,* 221–36. Chicago: Aldine.

Dumézil, Georges. 1988 [1948]. *Mitra-Varuna: An Essay on Two Indo-European Representations of Sovereignty.* New York: Zone Books.

Eidheim, Harald. 1969. "When Ethnic Identity Is a Social Stigma." In Fredrik Barth, ed., *Ethnic Groups and Boundaries,* 39–57. London: George Allen & Unwin.

Epstein, A. L. 1978. *Ethos and Identity: Three Studies in Ethnicity.* London: Tavistock Publications.

Erikson, Erik H. 1968. *Identity: Youth and Crisis.* New York: Norton.

———. 1980 [1959]. *Identity and the Life Cycle.* New York: Norton.

Escobar, Arturo. 1993. "The Limits of Reflexivity: Politics in Anthropology's Post-*Writing Culture* Era." *Journal of Anthropological Research* 49 (4): 377–91.

———. 1994. "Welcome to Cyberia: Notes on the Anthropology of Cyberculture." *Current Anthropology* 35 (3): 211–31.

Evans-Pritchard, E. E. 1977 [1940]. *The Nuer: A Description of the Modes of Livelihood and Political Institutions of a Nilotic People.* New York: Oxford University Press.

Ewing, Katherine Pratt. 1990. "The Illusion of Wholeness: Culture, Self, and the Experience of Inconsistency." *Ethos* 18 (3): 251–78.

———. 1998. "Crossing Borders and Transgressing Boundaries: Metaphors for Negotiating Multiple Identities." *Ethos* 26 (2): 262–67.

Fabricant, Carole. 1998. "Riding the Waves of (Post)Colonial Migrancy: Are We All Really in the Same Boat?" *Diaspora* 7 (1): 25–51.

Fanon, Frantz. 1967. *Black Skin, White Masks.* Trans. Charles Lam Markmann. New York: Grove Press.

Fawcett, James T. 1989. "Networks, Linkages, and Migration Systems." *International Migration Review* 23 (3): 672–80.

Fawcett, James T. and Fred Arnold. 1987. "Explaining Diversity: Asian and Pacific Immigration Systems." In James Fawcett and Benjamin Carino, eds., *Pacific Bridges: The New Immigration from Asia and the Pacific Islands,* 453–73. New York: Center for Migration Studies.

Featherstone, Mike. 1996. "Localism, Globalism, and Cultural Identity." In Rob Wilson and Wimal Dissanayake, eds., *Global/Local: Cultural Production and the Transnational Imaginary,* 46–77. Durham: Duke University Press.

Fegan, Brian. 1986. "Tenants' Non-Violent Resistance to Landowner Claims in a Central Luzon Village." *Journal of Peasant Studies* 13 (2): 87–106.

Feldman-Bianco, Bela. 1992. "Multiple Layers of Time and Space: The Construction of Class, Race, Ethnicity, and Nationalism Among Portuguese Immigrants." In Nina Glick Schiller, Linda Basch, and Cristina Blanc-Szanton, eds., *Towards a Transnational Perspective on Migration: Race, Class, Ethnicity, and Nationalism Reconsidered*, 145–74. New York: The New York Academy of Sciences.

Ferreira, Yoshiya Nakagawara and Alice Yatiyo Asari. 1986. "Algumas Considerações sobre a Atuação do Imigrante Japonês e seus Descendentes na comunidade Londrinense" (Some Considerations About the Achievements of the Japanese Immigrants and Their Descendents in the Londrina Community). In Massao Ohno, ed., *O Nikkei e Sua Americanidade* (The Nikkei and Their Americanness), 213–24. São Paulo: COPANI.

Festinger, Leon. 1957. *A Theory of Cognitive Dissonance*. Stanford: Stanford University Press.

Flores, Moacyr. 1975. "Japoneses no Rio Grande do Sul" (The Japanese in Rio Grande do Sul). *Veritas* 77:65–98.

Foner, Nancy. 1997. "What's New About Transnationalism? New York Immigrants Today and at the Turn of the Century." *Diaspora* 6 (3): 355–75.

Fordham, Signithia and John U. Ogbu. 1986. "Black Students' School Success: Coping with the Burden of 'Acting White.' " *The Urban Review* 18 (3): 176–206.

Foster, Robert J. 1991. "Making National Cultures in the Global Ecumene." *Annual Review of Anthropology* 20:235–60.

Foucault, Michel. 1982. "The Subject and Power." In Hubert L. Dreyfus and Paul Rabinow, eds., *Michel Foucault: Beyond Structuralism and Hermeneutics*, 208–26. Chicago: University of Chicago Press.

——. 1995 [1977]. *Discipline and Punish*. Trans. Alan Sheridan. New York: Vintage.

Frazer, Sir James G. 1911–15. *The Golden Bough*, 3rd ed. 13 vols. London: Macmillan.

Freyre, Gilberto. 1936. *Casa Grande & Senzala; Formação da Família Brasileira Sob o Regimen de Economia Patriarchal* (The Masters and the Slaves: The Formation of the Brazilian Family Under a Patriarchal, Economic Regime). Rio de Janeiro: Schmidt.

Fujisaki, Yasuo. 1991. *Dekasegi Nikkei Gaikokujin Rodosha* (Migrant Nikkei Foreign Workers). Tokyo: Akaishi Shoten.

Fujitani, Takashi. 1996. *Splendid Monarchy: Power and Pageantry in Modern Japan*. Berkeley: University of California Press.

Fukunaga, Patrick Makoto. 1983. *The Brazilian Experience: The Japanese Immigrants During the Period of the Vargas Regime and the Immediate Aftermath, 1930–1946*. Ph.D. diss., University of California, Santa Barbara. Ann Arbor, MI: University Microfilms International.

Gans, Herbert J. 1979. "Symbolic Ethnicity: The Future of Ethnic Groups and Cultures in America." *Ethnic and Racial Studies* 2 (1): 1–20.

——. 1992. "Second-Generation Decline: Scenarios for the Economic and Ethnic Futures of the Post-1965 American Immigrants." *Ethnic and Racial Studies* 15 (2): 173–92.

——. 1994. "Symbolic Ethnicity and Symbolic Religiosity: Towards a Comparison of Ethnic and Religious Acculturation." *Ethnic and Racial Studies* 17 (4): 577–92.

——. 1997. "Toward a Reconciliation of 'Assimilation' and 'Pluralism': The Interplay of Acculturation and Ethnic Retention." *International Migration Review* 31 (4): 875–92.

Geertz, Clifford. 1973. *The Interpretation of Cultures*. New York: Basic Books.

Gellner, Ernest. 1983. *Nations and Nationalism*. Ithaca: Cornell University Press.

Giddens, Anthony. 1984. *The Constitution of Society: Outline of the Theory of Structuration.* Berkeley: University of California Press.

——. 1989. *Sociology.* Cambridge: Polity Press.

——. 1991. *Modernity and Self-Identity: Self and Society in the Late Modern Age.* Stanford: Stanford University Press.

Gilroy, Paul. 1993. *The Black Atlantic: Modernity and Double Consciousness.* Cambridge: Harvard University Press.

Glick Schiller, Nina. 1997. "The Situation of Transnational Studies." *Identities: Global Studies in Culture and Power* 4 (2): 155–66.

Glick Schiller, Nina, Linda Basch, and Cristina Szanton Blanc. 1995. "From Immigrant to Transmigrant: Theorizing Transnational Migration." *Anthropological Quarterly* 68 (1): 48–63.

Glick Schiller, Nina and Georges Fouron. 1990. " 'Everywhere We Go, We Are in Danger': Ti Manno and the Emergence of a Haitian Transnational Identity." *American Ethnologist* 17 (2): 329–47.

——. 1998. "Transnational Lives and National Identities: The Identity Politics of Haitian Immigrants." In Michael Peter Smith and Luis Eduardo Guarnizo, eds., *Transnationalism from Below, Comparative Urban and Community Research,* 6:130–61. New Brunswick: Transaction Publishers.

Gmelch, George. 1980. "Return Migration." *Annual Review of Anthropology* 9:135–59.

Goffman, Erving. 1959. *The Presentation of Self in Everyday Life.* New York: Anchor Press.

——. 1963. *Stigma: Notes on the Management of Spoiled Identity.* Englewood Cliffs, NJ: Prentice-Hall.

——. 1967. *Interaction Ritual: Essays on Face-to-Face Behavior.* New York: Pantheon.

Gold, Raymond L. 1958. "Roles in Sociological Field Observations." *Social Forces* 36:217–23.

Gonzalez, Nancie L. 1986. "The Anthropologist as Female Head of Household." In Tony Larry Whitehead and Mary Ellen Conaway, eds., *Self, Sex, and Gender in Cross-Cultural Fieldwork,* 84–100. Urbana: University of Illinois Press.

——. 1989. "Conflict, Migration, and the Expression of Ethnicity: Introduction." In Nancie L. Gonzalez and Carolyn S. McCommon, eds., *Conflict, Migration, and the Expression of Ethnicity.* Boulder: Westview Press, 1–10.

Goodman, Roger. 1990a. "Deconstructing an Anthropological Text: a "Moving" Account of Returnee Schoolchildren in Contemporary Japan." In Eyal Ben-Ari, Brian Moeran, and James Valentine, eds., *Unwrapping Japan: Society and Culture in Anthropological Perspective,* 163–87. Honolulu: University of Hawaii Press.

——. 1990b. *Japan's "International Youth": The Emergence of a New Class of Schoolchildren.* Oxford: Clarendon Press.

Gordon, Milton. 1961. "Assimiliation in America: Theory and Reality." *Daedalus* 90 (2): 263–83.

——. 1964. *Assimilation in American Life: The Role of Race, Religion and National Origins.* New York: Oxford University Press.

Goza, Franklin. 1994. "Brazilian Immigration to North America." *International Migration Review* 28 (1): 136–52.

——. 1999. "Brazilian Immigration to Ontario." *International Migration* 37 (4): 765–89.

Graburn, Nelson. 1983. *To Pray, Pay, and Play: The Cultural Structure of Japanese Domestic Tourism.* Aix-en-Provence Cedex: Centre Des Hautes Etudes Touristiques.

Grasmuck, Sherri and Patricia R. Pessar. 1991. *Between Two Islands: Dominican International Migration.* Berkeley: University of California Press.

Guarnizo, Luis Eduardo. 1997. "The Emergence of a Transnational Social Formation and the Mirage of Return Migration Among Dominican Transmigrants." *Identities: Global Studies in Culture and Power* 4 (2): 281–322.

Guarnizo, Luis Eduardo and Michael Peter Smith. 1998. "The Locations of Transnationalism." In Michael Peter Smith and Luis Eduardo Guarnizo, eds., *Transnationalism from Below, Comparative Urban and Community Research*, 6:3–34. New Brunswick: Transaction Publishers.

Gupta, Akhil. 1992. "The Song of the Nonaligned World: Transnational Identities and the Reinscription of Space in Late Capitalism." *Cultural Anthropology* 7 (1): 63–79.

——. 1994. "The Reincarnation of Souls and the Rebirth of Commodities: Representations of Time in 'East' and 'West.' " In Jonathan Boyarin, ed., *Remapping Memory: The Politics of TimeSpace*, 161–83. Minneapolis: University of Minnesota Press.

Gupta, Akhil and James Ferguson. 1992. "Beyond 'Culture': Space, Identity, and the Politics of Difference." *Cultural Anthropology* 7 (1): 6–23.

Hagendoorn, Louk. 1993. "Ethnic Categorization and Outgroup Exclusion: Cultural Values and Social Stereotypes in the Construction of Ethnic Hierarchies." *Ethnic and Racial Studies* 16 (1): 26–51.

Hall, Stuart. 1990. "Cultural Identity and Diaspora." In Jonathan Rutherford, ed., *Identity: Community, Culture, Difference*, 222–37. London: Lawrence & Wishart.

Hallowell, A. Irving. 1955. *Culture and Experience*. Philadelphia: University of Pennsylvania Press.

Hamabata, Matthews M. 1990. *Crested Kimono: Power and Love in the Japanese Business Family*. Ithaca: Cornell University Press.

Hammarlund, Anders. 1994. "Migrancy and Syncretism: A Turkish Musician in Stockholm." *Diaspora* 3 (3): 305–23.

Handa, Tomoo. 1987. *O Imigrante Japonês: História de sua Vida no Brasil* (The Japanese Immigrant: The History of His Life in Brazil). São Paulo: Centro de Estudos Nipo-Brasileiros.

Hannerz, Ulf. 1987. "The World in Creolisation." *Africa* 57 (4): 546–59.

——. 1996. *Transnational Connections: Culture, People, Places*. London: Routledge.

Hansen, Marcus. 1952. "The Third Generation in America." *Commentary* 14:492–500.

Harootunian, Harry D. 1988. *Things Seen and Unseen: Discourse and Ideology in Tokugawa Nativism*. Chicago: University of Chicago Press.

Harris, Marvin and Conrad Kottak. 1963. "The Structural Significance of Brazilian Racial Categories." *Sociologia* 25:203–209.

Harvey, David. 1989. *The Condition of Postmodernity*. Cambridge, MA: Blackwell.

Herman, Simon N. 1970. *American Students in Israel*. Ithaca: Cornell University Press.

Herskovits, Melville. 1941. *The Myth of the Negro Past*. New York: Harper and Brothers.

Herzfeld, Michael. 1997. *Cultural Intimacy: Social Poetics in the Nation-State*. New York: Routledge.

Hirota, Yasuo. 1993. "Toshi Esunikku Comyunitei no Keisei to 'Tekiyo' no Iso ni Tsuite: Tokuni Yokohama-shi Tsurumi no Nikkeijin Comyunitei o Taisho to Shite" (About the Construction of Urban Ethnic Communities and the Phase of Adaptation: Especially Within the Nikkeijin Communities in Tsurumi, Kanagawa-ken). *Shakai Kagaku Nenpo* 27:289–325.

——. 1994. "Nikkeijin Kazoku no Ikikata" (The Lifestyle of Nikkeijin Families). In Michihiro Okuda, Yasuo Hirota, and Junko Tajima, eds., *Gaikokujin Kyojyusha to Nihon no Chiiki Shakai* (Foreign Residents and Japanese Local Society), 192–257. Tokyo: Akaishi Shoten.

Horowitz, Ruth. 1989. "Getting In." In Carolyn D. Smith and William Kornblum, eds., *In the Field: Readings on the Field Research Experience*, 45–54. New York: Praeger.

Hsu, Ruth Y. 1996. " 'Will the Model Minority Please Identity Itself?' American Ethnic Identity and Its Discontents." *Diaspora* 5 (1): 37–63.

IBGE (*Instituto Brasileiro de Geografia e Estatística*). 1983–92. *Anuário Estatístico do Brasil* (Annual Statistics of Brazil).

Inkeles, Alex. 1976. "Becoming Modern: Individual Change in Six Developing Countries." In Theodore Schwartz, ed., *Socialization as Cultural Communication: Development of a Theme in the Work of Margaret Mead*, 231–50. Berkeley: University of California Press.

Inkeles, Alex and David H. Smith. 1976. "Personal Adjustment and Modernization." In George A. De Vos, ed., *Responses to Change: Society, Culture, and Personality*, 214–33. New York: D. Van Nostrand.

Inoue, Neusa Emiko. 1994. "Desmistificando os Problemas Psicológicos" (Demystifying Psychological Problems). In Charles Tetsuo Chigusa, ed., *A Quebra dos Mitos: O Fenômeno Dekassegui através de Relatos Pessoais* (The Breaking of Myths: The *Dekasegi* Phenomenon Through Personal Accounts), 75–77. Atsugi-shi, Japan: International Press Corporation.

Institute of Statistical Research. 1993. *Nanbei Nikkeijin Shuro ni Kansuru Jittai Chosa* (Survey About the Employment of South American *Nikkeijin*). Tokyo: Institute of Statistical Research, 7–37.

Ishi, Angelo A. 1991. *Nikkei Burajirujin Dekasegi Rodosha no Ibunka Komyunikeshon ni Kansuru Kenyu* (Research About the Communication of Cultural Differences of the Brazilian Nikkei Workers). M.A. thesis, University of Tokyo.

——. 1992. "Burajiru Nikkei Dekasegi Rodosha to Nihon no Shinzoku" (Brazilian *Nikkei Dekasegi* Workers and Japanese Relatives). *Mare Nostrum* 5:69–72.

——. 1994. "Quem é Quem no Tribunal da Discriminação" (Who Is Who in the Tribunal of Discrimination). In Charles Tetsuo Chigusa, ed., *A Quebra dos Mitos: O Fenômeno Dekassegui através de Relatos Pessoais* (The Breaking of Myths: The *Dekasegi* Phenomenon Through Personal Accounts), 35–51. Atsugi-shi, Japan: International Press Corporation.

Iwabuchi, Koichi. 1998. "Marketing 'Japan': Japanese Cultural Presence Under a Global Gaze." *Japanese Studies* 18 (2): 165–86.

Ivy, Marilyn. 1995. *Discourses of the Vanishing: Modernity, Phantasm, Japan*. Chicago: University of Chicago Press.

Japan Immigration Association. 1995. *Statistics on Immigration Control*. Tokyo: Japan Immigration Association.

——. 1996. *Statistics on Resident Foreigners*. Tokyo: Japan Immigration Association.

Japan Institute of Labor. 1995. *Nikkeijin Rodosha no Jukyu Shisutemu to Shuro Keiken* (The Demand/Supply System and Employment Experiences of Nikkeijin Workers). Tokyo: Japan Institute of Labor.

Japan Statistics Research Institute (*Nihon Tokei Kenkyujo*). 1993. *Tokei Kenkyu Sanko Shiryo no. 38: Nikkei Burajirujin Shuro/Seikatsu Jittai Chosa* (Statistical Research Reference: Survey of Brazilian *Nikkeijin* Employment and Living Conditions). Tokyo: *Nihon Tokei Kenkyujo* (Hosei University).

Jaspars, J. M. F. and Suwarsih Warnaen. 1982. "Intergroup Relations, Ethnic Identity, and Self-Evaluation in Indonesia." In Henri Tajfel, ed., *Social Identity and Intergroup Relations*, 335–66. Cambridge: Cambridge University Press.

Jenkins, Richard. 1994. "Rethinking Ethnicity: Identity, Categorization, and Power." *Ethnic and Racial Studies* 17 (2): 197–223.

JICA (Japan International Cooperation Association). 1992. *Nikkeijin Honpo Shuro Jittai Chosa Hokokusho* (Report on the Survey of the Nikkeijin Working in Our Country). *Kokusai Kyoryoku Jigyodan* (International Cooperation Association).

Johnson, Chalmers. 1995. *Japan: Who Governs? The Rise of the Developmental State.* New York: Norton.

Joppke, Christian. 1998. "Multiculturalism and Immigration: A Comparison of the United States, Germany, and Great Britain." In David Jacobson, ed., *The Immigration Reader: America in a Multidisciplinary Perspective,* 285–319. Malden, MA: Blackwell.

———. 1999. *Immigration and the Nation-State: The United States, Germany, and Great Britain.* New York: Oxford University Press.

Kajita, Takamichi. 1994. *Gaikokujin Rodosha to Nihon* (Foreign Laborers and Japan). Tokyo: NHK Books.

Kaplan, Martha and John D. Kelly. 1994. "Rethinking Resistance: Dialogics of 'Disaffection' in Colonial Fiji." *American Ethnologist* 21 (1): 123–51.

Kardiner, Abram and Lionel Ovesey. 1951. *The Mark of Oppression.* New York: Norton.

Kawamura, Lili Katsuko. 1994. "Quem São os Brasileiros que Trabalham no Japao?" (Who Are the Brazilians Who Work in Japan?). In Charles Tetsuo Chigusa, ed., *A Quebra dos Mitos: O Fenômeno Dekassegui através de Relatos Pessoais* (The Breaking of Myths: The *Dekasegi* Phenomenon Through Personal Accounts), 15–23. Atsugi-shi, Japan: International Press Corporation.

Kearney, Michael. 1991. "Borders and Boundaries of State and Self at the End of Empire." *Journal of Historical Sociology* 4 (1): 52–74.

———. 1995. "The Local and the Global: The Anthropology of Globalization and Transnationalism." *Annual Review of Anthropology* 24:547–65.

Kelly, William W. 1993. "Finding a Place in Metropolitan Japan: Ideologies, Institutions, and Everyday Life." In Andrew Gordon, ed.. *Postwar Japan as History,* 189–216. Berkeley: University of California Press.

Kidder, Louise H. 1992. "Requirements for Being 'Japanese.'" *International Journal of Intercultural Relations* 16:383–93.

Kitagawa, Toyoie. 1992. *Gunma-ken Oizumi-machi ni Okeru Nikkeijin Rodosha Hiaringu Chosa: Eijjyuka Shikou to Ukeire Kibanseibi* (Survey Hearing of Nikkeijin Workers in Gunma-ken, Oizumi-machi: The Intention to Become Permanent and the Fundamental Framework for Their Acceptance). In *Hito no Kokusaika ni Kansuru Sogoteki Kenkyu: Tokuni Gaikokujin Rodosha ni Kansuru Chosa Kenkyu o Chushin ni* (General Survey on the Internationalization of People: Especially Focusing on the Survey Research About Foreign Workers). Tokyo: Toyo University, 89–154.

———. 1993. *Hamamatsu-shi ni Okeru Gaikokujin no Seikatsu Jittai/Ishiki Chosa: Nikkei Burajiru/Perujin o Chushin ni* (Survey of Living Conditions and Consciousness of Foreigners in Hamamatsu City: Focusing on Nikkei-Brazilians and Peruvians). Hamamatsu Planning Section/International Exchange Office.

———. 1996. "Hamamatsushi ni Okeru Nikkei Burajirujin no Seikatsu Kozo to Ishiki: Nippaku Ryokoku Chosa o Fumaete" (The Lives and Consciousness of the Brazilian Nikkeijin in Hamamatsu City: Based on Surveys in Both Japan and Brazil). *Toyo Daigaku Shakai Gakubu Kiyo* (Bulletin of the Department of Sociology at Toyo University) 34 (1): 109–96.

———. 1997. "Burajiru-taun no Keisei to Deasupora: Nikkei Burajirujin no Teijyuka ni Kansuru Nananen Keizoku Oizumi-machi Chosa" (Diaspora and the Formation of Brazil-town: A Continuing Seven-Year Oizumi Town Survey About the Settlement of Brazilian Nikkeijin).

Toyo Daigaku Shakai Gakubu Kiyo (Bulletin of the Department of Sociology at Toyo University) 34 (3): 66–173.

Kitano, Harry H. L. 1976. *Japanese Americans: The Evolution of a Subculture*. Englewood Cliffs, NJ: Prentice-Hall.

Klagsbrunn, Victor Hugo. 1996. "Globalização da Economia Mundial e Mercado de Trabalho: A Emigração de Brasileiros para os Estados Unidos e Japão" (Globalization of the World Economy and the Labor Market: Brazilian Emigration to the United States and Japan). In Neide Patarra, ed., *Migrações Internacionais: Herança XX, Agenda XXI* (International Migration: Legacy XX, Agenda XXI), 2:33–48. Campinas, Brazil: Programa Interinstitucional de Avaliação e Acompanhamento das Migrações Internacionais no Brasil.

Koga, Eunice Ishikawa. 1995. "Kyojyu no Chokika to Aidenteitei no Naiyo: Nikkei Burajirujin no Baai" (Long-Term Residence and the Content of Identity: The Case of the Brazilian *Nikkeijin*). In Takashi Miyajima, ed., *Chiiki Shakai ni Okeru Gaikokujin Rodosha: Nichi/O ni Okeru Ukeire no Genjyo to Kadai* (The Foreign Labor Problem in Local Societies: Issues and Realities of Acceptance in Japan and European Countries), 43–52. Tokyo: Ochanomizu University.

Kondo, Dorinne K. 1986. "Dissolution and Reconstitution of Self: Implications for Anthropological Epistemology." *Cultural Anthropology* 1 (1): 74–88.

———. 1990. *Crafting Selves: Power, Gender, and Discourses of Identity in a Japanese Workplace*. Chicago: University of Chicago Press.

Kornblum, William. 1989. "Introduction." In Carolyn D. Smith and William Kornblum, eds., *In the Field: Readings on the Field Research Experience*, 16. New York: Praeger.

Kritz, Mary M. and Hania Zlotnik. 1992. "Global Interactions: Migration Systems, Processes, and Policies." In Mary M. Kritz, Lin Lean Lim, and Hania Zlotnik, eds., *International Migration Systems: A Global Approach*, 1–16. New York: Oxford University Press.

Kuwahara, Yasuo. 1993. "Nikkeijin Rodosha ga Nihon Dekasegi ni Fumikiru Made" (The Road to Becoming Japanese Dekasegi for *Nikkeijin* Workers). In *Nanbei Nikkeijin Shuro ni Kansuru Jittai Chosa* (Survey About the Employment of South American *Nikkeijin*), 7–37. Tokyo: Institute of Statistical Research.

Laing, Ronald D. 1969. *The Divided Self*. New York: Pantheon.

Lamphere, Louis. 1992. "Introduction: The Shaping of Diversity." In Louise Lamphere, ed., *Structuring Diversity: Ethnographic Perspectives on the New Immigration*, 1–34. Chicago: University of Chicago Press.

Landes, Ruth. 1986. "A Woman Anthropologist in Brazil." In Peggy Golde, ed., *Women in the Field: Anthropological Experiences*, 119–39. Chicago: Aldine.

Leach, Edmund R. 1964. "Anthropological Aspects of Language: Animal Categories and Verbal Abuse." In E. J. Lennenberg, ed., *New Directions in the Study of Language*, 23–63. Cambridge: Cambridge University Press.

Lebra, Takie Sugiyama. 1976. *Japanese Patterns of Behavior*. Honolulu: University of Hawaii Press.

Lee, Changsoo and George A. De Vos. 1981. *Koreans in Japan: Ethnic Conflict and Accommodation*. Berkeley: University of California Press.

Lee, Reba. 1955. *I Passed for White*. New York: Longmans, Green.

Lesser, Jeffrey. 1999. *Negotiating National Identity: Immigrants, Minorities, and the Struggle for Ethnicity in Brazil*. Durham: Duke University Press.

Levine, Gene N. and Darrel M. Montero. 1973. "Socioeconomic Mobility Among Three Generations of Japanese Americans." *Journal of Social Issues* 29 (2): 33–48.

Levi-Strauss, Claude. 1966. *The Savage Mind*. Chicago: University of Chicago Press.

——. 1969. *Tristes Tropiques*. Trans. John Russell. New York: Atheneum.

Levitt, Peggy. N.d. "Transnational Migration: Taking Stock and Future Directions." Unpublished manuscript.

Levy, Daniel. 1999. *Remembering the Nation: Ethnic Germans and the Transformation of National Identity in the Federal Republic of Germany*. Ph.D. diss., Coumbia University.

Liberal Democratic Party. 1992. *Kokusaika Jidai ni Taio Shite: Omo to Shite Gaikokujin Mondai ni Kansuru Teigen* (In Response to the Age of Internationalization: A Proposal About the Foreign Labor Problem). Tokyo: Liberal Democratic Party.

Lie, John. 2001. *Multiethnic Japan*. Cambridge: Harvard University Press.

Liebkind, Karmela. 1982. "The Swedish-Speaking Finns: A Case Study of Ethnolinguistic Identity." In Henri Tajfel, ed., *Social Identity and Intergroup Relations*, 367–411. Cambridge: Cambridge University Press.

Lifton, Robert Jay. 1969. *Death in Life: Survivors of Hiroshima*. New York: Vintage.

——. 1983 [1976]. *The Life of the Self: Toward a New Psychology*. New York: Basic Books.

Linger, Daniel T. 1997. "Brazil Displaced: Restaurant 51 in Nagoya, Japan." *Horizontes Antropológicos* 3 (5): 181–203.

——. 2001. *No One Home: Brazilian Selves Remade in Japan*. Stanford: Stanford University Press.

Lopez, David and Yen Espiritu. 1990. "Panethnicity in the United States: A Theoretical Framework." *Ethnic and Racial Studies* 13 (2): 198–224.

Luhrmann, Tanya M. 1989. *Persuasions of the Witch's Craft: Ritual Magic in Contemporary England*. Cambridge: Harvard University Press.

——. 1994a. "The Good Parsi: The Postcolonial 'Feminization' of a Colonial Elite." *Man* 29 (2): 333–57.

——. 1994b. "Psychological Anthropology as the Naturalist's Art." In Marcelo M. Suárez-Orozco and George and Louise Spindler, eds., *The Making of Psychological Anthropology II*, 60–79. Fort Worth: Harcourt Brace College Publishers.

Lutz, Catherine. 1988. *Unnatural Emotions: Everyday Sentiments on a Micronesian Atoll and Their Challenge to Western Theory*. Chicago: University of Chicago Press.

Mackie, Vera. 1998. "Japayuki Cinderella Girl: Containing the Immigrant Other." *Japanese Studies* 18 (1): 45–63.

Maeyama, Takashi. 1982. *Imin no Nihon Kaiki Undo* (The Japanese Repatriation Immigrant Movement). Tokyo: NHK Books.

——. 1984. "Burajiru Nikkeijin ni Okeru Esunishitei to Aidenteitei: Ishikiteki Seijiteki Genjyo to Shite" (The Ethnicity and Identity of the Nikkeijin in Brazil: Politico-Cognitive Phenomena). *Minzokugaku Kenkyu* (Ethnicity Research) 48 (4): 444–58.

——. 1989. "Nikkeijin (Burajiru): Chukan Mainoritei no Mondai (Brazilian Nikkeijin: The Problem of Middlemen Minorities)." *Bunkajinruigaku* (Cultural Anthropology) 6 (1): 208–21.

——. 1996. *Esunishitei to Burajiru Nikkeijin* (Ethnicity and Brazilian Nikkeijin). Tokyo: Ochanomizu Shobo.

Malinowski, Bronislaw. 1954 [1948]. *Magic, Science, and Religion and Other Essays*. Garden City, NY: Doubleday Anchor Books.

——. 1961 [1922]. *Argonauts of the Western Pacific: An Account of Native Enterprise and Adventure in the Archipelagoes of Melanesian New Guinea*. New York: E. P. Dutton.

Malkki, Lisa. 1992. "National Geographic: The Rooting of Peoples and the Territorialization of National Identity Among Scholars and Refugees." *Cultural Anthropology* 7 (1): 24–62.

Mandel, Ruth. 1989. "Ethnicity and Identity Among Migrant Guestworkers in West Berlin." In Nancie L. Gonzalez and Carolyn S. McCommon, eds., *Conflict, Migration, and the Expression of Ethnicity,* 60–74. Boulder: Westview Press.

Marcus, George E. 1995. "Ethnography in/of the World System: The Emergence of Multi-Sited Ethnography." *Annual Review of Anthropology* 24:95–117.

Margolis, Maxine, L. 1994. *Little Brazil: An Ethnography of Brazilian Immigrants in New York City.* Princeton: Princeton University Press.

Martes, Ana Cristina Braga. 1997. "Respeito e Cidadania: O Ministerio das Relações Exteriores e os Imigrantes Brasileiros em Boston" (Respect and Citizenship: The Ministry of Foreign Affairs and Brazilian Immigrants in Boston). Paper presented at the First Symposium on Brazilian Emigration, Lisbon, Portugal.

——. 1999. "Os Imigrantes Brasileiros e as Igrejas em Massachusetts" (Brazilian Immigrants and Churches in Massachusetts). In Rossana Rocha Reis and Teresa Sales, eds., *Cenas do Brasil Migrante* (Scenes of Migrant Brazil), 87–122. São Paulo, Brazil: Boitempo Editorial.

——. 2000. *Brasileiros nos Estados Unidos: Um Estudo sobre Imigrantes em Massachusetts* (Brazilians in the United States: A Study About Immigrants in Massachusetts). São Paulo, Brazil: Editora Paz e Terra.

Mason, David. 1986. "Introduction: Controversies and Continuities in Race and Ethnic Relations Theory." In John Rex and David Mason, eds., *Theories of Race and Ethnic Relations,* 1–19. Cambridge: Cambridge University Press.

Massey, Doreen. 1992. "A Place Called Home?" *New Formations* 17:3–15.

Massey, Douglas S. 1988. "Economic Development and International Migration in Comparative Perspective." *Population and Development Review* 14:383–413.

Mato, Daniel. 1997. "On Global and Local Agents and the Social Making of Transnational Identities and Related Agendas in 'Latin' America." *Identities: Global Studies in Culture and Power* 4 (2): 167–212.

Maybury-Lewis, David. 1965. *The Savage and the Innocent.* Boston: Beacon Press.

McKeown, Adam. 1999. "Conceptualizing Chinese Diasporas, 1842 to 1949." *Journal of Asian Studies* 58 (2): 306–37.

Mead, Margaret. 1952. "The Training of the Cultural Anthropologist." *American Anthropologist* 54:343–46.

Medina, Laurie Kroshus. 1997. "Defining Difference, Forging Unity: The Co-construction of Race, Ethnicity, and Nation in Belize." *Ethnic and Racial Studies* 20 (4): 757–80.

Merton, Robert K. 1982. "Discrimination and the American Creed." In Norman R. Yetman and C. Hoy Steele, eds., *Majority and Minority: The Dynamics of Race and Ethnicity in American Life,* 34–47. Boston: Allyn and Bacon.

Minister of Labor Secretariat. 1995. *Rodo Tokei Yoran* (Labor Statistics Survey). Tokyo: Ministry of Finance Publishing Bureau.

Minister of Labor Secretariat Policy Planning and Research Department. 1993. *Rodo Keizai Doko Chosa Hokoku* (Survey Report on Trends in the Labor Economy). Tokyo: Ministry of Labor.

Ministry of Justice. 1994. *Shutsunyukoku Kanri Gyosei no Genjyo to Tomen no Kadai* (Administration of Immigration Control and Current Topics). Tokyo: Ministry of Justice.

Ministry of Justice Immigration Bureau. 1987–1995. *Kokusai Jinryu: The Immigration Newsmagazine* (monthly). Vols. 1–94.

Ministry of Labor. 1991. *Gaikokujin Rodosha ga Rodomento ni Oyobosu Eikyoto ni Kansuru Kenkyukai* (Research Group Study on the Impact of Foreign Laborers). Tokyo: Ministry of Labor.

———. 1992. *Gaikokujin Rodosha ga Rodomento ni Oyobosu Eikyoto ni Kansuru Kenkyukai Senmonbukai* (Expert Research Group Study on the Impact of Foreign Laborers). Tokyo: Ministry of Labor.

Mintz, Sidney. 1998. "The Localization of Anthropological Practice: From Area Studies to Transnationalism." *Critique of Anthropology* 18 (2): 117–33.

Mitchell, J. C. 1974. "Perceptions of Ethnicity and Ethnic Behaviour: An Empirical Exploration." In Abner Cohen, ed., *Urban Ethnicity*, 1–35. London: Tavistock Publications.

Miyajima, Takashi. 1993. *Gaikokujin Rodosha to Nihon Shakai* (Foreign Workers and Japanese Society). Tokyo: Akaishi Shoten.

Miyao, Sussumu. 1980. "Posicionamento Social da População de Origem Japonesa" (The Social Position of the Population of Japanese Origin). In Hiroshi Saito, ed., *A Presença Japonêsa no Brasil* (The Japanese Presence in Brazil), 91–99. São Paulo: Editôra da Universidade de São Paulo.

Moore, Donald S. 1998. "Subaltern Struggles and the Politics of Place: Remapping Resistance in Zimbabwe's Eastern Highlands." *Cultural Anthropology* 13 (3): 344–81.

Moreira da Rocha, Cristina. 1999. "Identity and Tea Ceremony in Brazil." *Japanese Studies* 19 (3): 287–95.

Mori, Hiromasa. 1994. "Nikkei Burjirujin no Nyushoku/Shuro Jyotai" (Working and Job Placement Conditions for Brazilian *Nikkeijin*). In *Kenkyu Hokoku* (Bulletin of the Japan Statistics Research Institute), 49–60. Tokyo: Japan Statistics Research Institute.

Mori, Hiromi. 1994. "Nikkei Shudanshi ni totte no 'Dekasegi' no Motsu Imi: San Nikei Shudanchi no Dekasegi Keitai to Eikyo no Taihi o Toshite" (The Meaning of "Dekasegi" for Areas of Nikkeijin Concentration: A Comparison of the Composition and Influence of Dekasegi in Three Nikkei Communities). *Ijyu Kenkyu* (Migration Research) 31:40–57.

Mori, Koichi. 1992. "Burajiru kara no Nikkeijin 'Dekasegi' no Suii" (Changes in the Nikkeijin Dekasegi from Brazil). *Ijyu Kenkyu* (Migration Research) 29:144–64.

Münz, Rainer and Rainer Ohliger. 1998. "Long-Distance Citizens: Ethnic Germans and Their Immigration to Germany." In Peter H. Schuck and Rainer Münz, eds., *Paths to Inclusion: The Integration of Migrants in the United States and Germany*, 155–201. New York: Berghahn Books.

Murphy-Shigematsu, Stephen. 2000. "Identities of Multiethnic People in Japan." In Mike Douglass and Glenda S. Roberts, eds., *Japan and Global Migration: Foreign Workers and the Advent of a Multicultural Society*, 196–216. London: Routledge.

Myerhoff, Barbara and Jay Ruby. 1982. "Introduction." In Jay Ruby, ed., *A Crack in the Mirror: Reflexive Perspectives in Anthropology*, 1–35. Philadelphia: University of Pennsylvania Press.

Naber, Nadine. 2000. "Ambiguous Insiders: An Investigation of Arab American Invisibility." *Ethnic and Racial Studies* 23 (1): 37–61.

Nader, Laura. 1972. "Up the Anthropologist: Perspectives Gained from Studying Up." In Dell Hymes, ed., *Reinventing Anthropology*, 284–311. New York: Pantheon.

———. 1986. "From Anguish to Exultation." In Peggy Golde, ed., *Women in the Field: Anthropological Experiences*, 97–116. Chicago: Aldine.

Nagata, Judith. 1981. "In Defense of Ethnic Boundaries: The Changing Myths and Charters of Malay Identity." In Charles F. Keyes, ed., *Ethnic Change*, 88–115. Seattle: University of Washington Press.

Nakagawa, Décio. 1994. "*Dekasseguis.*" Unpublished paper.

Nakagawa, Fumio. 1983. "Japanese–Latin American Relations Since the 1960s: An Overview." *Latin American Studies* 6:63–71.

Nash, Dennison and Ronald Wintrob. 1972. "The Emergence of Self-Consciousness in Ethnography." *Current Anthropology* 13:527–42.

Neary, Ian. 1997. "Burakumin in Contemporary Japan." In Michael Weiner, ed. *Japan's Minorities: The Illusion of Homogeneity*, 50–78. New York: Routledge.

NHK Service Center. 1993. *NHK Seron Chosa Shiryoshu Dai Roku Shu* (NHK Public Opinion Survey Compendium, No. 6). Tokyo: NHK Service Center.

Ninomiya, Masato, ed. 1992. *Dekassegui: Palestras e Exposições do Simpósio sobre o Fenômeno Chamado Dekassegui* (Dekasegi: Lectures and Expositions from the Symposium About the Phenomenon Called *Dekasegi*). São Paulo, Brazil: Editora Estação Liberdade.

Ninomiya, Masato and Rodosho Shokugyo Anteikyoku Gyomu Choseika (Ministry of Labor Employment Stability Bureau Business Regulation Section). 1994. *Nihon/Burajiru Ryokoku ni okeru Nikkeijin no Rodo to Seikatsu* (The Labor and Lives of Nikkeijin in Both Japan and Brazil). Tokyo: Nikkan Rodo Tsushinsha.

Nishioka, Lianha. 1995. *Nihon Shakai no naka no Nikkei Burajirujin: Ishiki Chosa kara no Kosatsu* (Nikkei Brazilians in Japanese Society: Considerations Based on Survey Data). Manuscript.

Nishizawa, Akihiko. 1995. "Nikkei Burajiru/Perujin Rodosha no Shakaiteki Sekai" (The Social World of Brazilian and Peruvian Nikkeijin). In *Inbei Sareta Gaibu: Toshi Kaso no Esunogurafi* (The Hidden Outside: The Ethnography of the Urban Underclass), 129–63. Tokyo: Sairyusha.

Nogueira, Arlinda Rocha. 1973. "Considerações Gerais Sobre a Imigração Japonesa para o Estado de São Paulo entre 1908 e 1922" (General Considerations About Japanese Immigration to the State of São Paulo Between 1908 and 1992). In Hiroshi Saito and Takashi Maeyama, eds., *Assimilação e Integração dos Japoneses no Brasil* (The Assimilation and Integration of the Japanese in Brazil), 32–55. Petrópolis, Rio de Janeiro: Editora Vozes.

———. 1983. *Imigração Japonêsa na História Contemporánea do Brasil* (Japanese Immigration in the Contemporary History of Brazil). São Paulo: Centro de Estudos Nipo-Brasileiros.

Nojima, Toshihiko. 1989. "Susumetai Nikkeijin no Tokubetsu Ukeire" (Proposal for the Special Admission of the *Nikkeijin*). *Gekkan Jiyu Minsu* (November): 92–99.

Nomoto, Hiroyuki, Satoshi Oga, Miyoko Goto, Regina Miyazaka, Kazunari Matsuo, Motoyasu Nakamura, Kazushi Yoshida, and Mioto Kato. 1993. *Zainichi Nikkeijin Oyobi sono Kazoku no Seikatsu Jittai to Nihongo no Gakushu ni Kansuru Chosa Hokoku* (Survey Report of the Living Conditions of the Resident Nikkeijin and Their Families and Their Study of Japanese). In *Nagoya Kyoiku Kenkyu Nenpo* (Nagoya Educational Research Annual Report), 10:136–95. Nagoya: Nagoya University Department of Education Social Education Research Center.

Obeyesekere, Gananath. 1981. *Medusa's Hair: An Essay on Personal Symbols and Religious Experience*. Chicago: University of Chicago Press.

———. 1982. "Sinhalese-Buddhist Identity in Ceylon." In George De Vos and Lola Romanucci-Ross, eds., *Ethnic Identity: Cultural Continuities and Change*, 231–58. Chicago: University of Chicago Press.

Ogbu, John U. 1974. *The Next Generation: An Ethnography of Education in an Urban Neighborhood*. New York: Academic Press.

———. 1978. *Minority Education and Caste: The American System in Cross-Cultural Perspective.* New York: Academic Press.

Ohnuki-Tierney, Emiko. 1984. *Illness and Culture in Contemporary Japan: An Anthropological View.* Cambridge: Cambridge University Press.

———. 1987. *The Monkey as Mirror: Symbolic Transformations in Japanese History and Ritual.* Princeton: Princeton University Press.

———. 1990a. "The Monkey as Self in Japanese Culture." In Emiko Ohnuki-Tierney, ed., *Culture Through Time: Anthropological Approaches,* 128–53. Stanford: Stanford University Press.

———. 1990b. "The Ambivalent Self of the Contemporary Japanese." *Cultural Anthropology* 5 (2): 197–216.

———. 1993. *Rice as Self: Japanese Identities Through Time.* Princeton: Princeton University Press.

Ong, Aihwa. 1987. *Spirits of Resistance and Capitalist Discipline: Factory Women in Malaysia.* Albany, NY: State University of New York Press.

———. 1993. "On the Edge of Empires: Flexible Citizenship Among Chinese in Diaspora." *Positions* 1 (3): 745–78.

———. 1996. "Cultural Citizenship as Subject-Making: Immigrants Negotiate Racial and Cultural Boundaries in the United States." *Current Anthropology* 37 (5): 737–62.

———. 1999. *Flexible Citizenship: The Cultural Logics of Transnationality.* Durham: Duke University Press.

Ono, Morio and Katsunori Wakisaka. 1973. "Cultura, Migração e Nissei" (Culture, Migration and Nisei). In Hiroshi Saito and Takashi Maeyama, eds., *Assimilação e Integração dos Japoneses no Brasil* (The Assimilation and Integration of the Japanese in Brazil), 531–38. Petrópolis, Rio de Janeiro: Editora Vozes.

Onuma, Yasuaki. 1987. *Tanitsu Minzoku Shakai no Shinwa o Koete: Zainichi Kankoku/Chosenjin to Shutsu Nykoku Kanri Taisei* (Beyond the Myth of Ethnic Homogeneity: Resident Koreans in Japan and the Organization of Immigration/Emigration Administration). Tokyo: Toshindo.

Ortner, Sherry B. 1995. "Resistance and the Problem of Ethnographic Refusal." *Comparative Studies in Society and History* 37 (1): 173–93.

Panagakos, Anastasia N. 1998. "Citizens of the Trans-Nation: Political Mobilization, Multiculturalism, and Nationalism in the Greek Diaspora." *Diaspora* 7 (1): 53-73.

Park, Kyeyoung. 1989. " 'Born Again': What Does It Mean to Korean-Americans in New York City?" *Journal of Ritual Studies* 3:287–301.

———. 1999. " 'I Am Floating in the Air': Creation of a Korean Transnational Space Among Korean-Latino American Remigrants." *Positions* 7 (3): 667–95.

Patarra, Neide L. and Rosana Baeninger. 1996. "Migrações Internacionais Recentes: O Caso do Brasil" (Recent International Migration: The Case of Brazil). In Neide Patarra, coordinator, *Emigração e Imigração Internacionais no Brasil Contemporâneo* (International Emigration and Immigration in Contemporary Brazil), 78–88. Campinas, Brazil: FNUAP.

Perlman, Joel and Roger Waldinger. 1997. "Second Generation Decline? Children of Immigrants, Past and Present—A Reconsideration." *International Migration Review* 31 (4): 893–922.

Pettigrew, Thomas Fraser. 1994. "New Patterns of Prejudice: The Different Worlds of 1984 and 1964." In Fred L. Pincus and Howard J. Ehrlich, eds., *Race and Ethnic Conflict: Contending Views on Prejudice, Discrimination, and Ethnoviolence,* 53–59. Boulder: Westview Press.

Piaget, Jean. 1967. *Six Psychological Studies.* Trans. Anita Tenzer. New York: Random House.

Pincus, Fred L. 1994. "From Individual to Structural Discrimination." In Fred L. Pincus and Howard J. Ehrlich, eds., *Race and Ethnic Conflict: Contending Views on Prejudice, Discriminaton, and Ethnoviolence*, 53–59. Boulder: Westview Press.

Piore, Michael J. 1979. *Birds of Passage: Migrant Labor and Industrial Societies.* Cambridge: Cambridge University Press.

Police Agency. 1994. *Police White Paper.* Tokyo: Ministry of Finance Printing Office.

Portes, Alejandro. 1978. "Migration and Underdevelopment." *Politics and Society* 8:1–48.

——. 1995. "Segmented Assimilation Among New Immigrant Youth: A Conceptual Framework." In Wayne A. Cornelius and Rubén G. Rumbaut, eds., *California's Immigrant Children: Theory, Research, and Implications for Educational Policy*, 71–76. San Diego: Center for U.S.–Mexican Studies, University of California, San Diego.

——. 1996. "Global Villagers: The Rise of Transnational Communities." *The American Prospect* 2:74–77.

——. 1998. "Divergent Destinies: Immigration, the Second Generation, and the Rise of Transnational Communities." In Peter H. Schuck and Rainer Münz, eds., *Paths to Inclusion: The Integration of Migrants in the United States and Germany*, 33–57. New York: Berghahn Books.

Portes, Alejandro and József Böröcz. 1989. "Contemporary Immigration: Theoretical Perspectives on its Determinants and Modes of Incorporation." *International Migration Review* 23 (3): 606–30.

Portes, Alejandro and Rubén G. Rumbaut. 1996. *Immigrant America: A Portrait.* Berkeley: University of California Press.

Portes, Alejandro and Alex Stepick. 1993. *City on the Edge: The Transformation of Miami.* Berkeley: University of California Press.

Powdermaker, Hortense. 1966. *Stranger and Friend.* New York: Norton.

Price, John. 1966. "A History of the Outcaste: Untouchability in Japan." In George A. De Vos and and Hiroshi Wagatsuma, eds., *Japan's Invisible Race: Caste in Culture and Personality*, 6–32. Berkeley: University of California Press.

Prime Minister's Office. 1985–1994. *Seron Chosa Nenkan: Zenkoku Seron Chosa no Genjyo* (Annual Public Opinion Surveys). Tokyo: Prime Minister's Office.

Putnam, Robert D. 1995. "Bowling Alone: America's Declining Social Capital." *Journal of Democracy* 6 (1): 65–78.

Rabinow, Paul. 1977. *Reflections on Fieldwork in Morocco.* Berkeley: University of California Press.

Rasmussen, Susan J. 1998. "Within the Tent and at the Crossroads: Travel and Gender Identity Among the Tuareg of Niger." *Ethos* 26 (2): 153–82.

Räthzel, Nora. 1995. *"Aussiedler* and *Ausländer:* Transforming German National Identity." *Social Identities* 1 (2): 263–82.

Reichl, Christopher A. 1995. "Stages in the Historical Process of Ethnicity: The Japanese in Brazil, 1908–1988." *Ethnohistory* 42 (1): 31–62.

Repak, Terry A. 1995. *Waiting on Washington: Central American Workers in the Nation's Capital.* Philadelphia: Temple University Press.

Ribeiro, Gustavo Lins. 1999. "O Que Faz O Brasil, Brazil: Jogos Identitários em São Francisco." (The Play of Identity in San Francisco). In Rossana Rocha Reis and Teresa Sales, eds., *Cenas do Brasil Migrante* (Scenes of Migrant Brazil), 45–85. São Paulo, Brazil: Boitempo Editorial.

Robertson, Roland. 1987. "Globalization Theory and Civilizational Analysis." *Comparative Civilizations Review* 17:20–30.

Rohlen, Thomas P. 1974. *For Harmony and Strength: Japanese White-Collar Organization in Anthropologial Perspective*. Berkeley: University of California Press.

———. 1981. "Education: Policies and Prospects." In Changsoo Lee and George A. De Vos, eds., *Koreans in Japan: Ethnic Conflict and Accommodation*, 182–222. Berkeley: University of California Press.

Roosens, Eugeen. 1994. "The Primordial Nature of Origins in Migrant Ethnicity." In Hans Vermeulen and Cora Govers, eds., *The Anthropology of Ethnicity: Beyond "Ethnic Groups and Boundaries"*, 81–104. Amsterdam: Het Spinhuis.

Rosaldo, Michelle Z. 1980. *Knowledge and Passion: Ilongot Notions of Self and Social Life*. Cambridge: Cambridge University Press.

———. 1984. "Toward an Anthropology of Self and Feeling." In Richard A. Shweder and Robert A. LeVine, eds., *Culture Theory: Essays on Mind, Self, and Emotion*, 137–58. Cambridge: Cambridge University Press.

Rosaldo, Renato. 1989. *Culture and Truth: The Remaking of Social Analysis*. Boston: Beacon Press.

Rossini, Rosa E. 1996. "O Retorno às Origens ou o Sonho do Encontro com o Eldorado: O Exemplo dos *Dekasseguis* do Brasil em Direção ao Japão" (Return to Origins or the Dream of Encountering Eldorado: The Case of Dekasegi from Brazil Headed to Japan). In Neide Patarra, coordinator, *Emigração e Imigração Internacionais no Brasil Contemporâneo* (International Emigration and Immigration in Contemporary Brazil), 104–10. Campinas, Brazil: FNUAP.

Roth, Joshua H. 1999. *Defining Communities: The Nation, the Firm, the Neighborhood, and Japanese-Brazilian Migrants in Japan*. Ph.D. diss., Cornell University.

Rothenberg, Jerome. 1977. "On the Microeconomics of Internal Migration." In Alan A. Brown and Egon Neuberger, eds., *Internal Migration: A Comparative Perspective*, 183–205. New York: Academic Press.

Rouse, Roger. 1991. "Mexican Migration and the Social Space of Postmodernism." *Diaspora* 1991 (1): 8–23.

———. 1995. "Questions of Identity: Personhood and Collectivity in Transnational Migration to the United States." *Critique of Anthropology* 15 (4): 351–80.

Rumbaut, Rubén G. 1997. "Assimilation and Its Discontents: Between Rhetoric and Reality." *International Migration Review* 31 (4): 923–60.

Rutherford, Jonathan. 1990. "A Place Called Home." In Jonathan Rutherford, ed., *Identity: Community, Culture, Difference*, 9–27. London: Lawrence & Wishart.

Ryang, Sonia. 1997. *North Koreans in Japan: Language, Ideology, and Identity*. Boulder: Westview Press.

Sahlins, Marshall D. 1985. *Islands of History*. Chicago: University of Chicago Press.

Said, Edward W. 1979. *Orientalism*. New York: Vintage.

Saito, Hiroshi. 1961. *O Japonês no Brasil: Estudo de Mobilidade e Fixação* (The Japanese in Brazil: A Study of Mobility and Settlement). São Paulo: Editôra Sociologia e Politica.

———. 1973. "A Margem da Contribuição de Japoneses na Horticultura de São Paulo" (At the Margins of the Japanese Contribution to the Horticulture of São Paulo). In Hiroshi Saito and Takashi Maeyama, eds., *Assimilação e Integração dos Japoneses no Brasil* (The Assimilation and Integration of the Japanese in Brazil), 189–200. Petrópolis, Rio de Janeiro: Editora Vozes.

——. 1976. "The Integration and Participation of the Japanese and their Descendants in Brazilian Society." *International Migration* 14 (3): 183–99.

——. 1978. *Gaikokujin ni natta Nihonjin: Burajiru Imin no Ikikata to Kawarikata* (Japanese Who Became Foreigners: The Lifestyle and Changes Among Japanese Immigrants in Brazil). Tokyo: Saimaru Shuppankai.

Saito, Júlia Kubo. 1986. "Auto-Estima e Auto-Conceito entre os Jovens Descendentes de Japoneses" (Self-Exteem and Self-Concepts among Japanese-Descent Youths). In Massao Ohno, ed., *O Nikkei e Sua Americanidade* (The Nikkei and their Americanness), 241–55. São Paulo: COPANI.

Saito, Toshiaki. 1986. "Brasileiros e Japoneses, Confronto de Identidade" (Brazilians and Japanese, Confrontation of Identity). In Massao Ohno, ed., *O Nikkei e Sua Americanidade* (The Nikkei and Their Americanness), 199–224. São Paulo: COPANI.

Sakurai, Célia. 1993. *Romanceiro da Imigração Japonesa* (Romances of Japanese Immigration). São Paulo: Editora Sumaré.

——. 1995. "A Fase Romântica da Política: Os Primeiros Deputados Nikkeis no Brasil" (The Romantic Phase of Politics: The First Nikkei Congressmen in Brazil). In Boris Fausto, Oswaldo Truzzi, Roberto Grün, Célia Sakurai, eds., *Imigração e Política em São Paulo* (Immigration and Politics in São Paulo), 127–77. São Paulo: Editora Sumaré.

Sales, Teresa. 1996. "O Trabalhador Brasileiro no Contexto das Novas Migrações Internacionais" (The Brazilian Worker in the Context of the New International Migration). In Neide Patarra, coordinator, *Emigração e Imigração Internacionais no Brasil Contemporâneo* (International Emigration and Immigration in Contemporary Brazil), 89–103. Campinas, Brazil: FNUAP.

——. 1998. *Brasileiros Longe de Casa* (Brazilians Far from Home). São Paulo, Brazil: Cortez Editora.

São Paulo Humanities Research Center (*Sanpauro Jinbun Kagaku Kenkyujo*). 1987–1988. *Burajiru ni Okeru Nikkeijin Jinko Chosa Hokokusho* (Population Survey Report About Nikkeijin in Brazil). São Paulo, Brazil: Sanpauro Jinbun Kagaku Kenkyujo.

Sasaki, Elisa Massae. 1999. "Movimento *Dekassegui*: A Experiência Migratória e Identitária dos Brasileiros Descendentes de Japoneses no Japão" (The Movement of *Dekasegi*: Migration Experiences and Identity of Japanese-Descent Brazilians in Japan). In Rossana Rocha Reis and Teresa Sales, eds., *Cenas do Brasil Migrante* (Scenes of Migrant Brazil), 243–74. São Paulo, Brazil: Boitempo Editorial.

Sassen, Saskia. 1988. *The Mobility of Labor and Capital: A Study in International Investment and Labor Flow.* Cambridge, England: Cambridge University Press.

——. 1996. *Losing Control? Sovereignty in an Age of Globalization.* New York: Columbia University Press.

——. 1998. *Globalization and Its Discontents: Essays on the New Mobility of People and Money.* New York: The New Press.

——. 1999. *Guests and Aliens.* New York: The New Press.

Scheper-Hughes, Nancy. 1992. *Death Without Weeping: The Violence of Everyday Life in Brazil.* Berkeley: University of California Press.

Schwartz, Morris S. and Charlotte Green Schwartz. 1955. "Problems in Participant Observation." *American Journal of Sociology* 60:343–53.

Scott, James C. 1985. *Weapons of the Weak: Everyday Forms of Peasant Resistance.* New Haven: Yale University Press.

Seeger, Anthony. 1981. *Nature and Society in Central Brazil: The Suya Indians of Mato Grosso.* Cambridge: Harvard University Press.

Sellek, Yoko. 1996. "The U-Turn Phenomenon Among South American-Japanese Descendants: From Emigrants to Migrants." *Immigrants and Minorities* 15 (3): 246–69.

———. 2001. *Migrant Labour in Japan.* New York: Palgrave.

Siddle, Richard. 1997. "Ainu: Japan's Indigenous People." In Michael Weiner, ed., *Japan's Minorities: The Illusion of Homogeneity*, 17–49. New York: Routledge.

Simpson, George Eaton and J. Milton Yinger. 1972. *Racial and Cultural Minorities: An Analysis of Prejudice and Discrimination.* New York: Harper and Row.

Smith, Anthony D. 1981. *The Ethnic Revival.* Cambridge: Cambridge University Press.

———. 1991. *National Identity.* Reno: University of Nevada Press.

———. 1995. *Nations and Nationalism in a Global Era.* Cambridge, UK: Polity Press.

Smith, Robert J. 1979. "The Ethnic Japanese in Brazil." *The Journal of Japanese Studies* 5 (1): 53–70.

Spiro, Melford E. 1955. "The Acculturation of American Ethnic Groups." *American Anthropologist* 57:1240–1252.

———. 1984. "Some Reflections on Cultural Determinism and Relativism with Special Reference to Emotion and Reason." In Richard A. Shweder and Robert A. LeVine, eds., *Culture Theory: Essays on Mind, Self, and Emotion*, 323–46. Cambridge: Cambridge University Press.

———. 1987. *Culture and Human Nature: Theoretical Papers of Melford E. Spiro.* Eds. Benjamin Kilborne and L. L. Langness. Chicago: University of Chicago Press.

———. 1996. "Postmodernist Anthropology, Subjectivity, and Science: A Modernist Critique." *Comparative Studies in Society and History* 38 (4): 759–80.

Stalker, P. 1994. *The Work of Strangers: A Survey of International Labour Migration.* Geneva: International Labour Office.

Staniford, Philip. 1973a. "Nihon Ni Itemo Sho Ga Nai: O Background, a Estratégia e a Personalidade do Imigrante Japonês no Além-mar" (There's No Use Staying in Japan: The Background, Strategy, and Personality of the Japanese Immigrant Abroad). In Hiroshi Saito and Takashi Maeyama, eds., *Assimilação e Integração dos Japoneses no Brasil* (The Assimilation and Integration of the Japanese in Brazil), 32–55. Petrópolis, Rio de Janeiro: Editora Vozes.

———. 1973b. *Pioneers in the Tropics: The Political Organization of Japanese in an Immigrant Community in Brazil.* London: Athlone Press.

Suárez-Orozco, Marcelo M. and Carola E. Suárez-Orozco. 1995a. "The Cultural Patterning of Achievement Motivation: A Comparison of Mexican, Mexican Immigrant, Mexican American, and Non-Latino White American Students." In Wayne A. Cornelius and Rubén G. Rumbaut, eds., *California's Immigrant Children: Theory, Research, and Implications for Educational Policy*, 161–90. San Diego: Center for U.S.–Mexican Studies.

———. 1995b. *Transformations: Immigration, Family Life, and Achievement Motivation Among Latino Adolescents.* Stanford: Stanford University Press.

Swidler, Ann. 1996. "What Anchors Cultural Practices." Paper presented at the Annual Meetings of the American Sociological Association, New York, August 16–20.

Taft, Ronald. 1973. "The Concept of Social Adaptation of Migrants." In *Migration: Report of the Research Conference on Migration, Ethnic Minority Status and Social Adaptation*, 105–14. Rome: United Nations Social Defence Research Institute.

Tajfel, Henri. 1982. "The Social Psychology of Minorities." In Charles Husband, ed., *"Race" in Britain: Continuity and Change*, 216–58. London: Hutchinson.

Tajima, Hisatoshi. 1995. *Laten Amerika Nikkeijin no Teijyuka* (The Settlement of Latin American *Nikkeijin*). In Hiroshi Komai, ed., *Teijyuka suru Gaikokujin* (Foreigners Who Settle), 165–98. Tokyo: Akaishi Shoten.

———. 1998. "Socio-Cultural Differentiation in the Formation of Ethnic Identity and Integration Into Japanese Society: The Case of Okinawan and Nikkei Brazilian Immigrants." *JCAS Symposium Series* 8:187–97.

Takahashi, Hidemine. 1995. *Nise Nipponjin Tanboki: Kaette Kita Nanbei Nikkeijintachi* (Report on Fake Japanese: South American *Nikkeijin* Returnees). Tokyo: Soshisha.

Takahashi, Yukiharu. 1992. *Yuko ka Modoro ka Dekasegi Japon* (To Go, or to Return, *Dekasegi* Japan). Tokyo: Kodansha.

Takenaka, Ayumi. 1996. "Limits of Ethnicity and Culture: Ethnicity-Based Transnational Migration and Networks of Japanese-Peruvian 'Sojouners.' " Paper presented at the Annual Meeting of the American Sociological Association, New York, August 16–20.

———. 2000. "Transnational Community and Its Ethnic Consequences: The Return Migration and the Transformation of Ethnicity of Japanese-Peruvians." In Nancy Foner, Rubén Rumbaut, and Steven Gold, eds., *Immigration Research for a New Century: Multidisciplinary Perspectives*, 442–58. New York: Russell Sage Foundation.

———. N.d. "Return Migration from Peru to Japan and the Question of Japanese National Boundaries." Unpublished manuscript.

Tambiah, Stanley J. 1969. "Animals are Good to Think and Good to Prohibit." *Ethnology* 8 (4): 423–59.

Tatum, Beverly Daniel. 1987. *Assimilation Blues: Black Families in a White Community*. New York: Greenwood Press.

Tedlock, Barbara. 1991. "From Participant Observation to the Observation of Participation: The Emergence of Narrative Ethnography." *Journal of Anthropological Research* 47 (1): 69–94.

Thompson, Stephen I. 1974. "Survival of Ethnicity in the Japanese Community of Lima, Peru." *Urban Anthropology* 3:243–61.

Tigner, James L. 1981. "Japanese Immigration Into Latin America: A Survey." *Journal of Interamerican Studies and World Affairs* 23 (4): 457–82.

Todaro, Michael P. 1969. "A Model of Labour Migration and Urban Unemployment in Less Developed Countries." *American Economic Review* 59:138–48.

Todorov, Tzvetan. 1984 [1982]. *The Conquest of America*. New York: Harper and Row.

———. 1995. *The Morals of History*. Trans. Alyson Waters. Minneapolis: University of Minnesota Press.

Tsuda, Takeyuki. 1993. "The Psychosocial Functions of Liminality: The Japanese University Experience." *Journal of Psychohistory* 20 (3): 305–30.

———. 1999a. "The Motivation to Migrate: The Ethnic and Sociocultural Constitution of the Japanese-Brazilian Return Migration System." *Economic Development and Cultural Change* 48 (1): 1–31.

———. 1999b. "The Permanence of 'Temporary' Migration: The 'Structural Embeddedness' of Japanese-Brazilian Migrant Workers in Japan." *Journal of Asian Studies* 58 (3): 687–722.

———. 2001. "When Identities Become Modern: Japanese Immigrants in Brazil and the Global Contextualization of Identity." *Ethnic and Racial Studies* 24 (3): 412–32.

———. 2002. "From Ethnic Affinity to Alienation in the Global Ecumene: The Ethnic Encounter Between the Japanese and Japanese-Brazilian Return Migrants." *Diaspora* 10 (1): 53–91 .

——. Forthcoming 1. "Homeland-less Abroad: Transnational Liminality, Social Alienation, and Personal Malaise." In Jeffrey Lesser, ed., *Searching for Home Abroad: Japanese-Brazilians and the Transnational Moment.* Durham: Duke University Press.

——. Forthcoming 2. *In Search of Homeland Abroad: Japanese-Brazilian Return Migration and the Transnational Condition.* Center for Comparative Immigration Studies Monograph Series. La Jolla: University of California at San Diego.

Tsuda, Takeyuki and Wayne Cornelius. Forthcoming. "Achieved Versus Ascribed Human Capital: A Comparative Analysis of Immigrant Wages and Labor Market Incorporation in Japan and the United States." In Jeffrey Reitz, ed., *Host Societies and the Reception of Immigrants.* Center for Comparative Immigration Studies Anthology Series. La Jolla: University of California at San Diego.

Tsuda, Takeyuki and George De Vos. 1997. "Socialization and Social Vitality: A Psychocultural Perspective." In Armand Clesse, Takashi Inoguchi, E. B. Keehn, and J. A. A. Stockwin, eds., *The Vitality of Japan: Sources of National Strength and Weakness,* 256–301. London: Macmillan.

Tsuzuki, Kurumi. 2000. "*Nikkei* Brazilians and Local Residents: A Study of the H Housing Complex in Toyota City." *Asian and Pacific Migration Journal* 9 (3): 327–42.

Turnbull, Colin M. 1986. "Sex and Gender: The Role of Subjectivity in Field Research." In Tony Larry Whitehead and Mary Ellen Conaway, eds., *Self, Sex, and Gender in Cross-Cultural Fieldwork,* 17–27. Urbana: University of Illinois Press.

Turner, Christena L. 1995. *Japanese Workers in Protest: An Ethnography of Consciousness and Experience.* Berkeley: University of California Press.

Turner, Victor. 1967. *The Forest of Symbols: Aspects of Ndembu Ritual.* Ithaca: Cornell University Press.

——. 1985 [1969]. *The Ritual Process: Structure and Anti-Structure.* Ithaca: Cornell University Press.

Utsumi, Americo. 1986. "A Contribuição da Comunidade Nipo-Brasileira ao Desenvolvimento da Agricultura" (The Contribution of the Japanese-Brazilian Community to the Development of Agriculture). In Massao Ohno, ed., *O Nikkei e Sua Americanidade* (The Nikkei and Their Americanness), 225–28. São Paulo: COPANI.

Valentine, James. 1990. "On the Borderlines: the Significance of Marginality in Japanese Society." In Eyal Ben-Ari, Brian Moeran, and James Valentine, eds., *Unwrapping Japan: Society and Culture in Anthropological Perspective,* 36–57. Honolulu: University of Hawaii Press.

Vandergeest, Peter. 1993. "Constructing Thailand: Regulation, Everyday Resistance, and Citizenship." *Contemporary Studies in Society and History* 35 (2): 133–58.

van Wolferen, Karel. 1990. *The Enigma of Japanese Power: People and Politics in a Stateless Nation.* New York: Vintage.

Verdery, Katherine. 1996. "Transnationalism, Nationalism, Citizenship, and Property: Eastern Europe Since 1989." *American Ethnologist* 25 (2): 291–306.

Verkuyten, Maykel. 1997. "Cultural Discourses in the Netherlands: Talking About Ethnic Minorities in the Inner City." *Identities: Global Studies in Culture and Power* 4 (1): 99–132.

Vieira, Francesca. 1973. *O Japonês na Frente de Expansão Paulista: O Processo de Absorção do Japonês em Marília* (The Japanese at the Forefront of the Expansion of São Paulo State: The Process of Absorption of the Japanese in Marília). São Paulo: Livraria Pioneira Editora.

Wagatsuma, Hiroshi. 1981. "Problems of Self-Identity Among Korean Youth in Japan." In Changsoo Lee and George A. De Vos, eds., *Koreans in Japan: Ethnic Conflict and Accommodation,* 304–33. Berkeley: University of California Press.

———. 1982. "Problems of Cultural Identity in Modern Japan." In George De Vos and Lola Romanucci-Ross, eds., *Ethnic Identity: Cultural Continuities and Change*, 307–34. Chicago: University of Chicago Press.

Wagley, Charles, and Marvin Harris. 1958. *Minorities in the New World*. New York: Columbia University Press.

Wallman, Sandra. 1986. "Ethnicity and the Boundary Process in Context." In John Rex and David Mason, eds., *Theories of Race and Ethnic Relations*, 226–45. Cambridge: Cambridge University Press.

Watanabe, Masako. 1992. "Burajiru kara no Nikkei Dekasegi Rodosha to "Nihon" tono Deai" (The Encounter Between Japan and Japanese-Descent Migrant Workers from Brazil). *Shakaigaku Chosa Jittshu Hokokusho* (Sociological Survey Report) 8:309–47.

———. 1995a. "Nikkei Burajirujin Jido/Seito no Zoka ni taisuru Kyoiku Genba deno Mosaku: Nikkei Burajirujin Shujyuchi no Hamamatsu-shi no Baai" (Attempts in Education to Respond to the Rapid Increase of Brazilian Nikkejin Children and Students: The Case of Hamamatsu City). *Shakaigaku/Shakai Fukushigaku Kenkyu* (Sociology and Social Welfare Review) 96:43–66.

———. 1995b. "Nikkei Burajirujin kara Mita Nihonjin no Amoru" (The Love of the Japanese, as Seen by the Nikkei Brazilians). *Socially* 3:99–100.

———, ed. 1995. *Dekasegi Nikkei Burajirujin* (Brazilian Nikkeijin Dekasegi), 2 vols. Tokyo: Akaishi Shoten.

Watanabe, Masako, and Shizue Teruyama. 1992. "Burajiru kara no Nikkei Dekasegi Rodosha no Jittai to Nihon Shakai no Taio" (Actual Situation of Japanese-Descent Migrant Workers from Brazil and the Response of Japanese Society). *Shakaigaku/Shakai Fukushigaku Kenkyu* (Sociology and Social Welfare Review) 89:1–66.

Watanabe, Masako, Masanori Ishikawa, Tomoko Anada, Harumi Yuge, Hiroyuki Watanabe, and Angelo Ishi. 1992. "Nikkei Dekasegi no Kyuzo ni Tomonau Nihon Shakai no Taio to Mosaku" (The Rapid Increase in Japanese-Descent Migrant Workers and the Resulting Response and Uncertainty of Japanese Society). *Meiji Gakuin Daigaku Shakaigakubu Fuzoku Kenkyujo Nenpo* (Meiji Gakuin University Sociology Division Affiliated Research Institute Annual Report) 22:55–85.

Watkins, Montse. 1994. *Hikage no Nikkeijin: Gaijin Kisha ga Mita Nanbei no Dekasegi Rodosha* (Shadowed Nikkeijin: South American *Dekasegi* Workers as Seen by a Foreign Journalist). Tokyo: Sairyusha.

Weber, Max. 1946. *From Max Weber: Essays in Sociology*. Eds. H. H. Gerth and C. Wright Mills. New York: Oxford University Press.

———. 1961. "Ethnic Groups." In Talcott Parsons, Edward Shils, Kaspar D. Naegele, and Jesse Pitts, eds., *Theories of Society*, 305–309. New York: Free Press.

Weidman, Hazel Hitson. 1986. "On Ambivalence and the Field." In Peggy Golde, ed., *Women in the Field: Anthropological Experiences*, 239–63. Chicago: Aldine.

Weiner, Michael. 1997a. "The Invention of Identity: 'Self' and 'Other' in Pre-War Japan." In Michael Weiner, ed., *Japan's Minorities: The Illusion of Homogeneity*, 1–16. New York: Routledge.

———. 1997b. "The Representation of Absence and the Absence of Representation: Korean Victims of the Atomic Bomb." In Michael Weiner, ed., *Japan's Minorities: The Illusion of Homogeneity*, 79–107. New York: Routledge.

Weinreich, Peter. 1983a. "Emerging from Threatened Identities." In Glynis M. Breakwell, ed., *Threatened Identities*, 149–85. New York: Wiley.

——. 1983b. "Psychodynamics of Personal and Social Identity." In A. Jacobson-Widding, ed., *Identity: Personal and Socio-Cultural*, 159–85. Atlantic Highlands, NJ: Humanities Press.

——. 1986. "The Operationalisation of Identity Theory in Racial and Ethnic Relations." In John Rex and David Mason, eds., *Theories of Race and Ethnic Relations*, 299–320. Cambridge: Cambridge University Press.

White, Merry. 1988. *The Japanese Overseas: Can They Go Home Again?* Princeton: Princeton University Press.

Whitehead, Tony Larry. 1986. "Breakdown, Resolution, and Coherence: The Fieldwork Experiences of a Big, Brown, Pretty-Talking Man in a West Indian Community." In Tony Larry Whitehead and Mary Ellen Conaway, eds., *Self, Sex, and Gender in Cross-Cultural Fieldwork*, 213–39. Urbana: University of Illinois Press.

Whitehead, Tony Larry and Mary Ellen Conaway. 1986. "Introduction." In Tony Larry Whitehead and Mary Ellen Conaway, eds., *Self, Sex, and Gender in Cross-Cultural Fieldwork*, 1–14. Urbana: University of Illinois Press.

Willems, Emilio and Herbert Baldus. 1942. "Cultural Change Among Japanese Immigrants in Brazil." *Sociology and Social Research: An International Journal* 26 (6): 525–37.

Williams, Raymond. 1977. *Marxism and Literature*. New York: Oxford University Press.

Williams, Thomas R. 1967. *Field Methods in the Study of Culture*. New York: Holt, Rinehart and Winston.

Willis, Paul E. 1981. *Learning to Labor: How Working Class Kids Get Working Class Jobs*. Hampshire, England: Gower Publishing Company.

Wilson, Rob and Wimal Dissanayake. 1996. "Introduction: Tracking the Global/Local." In Rob Wilson and Wimal Dissanayake, eds., *Global/Local: Cultural Production and the Transnational Imaginary*, 1–18. Durham: Duke University Press.

Wiltshire, Rosina. 1992. "Implications of Transnational Migration for Nationalism: The Caribbean Example." In Nina Glick Schiller, Linda Basch, and Cristina Blanc-Szanton, eds., *Towards a Transnational Perspective on Migration: Race, Class, Ethnicity, and Nationalism Reconsidered*, 175–88. New York: The New York Academy of Sciences.

Winnicott, Donald W. 1965. *The Maturational Processes and the Facilitating Environment: Studies in the Theory of Emotional Development*. Madison, WI: International Universities Press.

World Bank. 1992–94. *World Development Report: Development and Environment*. Oxford: Oxford University Press.

Yamanaka, Keiko. 1996. "Return Migration of Japanese-Brazilians to Japan: The *Nikkeijin* as Ethnic Minority and Political Construct." *Diaspora* 5 (1): 65–97.

——. 1997. "Return Migration of Japanese Brazilian Women: Household Strategies and Search for the 'Homeland.' " In Diane Baxter and Ruth Krulfeld, eds., *Beyond Boundaries: Selected Papers on Refugees and Immigrants*, 5:11–34. Arlington, VA: American Anthropological Association.

——. 2000. " 'I Will Go Home, but When?' Labor Migration and Circular Diaspora Formation by Japanese Brazilians in Japan." In Mike Douglass and Glenda S. Roberts, eds., *Japan and Global Migration: Foreign Workers and the Advent of a Multicultural Society*, 123–52. London: Routledge.

Yamanaka, Keiko and Eunice Koga. 1996. "Nikkei Burajirujin no Nihon Ryunyu no Keizoku to Ido no Shakaika no Shinto: Ido Shisutemuron o Tsukatte" (The Continued Inflow of Nikkei Brazilians and the Spread of the Socialization of Migration: Using Migration Systems Theory). *Iju Kenkyu* (Immigration Studies) 33:55–72.

Yamanaka, Keiko and Takashi Miyajima. 1992. "A Paradox of Skilled Workers 'Only': Japan's New Immigration Policies Regarding Foreign Labor." Paper presented at the 1992 Annual Meeting of the American Sociological Association, Pittsburgh, August 20–24, 1992.

Yamashita, Karen Tei. 2001. *Circle K Cycles*. Minneapolis: Coffee House Press.

Yancey, William L., Eugene P. Ericksen, and Richard N. Juliani. 1982. "Emergent Ethnicity: A Review and Reformulation." In Norman R. Yetman and C. Hoy Steele, eds., *Majority and Minority: The Dynamics of Race and Ethnicity in American Life*, 469–78. Boston: Allyn and Bacon.

Yinger, J. Milton. 1981. "Toward a Theory of Assimilation and Dissimilation." *Ethnic and Racial Studies* 4:249–64.

——. 1986. "Intersecting Strands in the Theorisation of Race and Ethnic Relations." In John Rex and David Mason, eds., *Theories of Race and Ethnic Relations*, 20–41. Cambridge: Cambridge University Press.

Yoshida, Teigo. 1981. "The Stranger as God . . .." *Ethnology* 20 (2): 87–99.

Yoshino, Kosaku. 1992. *Cultural Nationalism in Contemporary Japan: A Sociological Enquiry*. London: Routledge.

Zhou, Min. 1997. "Segmented Assimilation: Issues, Controversies, and Recent Research on the New Second Generation." *International Migration Review* 31 (4): 975–1008.

Zhou, Min and Carl L. Bankston III. 1994. "Social Capital and the Adaptation of the Second Generation: The Case of Vietnamese Youth in New Orleans." *International Migration Review* 28 (4): 821–45.

Index